a b r i e f h i s t

The Desert
From *Introduction*, page 27

GOD

a brief history

JOHN BOWKER

Yoruba Carving
From *Introduction*, page 25

DORLING KINDERSLEY

previous page
Humble Servant
From India, page 81

LONDON, NEW YORK,
MUNICH, MELBOURNE
and DELHI

DK Publishing, Inc.
Publisher   Sean Moore
Creative Director   Tina Vaughan
Art Director   Dirk Kaufman
Editorial Director   Chuck Wills
Production   Chris Avgherinos

Produced for DK Publishing, Inc.
by

studio cactus C

13 SOUTHGATE STREET WINCHESTER HAMPSHIRE SO23 9DZ

Project Manager   Kate Grant
Project Art Editor   Sharon Rudd
Project Editor   Donna Wood

First published in Great Britain in 2002
by Dorling Kindersley Limited,
80 Strand, London WC2R 0RL

This paperback edition first published
in Great Britain in 2003

Copyright © 2002
Dorling Kindersley Limited
A Penguin Company
Text copyright © 2002 John Bowker

A CIP catalogue record for this book is
available from the British Library

ISBN 1-4053-0490-1

Reproduced by Colourscan, Singapore.

Printed and bound in Hong Kong by
Wing King Tong.

See our complete catalogue at
www.dk.com

CONTENTS

THE AZTECS, FROM IN THE
BEGINNING, PAGE 48

LAOZI, FROM THE RELIGIONS OF
ASIA, PAGE 152

PRIESTS, FROM THE RELIGIONS
OF ABRAHAM,
PAGE 198

THE CAPPADOCIANS, FROM
THE RELIGIONS OF ABRAHAM,
PAGE 253

AUTHOR'S PREFACE

◈

THIS BOOK AND ITS TITLE WERE FIRST PROPOSED by Sean Moore of Dorling Kindersley as a parallel, no doubt, to *A Brief History of Time*. God and time do indeed resemble each other in two ways: neither exists as common-sense might imagine, and both have been central to human awareness and experience for as long as any evidence survives.

There has never been any human society in which God has not been a part, usually a controlling and creative part. That is true even of those societies that set out to be deliberately secular, such as:

- the embryonic United States when religion and politics were deliberately separated from each other (as was imposed also on the Philippines in 1902)
- Turkey in an amendment to its Constitution in 1928 (the amendment deleted the statement of the 1924 Constitution that "the religion of the Turkish State is Islam")
- Russia and China when the Marxist critique of religion was put into effect
- India at the time of Independence when its Constitution guaranteed freedom of conscience and religion (article 25.1), and at the same time followed the US as far as it could in separating the State from the endorsement or support of any one religion

In none of those countries has God disappeared. A comprehensive history of God, therefore, would have to be pretty well the history of everything – much as the schoolmaster observed in Alan Bennett's play, *Forty Years On*, "God, whatever else He is, and of course He is everything else, is not a fool".

Not surprisingly, this book is more modest. It is not a comprehensive history of all that has been thought and believed about God, nor does it record all the stories that have been told about God. Instead, I have described ways in which people have made their own discoveries of God

and have developed and changed our understanding of who and what God is, and of how God became real to them.

Most of the chapters follow a roughly chronological sequence, but even then it sometimes proved more coherent to deal with a sequence in one place (for example, Sikhs as a unit in the midst of Indian religion, Korea and Japan as sequences in the midst of Asian religion) rather than scatter small sections according to their dates. Brief timelines and maps pertinent to the topics discussed in each chapter are provided at the beginning of each to give a quick indication of the events and people mentioned: the chronological squence can be found there. An attempt has been made to explain beliefs and practices, but this book cannot be a history of religions: for that, see *An Illustrated History of Religions* (CUP, 2001). For context and background, DK's *World Religions* (1997) looks at religions through art and architecture; *The Oxford Dictionary of World Religions* (OUP, 1997) gives further details on the people, texts, beliefs, and practices mentioned in this book.

The book begins with an Introduction to the background to belief in God, showing the way in which that belief is deeply embedded in the human brain and body. It continues with a chapter called *In the Beginning*, which looks at early ways in which people explored the nature and meaning of God, in such things as art, sex, story, music, dance, architecture, ritual, sacrifice, and reverence for the natural world. Although these themes are early, they all recur throughout the book, and their later appearances can be traced through the Index.

The chapters then explore the ways in which belief in God began and has developed in the major religious traditions of the world, in three main groups: the religions of India, of Asia, and of (in origin) the Middle East and Mediterranean world; since these last (Judaism, Christianity, and

Islam) spread all over the world, it is perhaps simpler to think of them as the Abrahamic religions, since they all claim Abraham (in Islam Ibrahim) as their ancestor.

The names of source books and other quoted works and their authors are kept as brief as possible in the text: the author's name (or title of the work) is given in brackets, with a page reference of that work. Full details of all sources used can then be looked up in the Bibliography.

I have tried to explain words and terms that may be unfamiliar as they occur. The page on which the term is first defined is given in bold in the index.

Although each religion has its own dating system, dates in this book are given according to the western calendar (BCE = Before the Common Era, CE = Common Era).

This book could not have been written without the help of many people to whom I express my very great gratitude in the Acknowledgments. Above all, my thanks go to two people who brought this book into being: Sean Moore of DK who suggested it in the first place – his calm integrity is a rare gift; and Margaret, my wife: I have learnt more about God in her company than from anywhere else; this book is hers, and comes with gratitude and love.

The poet and novelist Thomas Hardy used to insist that an honest estimate of life required what he called "a full look at the worst". That is certainly necessary in the case of God, since so much folly, wickedness, and commercial exploitation swirl around what people make of God. Even so, it amazes me how many people and how much of the media look *only* at the worst in the case of God, and never recognize the landfall and lightning strike through which God changes people into goodness and grace. A poem by R.S. Thomas is quoted in this book (p.317) that ends with a plea for "the better ventilating of the atmosphere of the closed mind". It is my hope that this book will serve that purpose.

Introduction

---◇---

How God appears in human imagination and experience.

The God Hadad

In Assyria, different gods were believed to protect people against disaster. The king Esarhaddon (7th century BCE) is promised: "I strengthen your life like your mother who brought you into being: the sixty great gods stand with me and protect you" (Moscati, p.73).

The Death of God

Down the Chute

IN 1923, THE AMERICAN JOURNALIST H.L. Mencken (1880–1956) held a memorial service for the Gods, who, as he put it, had "gone down the chute". He asked:

"What has become of Sutekh, once the high god of the whole Nile Valley? What has become of:

Reseph	Isis	Anath	Ptah
Ashtoreth	Anubis	Baal	Addu
Astarte	Shalem	Hadad	Dagon
El	Sharrab	Nergal	Yau
Nebo	Amon-Re	Ninib	Osiris
Melek	Sebek	Ahijah	Molech?

All these were once gods of the highest eminence. Many of them are mentioned with fear and trembling in the Old Testament. They ranked, five or six thousand years ago, with Jahveh himself; the worst of them stood far higher than Thor. Yet they have all gone down the chute, and with them the following:

Bile	Iuno Lucina	Ler	Saturn
Arianrod	Furrina	Morrigu	Vediovis
Govannon	Consus	Pwyll	Cronos
Ogyryan	Enki	Dea Dia	Engurra
Gwydion	Belus	Manawyddan	Dimmer
Mu-ul-lil	Nuada Argetlam	Tagd	Uhargisi
Goibniu	Ubilulu	Odin	Gasan-lil
Llaw Gyffes	U-dimmer-an-kia	Lleu	Enurestu
Ogma	U-sab-sib	Mider	U-Mersi
Rigantona	Tammuz	Marzin	Venus
Mars	Bau	Ceros	Mulu-hursang
Vaticanus	Anu	Edulia	Beitis
Adeona	Nusku"		

The list continues for another page. Then Mencken asked:

"Where is the graveyard of dead gods? What lingering mourner waters their mounds? ... Men laboured for generations to build vast temples to them – temples with stones as large as hay-wagons. The business of interpreting their whims occupied thousands of priests, wizards, archdeacons, evangelists, haruspices, bishops, archbishops. To doubt them was to die, usually at the stake. Armies took to the field to defend them against infidels: villages were burned, women and children were butchered, cattle were driven off ... They were gods of the highest standing and dignity, – gods of civilized peoples – worshipped and believed in by millions. All were theoretically omnipotent, omniscient and immortal. And all are dead" (*Prejudices*). Mencken conducted a long war against God, whom in the *Minority Report* he referred to as "the immemorial refuge of the incompetent, the helpless, the miserable. They find not only sanctuary in His arms, but also a kind of superiority, soothing to their macerated egos; He will set them above their betters".

Mencken was far from being alone in declaring "the death of God". In fact his question, "where is the graveyard of dead gods?" had been answered 40 years earlier by an even greater antagonist against God, Friedrich Nietzsche (1844–1900). In *The Gay Science* (1887) he described a madman who ran into the market square on a bright morning carrying a lantern and shouting over and over again, "I seek God! I seek God!":

"A number of those who have no faith were standing around, so great laughter erupted. 'Is he lost, then?' said one; 'Has he lost his way, like a child?' said another, 'Or has he gone into hiding? Is he afraid of us? Has he gone on a journey? Taken up residence elsewhere?' So they shouted and laughed. The madman sprang into their midst, and cut through them with the look he gave them. 'Where has God gone to?' he cried, 'I will tell you: we have killed him – you and I.' It is said also that the madman on the same day went into a number of churches and sang there his *requiem aeternam deo*. His reply, when he was brought out to account for himself, is said to have been, 'What are these churches, if they are not the tombs and graves of God?'"

Nietzsche declared that the death of God was "a recent event", and in the 19th century many questioned God's existence. But that questioning, with the death of God that may follow from it, has occurred in every century, in most parts of the world. It occurred dramatically, for example, in India in the emergence of Jains and Buddhists (pp.69–71), for some Jews (p.225), and in China among the naturalists (p.150).

Worship in Assyria
This cylinder seal from the 9th/8th century BCE *depicts a scene of worship. The Assyrians were a dominating power in Mesopotamia from c.1900 to 612BCE. The chief God was Asshur, but other Gods and Goddesses were also worshipped.*

Rejecting God

Arguments for Atheism

THE DEATH OF GOD is not unusual. It occurs in every generation everywhere in the world. In the Mediterranean civilization, Diagoras became a typical example of those who deny God – according to Athenagoras (2nd century CE) "he chopped up a statue of Heracles in order to boil his turnips, and he proclaimed outright that God did not exist." Cicero (1st century BCE) used him as an example (see box, left).

If the death of God is so common, why does it happen? The reasons may be personal and linked to individual circumstances, but they may also be less specific and shared by many people. In general they can be grouped under the Three Rs for rejection, the first of which stands for *rebuttals*. These look at claims made on behalf of God and argue that the claims are incoherent, insubstantial, or false – claims, for example, that God made the world in six literal days when evidence, gathered through many centuries, suggests that the universe came into being over a much longer period; or claims that God is loving when the suffering of so many people and the fate of so many animals (much of it, evidently, undeserved) does not suggest love. This raises the question of what is known as "theodicy" (from the Greek *theos*, "god", + *dike*, "justice"): if God is, as is claimed, all-powerful and all-loving, why does God not use that power to create a world in which love ensures that there is no undeserved suffering? God is either not all-powerful or not all-loving. Rebuttal arguments against God also look at things people do in the name of God that seem, to say the least, undesirable – fighting wars, for example, or justifying the subordination of women to men.

The second of the Three Rs stands for *reductions*: these arguments accept that people believe in God, but offer reasons why they do so that do not involve the possibility that God exists. An example is H.L. Mencken (p.11) claiming that people believe in God because they are inadequate and seek consolation or power over others that they cannot get in any other way. This is a form of projection (creating outside ourselves something that deals with our deepest needs, and that we take to be real although it does not exist independently). Others who reduced God to a projection of this kind were

> "Diagoras the Atheist once visited Samothrace and a friend there said to him, 'You think the gods have no care for humans? Why, you can see from all these votive pictures here how many people have escaped the fury of storms at sea by praying to the gods, who have brought them safe to harbour.' 'Yes, indeed,' said Diagoras, 'but where are the pictures of all those who suffered shipwreck and perished in the waves?' On another occasion he was on a voyage and the crew became anxious and alarmed about the bad weather and began to mutter that it served them right for taking an atheist on board. Diagoras just pointed out to them a number of other ships on the same course which were in equal difficulties and asked them whether they thought that there was a Diagoras on the passenger-list of every one of them. The fact is that a man's character or way of life makes no difference at all to his good luck or his bad"
>
> (Cicero 3.89)

Ludwig Feuerbach
Feuerbach (1804–72) argued that "God" is the projection that people make of their highest ideals, the best they can imagine. Thus theology (thought about God) is really anthropology (the best we can hope for in a human life).

Feuerbach (see caption, left), Sigmund Freud (1856–1939), and, perhaps most famously, Karl Marx (1818–83), who claimed that "God" is nothing but the way in which the alienation between different classes in society is kept in being: "God" is used to justify the divisions of society and to keep the working class in its place. Reductionist arguments can themselves usually be reduced to "nothing buttery" – that is, God is really nothing but…. A more recent reductionist is biologist Richard Dawkins, who claims that God is nothing but a virus infecting one brain after another with damaging and unhealthy information.

The third of the Three Rs stands for *refutations*: these look at arguments leading to the conclusion that God exists and then argue against their cogency or validity. A classic example of arguments pointing to God are the Five Ways of Aquinas (p.267), all of which occur in other religions as well. Often an early form of such arguments is refuted, leading to the restatement of the argument, leading to a further refutation, and so on. In other words, although some arguments in favour of God have been conclusively refuted and have not been refined, many continue to be debated to the present day and will be in the future. Not all arguments pointing to the existence of God have been finally refuted. The issues are still open.

It remains the case that such arguments cannot be conclusive because whatever God may be (if anything), God is certainly a great deal more than the conclusion of an argument. What arguments can do is point to the probability of God (or otherwise), and to the far greater sense that can be made of many features in a universe like this (and as yet we do not have any others with which to compare it) on the assumption that God exists. If, however, that is so, why have human words about God varied so much and have seemed so often to be ourselves "writ large"?

That was the question of the little black girl.

Theodicy
Claims that God is all-powerful and all-loving are called into question by undeserved suffering, like that of starving children. Some suffering is caused by human evil, but much occurs in the natural order over which humans have no control.

The Images of God

Changes in Human Imagination

Shaw on Christ
"Why not give Christianity a trial? The question seems a hopeless one after 2,000 years of resolute adherence to the old cry of 'Not this man but Barabbas'... 'This man' has not been a failure yet; for nobody has ever been sane enough to try his way" (Androcles and the Lion).

THE LITTLE BLACK GIRL ASKED the missionary who had converted her "'Where is god?' 'He has said, "Seek and ye shall find me"' said the missionary." So begins the book by the Irish playwright, George Bernard Shaw (1856–1950), *The Adventures of the Black Girl in Her Search for God*. The black girl takes the advice literally, picks up her large stick or knobkerry in order to knock down any false idols, and sets off on her search. On her way she meets people who make many different claims about the nature of God (see box, below). At the end of her search, the black girl meets Voltaire cultivating his garden (see caption, right). Voltaire's *Candide* concludes that the only "answer" is to get on with what we can manage, cultivating our own garden: *"Il faut cultiver notre jardin".*

Shaw argued that "God" is not an answer to anything, because people have repeatedly challenged and changed prevailing ideas about God, to the point that "God" has no reality outside their ideas: "The Bible, scientifically obsolete in all other respects, remains interesting as a record of how the idea of God, which is the first effort of civilized mankind to account for the existence and origin and purpose of as

THE LITTLE BLACK GIRL

During her search for God, the little black girl meets:

+ **THE LORD OF HOSTS**: He demands sacrifice and blood.
+ **THE CREATOR FROM THE BOOK OF JOB**: He cannot tell her why so much of creation is badly done.
+ **THE PHILOSOPHER FROM THE BOOK OF ECCLESIASTES**: He can find no meaning in anything except enjoyment of the good things of this life.
+ **THE PROPHET MICAH**: He denounces the God of sacrifice.
+ **PAVLOV**: The psychologist tells her that God is a conditioned reflex.
+ **A ROMAN SOLDIER**: He says that God is the power of Empire.
+ **JESUS**: He tells her that God is within her.
+ **PETER**: He is carrying the Church on his back and has with him others "carrying smaller and

mostly much uglier paper churches" – but all of them assure the little black girl that their version of God is the right one.
+ **JEWS**: They are waiting for the Messiah.
+ **THE CARAVAN OF THE CURIOUS**: They have transferred belief to Natural Selection and for them God is a fable.
+ **A MUSLIM**: He believes that God is Allah: "Man's nature is manifold: Allah alone is one... He is the core of the onion, the bodiless centre without which there could be no body. He is the number of the innumerable stars, the weight of the imponderable air, the – ' 'You are a poet, I believe' said the image maker. The Arab, thus interrupted, coloured deeply; sprang to his feet; and drew his scimitar. 'Do you dare to accuse me of being a lewd balladmonger?' he said. 'This is an insult to be wiped out in blood'" (p.29).

much of the universe as we are conscious of, develops from a childish idolatry of a thundering, earthquaking, famine striking, pestilence launching, blinding, deafening, killing, destructively omnipotent Bogey Man, maker of night and day and sun and moon, of the four seasons and their miracles of seed and harvest, to a braver idealization of a benevolent sage, a just judge, an affectionate father, evolving finally into the incorporeal word that never becomes flesh, at which point modern science and philosophy takes up the problem with its *Vis Naturae*, its *Élan Vital*, its Life Force, its Evolutionary Appetite, its still more abstract Categorical Imperative, and what not" (p.69).

Shaw's point is that people always create God in their own image. It was indeed Voltaire's own remark that God created man in his own image (Genesis 1.26–7) and man promptly returned the compliment; according to his contemporary, Montesquieu (1689–1755), "If triangles had a God, God would have three sides." It is an observation at least as old as the Greek philosopher Xenophanes (6th/5th centuries BCE):

> *"Oxen, lions and horses, if they had hands with which to carve images, would fashion gods according to their own shapes and give them bodies like their own"*

(Fragment 15)

In more recent times, an attractive version of this was written by the poet Rupert Brooke (1887–1915) in his poem *Heaven* (see box, above right). All our language about God seems to be limited in this way. It is, to use the technical phrase, culturally relative – i.e., it relates to, and is an expression of, whatever ideas and words are available at any time in any particular culture. That is true even of words believed to be revealed in which people hear and read the Word of God. Sikhs (among others) treat the Book as though it is God on earth (p.126), but they do not make the mistake of supposing that the Book actually is God. The self-revelation of God has to be made (if it is) through words that people can understand, and these words necessarily belong to particular people and times and languages.

So if God cannot be described except in the image of ourselves, and those images change enormously from one generation to another, how, if at all, can we say anything that is independently reliable about God?

> *"Fish say, they have their Stream and Pond;*
> *But is there anything Beyond?…*
> *We darkly know, by Faith we cry,*
> *The future is not Wholly Dry.*
> *And there (they trust) there swimmeth One*
> *Who swam ere rivers were begun,*
> *Immense, of fishy form and mind,*
> *Squamous, omnipotent and kind;*
> *And under that Almighty Fin,*
> *The littlest fish may enter in….*
> *And in that Heaven of all their wish,*
> *There shall be no more land, say fish"*

(Brooke, pp.35f)

Voltaire

Voltaire (1694–1778) wrote Candide *after the Lisbon earthquake of 1755 to question the view that under God "all is for the best in the best of all possible worlds".*

Speaking of God

A Process of Correction

GEORGE BERNARD SHAW ARGUED that imaginations of God have been corrected and changed so often that little is left of what was once believed about God; indeed, he claimed, there is nothing left of God. The fact, however, that we cannot talk adequately about something does not mean that there is nothing to talk about. Scientists cannot talk adequately about the universe, but that does not mean that there is nothing to talk about. In fact, scientists are always revising what they say about particular features of the universe. Science develops by correcting itself as it goes along – it is corrigible: its statements are, to use the technical words, approximate, fallible, corrigible – and often wrong from the point of view of later generations. The corrigibility of science has led to massive corrections of its own past, as the sequence from Newtonian absolutes of space and time, to Einstein and relativity, to Bohr and quantum mechanics, illustrates.

It also illustrates the vital point that Newton did not become completely "wrong": the older theory remains valid enough (in the kind of time and space in which human beings live) for it to be reliable for many practical purposes (see caption). Nevertheless, some claims about the universe have been discarded completely, although for generations they seemed secure and necessary. Spissitude, phlogiston, caloric, and ether were all, in their time, believed to be real. They were thought necessary in order to explain processes such as combustion and the propagation of light: "All space", wrote Newton, "is permeated by an elastic medium or aether, which is capable of propagating vibrations of sound, only with far greater velocity." Yet all of them have had to be rejected: the unfamiliarity of the terms shows how completely they have been abandoned.

It is easy to find examples of the corrigibility of science: there was a time when the earth was thought to be static and somewhere near the centre of the universe; when insects and mice, fish, and frogs were spontaneously generated from decaying matter; when the blood flowed in two systems, the venous and the arterial, passing from one to the other through invisible pores in the septum of the heart, and through anastomoses, or minute openings, between the veins and the arteries. They were, as Mencken (p.10) would have put it, scientific entities of the highest eminence, and they have all gone down the chute. And the process of correction continues.

The conclusion we draw from this is not that science has changed its past pictures so often that we cannot any longer trust it. In fact, exactly the reverse is true. Because science is open to correction and concerned with what may be said truly, it turns out to be reliable, even though on particular matters it happens to have been wrong. In other words, what scientists say may be approximate, provisional, corrigible, fallible, and

Newton's Laws
The operational success of satellites and space probes is witness to the enduring validity of Newton's laws, even though in other ways his conception of the physical universe has been superseded by the (also incomplete) insights of quantum mechanics.

often wrong, but it is, nevertheless, *wrong about something*. No scientist can say finally and completely what the universe is like, but what there is in the case of the universe allows approximate and changing pictures to be given and to be found reliable. From the evidence, therefore, of experience, much of it experimental, scientists create provisional pictures of the universe and of ourselves. By no means all of this can be based on direct observation. No one, for example, can see neutrinos directly, nor observe evolution as it happened millions of years ago. But by the kind of argument known as "abductive inference" (p.266), they infer from conducive properties (or evidence) in what *can* be observed the (provisional) truth of neutrinos and evolution.

Something like this is true also of God. What people say about God is bound to be approximate, provisional, corrigible, and often wrong. That is so, because "no one has ever seen God" (John 1.18). Why not? Because God is not an object like other objects in the universe, open to observation. By abductive inference, we may conclude, from our experience of the universe and of ourselves, that God is. This means that God can be experienced *directly* (as being present to us), but God cannot be observed *immediately* (but only as mediated through the things we sense and our subsequent reflection; see also p.20).

On the basis of experience and argument, people have corrected and changed the provisional pictures of God: like spissitude and phlogiston, some things that used to be claimed about God are simply wrong (see caption, right). We are now correcting the view that God is male: in this book, outside quotations, the masculine pronoun is not used of God.

But this does not mean that God is not there to be talked about. As with science and the universe, so with God. Our pictures are approximate, provisional, corrigible, and often wrong. But the possibility remains that they are *wrong about some One*. No one can tell you finally and completely what God is like, but the long engagement with God, in the many ways described in this book, has sifted and winnowed human understanding. That has happened only because people have found sufficiently what there is in the case of God for approximate and changing pictures to be given and to be found reliable and trustworthy as a foundation for the approach to God in prayer and other ways of worship. Experiencing the world leads to the recognition of God.

God Created Adam
Long-held views about God are constantly being changed and corrected. It is not a matter of fact that God is an old man with a long white beard sitting on a cloud a few thousand feet above the earth. Nevertheless, traditional images retain their power in human imagination, not only in poetry and art, but also in prayer and worship.

Experiencing the World

The Human Response

The Grand Canyon
In Native American myth, the Canyon is the path made by Ta-Vwoats when he took a mourning chief to find his wife in the spirit world. It was a place of fear until the river was added as a barrier against harmful invaders.

WHEN THE WRITER BILL BRYSON (born 1951) made his "travels in small town America" for his book *The Lost Continent*, he decided to revisit the Grand Canyon. When he got there, everything was covered with a thick fog. Even so, he decided to walk to a look-out point on the edge of the Canyon:

"Eventually I came to a platform of rocks, marking the edge of the canyon. There was no fence to keep you back from the edge, so I shuffled cautiously over and looked down, but could see nothing but grey soup. A middle-aged couple came along and as we stood chatting about what a dispiriting experience this was, a miraculous thing happened. The fog parted. It just silently drew back, like a set of theatre curtains being opened, and suddenly we saw that we were on the edge of a sheer, giddying drop of at least a thousand feet. 'Jesus!' we said and jumped back, and all along the canyon edge you could hear people saying 'Jesus!', like a message being passed down a long line. And then for many moments all was silence, except for the tiny fretful shiftings of the snow, because out there in front of us was the most awesome, most silencing sight that exists on earth"

What was happening inside Bill Bryson's brain and body at that moment? External receptors in his eyes and ears were transmitting sensory

THE LONG ROUTE AND THE SHORT CUT

How the brain converts sensory inputs into feelings and reactions.

✤ **THE LONG ROUTE**: In this route the brain sends the inputs via the cortex to the amygdala so that there can be some sifting of what is going on. Although it happens very fast, there is a sense in which we stop to think about it before our emotions come into play.

✤ **THE SHORT CUT**: In some circumstances (for example, facing a snake about to strike), those who stop to think may stop thinking for ever – they will be dead. So the brain has a short-cut route, from the thalamus to the amygdala which initiates the response at once.

messages to specific areas of the thalamus, and these processed the signals and sent the results to specialized areas of the cortex. The cortex then sorted out what was going on and alerted another part of the brain, the amygdala, to initiate appropriate responses throughout the body. A direct seeing and hearing of external circumstances was interpreted in such a way that he jumped back in fear, and had profound feelings of beauty.

That is a very over-simplified account, and, in any case, brain research in these areas is still at a very early stage. Nevertheless, we do know that the way our brains and bodies respond with feelings and emotions to what goes on around and within us is absolutely fundamental, not just for our survival, but for what we are as human beings. We sense the world, not simply as cameras recording mechanically whatever passes through the lens, but as people who respond with interpretation and feeling, and who thus *experience* the world and themselves. These experiences often come from a direct seeing of the world (see box, right).

Of course, our immediate emotions may be mistaken. When we think about it, we may conclude that there was no need for fear (there is less in this than meets the eye), or, when our emotions come into play later on, we may conclude that something that seemed dull is actually very moving (there is much *more* in this than meets the eye). This means that the brain relates sensory inputs (what we see, hear, touch, etc) to our feelings and reactions in two connected ways, known as the long route and the short cut (see box, below left). The feelings and experiences that make us human and keep us alive may happen in a very direct way, or they may happen through a process of thinking and reflection. It is the second process that allows us to build the worlds of our imagination on the basis of our emotions: we write books and music, for example, or we compose poems and pictures.

We never see "fear" or "beauty" as such, however. We sense (see, hear, etc) things that carry within themselves the signals that evoke our various emotions. The signals are known technically as "conducive properties" (Latin *duco*, "I lead towards"): conducive properties are those features that lead to one emotional response rather than another. People watching a horror film can be genuinely frightened because the film-maker has deliberately put before their eyes the conducive properties that will create the emotion of fear. So also with God: we do not see "God": we see conducive properties in the world around us and in other people that produce the appropriate emotion and response of awe, wonder, worship, thankfulness – and, to a degree, of fear. Rudolf Otto (1869–1937) described the feeling as *mysterium tremendum fascinans et augustum,* an overwhelming mystery that is awe-inspiring but also attracting. It is a feeling or emotion of being in the presence of transcendent and awe-inspiring Otherness who nevertheless is present with us in a personal way and who draws us into ever deeper relationship. It is, therefore, a feeling of profound meaning and purpose. It is the natural sense of God.

The British poet Norman Nicholson recalled standing in the Ruskin museum in the Lake District when two children from the village came in and went to a case of minerals. One of them pointed to "a strange piece of quartz, golden, glittering and contorted as a Chinese lizard: 'That's my favourite,' said one. 'Smashing, isn't it?' replied the other" (Nicholson, p.194). That is a direct seeing of something which evokes the experience of beauty.

Experiencing Beauty
Observing a thing of beauty, such as a perfect flower, we do not see "beauty", we see conducive properties that produce the appropriate response.

Experiencing God

A Fundamental Awareness

Rodin and Rilke
The poet Rilke (p.277) so admired the work of Rodin (the work below includes The Hand of God) that he studied with him in 1902 in order to create in words the power of Rodin's sculpture: "But now and then the curtain of the eyelid Lifts soundlessly – An image enters then, Runs through the quiet tension of the limbs, Reaches the heart – and ceases to exist" (Sämtliche Werke, I, 505).

THE WAY THAT HUMAN BODIES and brains are built leads us to see and experience the world (and our own inner nature) in both emotional and rational ways. Where God is concerned, this means that we see directly the conducive properties that lead to the emotion and experience of God, although we never see God *im-mediately* – that is, not mediated through the world and its objects. We may then also use the neocortex to think and reflect on this experience. We may, for example, think that we were after all mistaken: we *felt* it was an experience of God, but we now think that it was an experience of, shall we say, profound beauty. On the other hand, we may think and reflect on this experience, and trust it; we may then extend and deepen it in such things as prayer and praise, theology and the theatre of ritual (p.42) – and also in valuing the world and other people in such a new way that it changes how we live.

Fundamentally, therefore, we see and experience God directly (though not immediately) through the occasions of the world because our brains and bodies are built in the way they are. We can no more *not* feel God than we can *not* feel fear. Rationally we may reconsider almost any emotion and reinterpret or even suppress it. But the experience of God will still remain a possibility and an opportunity for brains and bodies of the kind that we have. It still makes sense to say, "Let us pray".

On this basis, many people claim to have a sense of God, or experiences of God, or at least experiences that point to the reality of God. Particular experiences may not be all that important in religions, not least because we can so often be mistaken about them and their meaning. Even so, we cannot know about the

A. Rodin

existence of anything except on the basis of experience: we cannot know that the world exists except on the basis of some experiences of it – experiences that we can share with each other of such a kind that it is reasonable to conclude that the world exists (though some philosophers have disputed this). The same applies to God: if we cannot have any experience of God, the question of God's existence cannot seriously arise.

Arguments from experience are never a simple matter, and philosophers warn how difficult it is to cross the bridge from claimed experience to the truth or reality of what is claimed to have been experienced: the fact that people claim to have been abducted by aliens does not lead automatically to the conclusion that aliens actually exist outside their imagination.

Even so, we have nothing else except our experiences (and our reflections on, and sharings of, them) on which to build our understandings of the world, the universe, and God. Certainly we need to make clear the reasons why we make particular claims, and others can then decide whether we have offered sufficient warrants for our assertions, always reminding ourselves of the credulous nature of human beings – i.e., our willingness to believe what we are told, especially if it is fantastic or incredible!

But where warrants for particular assertions *are* offered, where there is supporting evidence for them (e.g., from the witness of other people), and particularly where we are able to make some check of them for ourselves, then we have good reason for trusting what is being claimed, even if those claims are as always expressed in approximate and corrigible words. This means, therefore, that there is, from a philosophical point of view, a serious argument based on experience pointing to the existence of God – an argument summarized in the box, right.

> "We can now put the view that religious experience provides evidence in favour of [the claim that] God exists *along these lines*: If one has an apparent experience of God under conditions in which there is no reason to think either that one would seem to experience God even if there were no God or that one could not discover, if God does not exist, that this is so, then one has experiential evidence that God exists"
>
> (Yandell, p.17)

Clearly, therefore, a fundamental reason why belief in God continues, despite the Three Rs of rejection (pp.12–13), is that many people either have awareness and experiences which they take to be of God, or they rely on the experiences of others whom they trust; and they (or at least many of them) find that, when they trust and live with the truth and consequence of this, their lives are made different in hugely important ways.

From all this, it is clear that the awareness of God, in human experience and reflection, is fundamental. If that awareness did not occur extremely commonly in every society and every generation (as it has most certainly done), there could not have been the constant change and correction, to which Bernard Shaw drew attention, in the ways that people have imagined God.

The human story of God is the story of people being drawn more deeply into the presence of God as they have learnt more profoundly the nature of the One who has invited and drawn them on. The story of science is a fascinating tribute to the integrity of the human spirit. So too is the story of God. But if the experiencing of God is so fundamental, what does that actually mean? It is the work of what is known as phenomenology to answer, or attempt to answer, that question.

Phenomenology

The Nature and Cause of Experience

Belief in God rests on much more than claims to an experience of God. In fact, claims to specific experiences of God have been treated with great caution in virtually all religions, because they can so often be confused with aberrant states of the brain, including the influence of drink and drugs. Even so, many people do have a sense of the presence of God that is not private (belonging to them exclusively and alone), but rather is shared with many others.

What experiences are they? An immense variety, as this book shows. The task of describing these belongs to what is known as phenomenology – from the Greek *phainomena*, "appearances", + *logos*, "word", "reason", "reflection". Phenomenology exists on two levels (see box, below): it sets out to describe, first what people report as their own experience, and second, what we have to infer or accept as the basis for those experiences – what has brought them into being. Phenomenologists may seem to talk about chairs (see box) or for that matter, Father Christmas, in an extremely

THE TWO LEVELS OF PHENOMENOLOGY

Describing and accounting for appearances.

✤ **THE FIRST LEVEL**: This tries to describe the things that people report having experienced (the appearances in their own awareness or consciousness) without entering into the truth or value of what they report. So, when the poet Henry Vaughan wrote, "I saw eternity the other night, Like a great ring of pure and endless light", the phenomenologist records, "Henry Vaughan has reported the appearance in his consciousness of what he describes as a ring of pure and endless light, and he reports that this appeared to him to be eternity." At this level, a phenomenologist simply records what people report without commenting on its truth or existence. People may report that they saw Father Christmas on the night before Christmas: a phenomenologist at the first level simply records that these are the appearances that people report, without commenting on whether Father Christmas truly exists and comes down chimneys.

✤ **THE SECOND LEVEL**: This asks what we are entitled to infer as necessarily being in existence for the reports at the first level to be so consistently made. Many people report appearances in their awareness that they describe as chairs. The phenomenologist at the first level makes no comment on whether chairs do or do not exist. When many reports come in confirming each other and exhibiting a great consistency in the features that constitute "chairs", phenomenologists at the second level ask, what must be the case in a world of this kind for reports of such consistency to come in? In that way, they and others can use the word "chair" with a clear sense of the kind of appearance in consciousness to which it refers, of how to use the word "chair", and of the circumstances in which it is an appropriate word to use – when people have an appearance in their consciousness or awareness of an object with four legs, a seat, and a back.

complicated way, but it shows how important it is to "make haste slowly". Many people claim that belief in God is like belief in fairies or Father Christmas – something we believe in as children but grow out of when we understand things better. Phenomenologists are wiser: at the first level they record the belief (without commenting on its truth or value) of children that Father Christmas exists and brings them gifts. They also record that children grow out of that belief.

That, however, is not the end of the story. At the second level, phenomenologists ask what in reality has brought that belief into being, and point out that what gives rise to that belief is the expectation of children at a particular time of year, and the experience of someone dressing up in recognizably symbolic clothes and distributing presents.

It is immediately obvious that the reported experience of God is not remotely like the reported experience of Father Christmas. In the case of God, phenomenologists at the first level record, as does this book, what people report. At the second level, they (along with anyone concerned with the truth of what we are and of what we are able to become) do not just *describe* those reports; they ask, what must we infer to be truly the case for reports of that kind to be so consistently made? What in human experience has evoked the word God, allowing us to use it in ways that others can understand? Not something as obvious as a hand in front of my face. But something – or some One – unmistakably real.

Maybe it seems obscure, but Tom Stoppard, in his play, *Jumpers*, caught the point exactly. George Moore, a philosopher, reflects on what he can know of God – and having just touched on phenomenology, we may well have some sympathy with the difficulties he gets into. Then he remembers why he goes on with the struggle to understand:

Father Christmas
The claim is sometimes made that belief in God is like belief in fairies or Father Christmas: we may believe in such things when young but grow out of them when we are older and wiser. Phenomenology at the second level shows why that claim is wrong.

"How does one know what it is one believes when it's so difficult to know what it is one knows? I don't claim to know that God exists, I only claim that he does without my knowing it, and while I claim as much I do not claim to know as much; indeed I cannot know and God knows I cannot. (Pause.) And yet I tell you that, now and again, not necessarily in the contemplation of rainbows or newborn babes, nor in extremities of pain or joy, but more probably ambushed by some quite trivial moment – say the exchange of signals between two long-distance lorry-drivers in the black sleet of a god-awful night on the old A1 – then in that dip-flash, dip-flash of headlights in the rain that seems to affirm some common ground that is not animal and not long-distance lorry-driving – then I tell you I know" (p.71)

God and Values

Beauty, Truth, Goodness, and Love

> "Euclid has fully explained all the qualities of the circle; but he has not, in any proposition, said a word of its beauty. The reason is evident. The beauty is not a quality of the circle. It lies not in any part of the line whose parts are equally distant from a common centre. It is only the effect, which that figure produces upon the mind, whose peculiar fabric or structure renders it susceptible of such sentiments"
>
> (Hume, App. 1§3)

THE "KNOWING" DESCRIBED by George Moore (p.23) shows how humans can experience events, objects, and people in ways that transcend their ordinary nature. The human brain and body allow us to discern truth, beauty, and goodness as having an independent and absolute value. This sense of absolute value encourages many to recognize (direct seeing, p.17) God as its foundation and guarantee. Others dispute this.

When Pope Benedict XI was choosing an artist for St Peter's in Rome, Giotto simply drew for him a circle. The Pope and his advisors saw not just skill but beauty in the circle and chose Giotto. Four centuries later, a Scottish philosopher, David Hume (1711–76) questioned their judgement arguing that everyone can agree, if they make the right measurements, whether a line before them forms a circle, but they cannot agree whether it is beautiful (see box, top left).

Hume argued that not only are aesthetic judgements (judgements about what is beautiful or ugly) subjective, so also are moral judgements (judgements about what is good, and about how we ought to act): "If we can depend upon any principle which we learn from philosophy this, I think, may be considered as certain and undoubted, that there is nothing, in itself, valuable or despicable, desirable or hateful, beautiful or deformed; but that these attributes arise from the particular constitution and fabric of human sentiment and affection."

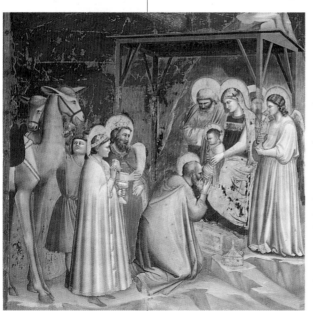

Giotto di Bondone
Giotto (c.1267–1337) painted this fresco of "The Adoration of the Kings" circa 1303–10. Admired as "a painter who surpasses all others" (Sacchetti, 14th century), his most famous works are the frescoes; possibly on the life of Francis (pp.264–5) in Assisi, and of the Holy Family in Padua.

If judgements about goodness and value are not "seen" but simply imposed on what we see, then, Hume argued, that is why we all disagree about what counts as good or as beautiful. "What is true on one side of the Pyrenees," observed Pascal (p.311) "is not true on the other." Hume argued that our disagreements about God point to the same lack of objectivity, and for the same reason: we do not see God in the same way that we see a circle; and Hume went on to argue, in *Dialogues Concerning Natural Religion* (1779), that the classic arguments pointing to the existence of God are fundamentally flawed.

But Hume did not distinguish between measurable properties (like circularity) that entail (make necessary) shared judgements, and conducive properties that lead to shareable judgements but are not *necessarily* coercive (i.e., judgements that everyone has to share). The basic fact remains that humans, with the kind of brains and bodies that they have, do make shareable judgements about beauty, goodness, and God, and that these judgements relate to the facts they see. The judgements are corrigible and fallible (pp.16f), but they are nevertheless objective, because the conducive properties are seen directly and entail shareable judgements – though the entailment is nothing like so strong as it is in the case of circularity. But that is true of virtually every judgement we make in the course of our everyday lives.

This means, to take an example, that the Yoruba in Africa make aesthetic judgements of beauty (see box, right) although what they and, let us say, people in China regard as beautiful is different. For the Yoruba, there are particular properties that lead to the response of "beauty":

"Beauty is seen in the mean (iwontúnsuonsi) – *in something not too tall or too short, not too beautiful (overhandsome people turn out to be skeletons in disguise in many folktales) or too ugly. Moreover, the Yoruba appreciate freshness and improvisation per se in the arts. These preoccupations are especially evident in the rich and vast body of art works celebrating Yoruba religions"*

(Thompson, p.5)

Built as we are, we cannot help but interact with and respond to the world in these ways. We know what truth, beauty, and goodness are absolutely, because we recognize them in any of the many different circumstances in which they occur; and they remain absolutely what they are (truth, beauty, or goodness) even though we disagree on what counts as beautiful or good (less so in the case of truth). In the same way, but greater than all three, is love – greater because it compels us into behaviours in which we forget ourselves for the good of others.

It is here that many people recognize God. The fact that we experience absolutes in the course of this life is very odd if the universe is a matter of chance and accident. It is not at all odd if they come from the One who is Absolute (complete and needing nothing to add to its perfection) creating and holding in being a world like this – one in which absolutes constitute us in all the finest aspects of our being. When we recognize these values, and live our lives on the basis of them, we begin to realize, even to know, *that* God is, the source and meaning of transcendence. Even so, we do not know *what* God is, and so the way people talk about God will be as varied as the way they talk about beauty. But the human ability to experience truth, beauty, goodness, love, and God will be the same for all who are built as humans are.

"The Yoruba assess everything aesthetically – from the taste and colour of a yam, to the qualities of a dye, to the dress and deportment of a woman or a man. An entry in one of the earliest dictionaries of their language, published in 1858, was amewa, literally 'knower-of-beauty', 'connoisseur', one who looks for the manifestation of pure artistry"

(Thompson, p.5)

Yoruba Carving
The 24 million Yoruba live mainly in Nigeria and are known for their craft skills and their strong religious belief. Shango (p.303) was important among their Gods.

The Death and Life of God

Opportunity and Imitation

GEORGE MOORE'S "KNOWING" (p.23) is also a reminder that most people who live their lives in the presence of God are not philosophers, as Jean Grou (1730–1803), writing in the Christian tradition, makes clear (see box, left).

Even so, philosophers are important in setting boundaries to what can and cannot be reasonably said or claimed on the basis of experience, and that has undoubtedly contributed to the winnowing process through which the human imagination of God (and language about God) has changed.

That is important, since it is not easy to speak about God: to speak fluently and fervently (as Grou put it, left) is not in itself a guarantee against speaking fervent and fluent nonsense. The major problem here is that God is not an object among other objects in the universe, and therefore cannot be produced for immediate observation, no matter how much people report a direct sense of God. People, in the present as much as in the past, do report a direct sense of God mediated through the world and other people; and many also report passing beyond words to the reality to whom their words inadequately point.

Some conclude from this that God is the universe, or that the universe is the body or the process of God (i.e., that "God" is a word to describe the transcendent nature of the universe in relation to ourselves). Far more often it is recognized that if God does indeed exist, it must be in a way that is independent of this or any other universe. God remains independent of the circumstances that give rise to the feeling or emotion of God (which can be the entire universe in a feeling, very commonly reported, of identity with the whole cosmos), just as, for example, the snake remains independent of the feeling or emotion of fear. Neither God nor the snake is simply an emotion. That at once makes clear why the death of God occurs repeatedly. It is hard enough to describe the nature of a snake, even though we can capture, observe, and dissect it. It is impossible to capture, observe, and dissect God: all human attempts to describe the essential nature of God in words must necessarily fail. The dilemma is that *some* words nevertheless always remain necessary. Otherwise we would not be able to share with each other the consequences of the fact that the feelings and emotions evoking and bearing witness to the reality of God are so deeply embedded in human nature: they are a consequence of what the genes and proteins build.

"The Christian's knowledge of God is not an endless course of reasonings on God's essence and perfections, like those of a mathematician on the circle and the triangle. Many philosophers and theologians, who held grand and noble ideas of the divine nature, were none the more holy or virtuous in consequence...
The soul is better instructed concerning divine things by prayer alone than wise men are by all their study. Many simple and unlearned persons, taught in the school of God, speak more fitly of him, more nobly, and fluently, and fervently, than the ablest doctors who, not being men of prayer, speak and write of heavenly things in a dry and painful way... St Antony (p.252) knew God after this sort when he complained that the sun rose too early, and put an end to his prayer; and so did St Francis (p.264) when he spent whole nights repeating with wonderful delight those words: 'My God, and my All.' The sense of God, this experimental knowledge, was the desire of all saints, and the fruit of their union with him"

(Grou, §1)

So the inadequacy of words means that the death of the characterizations of God is inevitable – those many Gods and Goddesses who have, in Mencken's words (pp.10–11) "gone down the chute"; and for some that means the death of God as such: in their view, characterizations of God fail because there is nothing in existence for those characterizations to describe. But far more often the death of the characterizations of God has proved to be not the death of God but the life of God – the continuing life and liveliness of God in human experience and imagination because through the death of the inadequate, people move into a new understanding and vision of God.

This is true even where people claim that God's self-revelation has supplied a kind of stability in the human understanding of God. Some understandings of God do become stable, but in revelation they are still expressed in human languages that people can understand. That is why religions based most strongly on revelation nevertheless make it clear that the essence (essential nature) of God is not identical with, or captured in, the words of revelation, however much they also claim that the words of revelation are the bridge between people and God. So the history of God cannot be told from God's point of view, since God is, by definition, without beginning or end, and stories without beginning or end are hard to tell. But the history of God from a human point of view is one of heroic and fascinating struggle to enter into the opportunity of God and to tell something of the wonder and glory of what happens. Even then, every statement about God and every act of worship has to end with the words, *Deus semper maior*, "God is always greater".

The opportunity of God is universal because all humans are built in the same way by genes and proteins so that we experience the world with feelings and with reflection on what those feelings mean. Mediated *through* the world, people have also experienced God. What, then, *have* they said about the ways in which God has become real and vivid for them? How has the human understanding of God been deepened and winnowed through time? That is the story this book will try to tell.

The Desert

The desert is a hostile and dangerous place, but it is to the desert that people go who seek to be alone with God. The American poet Stephen Crane (1871–1900) wrote:
"I walked in a desert.
And I cried,
'Ah, God, take me from this place!'
A voice said, 'It is no desert.'
I cried, 'Well, but –'
A voice said, 'It is no desert'"
(Williams, p.227).

In the Beginning

Early and persisting foundations in the human search for God.

IN THE BEGINNING

T HE HUMAN SEARCH FOR GOD began long before the invention of writing and (much later) of printing. In the earliest stages, therefore, ideas, stories, and beliefs had to be remembered and passed on by word of mouth (oral tradition). Much information is still preserved and transmitted in this way, but it is impossible for us to know how old it is or how much it has changed over time.

This makes it equally impossible to know what the earliest beliefs about God and Goddess were. Archaeologists recover artefacts and uncover the remains of buildings. Many of these resemble those of later periods when surviving texts suggest what they meant to the people who used or built them. From the known we infer what the beliefs and practices of the earlier times may have been, but there cannot be any certainty about it.

For the earliest periods, therefore, without the controlling record of text or inscription, there can be wild guesses and extreme statements, of which there are many in the case of early beliefs about God.

To take only one example: the Nasca lines (sometimes called "the eighth wonder of the world") were laid out over nearly 400 square miles of desert in Southern Peru. They are so extensive and complicated that the overall design can be seen only from the air. What did they mean to those who created but could never see them? Some have claimed that they were runways made for visitors from outer space who were then believed to be supernatural beings – the first gods. The archaeologist Anthony Aveni mapped them onto water supplies and suggested that they demarcated access to water under the auspices of guardian spirits (many designs are of

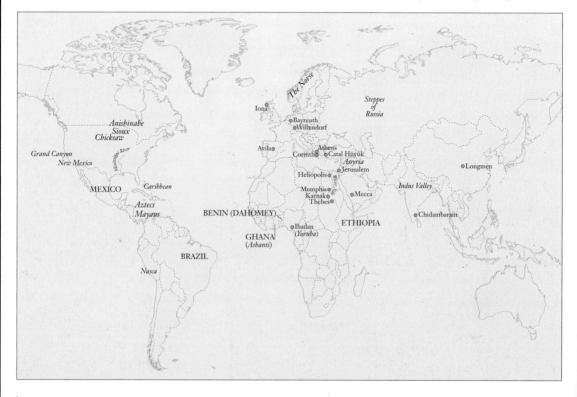

birds and animals). There is no final proof, but some suggestions remain much more probable than others.

But although meanings may be hard to recover, the forms through which our ancestors encountered God have endured: the content changes, but sex, fertility, nurture, nature, signs, symbols, music, trance, ecstasy, ritual, myth, sacrifice, architecture, and art remain as important today as ever. All these are deeply embedded in human brains and bodies, on the basis of which culture is built and treasured.

Nasca Lines
Some believe the Nasca lines in Peru served as a calendar for the Paracas and Nasca cultures, others that they were ritual walkways from ceremonial sites. Some even think they were created by alien spacecraft.

Palaeolithic	c.35,000– 10,000
Willendorf carving	c.19,000
Native Americans settle	c.7000
Catal Hüyük	c.6500– 5500
Cave art	2000– 1500
Amenophis IV · Hymn to Aten · Norse myths · Seti I	1500– 1000
Xenophanes · Acropolis	1000–500
Cicero	500–000
Athenagoras · Tang	000–1000
Giotto · Aztecs; Mayans	1250–1500
Newton · Montesquieu	1500–1750
Voltaire · Hume · Schopenhauer · Grou · Schelling · Feuerbach · Wagner · Marx · Peirce · Rodin · Nietzsche	1750–1850
Shaw · Freud · Husserl · Otto · Ghost Dance · Rilke · Jung · Einstein · Brooke · Wittgenstein · Revival of Wicca	1850–PRESENT

Goddess

Mother of All Things

THE STORY OF GOD BEGINS with the story of Goddess, as at least an equal part of it. Some go further and say that the story began *as* the story of Goddess, with the imagination of Deity as female, and with the male God as at best a subordinate partner.

Why is that claim made? Mainly because of the widespread finds by archaeologists of small female figures and cave paintings, many of which, from Palaeolithic times (c.35,000–10,000BCE) and later, emphasize the breasts, the pregnant womb, and the vagina, exactly those parts of women most obviously associated with the production of new life and its nourishment. For a long time, these figures were called Venuses, after the Roman Goddess associated with sex and love.

The common occurrence of Venuses, sometimes to the exclusion of male counterparts, led to the argument that the earliest human imagination of Deity was of Goddess, and to claims as extreme as this:

"Death is the powerful dramatic mystery equal to Birth – and both are overarched and contained by the Great Mother. This concept of a female earth as the source of cyclic birth, life, death, and rebirth underlies all mythological and religious symbology: it is the source of all religious belief. It is important to grasp the time dimension involved: God was female for at least the first 200,000 years of human life on earth. *This is a conservative estimate; wooden images of the Mother God were doubtless carved long before the stone Cro-Magnon Venuses, but wood does not survive"*

(Sjöö and Mor, pp.48f)

Was there once a religious civilization in which the focus, through the cult of Goddess, was on agriculture, not on killing? That was the suggestion of James Mellaart who, during the 1960s, excavated a town at Catal Hüyük in Turkey that flourished as a settlement between c.6500 and 5500BCE. Although hunting scenes are portrayed, neither weapons nor traces of animal slaughter were found in the excavations. There are rooms in which only Goddess is shown in paintings and reliefs, suggesting a religion and understanding of the world and its origins reflecting the importance of women in fertility and the sustaining of life. In some rooms, there are pictures of female vultures standing near headless bodies, suggesting a belief that Goddess takes back into herself (as in burial) the

Goddess of Willendorf
This small figure carved from limestone was found at Willendorf in Austria, and used to be called "the Venus of Willendorf". It is a striking early (c.19,000BCE) example of the acknowledgment of Woman as the source of life and fertility. The seven lines around the head may reflect the widespread recognition of the number seven as sacred.

bodies of the dead in order to bring about new life. These arguments were given focus by Marija Gimbutas (1921–94) who in her work *The Living Goddesses* claimed, on the basis of archaeological finds, that there had been an old European culture in which the people were "relatively peaceful, agrarian, artistically creative, probably equalitarian in social structure, and goddess worshipping". These people were overcome by invaders from the steppes of Russia who were "a patrilineal, pastoral, and semi-nomadic group of peoples… They were militaristic, produced weapons, and rode horses. Their religion centred upon male gods". If true, that would reproduce the way in which the Aryans took over the culture and civilization of North (and eventually virtually all) India (p.60).

The reconstruction of beliefs before the invention of writing is always a matter of guesswork. Only rarely in the case of early archaeology is any inscription found with the artefacts indicating what the beliefs associated with them were. And only very much later do any texts survive in which people tried to express what their beliefs about Goddess and God were, and what they meant: sometimes when texts are discovered they contradict the interpretations offered previously; thus women were portrayed in early Egypt holding their breasts, and this was interpreted as evidence of a fertility cult, but when the decipherment of hieroglyphs was achieved, it was clear from texts that this was a gesture of mourning.

This means that many claims about early religion are made, some of which are far too confident – for example, the claim in the quote (left), that rebirth is the source of all religious symbology and of all religious belief. In "The Discovery of the Modern Goddess", Ronald Hutton shows that many claims about Goddess are statements about people in the present, not the past. Nevertheless, it is obvious from both artefacts and texts that Goddess was widely displaced by God: in the case of North India, the disappearance of the Indus Valley images of Goddess is paralleled by the virtual disappearance of Goddess in the Vedas (p.62). That process of displacement continued from early times and produced the dominant masculine imagination and characterization of God.

Although humans could once portray Goddess or God directly and with confidence, it has become increasingly obvious that words and imagination will always fall short (p.17). Nevertheless, something, however provisional or inadequate, *has* to be said to give some sort of expression to what is so true and marvellous in human experience. The question has become increasingly urgent – and for some religious people increasingly tense – how the characterization of Deity from the experience of women can be reaffirmed within the largely masculine characterization of God. For some, it can't happen. Religion has been so patriarchal for so many centuries that "God" is a dead image. For them, the recovery of

Mother Goddess
Jung (p.39) was so impressed by the widespread occurrence of figures like this (found in ancient Turkey c.6000BCE) that he regarded the Great Mother as "the first, strongest, and most lasting of all the archetypes" (Husain, p.19).

THE POSITIVE ROLE OF WITCHES

Anthropologists have argued that witches benefit small-scale societies in a number of important ways:

✤ **HEALING**: They have been active in healing and in the use of herbal medicine.
✤ **RESOLVING DISPUTES**: They have the authority to resolve disputes.
✤ **ALTRUISTIC ACTIONS**: They force a society into altruistic actions: for

example, the belief that the old, if not looked after, may decide to become angry witches leads to better care for the aged.
✤ **EVIL EYE**: They allow the possibility of some action in otherwise impossible circumstances, such as casting the evil eye on an enemy.

Deity means the recovery of Goddess, whose cult anyway, it is claimed, never disappeared but simply went underground. One example among many of that claim is Wicca, from the Old English root meaning "to bend" or "to shape". Wicca rests on a belief that human affairs and features of the environment can be ordered, controlled, and changed by skilled practitioners whose powers are usually believed to be innate. The emphasis is on the application of power, derived especially from Goddess, to change existing circumstances, above all by changing one's inner life – "the power within oneself", as Margot Adler described it in her book *Drawing Down the Moon*, "to create artistically and change one's life".

Witchcraft is closely associated with the use of magic, but its techniques are derived from within, or else bestowed by a supernatural agent, rather than (as often with magic) learnt. The belief that the agent was the devil led to a ferocious persecution of witches in medieval Europe, an antagonism reinforced by the fact that witches were often women and therefore seemed to be exercising powers that men could not control.

Because of this antagonism, witches were usually described in a hostile way. More recently, anthropologists have described their activities in more positive terms (see box, above). Witches are certainly threatening, but that means that they can provide sanctions to help control aberrant behaviour.

The increasing emancipation of women from the control of men, both in society and in religions, has also led to a re-evaluation of the role and meaning of witches. All this underlies the claim that witchcraft is the enduring way in which Goddess has been preserved as a living truth, so that present-day Wicca is simply the latest stage so far in an unbroken religious tradition. According to Starhawk, a leader of the recovery of Wicca at the end of the 20th century, "Followers of Wicca seek their inspiration in pre-Christian sources, European folklore, and mythology. They consider themselves priests and priestesses of an ancient European shamanistic [for Shamanism, see pp.160f] nature religion that worships a goddess who is related to the ancient Mother Goddess in her three aspects of

White Witches
Kevin Carlyon, High Priest of British white witches, binding two new initiates into the Covenant of Earth Magic in 1999.

Maiden, Mother, and Crone." In *The Spiral Dance* (1979) she protested against the caricature of witches as "members of a kooky cult", and claimed that Wicca has "the depth, dignity, and seriousness of purpose of a true religion".

In this religion, Goddess is the focus of worship, and worship and liturgy (Greek *leitourgia*: for the meaning, see p.214) are themselves among the most important ways in which the human experience of Deity is expressed. Margot Adler quoted a ritual for the opening of a sacred circle in which people can then "shape" their own worship (see box, right). Often, but not always, such worship separates Goddess from God.

Not everyone has found the separation of Goddess from God necessary if the experience and insight of women is to win its way into the characterization of Deity. This may seem impossible in religions where masculine language and imagination of God are, and always have been, dominant. Some people do find it difficult to think of God except in the way that they and their tradition have imagined *Him*.

The masculine pronoun makes the point. In 1851, Herman Melville (1819–91) wrote in a letter to Nathaniel Hawthorne about the common dislike of God: "The reason the mass of men fear God and at bottom dislike Him, is because they rather dislike His heart, and fancy Him all brain, like a watch." He then added in a bracket: "You perceive I employ a capital initial in the pronoun referring to the Deity: don't you think there is a slight dash of flunkeyism in the usage?" (p.559). What this book shows, however, is that flunkeyism is not the same as adoration, worship, and prayer: the closer people have been drawn to Goddess or God, the more they have known that their images and words fall far short of the One to whom their words are pointing.

This means that metaphors and analogies, inadequate and approximate as they are, become inevitable when humans try to say something about Goddess or God. Among these, the most powerful and widespread metaphor to describe what the union with Goddess or God feels like has been that of sexual union, since that is so much more than a physical event. Even so, the physical is important, and for that reason the practice of sexual union was incorporated into ritual in many religions as an introduction to union with Deity.

Given, therefore, the profound importance of the union of male and female as a metaphor and practice of union with Goddess or God, it is not surprising that people have found it liberating to use feminine as much as masculine words and images in approaching Deity in whom gender does not exist: all words fall short of the essence (the essential nature and being) of the One that is, but all can catch something of the experience involved – and can extend that experience into vision.

"A circle should be marked on the floor, surrounding those who will participate in the ceremony. An altar is to be set up at the centre of the circle. At the centre of the altar shall be placed an image of the Goddess, and an incense burner placed in front of it... When all the people are prepared they shall assemble within the circle. The woman acting as priestess shall direct the man who acts as priest to light the candles and incense.
She shall then say:
'The presence of the noble Goddess extends everywhere. Throughout the many strange, magical, and beautiful worlds. To all places of wilderness, enchantment, and freedom.'
The goddess is then worshipped at four quarters, and the people present are sealed in the circle with these words:
'The circle is sealed, and all herein
Are totally and completely apart
From the outside world,
That we may glorify the Lady whom we adore.
Blessed Be!
All repeat: Blessed Be!...
As above, so below:
As the universe, so the soul.
As without, so within.
Blessed and gracious one,
On this day do we consecrate to you
Our bodies, Our minds,
And our spirits. Blessed Be!...

"Our rite draws to its end.
O lovely and gracious Goddess,
Be with each of us as we depart.
The circle is broken!'"

(Adler, pp.470–2)

The Natural World

Walking with Care

Sun Dance

A hide painting with a representation of the Sun Dance. Among the Pueblo Indians of New Mexico, the power of the source of life (identified with the sun) was mediated into the world by the Inside Chief who "controlled the sacred". According to R.Gutierrez (see Bibl.) his role was to keep the cosmos properly balanced by ensuring that humans did not go their own way, and that the ties of reciprocity between humans, animals, natural forces, and supernatural spirits were not disturbed.

WHEN THE ANISHINABE (a Native American people from the area of the Great Lakes) go hunting, they go gently. Certainly the hunted animal dies, but hunting is regarded as an act of communication between human and animal *persons*: animals, who have their own languages, need to be persuaded to give up their bodies by the assurance that humans will make restoration so that the spirit of the dead animal will be reborn: through rituals the hunter and the hunted are connected to each other.

"Walking with care" is a Native American way of talking about the sacred nature of the world. The Sioux (a group of Native Americans living originally in the area of the upper Mississippi river) address the Earth as Mother: "Every step that we take upon you should be done in a sacred manner; each step should be as a prayer."

Native Americans inhabited every part of North America, from the Arctic to the deserts in the south, in many different tribes speaking many different languages, so it is unwise to generalize about Native American religion. Nevertheless, some fundamental themes recur, many of which agree with the beliefs of primal religions (see box, below), certainly that of humans living in a network of relationships with all that exists.

What European settlers regarded as a wilderness (perhaps from Old English "wild deer-ness" or simply "wild + ness"), Native Americans regarded as a spirited and living being (see box, top right).

The "Great Mystery" referred to by Luther Standing Bear was the equally widespread belief that all things come from the High God, the One source of life as gift, the unproduced Producer of all that is.

The High God, with different names in different tribes, is known through the many manifestations of life and creation, all of which are

PRIMAL RELIGIONS

H. Turner (see Bibl.) claimed that primal religions underlie all later religions, with six common features:

✣ **KINSHIP**: A sense of kinship with nature.
✣ **CO-EXISTENCE**: A realistic sense of being a creature not self-sufficient on its own.
✣ **SPIRITS**: A belief that humans are not alone or isolated but are surrounded by a personalized world of helpful and harmful spirits.
✣ **RELATIONSHIP**: An ability to enter into

relationship with these spirits, to receive blessing and protection.
✣ **AFTERLIFE**: A sense that these relationships continue beyond death.
✣ **SACRAMENT**: A belief that humans live in a sacramental world in which the material and physical both contain and carry the spiritual.

bearers of the same spirit. These agents of God are not introduced as a kind of primitive science, as a means, for example, of explaining natural phenomena. They are, rather, the means through which Native Americans enter into a relationship with God through sight, sound, and hearing, as in the Sweat Lodge ceremonies, described by Linda Hogan (p.224) of the Chickasaw (who lived originally on the banks of the Mississippi):

"By late afternoon we are ready to enter the enclosure. The hot lava stones are placed inside. They remind us of earth's red and fiery core, and of the spark inside all life. After the flap, which serves as a door, is closed, water is poured over the stones and the hot steam rises around us. In a sweat lodge ceremony, the entire world is brought inside the enclosure. The animals come from the warm and sunny distances. Water from dark lakes is there. Wind. Young, lithe willow branches bent overhead remember their lives rooted in ground, the sun their leaves took in. They remember that minerals and water rose up their trunks, and birds nested in their leaves, and that planets turned above their brief, slender lives. Wind arrives from the four directions. It has moved through caves and breathed through our bodies. It is the same air elk have inhaled, air that passed through the lungs of a grizzly bear. We sit together in our aloneness and speak, one at a time, our deepest language of need, hope, loss, and survival. We remember that all things are connected. [We] say the words, 'All my relations', before and after we pray; those words create a relationship with other people, with animals, with the land."

Seeing God in and through the natural order is common throughout the world. If the world is regarded *as* God – for example, as the body of God – the result is called pantheism (cf. panentheism, p.317). But even if God is believed to be distinct from the natural order, it is still common for the natural order to be received as the gift of God and to be read like a revelation alongside scripture (as in the poem on p.255), a book that reveals the purpose and meaning of God.

"We did not think of the great open plains, the beautiful rolling hills, and winding streams with tangled growth, as 'wild'. Only to the white man was nature a 'wilderness' and only to him was the land 'infested' with 'wild' animals and 'savage' people. To us it was tame. Earth was bountiful and we were surrounded with the blessings of the Great Mystery"

(Luther Standing Bear, p.38)

The Ghost Dance

Ghost Dance movements (from 1870 and 1890) looked to a restoration of the old order, including the dead being brought back to life: "The time will come when the whole Indian race, living and dead, will be reunited upon a regenerated earth, to live a life of aboriginal happiness, forever free from death, disease, and misery" (Mooney, p.75).

Symbol and Sign

Finding a Common Language

Symbol
This stained glass window depicting the Virgin Mary with blue robe and halo is (in Peirce's sense, see text) a symbol of her.

Icon
The ivory figure of the Virgin Mary shows the Asian features characteristic of religious carvings created in the Orient. It is (in Peirce's sense, see text) an icon of her.

AT THE CENTRE OF THE WORLD stood Yggdrasil, "the ash tree house of Ygg", on whose growth and fertility the nine worlds depended – so, at least, the old Norse sagas (for example, the *Prose Edda* of Snorri Sturluson) relate. Even the Aesir gods depended on the Tree's survival.

The Tree was supported by three roots: the first reached down to Jotunnheim, the land of the giants; the second to Niflheim, the lowest of the nine worlds; and the third to Godheim and the city of Asgard, the home of the gods such as Thor and Odin. But the Tree was not secure: each day the dragon Nidhoggr and smaller serpents gnawed at its root, and goats nibbled its leaves and branches. So each day the three Norns, Urdr, Verdandi, and Skuldr (Fate, Being, and Necessity) watered Yggdrasil with water from a sacred pool, and plastered its cracks with mud to keep it alive (the Norns too are essential to the survival of the Aesir gods: when they decree it, the gods die). For that purpose also, sacrifices were made to Yggdrasil, often by hanging victims on trees. The supreme offering was made by the god Odin, who stabbed himself with his own spear and hung on Yggdrasil as a corpse for nine days in order to learn the secrets of the runes.

The runes were wisdom and secrets secured in the earliest writing system: as twigs fell off the tree, they were arranged by the Norns into letters and words so that they could record their understanding of how to live and how to overcome evil and danger. Odin used the runes to bring himself back to life, but his self-sacrifice had been necessary for the secret of the runes to become known and shared with others.

Many more stories were told about the tree Yggdrasil, all of them extending the meaning of the Tree as the great symbol of the cosmos as a dynamic process, and the symbol also of the constant struggle between life and death: the destructive dragon at Yggdrasil's root was balanced by the guardian eagle at its summit.

Symbols, like that of the Tree, appear in all the religions of the world. Trees appear frequently as the *axis mundi*, the central pole or hub around which the world revolves. Trees are natural symbols of growth, death, and rebirth in the unending sequence of new seasons. A tree contains within itself the power of God to create and to destroy.

The Tree is only one of a vast treasury of symbols through which humans have told their stories of God, of the universe, of life and death – and in fact of every way in which people have experienced their lives. Symbols are visible expressions of the feelings and thoughts that humans have had about their world and about their situation in it. The power of symbols is that they form a common language that all people understand.

The power of this language and the fact that the same symbols are found in different cultures and different ages led Carl Jung (1875–1961) to argue that the God-image belongs deeply within all human beings: "it corresponds to a definite complex of psychological facts" (8.528) – though he was careful to say that "what God is in himself remains outside the competence of all psychology".

Jung was certainly correct in saying that symbols have been particularly important in the human search for God, because they not only represent God and the attributes of God: they are believed also to carry something of the reality of God in themselves. This was a point made by US logician C.S. Peirce (1839–1914) when he related the understanding of symbols to the study of signs known as semiotics (Greek *sema,* "sign"). Peirce drew a distinction between three types of sign: icon, index, and symbol. An icon is a sign containing some of the qualities associated with the thing signified (e.g., maps and diagrams); an index is a sign which is in a dynamic relation with the thing signified and calls attention to what is signified (e.g., the column of mercury in a thermometer measuring temperature and indicating health or illness); a symbol is a conventional sign with an agreed meaning. Thus a statue of a saint is an icon; a relic of that saint is an index; and a halo is a symbol, pointing to holiness.

The more clearly it came to be realized that God is far beyond human sight and description, the more the visual representations of God moved from icon (in Peirce's sense) to symbol. But all signs, in their different forms, carry the meanings that people associate in their tradition with "God" in ways that allow or encourage them to enter into relationship with God. This means that signs associated with God are stable, but they are not necessarily fixed in meaning for all time. Just as the characterizations of God change dramatically through time, so also do the meanings of particular signs. Important signs and symbols, therefore, have a life of their own. When Christianity converted the people of Northern Europe, it converted also their symbols. The self-sacrifice of Odin on the tree became the sacrifice of Jesus on the cross; and the Galilean teacher became the young hero who conquers death and reveals the meaning and purpose of life. In *The Dream of the Rood* ("rood" is an Old English word for "cross"), the Anglo-Saxon poet wrote:

"Then the young warrior, he was God Almighty,
Stripped himself, firm and unflinching; he climbed
Upon the cross, brave before many, to redeem mankind.
A rood was raised up; I bore aloft the mighty king, the lord
of heaven"

Index
Reliquary of the Virgin Mary from Limoges. A reliquary contains some relic (some item) of the person or object (e.g., part of the cross of Jesus). A reliquary of Mary is (in Peirce's sense, see text) an index of her.

Music

Ecstasy and Trance

Indian Trance and Dance
"The art of dancing arose when the god Vishnu [p.90] killed the demons, and Lakshmi [p.116] noticed the graceful movements of her Lord and asked to know what was meant by them" (Anand, p.239). In India, there are more than 200 classical forms of dance in union with God, many shown on carvings on the temple of Chidambaram.

"Music stands quite alone. It is cut off from all the other arts ... It does not express a particular and definite joy, sorrow, anguish, horror, delight, or mood of peace, but joy, sorrow, anguish, horror, delight, peace of mind themselves, in the abstract, in their essential nature, without accessories, and therefore without their customary motives. Yet it enables us to grasp and share them fully in this quintessence"

(Schopenhauer)

ACCORDING TO CONTEMPORARY MUSICIAN Lee "Scratch" Perry, reggae music is called by some people "an explosion": "But I call it Deep Roots Music… As seventy-two nations [the number of the nations in the Jewish Bible] must bow to reggae music, rock steady music, ska music, meringue music, calypso music, jazz music – don't care what the music might be, but music is the only comforter, I'm telling you the truth, man" (Johnson and Pines).

Reggae is music associated originally with the Rastafarians, a religious movement that developed in the Caribbean affirming the worth and value of Africa, and acknowledging Hailie Selassie, the descendant of Solomon and Sheba, as the messianic (pp.198, 203) representative of God on earth. Reggae was born out of the great suffering and injustice of slavery, and became even more than a comforter. Johnson and Pines also quote Big Youth:

"Them have reggae music as a little sacred dance music. But there's a form of reggae music called Jah [the name of God in the Jewish Bible] music… That is the music that inspire black people. The music is philosophical, so much so that it brings people out of darkness. Jah music tells people about themselves"

Music does this or something like it to all people. Music in its many different forms allows people to express their feelings and emotions, and it also evokes emotional responses from them, as Schopenhauer (1788–1860) commented (see box, left). Because music is connected so directly to feelings and emotions, it is a paramount way in which people have expressed their feelings of and about God. In particular, it is connected with trance (a state in which union with God is often claimed) and perhaps, though less certainly, with ecstasy – less certainly, because it depends on how trance and ecstasy are defined.

In general, those words are often used as though they both mean the same thing: a state in which brain and body are dramatically and visibly altered, giving the impression that the people involved have either left their ordinary way of living in the world (Greek *ekstasis*, "standing outside"), or have been taken over or possessed by outside agents, ranging from devils to God.

To reduce confusion about these very different states, Gilbert Rouget, in *Music and Trance*, suggested that the word "ecstasy" should be used for those states in which people move into conditions of bliss and attainment of God (often with dramatic and visible consequences) in isolation, immobility, and quiet; and that the word "trance" should be used when equally dramatic and visible consequences are produced, but this time in public, often accompanied by chanting, drums or other music, and by dance.

To exemplify the differences, Rouget offered the example of Saint Teresa of Avila (cf. p.292) because she experienced both. What she reports is not as precise as Rouget's definitions, and she called everything "ecstasy" (Spanish *extasis*). Nevertheless, she recognized distinctions between union (*union*, Rouget's trance) and rapture or ravishment (*arrobamiento*, Rouget's ecstasy): the latter (ecstasy) produces "phenomena of a higher degree", and in this state, in utter aloneness before God ("That desert and solitude seem to the soul better than all the companionship of the world") she felt pain and glory.

Looking worldwide, other distinctions, as well as the contrast between private and public, become clear:

❖ Ecstasy produces visions and sounds, trance does not
❖ Ecstasy is produced by sensory control or deprivation, trance by over-stimulation of the senses
❖ People coming out of ecstasy remember what has happened, coming out of trance they often do not

An important difference between trance and ecstasy observed by Rouget is that trance, but not ecstasy, is accompanied by music. The relevance of music is not that it causes trance by a direct effect on the brain, but that it helps to create the social approval and endorsement of the behaviours that lead to trance – behaviours that without a context of social approval might be regarded with fear and terror. In his conclusion, Rouget asks why music is indispensable to trance, and answers:

"Because it is the only language that speaks simultaneously to the head and legs; because it is through music that the group provides the entranced person with a mirror in which he can read the image of his borrowed identity; and because it is the music that enables him to reflect this identity back again to the group in the form of dance. There is no mystery to it at all. Or, if there is, then it lies in the trance state itself, as a special state of consciousness; and if we must seek for an explanation of this, it may be found in the overriding power of a certain conjunction of emotion and imagination. This is the source from which trance springs. Music does nothing more than socialize it, and enable it to attain its full development" (pp.325ff)

"Music can draw the hearer in chains of gold to the consideration of holy things"

(Thomas Morley)

St Teresa's Ecstasy
Bernini's sculpture shows Teresa in ecstasy: "The whole body is paralysed. One is unable to stir with either the feet or the arms. Rather, if one is standing, one sits down, like a person being carried from one place to another, unable even to breathe" (Teresa, p.251). She knew also of public occasions of union/trance when she felt herself leaving her body and the other sisters were aware of it; or when singing with the sisters, "the effect upon me was so great that my hands began to grow numb" (ibid., p.389).

Ritual

Behaviours Embedded in the Brain

Baptism
*Baptism is ritual as an
enacted sign in which the
person baptised, whether
infant or adult, becomes part
of the body of Christ
(pp.235, 241) and is thus
taken by God to a life
beyond death, even though
this life still continues. In
Christ, death has already
happened, and Paul could
say, "You are already dead,
and your life lies hidden
with Christ in God"
(Colossians 3.3).*

ALL PEOPLE LIVE THEIR LIVES facing "a choice of catastrophes" –
the title of a book by the science-fiction writer Isaac Asimov
reviewing "the disasters that threaten our world". They range
from the remote (the heat death of the universe) to the near at hand
(the change of climate and the depletion of resources). On a smaller
scale, individuals also face threats to their lives, from crossing the road
to catching a virus. Living organisms are vulnerable, and need to be
defended if they are to live long enough to create the next generation.

Humans have many defences protecting their proteins and genes.
Some are biological, like cells and the skin inside which they live; others,
like culture, humans have created – the arrangements they have made to
live successfully in families, groups, nations, and empires. Culture, as a
defensive "skin", comprises such things as writing and books, traffic lights
and schools, and religions.

Religions are the earliest cultural systems we know about that helped
to protect both the bringing into being of children and their protection
and instruction. That is why many religions have such strict rituals and
rules in matters of sex, marriage, and food (see Bowker, pp.3–108).

Among the many ways in which religions have protected what is, in
more up-to-date language, gene-replication and the nurture of children,
one of the most important is ritual. Rituals are learned and repeated
behaviours that people in a particular group or religion practise, either
individually or more often together. Rituals are so important for human
life that they occur as much in non-religious ways (for example, in the
parades and ceremonies of Communist societies) as they do
in religious acts of worship or in rites (rituals) of passage (at
birth, puberty, marriage, and death).

Through ritual, religions tie culture strongly to God, to the
purpose and protection of God. Religions agree that survival
is important, but they also ask, "Survival for what?" For what
purpose is life lived in the context of such vulnerability?
Rituals are a common and usually non-verbal way of enacting
the overriding purposes and meanings of life and of death.
Rituals are thus repeated patterns of action and behaviour
undertaken for an immense number of purposes – for example, to
celebrate the birth of a child or to lament the passing of an elder; to
give thanks for the life-giving presence of food and water or to bring a
death-dealing disaster on enemies; to offer praise or to express
penitence; and certainly to recognize and come into the presence
of God. For this to work, rituals have to be recognized and
understood at the deepest levels of human understanding, so

not surprisingly they are embedded in the human brain and body: ritual behaviours are natural in the kind of brains and bodies that humans have – as indeed they are to some extent in other animals: people who study animal behaviour (ethologists) often speak of "ritual displays" in the approach to mating, or the defence of territory.

This "naturalness" does not imply that ritual behaviours are determined by genetic programs, as some have claimed. Rather, rituals are widely employed in human cultures because they hold together the interactions between two major ways in which human brains process information as they respond to the world: *associative learning* and *symbolic cognition*.

Associative learning means forming associations between representations of events in the world, and is present in all animals in differing degrees of complexity. The human brain has been formed by evolution to process some stimulus events as intrinsically rewarding (e.g., sweet tastes) or to be avoided (aversive, e.g., very bitter or sour tastes). Such unlearned stimuli are called *primary reinforcers*. The brain rapidly identifies *neutral stimuli* which are linked in time or space to primary reinforcers, so that they evoke similar responses in terms of emotions and of motivation to act. These neutral stimuli become *secondary reinforcers*. The amygdala (p.44) and orbofrontal cortex are the key brain structures representing the feelings associated with primary reinforcers, as well as memorizing associations with secondary reinforcers.

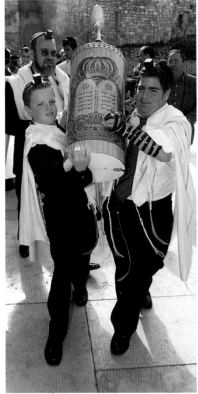

At one level, rituals employ many stimuli which human brains find intrinsically rewarding or aversive (thus heightening emotion when rituals are performed) in addition to setting up learned associations between stimuli which may be remembered for a lifetime. Examples of intrinsically arousing or attention-grabbing stimuli used in rituals include: motion, colour, luminosity, emotive facial expressions of masks, accentuated sexual characteristics (cosmetics, oils), sudden loud noises (fireworks, bells), styles of language (singing, chanting), pain (flagellation, circumcision), temperature (baptism by immersion), smells (incense, perfumes), and taste (ritual foods), among many others.

Humans, however, do not simply respond to stimuli; they interpret them and identify them to themselves and to each other using *symbol-based cognition*. Humans are able to think with signs (pp.38–9), creating the possibility of, for example, using metaphor to represent God as a Judge or King, and then depicting this conception through signs, symbols, and icons such as paintings or sculpture.

The brain represents a concept such as "king" by splitting it up into component parts (e.g., visual appearance, vocal quality, emotional connotations), which are each stored in specialized regions, and by then binding this information together in multimodal processing areas (such as the temporal lobe memory system and prefrontal cortex) when the concept

Bar and Bat Mitzva
These Jewish ceremonies are rites (rituals) of passage, in which boys and girls (though not girls for all Jews) move from childhood to accepting the responsibility of the Covenant (p.176): they become "a son (or a daughter) of the commandment". The 613 commands and prohibitions of Torah (p.200) become the way in which Jews can say "Yes" to God.

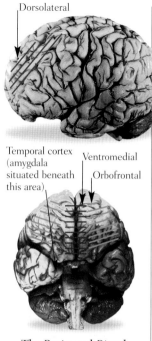

Dorsolateral

Temporal cortex (amygdala situated beneath this area)

Ventromedial

Orbofrontal

The Brain and Ritual
In ritual, the brain draws together stored information to create meaningful responses (e.g., thoughts, memories, images). Temporal lobe structures are very important in binding this information together. The ventromedial prefrontal cortices help to link these meanings with emotions, often profound.

is activated by reading the word "king", by a thought of a king, and so on. By imagining God as King, we are using existing brain-based representations to create a specific sense of what God is like, linking God to a potentially vast network of associated meanings which can be explored in many ways (for example, in ritual symbolism, religious art, prayer, poetry, and the many other ways described in this book). In this way, religious symbolism at a cognitive level corresponds to the ways in which rituals use stimuli at an associative level to evoke sensations and emotions, and they too contribute to the emotional experience of the ritual performance.

Our capacity for symbolic cognition has arisen out of the long-running co-evolution of culture and the brain (particularly the prefrontal cortex, which co-ordinates the complex cognitive processes which support symbolic representation and learning: see Deacon, 1998). Symbolic cognition allows culturally prominent symbols (such as the Christian cross or Shiva as Nataraja, the Lord of the Dance, p.104) to be created and to become the focus of layers of associated thoughts, memories, and emotions during the course of a religious lifetime. Thus human brains not only form associations between stimulus events, as other animals do, but also interpret stimuli as *meaningful* by using symbols to create representations of what is going on, both in public expressions (e.g., speech and mime) and in private experience. In this way, meanings can become associated with experience and can resonate emotionally (for example, when the image of the Resurrection is used to express faith that adversity can be overcome, or when loss of life is accepted as part of the creative and destructive Dance of Shiva). Rituals, therefore, orchestrate the interaction between associative and symbolic learning processes by manipulating the sensory characteristics of symbolic displays. In this way, primary and secondary reinforcers heighten arousal, feelings, sensations, and attention, interacting with the concepts encoded and evoked by the sign stimuli of the ritual (symbolic and iconic objects, gestures, mime, language, etc.) so that they are experienced and *felt* as especially powerful, relevant, and memorable.

THE SOMATIC MARKER HYPOTHESIS

Quinton Deeley explains this theory linking cognition and emotion:

This hypothesis links cognition and emotion by proposing that cognitive abilities such as decision-making, self-awareness, and empathy are influenced by bodily or *somatic* states which *mark* cognitive representations (e.g., of an imagined course of action) with feelings or responses based on prior emotional conditioning. The ventromedial prefrontal cortices are thought to reactivate the somatic states originally associated with a given stimulus pattern or mental representation, co-ordinating the activity of emotional networks. From this perspective, ritual performances join symbolic representations with distinctive somatic states. When ritual symbols or associated concepts are re-encountered, the ritually inculcated somatic states are partially or fully reactivated. This may then manifest itself in unconsciously motivated or fully conscious attitudes or behaviours (e.g. avoiding ritually unclean foods, or an attitude of reverence to religious icons or symbols): see Damasio, 2000.

Rituals are thus extremely common in different religions and societies (many rituals are secular and have nothing specifically to do with religion) because they are a dramatically effective way in which people can find powerful (often transcendent) meaning in the local circumstances of their lives. Rituals create distinctive emotions and feelings, almost like a tone or colour, whether the emotions are of joy, awe, reverence, ecstasy, fear, grief, or sadness. A current theory that helps to explain how ritual joins symbolic cognition and emotion is the *somatic marker hypothesis* (see box, below left).

Meaning is thus constructed, remembered, and reinforced in extremely complex ways, so it is not surprising that humans fill their environments with signs and symbols as well as ritual practices. Through this process even the most abstract ideas, like time, space, and God, can be personalized and interacted with. They can be related to the experienced world, even though they are known to be "not exactly like that". This is precisely what happens in all religions in relation to God, who is known to be beyond words and description and yet is clearly knowable and approachable through signs and rituals. It is indeed the role of analogy to make the abstract conceivable in terms of the familiar (see, e.g., Aquinas, p.268).

On this basis, it is obvious why rituals are so important in human evolution. They are a fundamental part of building a protective culture, because they connect people through the opportunity of what human brains and bodies have in common. None of this *diminishes* the beauty and importance of ritual; indeed, it explains why ritual is so indispensable, even if one thinks in terms of human evolution alone. Rituals are the world that people live in common with their neighbours, bound together by them in a shared enterprise of life.

Ritual is thus another of the profound and natural "languages" through which people throughout history have given expression to their feelings and understandings of God, not least as the One who confers ultimate meaning on every aspect of life and of death.

Funeral
Rituals surrounding death may help those who mourn in their grief, but their purpose is to help the one who has died. In the Gita (p.92), Krishna says of himself, "Whoever at the hour of death, when abandoning his body, bears me in mind, rejoins my being, there is no doubt of this at all" (8.6). Death rituals aid these transitions, so that the person "escapes even the furthest outreach of Yama's [Death's] ranging hounds" (Bowker, Meanings p.167).

Myth

Transcending Scientific Analysis

"I do not know if Mawu is a man or a woman. History tells that Mawu created the world. Then when the world was created, Mawu withdrew from the earth and went to live in the sky. After living in the sky, Mawu did not care to come down and live on earth again. But on earth nothing went well.

Human beings did not understand how to do things for themselves. They quarrelled. They fought. They did not know how to cultivate the fields, or how to weave cloth to cover their bodies.

So Mawu sent her only son down to earth, whose name is Lisa; and to her son Lisa, Mawu gave metal, Gu, and she told Lisa to go down to the earth and cut the bush with this metal, and teach men how to use it to make useful things"

(Courlander, p.166)

Myth in Africa
Isidore Okpewho (p.68) identified the growth cycle of African myth in relation to fact and fiction in this simple diagram.

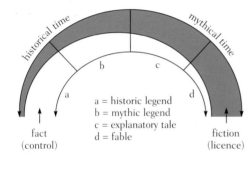

a = historic legend
b = mythic legend
c = explanatory tale
d = fable

fact
(control)

fiction
(licence)

THE STORY ON THE LEFT IS TOLD BY THE FON PEOPLE of Dahomey in Africa about the coming of metal – and of swords – to the earth. Stories such as this are far older than the written or printed word: they have been treasured by people in all parts of the world and repeated to each generation.

They take the form of legend, folklore, epic, riddle, and myth – and although the definition of those words is not agreed, they reflect the way in which these stories may deal with everything, from known events to the unknown origins of creation and time, from entertainment to instruction, and much more.

Stories as myth are the common property of groups like families, tribes, or nations – the glue that helps to hold them together. Oyekan Owomoyela records how families gather together in Ibadan (in Nigeria) to tell riddles and stories:

"Apart from such concessions to progress as the use of electricity, pipe-borne water, and the Rediffusion box that brings a fixed radio programme by wire from a local transmitting station, the household remains a redoubt of tradition. After the evening meal, the members of the family gather on a porch [where] …the entertainment begins with riddles. What dines with an oba *(paramount chief of a community) and leaves him to clear the dishes? A fly. What passes before the oba's palace without making obeisance? Rain flood. On its way to Oyo its face is towards Oyo, on its way from Oyo its face is still towards Oyo. What is it? A double-faced drum. After a few riddles, the tales begin…"*

(Lindfors, p.264)

Myth is the way in which the story of any individual life is set in the context of far larger stories – narratives of the family or tribe or nation to which the individual belongs, and of the whole world, past, present, and future. Myth is supremely the way in which the human mind is able to explore and imagine God; and religions are communities with a common narrative and story in their shared mythology. This may seem hard to understand now, when so many people use the word myth to mean "false". What in fact is false is the belief that there is only one way of telling truth – for example, through science. Myth is an early reminder that truth can be told as much in fiction as in scientific fact, as much in poetry as in a mathematical proof – indeed, more so, because, myth enables people to record and share the ways in which they transcend the strict scientific analysis of what they are, as J.A. Ramsey put it, "mammals as highly tuned physiological machines carrying out with superlative efficiency what the lower animals are content to muddle through with" (Mackay, p.127). The philosopher F.W.J. Schelling (1775–1854) commented in his *Dialogue on Poetry*, "What is every beautiful mythology but a hieroglyphic expression of surrounding nature in a transfiguration of imagination and love?"

Schelling lived at a time when increasingly confident claims were being made that science would give the true explanation and account of everything – a view known as "scientism". Against this misplaced over-confidence, Richard Wagner (1813–83) began to write his "total art-works", operas in which he deliberately drew on past myths in order to create a new myth that would bear the weight of meaning in his own time.

Wagner did not doubt that physics (and the other sciences) answer many questions. But not all questions: why do people suffer? How are their sufferings related to what they or others have done in the past? How can they be rescued or redeemed from evil they have done in the past? In *Parsifal*, Wagner explored the theme of redemption and the way in which it is linked to suffering (*see caption*).

Wagner's *Parsifal* is one example. Far more widely, myth is a supreme human achievement, enabling people to share their deepest insights with each other, their hopes and their fears, and their experience of God.

Parsifal

In Wagner's *Parsifal*, *the theme of* mitleid (*"suffering with"*) *is explored. Parsifal does not merely pity Amfortas who, in bitter penitence, longs for death to be "a small atonement for a sin like mine" (Act 3.249). Parsifal enters into that suffering and shares it, and by doing so, he begins to acquire an understanding of himself that opens up the way to his own redemption. It is* mitleid, *suffering with others, that alone marks out the long-awaited redeemer: "Before the wrecked sanctuary Amfortas lay in fervent prayer, Begging a sign of pardon: Made wise through* mitleid *The blameless simpleton: Wait for him, the one I choose" (1.1.234ff)*

Sacrifice

Securing Life and Order

L ONG AGO, THE HUMAN RACE died out. The gods had given humans many things, but they had failed to give them the power, or at least the knowledge, to reproduce. Two of the gods, Quetzalcoatl and Xolotl, decided to rescue them. Quetzalcoatl went down into the underworld and gathered up the scattered bones of dead humans and took them back to the upper world. There, he ground them to dust, but there was still no life in them. He therefore cut open his own vein and mixed his own blood with the dust. Xolotl moulded the dust into human shapes, and Quetzalcoatl breathed life into them. Having given his life-blood for this creation, Quetzalcoatl then protected it, teaching people how to reproduce, how to measure time, and how to farm, write, and understand the stars.

That story from the Aztecs shows how deeply blood, life, and sacrifice are connected. Those who have received life through the shedding of blood on the part of God can show their gratitude most effectively by offering blood in return. Sacrifice was therefore prominent in Aztec religion. Priests repeatedly shed their own blood by passing barbed cords through their tongues and ears. Beyond that, humans were sacrificed, in rituals and ceremonies of great drama, and the Aztecs increasingly went to war with their neighbours in order, among other reasons, to obtain victims for sacrifice.

Sacrifice is one of the most important ways in which humans have expressed their feelings about God. It occurs in all religions – often criticized and changed, and sometimes given new form and meaning – but always appearing as one of the fundamental ways in which humans understand their situation and do something about it. "No man is an island", and sacrifice is one of the most powerful ways in which humans express the worth and cost of their relationships – above all their relationship with God. Sacrifice is thus the means through which life and order are secured; it is the enacted language through which humans recognize their precarious situation (threatened always by death) and express their

The Aztecs
The shedding of blood was important to the Aztecs, a race descended from Mexican warriors who, in about 1325CE, established a foothold on an island, Tenochtitlán, in Lake Texcoco. Calling themselves Aztec from the legendary land in which their ancestors lived, they established a flourishing empire until the 16th century CE when the Europeans arrived.

needs and their hope. Even among the Maya, predecessors of the Aztecs in Central America, this was true. The early discovery of the Maya suggested a peaceful people whose religion involved the stars and led to impressive discoveries in mathematics and astronomy. But as the Mayan hieroglyphic writing was deciphered, it became evident that the Mayans engaged in warfare, taking prisoners, many of whom were then mutilated and sacrificed. Human blood was thought to be essential as an offering if the relationship with the gods was to be maintained.

But human sacrifice is only one, relatively small, part of the way in which sacrifice has contributed to the story of God. Generally speaking, sacrifice is the offering in a ritual way of something that may be living or may be an inanimate object. The life or the object that is offered does not have to have great value in itself: it gains its value by being offered.

There are many reasons why it is done, and more than one reason may obtain in any particular sacrifice. It may be offered to deal with the fact of offence or sin, either by way of expiation (accepting that a price has to be paid) or of propitiation (calming down the legitimate anger of God); it may be offered as a substitution for something that belongs to God (for example, the first-born); it may be offered in order to establish communion among those who participate and union with God; it may be offered in expectation of receiving something in return (the principle known in Latin as *do ut des*, I give in order that you may give); it may be offered to cleanse some thought or defect; or as a way of saying thank you; or to turn away some threat or disaster, such as famine, drought, floods, or infertility. Sacrifice may be offered as a means of celebration and of holding a whole community together in common and familiar actions.

The importance of sacrifice has not led to its remaining unchallenged. In India, both Jains and Buddhists (pp.68–71) questioned whether sacrifice actually achieves what it is claimed to achieve. In their view, the characterization of God as one who responds to people only if they pay him well enough to do so was ludicrous. Even then, they recognized how important sacrifice is as a language through which to express feelings of worth and value. They therefore introduced *dana* (gift) as an equivalent to sacrifice: in Buddhism *dana* is the gift by lay people to Buddhist monks of food, drink, clothing, and other necessities and it is one of the most important works of merit.

Even in religions which give a high value to sacrifice, its worth, or the way in which it is done, has been repeatedly questioned. But at the heart of sacrifice remains the insight that some things, or some people, are of such inestimable, or even infinite, value that it is worth sacrificing something or everything for them. There is no greater love than to give up one's life for a friend, except possibly to give one's life for an enemy.

Sacrificial Sheep
Muslims are under obligation to sacrifice animals (a sheep, camel, cow, or goat). The sacrifice at the Great Festival (alId alKabir, also known as Id alAdha) commemorates Ibrahim's (Abraham's) sacrifice of a ram in place of his son. It takes place on the tenth day of Dhu 'lHijjah, and illustrates for Muslims the mercy of Allah in accepting a substitute for what rightfully belongs to Allah.

Architecture

◆

Buildings of God

Cave Temples

The story of God is told even when the place is not a building, but is the adaptation of a natural feature, like a cave. The earliest paintings lie deeply hidden in caves, and although their meaning is not fully understood, it is likely that features of the decoration have connections with shamans (p.160) and rituals. Caves continued to be adapted by different religions, for example in Buddhist chaityas, and in Byzantine cave churches. Shown here, the Longmen cave-temple complex on the Yi River has 1,352 caves, and about 40 pagodas of various sizes, containing more than 100,000 Buddhist images. Work on the caves continued well into the Tang period.

T KARNAK, ON THE BANKS of the River Nile, not far from Luxor, the Pharaohs of Egypt built many temples. Into the largest of the buildings, the huge Hypostyle Hall of Seti I (c.1318–1304BCE), the largest churches of Christendom would easily fit, with space to spare. The palaces of the Pharaohs were splendid, the temples even more so.

That is true of religious architecture throughout the world. Buildings devoted to God use the best skills and technology of their time. Vast fortunes have been spent on them, employing the greatest craftsmen, sculptors, and artists of their day. Through architecture, people tell, not only the story of God, but also the worth and cost of their devotion. In addition, through the decoration of these buildings, the story of God is often told directly – in carvings, paintings, and glass.

Humans have deliberately constructed buildings to make possible their approach to God in worship, ritual, and prayer. There has often been argument about whether God needs a building: how can God, supposedly surveying the whole world, be confined within walls? But frequently the building protects the image (the visible imagination) of God. In most temples, the worshipper moves through successive stages, often courtyards and halls, leading to a darker and more mysterious interior. At the centre lies the holiest place, where the presence of God is to be found.

In another way, also, buildings have helped humans to tell the story of God: they provide a place where people can come together in the presence of God. Prayer, ritual, and worship do not require a building. They can take place anywhere. But a building draws people together and provides a degree of permanence for ritual and for the telling of the stories of God. Thus the word "synagogue" means "a place of assembly": it is the place where Jews gather together to hear the word of God read and interpreted, and where they turn towards Jerusalem, the place where the Temple was originally built (pp.190f).

That simple fact is a reminder that buildings tell the story of God through their design. Christian churches are often in the shape of a cross; Muslim mosques are focused on the pulpit, from which the word of God is proclaimed, and on the niche (*mihrab*) which points the worshippers in the direction of Mecca; Hindu temples express the cosmos in miniature form so that the created and the Creator can meet on holy ground; Chinese temples are laid out so that their entrances lie on the four cardinal points, and so that the good forces and influences can flow into them; and Greek temples were built on sites associated with the gods, often on a high place close to the home of the gods, as most obviously on the Acropolis (Greek "upper city") in Athens.

In one other important way, buildings reveal much about the story of God. Buildings are not static: they are constantly being changed, and the changes tell us much about the ways in which the human imagination of God has also changed. Buildings may even be pulled down, and others built in their place. Thus the Temple site at Karnak was developed over a period of about 2,000 years. Egypt is an oasis, 600 miles long, made fertile by the Nile. To rule over this vast country, the Pharaohs had to secure the co-operation of the many different inhabitants. They did so, in part, by linking local gods to themselves and to their own worship, until the Pharaohs became for all people the manifestation of God.

So the Sun God Re (or Ra) of Heliopolis ("City of the Sun") was linked with the Pharaohs, who were called the Sons of Re and were thus associated with the splendour and power of the Sun. The Gods of other major places, such as Thebes and Memphis, were then made the allies of Re. So when a dynasty from Thebes became the Pharaohs, they brought their God, Amun, with them, and this produced Amon-Re. Attempts were then made to organize the gods into families and hierarchies, and one of the Pharaohs, Amenophis IV (1379–62BCE), declared that Aten, the Sun giving heat and life to the world, was the supreme God. He changed his name to Akhenaten, the one who serves Aten, and he closed the temples of other gods. Even the names of those gods were hacked out of the walls where they had been inscribed. Despite all this, immediately after his death the temples were demolished, and many of the building blocks were used for the reconstruction of temples to the other gods. Something like this is true of many religious buildings: they reflect the human experience of God, but their history tells also of the ways in which the human imagination of God changes.

Karnak Temple Complex
During the first five years of his reign, Amenophis extended the Temple complex at Karnak, dedicating it to Aten, and called it pr-itn, *"the domain of Aten". He also composed a famous hymn that celebrates the life-giving power of the Sun: "You rise in perfection on the horizon of the sky, living Aten, who started life...You are my desire" (Simpson, p.290).*

Art

Pointing to the Truth

"The lunatic, the lover,
and the poet
Are of imagination all compact...
Such tricks hath strong
imagination,
That if it would but apprehend
some joy,
It comprehends some bringer
of that joy;
Or in the night, imagining
some fear,
How easy is a bush
supposed a bear!"

(A Midsummer Night's Dream, 5.1.7)

Hand Outlines

*In caves from as early as the
Palaeolithic era, people
painted pictures of animals
that may have connections
with shamanism (p.160);
they also placed hands
against the wall and drew
round them.*

LONG AGO IN CORINTH, a young woman called Butades faced the prospect of being separated from her lover, so before he left her, she made him stand so that his shadow fell on the wall. She then traced the outline of his shadow so that she would have a copy of him in his absence. The French artist J-B. Suvée painted this incident and called the painting *The Origin of Drawing*.

In the ancient Mediterranean world, that was believed to be the origin of art – in which case the outline of hands on cave walls is the true beginning of art. When Pliny the Elder wrote his *Natural History* in the first century of the Christian era, he reported that no one could tell whether it was the Egyptians or the Greeks who invented art, but at least, he wrote, "all agree that art began with tracing an outline round a person's shadow". So, in the Mediterranean world from which the great traditions of Western art are derived, the initial purpose of art was *mimesis*, a Greek word meaning "imitation".

But copying and imitation were not sufficient on their own. Plato insisted that while perfect imitation is indeed the aim, the skill of an artist lies in suggesting the truth of what has been copied by *not* copying exactly: it is the skill of an artist to suggest an image instead of producing an exact copy.

The word "image" suggests immediately the word "imagination" (see box, above left). Artists are those who, by using imagination, take something from a wall before they put anything on a wall. That at least is what Leonardo da Vinci thought important in the training of any artist: "I will not refrain from setting among these precepts a new device for consideration which, although it may appear trivial and almost ludicrous, is nevertheless of great utility in arousing the mind to various inventions. And this is that if you look at any walls spotted with various stains or with a mixture of different kinds of stones, if you are about to invent some scene you will be able to see in it a resemblance to various different landscapes adorned with mountains, rivers, rocks, trees, plains, wide valleys, and various groups of hills. You will also be able to see divers combats and figures in quick movement, and strange expressions of faces, and outlandish costumes, and an infinite number of things which you can then reduce into separate and well conceived forms. With such walls and blends of different stones it comes about as it does with the sound of bells, in whose clanging you may discover every name and word that you can imagine."

Imagination was equally paramount in the very different world of China. In China, poetry and painting belong to each other as "the host and the guest". Both are marked for excellence, not by what they put in, but by what they leave out. It is rare to see a shadow in a Chinese painting, even when the sun or the moon are clearly evident, for Chinese paintings are not attempting to represent, or re-present, a scene realistically, as a photograph might attempt to do; they are trying to convey the inner identity and unity of all nature and appearance (cf. the Dao, p.152), and this can more effectively be done by allusive suggestion than by reproduction of the superficial appearance. When the Emperor Hui Sung set an exam for his would-be civil servants, he chose a line of poetry for them to illustrate: "When I returned from trampling on flowers, the hoofs of my horse were fragrant." The winning painting portrayed no meadows full of flowers: the horse is walking on a path, but with two butterflies fluttering round its hoofs: the meadows and the flowers must be somewhere near, but they are not directly visible.

Throughout the world, human emotions and feelings have been both expressed and evoked by art in which skill and imagination are combined. Inevitably, therefore, art has been a major "language" through which people have tried to say something – many very different things – about God. God has been directly portrayed, even though people are well aware that God cannot be set in front of a wall or a canvas and copied. More often, therefore, images of Goddess and God are suggested through the symbols associated with them.

Art may also express the feelings that people have about Goddess and God, from penitence to praise. It may be teaching and instruction, it may be propaganda: sometimes it tries to coerce people into belief, offering terrifying pictures of the punishments awaiting the wicked after death, and of the agents of those tortures. But far beyond all that, art is capable of pointing to the truth of God by the way it connects with the common sensing of God through the occasions of the world. It does not coerce the emotion, but allows it, even evokes it. Art may, and often does, become a window through which people look – and as they look, so, at least on occasion, they see. Even so, for some religious traditions, it is a radical contradiction to suppose that God can be portrayed in any way: it comes close to idolatry, the worship of an image instead of the unseen and unseeable reality. In India however, the image is one of the life-giving ways in which the unseen is able to be seen – so much so, that a common Indian word for "worship" is *darshan*, meaning literally "seeing". What, then, do Indians "see" in the case of God?

Chinese Art
"To the Chinese the theme of a painting is inseparable from its form, and both are the expression of an all-embracing philosophical attitude towards the visible world... The educated Chinese painter was, unlike his European counterpart, never just a painter. He was something of a philosopher, too; and being a philosopher, his vision did not fade with the passing of his youth, but strengthened and deepened as he grew older" (Sullivan, pp.1,11).

India

---◇---

A tapestry of different ways to God.

INDIA

The name Hinduism was given in the 19th century to the coalition of religions that exists in India. The word comes from the Persian *hindu*, Sanskrit *sindhu*, meaning "river", referring to the inhabitants of the river Indus valley. It therefore means Indian. Of India's more than one billion people, about 80 per cent are Hindu, with about 30 million more dispersed throughout the world, but there is no single religion that can be called "Hinduism". The beliefs and practices of Hindus have many common characteristics, but they are expressed in different ways: village religion, for example, is very different from philosophical religion.

Historically, Indian religion is seen as unfolding through stages, but that again is misleading, because some of the earliest forms have lasted to the present day and may be little affected by later innovations. The roots are in the traditions of the early inhabitants of India:

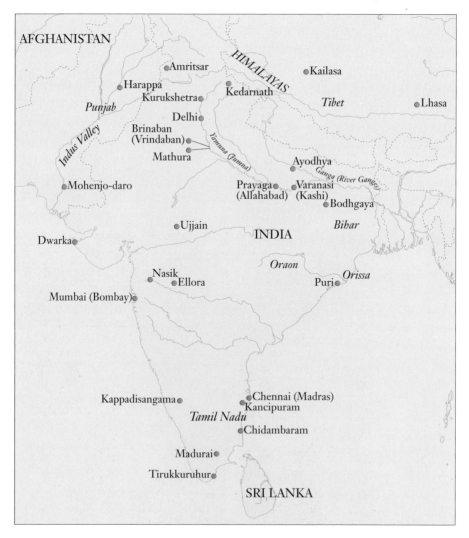

the Indus valley civilization (c.2500–1800BCE); the Dravidian culture that persists among the Tamils in South India; and the Aryans, who entered North-west India from c.1500BCE. Aryan religion became the mainstream Vedic religion, based on sacrifice and the sacred texts known as Vedas and Vedanta.

Within the Indian coalition, some movements (Jains, Buddhists, and Sikhs) became separate religions; others developed their own traditions without becoming so independent. Noteworthy are Vaishnavites (devoted to Vishnu and the incarnate forms of Vishnu, especially Krishna and Rama), Shaivites (devoted to Shiva and Shiva's consorts), and Shaktas (devoted to Goddess). Beliefs held in common now (though differently understood) include: God or the Absolute source of all appearance becoming manifest in many ways, including different Gods and Goddesses, so that people can approach, understand, and worship different manifestations; rebirth continuing, perhaps through millions of lives, until the chain of ignorance (*avidya*) is broken and release (*moksha*) is attained; the form rebirth takes being controlled by karma, a moral law as impersonal and inevitable as gravity; necessity for the order of society and the universe being maintained (Dharma, p.68, and *rita, p.62*). There are many equally valid ways to move toward *moksha*; important among these are worship of the visible form of the Deity in *darshana* (direct "seeing"), and *puja* (worship).

Worship
Deity becomes manifest in India in many forms. In temples, they are welcomed as honoured guests in forms of worship known as puja *(p.94).*

INDIA TIMELINE		
Indus Valley · Tamil Gods & Goddesses · Aryans	2500–1500
Vedic period	1500–1000
Brahmanism · Samkhya · Upanishads · Bhagavadgita	1000–500
The Buddha · The Epics (*Ramayana & Mahabharata*) · Kanada & Vaisheshika · Nyaya	500–000
Nagarjuna · Patanjali	0–250
Puranas	250–500
Founding of Nyingma · Nalvars/Nayanars	500–750
Shankara · Nammalvar (Maran) · Shantideva · Founding of Kagyu · Founding of Sakya	750–1000
Vacana poets · Shrividya · Ramanuja · Jayadeva · Madhva · Devi Gita · Jagganath temple · Shinran	1000–1250
Founding of Geluk Sants	1250–1500
Guru Nanak · Kabir · Vallabha · Surdas · Caitanya · Mirabai · Guru Arjan · Tulsi Das · Tukaram · Rupa · Krishnadasa Kaviraja · Golden Temple · Guru Granth Sahib installed · Guru Gobind Singh	1500–1750
Ram Mohan Roy · Brahmo Sabha/Brahmo Samaj · Ramakrishna · Rabindranath Tagore · Vivekananda · Gandhi · Aurobindo · World Parliament of Religions · Largest-ever Kumbhamela at Prayaga	1750–PRESENT

Tamil Nadu

Where the Gods Meet

TAMILS IN SOUTH INDIA tell the story of a Brahman (see below) called Jamadagni who married a woman of such purity and concentration of mind that she could carry as much water as she wanted in nothing but a piece of cloth. One day, carrying water from the river, she saw reflected in it some Gandharvas (musicians and singers to the Gods) flying above her. Moved by their beauty, she lost her concentration, and at once the water poured away.

Jamadagni questioned his wife about this and, when she confessed that she had been moved by the beauty of the Gandharvas, he ordered their son, Parashurama, to take her into the wilderness and cut off her head. At the place of execution, she embraced for protection a woman who was a *paraiya* (Tamil for "outcaste", hence the English "pariah"). The son promptly cut off both their heads but then returned to his father overwhelmed with grief.

Jamadagni admired his son's obedience and promised him whatever he most desired as a reward. The son asked that his mother should be restored to life. He was told to put the heads back on their shoulders, and both would live again.

The son did so, but put the Paraiya head on the Brahman body and vice versa. The woman with the Brahman head and Paraiya body became the Goddess Mariamma, to whom goats and cocks are sacrificed, but not buffaloes; the woman with the Paraiya head and Brahman body became Ellamma, to whom buffaloes are sacrificed, but not goats and cocks.

The story of misplaced heads is told in many parts of India for different purposes (see Ganesha, p.108). Henry Whitehead, who first heard this particular story in South India, pointed out how it reflects the way in which two originally separate religions, those of the Brahmans and of the Tamils, came together as one and yet retained many of their independent traditions and practices.

"Brahmanism" (from Brahmans, controllers of rituals and sacrifices) is a name given to the early form of religion developed from the beliefs and practices of the Aryans who entered North India from c.1500BCE onwards (p.60). From them come the sacred texts known as the Vedas, so that this early religion is also known as Vedic religion.

Brahmanism, with its sacred language of Sanskrit, gradually spread throughout India, and its beliefs, Gods, and practices became dominant without eradicating alternative faiths. The Brahman head could be put on the native body, but equally the native head could be put on the Brahman body, as with the way of worship known as *puja* (p.94). Either way round, the fusion of independent beliefs repeatedly created for the

Sacred Language
Sanskrit (see script, above) became the sacred language of India, but many Indian religions have their own sacred languages including the Dravidian languages of great importance in South India.

Indian people dramatic new ways both of understanding and of worshipping God.

The way Brahmanism spread has been described as "the great tradition" in relation to "the little tradition" (Redfield) but that phrase has been abandoned because it was resented by those belonging to the regional religions: it made them sound like junior partners. This has become a deeply serious and political issue in India as areas like Tamil Nadu, speaking one of the Dravidian languages, seek increasing autonomy or independence. The Tamil names for God have become markers of Tamil identity, even though Tamil Gods and Goddesses have long been associated with Brahmanic and other Deities.

This is particularly true of the God Murukan, to whom three of the six major temples in Tamil Nadu are dedicated. Tamils use the word *teyvam* to speak of all that constitutes the nature of God: it is *teyvam* that becomes manifest in all the many forms in which God appears. Within that nature lie beauty and loveliness, all manner of sweetness, unending youth – all, in other words, that is summed up in the word *muruku: muruku* is *teyvam*, and *muruku* (an abstract, neuter noun) becomes real and personal as Murukan.

Goddess Pattini
The cult of the Goddess Pattini moved from South India to Sri Lanka where both Buddhists and Hindus (otherwise so divided) equally revere her. But in South India she is no longer worshipped extensively in her own right because her cult has become assimilated with that of Kali (p.117).

Murukan is a Tamil understanding of God that predates the arrival of Brahmanism from the North. Murukan is linked to that religion by being regarded as the son of Shiva (p.108), who was early connected with Rudra (p.105). Murukan is identified with Skanda (p.109) the great warrior and is accepted by the devotees of Shiva as the one who leads to Shiva and brings release from the world.

This process through which different approaches to God adjust to each other, so that they change and reinforce each other in a new vision, is fundamental to the Indian story of God. Particular manifestations of God/Goddess can be extremely stable across many centuries, and yet the imagination of God is always, both literally and metaphorically, on the move (see Pattini, right).

Approaching the Indian understanding of God through Tamil Nadu is therefore a reminder that many different strands are woven together; that village religion is one of the most important though least well-known of those strands; that the telling of stories is fundamental for all Indian religions; and that what matters is not the conquest of one God by another but the conquest of ignorance by all. There are at least three hundred and thirty three million Gods among the Indians (since every form of life can be a manifestation of God, and traditionally there are that many forms of life) but there is, beyond image and metaphor, only the One who in these different ways becomes known. So wrote the Tamil poet Allama (see box, right):

"Looking for your light,
I went out:
It was like the sudden dawn
Of a million million suns,

A ganglion of lightnings
For my wonder.

O Lord of Caves,
if you are light,
there can be no metaphor"

(Ramanujan, p.52)

Indus Valley

The Coming of the Aryans

A MONG THE MANY STRANDS that make up the Indian understanding of God, one of the earliest is that of the Indus Valley civilization which flourished c.2500–1800BCE. Archaeologists have found buildings, small figures, and seals from this era, but the script has not yet been deciphered and it is not clear exactly what the beliefs were. It is not even certain whether the language used was Dravidian (p.58) or an early form of Indo-European. However, the findings appear to show a number of anticipations of later religious developments (see box, right).

Study of the buildings and artefacts left by the Indus Valley civilization shows that they embraced a number of religious themes that seemed to disappear (only later to reappear) when the beliefs and practices of a new people, the Aryans, came to dominate the Indus Valley – and eventually the whole of India.

The Aryans (*arya* = "noble") came from central Asia and, because of their skill with horses and chariots, they spread into Europe and North India – a reason why there are connections between Indian and European languages: the word "God", German *Gott*, is Teutonic, but from the Aryan *dyaus* come Zeus, *Deus, Dieu,* Deity, etc. They entered India from c.1500BCE onwards – it was once thought by invasion, but some now argue by more peaceful infiltration, in which Dravidian beliefs were not displaced or destroyed, but absorbed and changed.

The Aryans lived in a world in which life was sustained through a powerful relationship of exchange between Gods and humans. That relationship was maintained primarily through sacrifice, and it was expressed in their sacred texts, known as the Vedas.

The Vedas (from *vid*, "knowledge") are believed to be not human compositions but eternal truth revealed to the world through *rishis* ("those who see"). Over many centuries, they were not written down, but were passed on orally, hence they are called *shruti* ("that which is heard"). There are four basic collections (*samhitas*); Rig Veda, containing 1,028 hymns divided into ten mandalas; Sama Veda, in which verses from the Rig Veda are arranged for the use of priests in sacrifice; Yajur Veda, containing sacrificial chants; and Atharva Veda, composed of charms, curses, and hymns intended for healing.

To the Vedas, and also regarded as a part of Shruti (Scripture), were attached first the Brahmanas, containing ritual texts and

The Proto-Shiva Seal
It is thought by some that this may be an early portrayal of Shiva. The animals surrounding the central figure suggest his role as Pashupati, the Lord of Animals.

INDUS VALLEY FINDINGS

Some of these features are found in later beliefs and practices:

---◆---

- ❧ **WATER**: Baths near buildings suggest the concern with water and ritual purification of later Hindu temples.
- ❧ **GODDESS AND MOTHER**: Many female figures suggest the importance of Goddess and Mother as the source of fertility and life.
- ❧ **YONI AND LINGA**: Stone rings and phallic-shaped stones suggest the later focus on the yoni and the linga (the female and male organs of generation) as the sources of life and strength.
- ❧ **SHIVA**: One seal may be a seated bull but has been seen by some as the forerunner of the God Shiva (pp.104ff), and is therefore sometimes called the proto-Shiva seal. It depicts a figure sitting in a position that resembles yoga (p.77), surrounded by animals, which has led to it also being called the Pashupati seal, since Shiva is regarded as Lord of the Animals (*pashupati*).
- ❧ **PROTECTED TREES**: Trees are depicted as the focus of worship and were protected, much as they still are in village religion.

Mother Goddess
Figures of Mother Goddess are common in the Indus Valley civilization, but Mother Goddess is not prominent in the Aryan Vedas.

explaining the sacred power contained in the chants and hymns (*mantras*), and then the Aranyakas, containing explanations of the inner meaning of the rituals and sacrifices. Beyond the Aranyakas but serving the same purpose of explanation are the Upanishads (p.84), the end or culmination of the Vedas and known therefore as Vedanta (Vedanta as the foundation of later commentary also includes Badarayana's *Brahma* or *Vedanta Sutra*, an elliptical summary of the teachings of the Vedas and the Upanishads, and *Bhagavadgita*, p.92). These works came into being over a period of many centuries, c.1200–300BCE.

From these texts it is obvious that relating humans to the Gods through sacrifice was fundamental to Aryan or Vedic religion. *Rig Veda* 10.90 describes all creation and every aspect of society coming from the sacrifice and dismemberment of a primordial Man (*purusha*). The order of society is a natural part of the order of the cosmos, and sacrifices maintain and express that order. The Gods are described as having appetites and desires like humans, so they can be invited as guests to sacrifices, share in the ritual meals, and be addressed in hymns with the hope that their anger might be abated or their favour secured, so that material benefits like sons or cattle might be gained.

The aim was not immortality but success in this life and its extension, if the Gods approved, to a span of 100 years. Some sacrifices, known as *shrauta*, were public and often on a grand scale. Others, known as *grihya* (belonging to the household) concerned individuals and families. Eventually, as the sacrifices became more numerous and complicated, a class of priests known as Brahmans came into being to supervise the rituals; and from them this developed stage of Vedic religion received the name of Brahmanism.

Sacrifice

The Vedic Gods

Agni

Agni mediates between humans and Gods. His threefold nature reflects the three sacrifices. He is accompanied by a ram and sometimes rides it. More often he is seven-tongued, golden-toothed, with 1,000 eyes and flaming hair, dressed in black and carrying a flaming spear. His smoke-bannered chariot is drawn by red steeds; its wheels are the seven winds.

"You, Soma, the guardian of our bodies,

Make your dwelling in each part of us, Lord of lords.

Though we go against your firm rule so often,

Have mercy on us, be kind and gracious"

(RV 8.48.9)

ACCORDING TO THE RIG VEDA, there are 33 Gods. In fact, the names of many more Gods are mentioned in the Vedas, and no explanation of the number 33 is given. Even so, this number became the basis of a later classification of the Gods in the Brahmanas (pp.60f), in which the various parts of the cosmos are seen as (to put it in terms of modern theatre) a series of stage sets on which the vast epic of life is played out.

The box (top right) makes clear the way in which the Gods in Vedic and Brahmanic religion express the power and energy of the natural order, and in which energy is transformed into new outcomes in regular, and at least to some extent, predictable ways. The Gods maintain the fundamental order of the universe, an order that is known as *rita*.

In this way, Vedic religion made personal as Gods what we would call the invariable laws of nature (the Adityas) and the constituent conditions of life (the Rudras), along with all the myriad transformations of energy. The result was that people could interact with them and came to realize that by co-operation with the Gods, they too could play their part in maintaining the *rita* (harmony and order) of the universe. This state of communication and co-operation they achieved through sacrifice.

Sacrifice in Vedic religion expressed the fundamental observation that death is the necessary condition of life: there cannot be any life in a universe of this kind without death. Today, we observe this in such things as the death of stars releasing heavier elements for new planets and organic life, or the death of succeeding generations creating the opportunity of evolution. The Vedic Aryans observed it more simply in the way that plants and animals are killed in order to provide food. They also observed that the one who eats may then become food for another. As one of the Upanishads (pp.84f) put it, "This whole [world] is just food and the eater of food" (*Brihad-aranyaka Up.* 1.4.6). That passage immediately goes on to state that "Soma is food and Agni is the eater of food", which at once points to two of the major Gods of the Vedas.

Soma, associated with the Moon as the cup of Soma, is the food of the ritual fire and thus the food of the Gods. Strictly speaking, anything that is offered to the Gods through the ritual fire is Soma, but the name is more often used of one particular offering, a plant or substance that was able to produce powerful hallucinogenic or intoxicating results. That this was the "magic mushroom", *Amanita muscaria*, was a popular guess, but it was

THE THIRTY THREE GODS

The names printed in bold are the Gods reckoned among the 33, to whom was added Prajapati,
the Lord of Creatures. He was regarded as the source and creator of all things.

Stage Set	Leading Actor	Supporting Cast	Director
Earth	**Agni** (Fire)	Five elements	Ashvins (Gods of agriculture)
Space	**Vayu** (Wind)	**11 Rudras** (life-giving energies)	**Indra**
Sky/Heaven	**Surya** (Sun)	**12 Adityas** (ruling laws)	Mitra/Varuna
Constellations	**Soma** (Moon)	The Ancestors	Svayambhu & Parameshtihin

more likely the plant *Ephedra*, which contains amphetamine. Soma, identified also with semen, is portrayed as the giver of life, the healer of diseases, and the Lord of all the other Gods: without Soma they would cease to be. All the hymns of Mandala 9 of the Rig Veda are addressed to Soma, and to him is dedicated the whole of Sama Veda (p.60). Soma, by entering those who sacrifice, connects them to God. Soma easily enters humans and affects them, but how does it enter the Gods? Through fire, or, to put it personally, through Agni (cf. Latin *ignis*, "fire": see caption, left). The whole process of the universe is given visible form in Agni. He is the heat of the sun, the flash of lightning, the fire of the hearth at home, and the fire of the ritual of sacrifice. He both brings life and consumes it. Through Agni as the heat of passion, the generation of life is possible and, by means of the funeral pyre, Agni carries from the earth all that remains of a dead body (a memory as thin as smoke).

The Vedic Gods maintain the natural order and operate in clearly defined domains. But how are they related to each other? That became an increasingly pressing question.

"Agni I extol, the household priest, the divine minister of the sacrifice, the chief priest, the bestower of blessings.

May that Agni, who is to be extolled by ancient and modern seers, conduct the gods here.

Through Agni may one gain day by day wealth and welfare which is glorious and replete with heroic sons.

O Agni, the sacrifice and ritual which you encompass on every side, that indeed goes to the Gods…

Presiding at ritual functions, the brightly shining custodian of the cosmic order (rita), thriving in your own realm,

O Agni, be easy of access to us as a father to his son. Join us for our wellbeing"

(RV 1.1)

Sun God
Surya the Sun God riding through the heavens in his horse-drawn chariot.

Three and One

Manifestations of God

AN EARLY VEDIC HYMN (*RV* 5.3.1) draws together different Gods and declares that they are each the same reality in different stages or modes of manifestation (see box, p.66):

"At birth, Agni, you are Varuna; when set alight you become Mitra: in you, son of strength, all Gods find their centre; to those who worship, you become Indra"

The Gods of the Vedas appear in and through the natural order that they sustain, but not *as* the natural order: they are not personifications of natural phenomena. They can be approached, particularly through sacrifice, in their respective domains, but it was already coming to be realized, even during the Vedic period, that they can better be regarded as manifestations of the One who is behind all appearance as its source and guarantee:

"Here, the Lord of tribes I behold, A benign, grey-haired priest, with seven heroes as sons, Flanked by his true brothers; Lightning and the oil sprinkled Fire.

Who was there to see the structured one When the unstructured one first bore him? Where was the Earth's life, her blood, her breath? Who may seek some light on this from a sage?

I, simpleton, asking this in ignorance, Meditate on the footprints set down by the Gods. Wise singers have spun a seven-stranded tale Around the Sun, this calf from heaven.

I, ignorant, unknowing, seek knowledge From those seers who may know. What was the One? Who was the Unborn One Who propped apart the six regions?...

Indra
Indra embodies the qualities of the other Gods: "Indra was made up of all the other Gods, and so he became the greatest" (Avyakta Up. 5.1).

Speech is divided into four levels,
The wise singers know them all.
Three levels are hidden, and men never attain them.
Men speak only the fourth.

They call it Indra, Mitra, Varuna,
Agni and Garutman [the Sun], the heavenly bird.
Of the One the singers chant in many ways;
They call it Agni, Yama, Matarishvan.

The yellow birds soar high to heaven,
Along the dark path, clothed in waters.
They have returned here from rita's home,
The earth is soaked in prosperity"

(RV 1.164. 1, 4–6, 45–7)

In the Vedas, the One who created all things is known as Prajapati:

"In the beginning was the Golden Womb [Hiranyagarbha,
the egg-like source of all creation],
Only-Lord of all that was born.
He upheld the heaven and earth together.
[To] what God shall we sacrifice?

He is the giver of life's breath, power and vigour;
His command all Gods obey.
He is the law of death, whose shadow is life immortal.
[To] what God shall we sacrifice?

Of whatever breathes, moves or is still,
He, through his power, is the ruler.
He is the God of men and cattle.
[To] what God shall we sacrifice?

May the earth's father never harm us,
For he made the heavens and followed Dharma.
He released the powerful and crystal waters.
[To] what God shall we sacrifice?

Prajapati, you alone embrace all these
Created things and none other beside you.
Grant us the wishes of our prayer;
May we have a store of wealth in our hands"

(RV 10.121.1–3, 8f)

The Care of God
"He who makes the swans
white, parrots green, and
peacocks of every colour,
He will support you in life.
Do not long for riches
when you are poor,
Do not exult
when you are rich:
All must receive the reward
of past deeds [karma, p.92],
whether they are
good or bad"
(Pancatantra 2.69).

OPPOSITE:

Varuna
Naga King Varuna sits on a
lotus lifted by serpents. In
the background is his
manifestation as the
God of rain.

But, in truth, the One who lies behind all things as their unproduced Producer is far beyond human language to describe or human intelligence to understand:

> *"Neither existence nor non-existence was as yet,*
> *Neither the world nor the sky that lies beyond it;*
> *What was covered? And where?*
> *And who gave it protection?*
> *Was there water, deep and unfathomable?*
>
> *Neither was there death, nor immortality,*
> *Nor any sign of night or day.*
> *The ONE breathed without air by self-impulse;*
> *Other than that was nothing whatsoever....*
>
> *Who really knows? Who can here say*
> *When was it born and from where creation came?*
> *The gods are later than this world's creation;*
> *Therefore, who knows from where it came into existence?*
>
> *That from which creation came into being,*
> *Whether it had held it together or it had not*
> *He who watches in the highest heaven*
> *He alone knows, unless – He does not know"*

(RV 10.129.1f, 6f)

This spirit of questioning and quest continued into the Upanishads (pp.84f). Among some it led also to devastating criticisms of the ways in which the Gods had been characterized: it led indeed to new religions.

VEDIC GODS

The Gods related to Agni in RV 5.31 (the hymn on page 64) are as follows:

⅗ **VARUNA** maintains the cosmic order of the heavens, guaranteeing the regularity of the seasons – above all the rainy season. He is the Lord of *rita* (p.62), and therefore also of Dharma (p.68). Understanding the inner meaning of things, he watches over humans with a thousand eyes: "The wise, law-keeping Varuna is enthroned as king, ruling all and beholding all things that have been or shall be." (RV 1.25.9).

⅗ **MITRA** (in Europe, Mithras, p.233) is so closely associated with Varuna that they often appear with the single name, Mitra-Varuna. Only one hymn is addressed in the Vedas to Mitra alone. Mitra's role is to ensure that the order guaranteed by Varuna is respected by humans, he ensures that people keep their promises and sustain the bonds of friendship.

⅗ **INDRA** is the ruler of the Gods, to whom more hymns are addressed in the Vedas than to any other except Agni. His strength (represented by the *vajra*, "thunderbolt") is maintained by Soma (p.62), of which he is the main recipient. He becomes the source of strength for other beings.

Criticisms of God

Buddhists and Jains

ONCE, LONG AGO, there were four kings of neighbouring kingdoms, each of whom had different experiences of what life is like (see box, below). When the kings witnessed how greed and lust lead to conflict and destruction, they renounced the world and went off without any possessions.

World-renouncers (*shramanas*) are common in two Indian religions, but they are not all the same. Some, for example, seek, as in Yoga, to activate the energies (*chakras*) that lie latent within the human body; others develop powers that enable them to perform miracles that otherwise only the Gods can perform. All of them are able, if they wish, to seek their goals in a state of independence from the rituals and sacrifices of Brahmanism. Some go further and reject the Gods who go with those things. Often they reject what is known as Dharma.

In Brahmanic belief, sacrifice and ritual help to keep the universe "running on time", that is, functioning in the way that it should. So too does Dharma. Dharma is a word that means many things, but at the heart is the sense of living and behaving in the way that is appropriate for who (or what) you are. Dharma is so fundamental that Indian religion and life are often known as *sanatana dharma*, "everlasting Dharma". A vast Dharma-literature grew up describing what exactly Dharma means in the many different circumstances of life. Inevitably, therefore, Dharma controls the ways in which its followers approach God: for example, only the Brahmans and other priests can undertake the major sacrifices.

THE FOUR KINGS

Seeing greed, lust, and conflict all around them, the four kings turned their backs on wealth and power and renounced the world:

❧ **THE FIRST KING**: He saw a mango tree in a grove bearing much fruit. A crowd came and, in their greed, they chopped down the tree to get at the fruit; and at once the king renounced the world.

❧ **THE SECOND KING**: Each day he saw a beautiful woman pass by with an exquisite bangle on each arm; but one day she wore them both on the same arm, and, by their jangling noise, she drew the eyes of all men after her; and at once the king renounced the world.

❧ **THE THIRD KING**: He saw a bird feeding off carrion, but in a moment dozens of other birds fell on it and on each other in a ferocious battle for the food; and at once the king renounced the world.

❧ **THE FOURTH KING**: This king noticed a fine bull in a herd. Suddenly, it was viciously attacked by all the younger bulls who desired the cows for themselves, and at once the king renounced the world.

(from a story told by Buddhists and Jains)

Dharma creates a highly ordered society and a well-organized relationship between humans and the Gods. But the story of the four kings, set as it is in legendary times, is a reminder that alongside Brahmanism, and predating it, are approaches to God that are independent – as in the case of Yoga, if the interpretation of the proto-Shiva seal (p.60) is correct.

Not only that, but some of those independent forms of belief radically criticized and rejected Brahmanism and its understanding of God. The story of the four kings is told by Buddhists, and they tell a similar story of a young prince called Gautama. He had been sheltered by his father in the palace to protect him from disturbing experiences, but one day he was taken out for a drive and he saw, on separate occasions, a sick man, an old man, and a dead man. Disturbed by the thought that these conditions were waiting for him, Gautama wondered how to escape them. On a fourth trip, he saw a Shramana (world-renouncing ascetic), emaciated but glowing and smiling serenely. Seeing the possibility that he and those like him had conquered the threats to life, Gautama abandoned his wife and son and went off to the forest where he embraced extreme asceticism. He discovered that such practices lead to extraordinary powers and attainments, but that is all: they attain their goal, but no more than their goal; and those goals do not lead to escape from suffering and death.

I n disillusionment at the true but limited attainments of asceticism, Gautama looked for "the middle way" (a common name for Buddhism) between asceticism and ritual, and sat beneath a tree concentrating on what he called later "seeing things as they really are". There he passed through the four stages or layers of progressive insight (*jhanas*), and finally reached enlightenment. From that moment he became the Buddha (i.e., the Enlightened One). He now saw exactly how suffering (*dukkha*) arises and how (and to what) we can pass beyond it. This core of enlightenment is summed up in the Four Noble Truths (see box, p.70). Where, however, in this system of belief, is God? Not quite nowhere, but nowhere outside the whole process of appearances coming into being and ceasing to be. The Buddha never denied the reality of God. Indeed, it was God (Brahma) who, when the Buddha sat motionless beneath the enlightenment tree (Bo Tree), persuaded him to get up and share his insight with others.

What the Buddha did deny was the belief that there is in reality God who is somehow outside this universe, who survives even when this universe ceases to be, and who is the Source and Creator of all things. Brahma, who was believed in Brahmanism to be the Creator, had simply made a mistake: he was the first appearance when this new universe came into being, and he thought that by being first, he must be the origin or creator of everything else. The Buddha also denied the efficacy of sacrifices. Jataka stories (stories of Gautama in his previous appearances on earth) record incidents

Emaciated Buddha
Gautama is shown after his asceticism in the forest, and before his enlightenment. His naturally glowing skin was made dull by his efforts.

Jain Shrine
Of the two major groups
among Jains, Digambaras go
naked and their images of
the Tirthankaras are naked
with downcast eyes, dead to
the world; Shvetambara
images wear a loin-cloth and
are alert to the world with
a single eye.

in which the unreliability of sacrifices to produce predictable consequences demonstrates that the Gods cannot be relied on. One story tells how the parents of Brahmadatta, a Brahman, encouraged him to tend the sacrificial fire in order to attain the realm of Brahma. One day he was given an ox for sacrifice, but, lacking the necessary salt, he went to a nearby village to get some. While he was away, some hunters came by: they killed the ox and ate it, leaving only the hide and entrails behind. When Brahmadatta returned, he realized how impotent Agni (p.63) was. He cried out, "My Lord of Fire, if you cannot protect yourself, how will you protect me? The meat being gone, you must make do with this!" Throwing the hide and the offal onto the fire, he took himself off to become a renouncer (*shramana*).

So the Gods are limited but as real as anything is real in Buddhist belief: God and the Gods are one of the many ways in which the flow of transient appearance takes shape, along with everything else. Of course they are appearances on a very high level of attainment, enduring through many aeons of time, but they too are seeking Nirvana.

But while they are in being, they may be very helpful, in, for example, answering prayers. That is why Buddhism as lived around the world is a religion in which the Gods are extremely important. Buddhism absorbed most of the Indian Gods (e.g., Pattini, p.59, Yama, p.72), and then took on many more from the countries to which it spread.

There is nothing contradictory or paradoxical about this. It simply means that on the way to enlightenment and Nirvana (and that may take many thousands or millions of reappearances), the Buddha accepted that it may be wise to seek the help of Gods and Goddesses, or to seek to attain their domain (*devaloka*, "heaven") after death, or even to become a God or Goddess – a possibility since they are only one form of appearance among many on the way to enlightenment.

This means that it is profoundly wrong to call Buddhism, as is often done, "a non-theistic religion", or even "a philosophy and not a religion". The later forms of Buddhism (known collectively as Mahayana)

THE FOUR NOBLE TRUTHS

From suffering to enlightenment:

❦ **ONE**: The fact of *dukkha* (suffering): all things are transient (*anicca*): as soon as they come into being, they are on the way to ceasing to be: there is nothing to be found anywhere that is permanent, not even a soul to survive death.

❦ **TWO**: The cause of *dukkha* (seeking or desiring something permanent): seeking something permanent in the midst of this leads inevitably to *dukkha*, the anguish and dissatisfaction that arises when we never find it.

❦ **THREE**: When we truly understand this, we see things as they really are, and we are no longer disturbed or affected by them. To be, but to remain unaffected by "the slings and arrows of outrageous fortune" (or by anything else) is to enter into the condition of Nirvana.

❦ **FOUR**: Seeing and understanding these truths enables us to trace the eight-step path (*ashtangika-marga*) that leads to that final condition of enlightenment.

developed many forms of appearance who help humans (and others) in vital ways, above all Buddhas and Bodhisattvas (those who have attained enlightenment but turn back from Nirvana to help those who are still suffering in the world). Important examples (among literally, from a Buddhist point of view, millions) are Tara, the mother of all the Buddhas, who has vowed never to relinquish her female form (pp.73, 74); Amitabha/Amida (p.74); Bhaishya-guru, the Healing Buddha; Hachiman Daibosatsu (p.165); and Kshitigarbha/Di Zang who helps children and who rescues the tormented from hell.

Cults of devotion and trust exist in relation to these, often indistinguishable from the way that other people worship God as one who is eternal and distinct from this or any other universe. Even so, the Buddha knew very well how a false trust in God or Goddess can lead away from the path to enlightenment. He was fiercely critical of ritual and sacrifice if they lead to a false belief that the Gods are *ultimately* real, or that they consume the sacrifices like hungry ghosts, or if they lead to exploitation of credulous and needy people. The Buddha saw himself not as God or as an intermediary between Gods and humans but rather as a physician who diagnoses illness and offers the cure. Those who use God to continue the illness and make money by exploiting people's need are denounced in no uncertain terms.

So already by the 5th century BCE, the Buddha was offering a radical critique of Brahmanic religion. He was not alone. The Jains also told the story of the four kings (*Uttaradhyayanasutram* 18.45–7) and, like the Buddhists, followed the world-renouncers in rejecting the Brahmanic characterization of the Gods, along with their sacrifices and rituals. They also rejected the belief that God is the creator of all things who remains independent of creation.

But Jains equally reject the accusation that they do not believe in God. God is the One in whom all the perfected ones (*siddhas*) and all the guides (*jinas*) subsist, so that God is both many and yet only what there truly is, and hence One. So Jains developed their own rituals and worship, not least of the 24 Tirthankaras, the ford-makers who show the way to attaining the goal, but also of the *siddhas*, for they are what God is, the final truth. To them as One they sing hymns that take over Indian ways of describing and praising God: "You are imperishable, mighty, unknowable, uncountable, primordial, Brahma, Ishvara, infinite: the saints call you by these names" (*Bhaktamara Stotra* 24).

Both Jains and Buddhists (with other renouncers) raised deep criticisms of the ways in which the Indian understandings of God were unfolding. Even so, they looked for ways in which the fundamental human recognition of God could find a natural and legitimate expression. Those ways developed as Buddhism spread beyond India.

Buddha's Feet
Once the Buddha attained Nirvana, it cannot be said whether he is or is not, since Nirvana is beyond the dimensions of human understanding. The Buddha, therefore, cannot be worshipped, since he is not God and is not available for worship. He can, however, be kept in mind, and images of the Buddha exist so that people can express gratitude for his teaching. The Taliban destruction in 2001 of the vast statues of the Buddha at Bamian completely misunderstood Buddhist gratitude and identified it, absurdly, with idolatry.

The Fierce Deities

Tara the Tear of Compassion

Fierce Deity
Yama is the Lord of Death for Hindus and Buddhists. For Hindus he is judge and gaoler (of the wicked) after death, but for Buddhists, karma (p.92) is the only judge, and Yama simply reveals what a life has been.

IN BUDDHISM, God, Gods, and Goddesses are as real as any other of the myriad forms of appearance, but they are no more real than that. What is true of humans – that there is no self or soul in humans, but only the coming together of transient forms of appearance – is true of the whole universe.

As the Mahayana philosopher Nagarjuna (c.150–250CE) put it, all phenomena are empty of a self or self-essence of any kind. When properly understood, all things – including humans and God – are empty or devoid of characteristics, and this emptiness is known as *shunyata*. This emptiness is, in fact, the nature of what the Buddha is – in other words, it is the Buddha-nature (see box, below left).

Conscious forms of appearance are privileged, because they have the opportunity to realize the truth that they are nothing other than the Buddha-nature already (there is nothing else to be, despite appearances to the contrary). By overcoming ignorance and bad impediments in their lives, they achieve this realization and become enlightened themselves.

The major role of Gods and Goddesses in Mahayana Buddhism is, like that of Buddhas and Bodhisattvas, to protect from all that threatens the realization of truth, and to bring practical help in attaining it. In Tibet, Deities are often imagined and portrayed as fierce: they have ferocious faces, and their many arms carry different weapons, as well as the heads or limbs of their victims. If they were not fierce, they could not protect those who look to them for help from the many dangers – of mind, body, or spirit – that would otherwise overwhelm everyone.

Supreme over all is the Lord of Knowing, the One who embodies the defeat of ignorance and thereby opens the way to insight and enlightenment. In most Tibetan monasteries, there is a room devoted to him where vigil is kept to engage him as protector of the monastery and the surrounding area (see box, far right). It is he who passes on to the Fierce Deities the offerings and the weapons that they need – skulls filled with blood for them to drink and the skin of flayed corpses for them to wear. We need protection from things worse than death.

The Fierce Deities become protectors through two different types of ritual: offerings and visualization. Visualization is an arduous ritual practice through which those who engage in it, the yogins, attain identity with the Deity: they become what the Deities are, not by facile thought (as with Nero, who, as he lay dying after a lifetime of being regarded as the representative of

*"Since he is by nature empty,
The thought that the Buddha
Exists or does not exist
After nirvana is not
appropriate…*

*Whatever is the essence of the
Tathagata
That is the essence of the world.
The Tathagata has no essence.
The world is without essence"*

(Nagarjuna, *Mulamadhyamakakarika*,
22.14, 16)

God on earth, said, "I think I am becoming a god!") but by rigorous discipline of contemplation that may take a lifetime to complete. However, even during the attempt, the power of the Fierce Deities is drawn into life.

This is only possible because in this exercise the yogins are putting into practice the truth of *shunyata*: all appearances, including those of the Fierce Deities and of humans, are of the same nature, devoid of differentiating characteristics, even though they appear to be so different. They already share the same Buddha-nature. Union with Truth already exists; it just remains to be realized.

For Tibetans (and many other Buddhists), this protection and help is focused in Tara, "She who saves". Tara was believed to have been born from a compassionate tear shed by Chenrezi Avalokiteshvara (p.158) when he beheld the sufferings of the world. Tara identified herself with the most defenceless and abused in the world. When she reached enlightenment, she was offered as a reward the chance to become a man. She replied, "There is neither 'male' nor 'female', any more than there is 'self' or 'person' [the teaching of *shunyata*]: bondage to 'male' and 'female' is destructive. And since there are many men aiming for enlightenment, but fewer women who have the opportunity, I will help all beings in the body of a woman until the emptiness of the world is completely realized."

Tara is the helper who is always accessible – so much so that the rituals of access to her are practised daily, not just annually, and she herself is taken to the villages by actors who perform the stories of the help she brings. These performances (known as *ach'e lhamo*) can last for days, with a reciter supporting dance and songs, and with the whole village taking part. These songs and dances "arouse her heart of compassion". Arousing the heart of compassion is also true of other manifestations in Buddhism.

Most Tibetan monasteries have a shrine to the Lord of Knowing:

"At the entrance are hung the decomposing bodies of bears, wild dogs, yaks, and snakes, stuffed with straw, to frighten away the evil spirits who might desire to pass the threshold. The carcasses fall to pieces, and the whole place is as disgusting as a space under a flight of stairs with us would be if it were full of rubbish covered with cobwebs, ancient umbrellas that belonged to great-grand-father, and fragments of bedraggled fur that had been worn by a dead aunt.... Pictures of the gods are painted on the walls. At first sight you would say they are demons, monsters, infernal beings. They are, however, good spirits, protectors, who assume these terrifying shapes to combat the invisible forces of evil....[It is a] dark, dusty pocket of stale air,... containing greasy, skinless carcasses, with terrifying gods painted on the walls riding monsters, wearing diadems of skulls and necklaces of human heads, and holding in their hands blood-filled skulls as cups"

(Maraini, pp.50f)

White Tara

Each Tibetan School is linked to a different form and colour of Tara (p.74). The mantra (p.129) of Tara, om tare tuttare ture svaha, is much used by Tibetans seeking protection.

Amitabha

The Pure Land

"As long as beings who are still reappearing suffer, may I become their medicine, their doctor and their nurse, until everyone is healed. In order that all beings may attain their goal, I shall give up without reserve my body, and all my accumulated virtue of the past, present and future, to be used for this purpose"

TARA REACHED ENLIGHTENMENT, but turned back to save those who still suffer in this world. Such saviours are known as bodhisattvas, (those who reach enlightenment but then turn back to help others). The poet and philosopher, Shantideva (8th century CE) summarized their vow (see box, left).

Since the Buddha-nature manifests itself in whatever different forms there are, Tara can appear as Goddess. In *Homages to the Twenty One Taras*, a text brought to Tibet from India in the 11th century CE, each of the 21 forms of Tara as Goddess has a different role, such as averting disasters, fulfilling desires, increasing wisdom, and healing the sick, and each of them is associated with a different colour. The Geluk (in Tibetan *dge.lugs.pa*, Virtuous Way) school of Tibetan Buddhism, to which the Dalai Lama belongs, reveres and worships Green Tara.

Buddhas and bodhisattvas, therefore, attract to themselves the worship that people in other religions offer to God, because Gods and Goddesses are among the many ways in which the Buddha-nature comes into appearance. In the form of God or Goddess, they bring help and deliverance to the world. Among the most notable and widely revered is Amitabha ("Infinite Light"), known in China as A-mi-t'o, from the Sanskrit Amita, and in Japan as Amida. He is also known as Amitayus, "Infinite Life". Amitabha offers to those who come to him in trust and faith the reward of reappearance in the Pure Land of Sukhavati, the Buddha-land or Paradise that lies in the West.

The story goes that long ago a king heard the preaching of a Buddha: he renounced his throne and became a monk, taking the name Dharmakara (in Japan Hozo). Instructed by the Buddha Lokeshvararaja, he resolved with 48 vows to found a Buddha-land. He surveyed many existing lands, noting the perfections of each, in order to create one land containing them all. The Land he eventually produced is Sukhavati, of which he became ruler. For immeasurable lengths of time, he devoted himself to good deeds and the service of others, and eventually by this practice he became the Buddha Amida.

He sits now on a lotus, emitting rays of golden light, surrounded by an aura larger than a billion worlds. He is attended by the bodhisattvas Avalokiteshvara and Mahasthamaprapta, and he bears the 84,000 auspicious marks, the materialization of the virtues that correspond to them. In particular, Amitabha has vowed to appear to all dying beings who truly long for enlightenment and who call on him at that moment, in order to lead them into the Western Paradise. The way of commitment and faith is known as *nembutsu* (Chinese *nien-fo*), "mindfulness of the

Buddha", and that in turn became concentrated in the words *Namu Amida Butsu* (Chinese *Nan-mo A-mi-tuo fo*), "I take refuge in the Buddha Amida". According to the Japanese teacher, Shinran (1173–1262CE), effort to achieve the Pure Land is a major obstacle preventing people from getting there: what is required is faith (*shinjin*) that Amida offers his help – and not even faith as a work of merit: all that is required is trust in the grace and goodness of Amida (cf Luther on faith alone, p.291).

Shinran became a Buddhist Tendai monk at the age of nine, but when his teacher Honen was exiled in 1207CE, Shinran rejected monastic life. He married and fathered children, and established the community of followers that eventually became Jodo Shinshu, the True Pure Land School. He believed that the buddhas and bodhisattvas fulfil all their commitments and vows to help those in need, so that all "ways of effort" are strictly unnecessary. The most that effort shows us is that effort gets us nowhere, because everyone always fails. Not even repeated calling on Amida's name (*nembutsu*) is strictly necessary: one plea sincerely meant will bring Amida's help: "If there is aroused even once in us one thought of joy and love through Amida's vow, we turn, just as we are, with our sins and lusts upon us, toward nirvana."

It follows that faith for Shinran is not an act of will, a conscious decision that we will put our trust in Amida. Faith is the single-minded acceptance that we are already held in the saving embrace of Amida, and that there is nothing to do except rest in that love. He drew the contrast between effort and faith in a letter: "The [expectation of] being ushered into Pure Land [by Amida] belongs to those who seek birth in Pure Land through religious practices. Their practices are grounded in self-effort. Death is also [seen as the crucial moment] to those who seek birth through religious practices. They still have not attained true faith… Believers of true faith, because they are embraced [by Amida] never to be forsaken, reside *already* at the stage whereby they are truly assured [of enlightenment]. For that reason, they have no need to look toward death or to depend on being ushered into Pure Land. When faith is established in them, birth in Pure Land is likewise established. They do not have to look toward the [deathbed] ceremony of being ushered into Pure Land" (Dobbins, pp.282f).

Green Tara
A painting on cloth depicting Green Tara. "The colour green is made by mixing white, yellow, and blue; so Green Tara unites pacifying, increasing, and destroying" (Buddhaguhya).

Early Philosophies

Samkhya-yoga

BUDDHISTS AND JAINS envisage a universe in which there is no place for God as creator, though that does not mean that Gods and Goddesses are unimportant, still less that they are impotent. By Hindus, therefore, Buddhism and Jainism are regarded as interpretations (*darshana*) of truth, but interpretations that happen to be wrong on this as well as other points. Thus they can be thought of as *nastika darshana* instead of *astika*.

Even so, among the six *astika darshanas* there are three interpretations in which, although they accept the authority of the Vedas, God is marginal or unimportant to the system. Vaisheshika, founded by Kanada (c.2nd century BCE), is an analysis of the six ways in which appearances come into conscious awareness – adding later the status of that which has ceased to be. Nyaya, close to Vaisheshika, developed the logic necessary to draw valid conclusions about the categories; Udayana (1025–1100CE) used that logic to put forward nine arguments for the existence of God, of which two (*karyat* and *ayojanat*) resemble the first and second of Aquinas (p.267) and another (*adrishtat*) is a moral argument, which states that value cannot be derived from inert matter.

Samkhya (traditionally founded by Kapila, c.6th century BCE) attempted to account for the appearing of the universe itself. Samkhya starts from an observation of the radical difference between conscious awareness (*purusha*) and inert matter (*prakriti*). Purusha is the conscious, intelligent self or essence; Prakriti is the eternal, unconscious potentiality of all being or appearance. In itself, Prakriti rests in a state of perfect balance or equilibrium, composed of three strands (*gunas*): *vattya* (the subtle principle of potential consciousness), *rajas* (the principle of activity), and *tamas* (the principle of passivity). The unfolding or evolution of Prakriti from its state of equilibrium occurs when Purusha becomes present to it, creating the duality of subject and object. The union of the two is compared to a lame man with good sight being carried on the shoulders of a blind man with sound legs. The "blindness" of Prakriti means that it is not conscious of the process of evolution, although all the time it produces all appearances: their variety is a consequence of the different proportions of the gunas: for example, if *vattya* predominates, mind (*manas*) is produced; but this is not the self. The true self is Purusha, still in association with the products of Prakriti, but unmoved, unchanging, imperturbable.

Meditation
In India, meditation is usually accompanied by careful ritual, and often by worship. This is true even in systems that do not focus on God.

By the light of the consciousness of Purusha, humans are able to become aware of Prakriti. If Purusha in humans forgets its true nature and regards the body or mind as the true self, then it remains attached to material things, Prakriti. Salvation or release is simply to recognize what is already the case, namely, that the true self (Purusha) within us was always independent and free and remains so now.

Freedom is thus obtained by discriminatory knowledge (*samkhya*), which is practical as well as theoretical; and that is why yoga became attached to Samkhya, producing the so-called Samkhya-yoga of Patanjali. In this dynamic philosophy, there is no need for God: everything is linked in chains of cause-and-effect for which there are observable and natural explanations, since everything arises from the imbalance between Purusha and Prakriti. From this it follows that every effect or manifestation is actually already present in the preceding cause, since otherwise those causes might produce not stable or predictable effects, but completely random ones.

In this scheme, God is not necessary. But then what does become necessary is to account for the human experiences of God and Goddess, given their distinct quality. Samkhya therefore developed different ways to show how God and Goddess come into being: one explanation was that they are simply one among the many products of Prakriti (a solution close to that of Buddhism); another explanation was to identify God with Purusha, the eternal source, the unproduced Producer of all that is through the secondary producer of causes, Prakriti. What Samkhya did not allow for was any possibility that God was somehow outside the system, outside Purusha and Prakriti, as an independent Lord and producer even of them.

Yoga
Yoga (from yuj, *to yoke or join) involves extreme commitment, along with acts of asceticism and concentration, in order to leave the world and join oneself with God or the object of devotion.*

Samkhya was cautious about God and Goddess, even at the earliest stages of Indian religion. Like all Indian schools or systems, its main focus is salvation or release from the prison in which people are held. That release is not achieved by an intervention from God; it is achieved by right understanding and insight – because the prison from which we need release is ignorance.

However, the fact that Samkhya, like Buddhism and Jainism, allowed a place for God and Goddess shows how insistent the human experience of God and Goddess is. It is of such a kind that it does not have to compete with naturalistic explanations of appearance, whether those of modern science or of these earlier philosophies, but can simply be stated alongside them in ways that are coherent, and can actually reinforce each other. The reinforcement of God came to be powerfully expressed in works known collectively as Itihasa ("so indeed it was"), works that gather the stories, beliefs, and practices that have sustained among countless Indians their devotion to God.

Among these works are the Puranas (pp.82f) and the great epics, *Mahabharata* (pp.92f) and *Ramayana*, the much-loved story of the adventures of Rama, India's favourite hero-prince.

Rama and *Ramayana*

The Defeat of Evil

LONG AGO, SO THE STORY GOES, a man who had been a thief was changed when he was taught to meditate – very effectively, because he sat still, lost to the world, for so long that ants built their anthills all over him. From that time, he was called Valmiki, "born of an anthill".

Valmiki is traditionally the author of *Ramayana*. He was inspired to write the epic in seven books (*kandas*) of 24,000 verses when he witnessed a hunter kill one of a pair of birds, and saw the survivor circling in grief. Valmiki cried out:

"Hunter, your soul in circling years no peace, no rest will ever find

Because no thought of love or mercy made you stay or hold your hand"

Forest Exile
Ramayana 3 *deals with the exile of Rama. The forest was portrayed as a place for meditation and struggle:* "Those who practise tapas and faith in the forest, the tranquil knowers who live the life of a mendicant, depart freed from sin, through the door of the sun to where dwells the immortal, imperishable person" (Mundaka Up 1.2.11).

He had never spoken like this before, and this miraculously given eight-beat metre became the way in which he spoke *Ramayana*.

Although *Ramayana* is attributed to Valmiki, it grew through a process of many centuries, reaching its present form c.4th–2nd centuries BCE. The book tells of the adventures and misfortunes of Rama who, as a result of the God Vishnu's help, was born in Ayodhya with his three brothers to Dashartha, King of Kosala.

Ramayana is basically an epic story in which the characters (especially Rama, Lakshmana, and Sita) exemplify Dharma (the appropriate way to live and behave), whether in good times or in bad. It is a classic story of the triumph of good over evil.

Ramayana also illustrates how Rama generated the power to follow the path of Dharma in all circumstances by the discipline and asceticism that produce *tapas* ("heat"). *Tapas* in the Vedas is the power used by the Gods (not created by them) to bring the created order into being (e.g., RV 10.129.3). It could be brought into being through the fire sacrifice, evidenced in the sacrificing priests pouring with sweat. It then became the power generated especially through asceticism, chastity, and yoga, through which an immense store of energy is concentrated in the body leading to release (*moksha*).

For all those many reasons, *Ramayana* is a treasured book. Its stories have passed deeply into Indian life: they are widely known, and every year they are sung and acted out in festivals throughout India known as

Rama Lilas. It is said, "Whoever reads and recites the holy and life-giving *Ramayana* is freed from fault and reaches heaven." The same is achieved by saying the name of Rama in a dying person's ear, or by a dying person speaking that name – as Gandhi did when he was assassinated. So deeply is *Ramayana* revered that many new versions were made developing its themes.

Of these, *Adhyatma Ramayana* (date and author unknown) developed the concept that Rama is much more than a great hero, and that both he and his beloved Sita are Avatars, "incarnations" (*avatara*, "descent", p.91) of Vishnu. They are in their essence the two aspects of Brahman (pp.86f): Rama is the impersonal source of all appearance: Sita is the way in which Brahman becomes manifest and creative. The evil Ravana worships God in them even though he is the enemy of God: to have God in mind may lead to the hatred (or death) of God, but it is still God that is in mind.

In *Adhyatma Ramayana*, the events become allegories of all that happens in the human search for God (including the yearning for God when God seems absent or far away, later to become so important in devotion to God, p.96). The major characters exemplify the way in which God/Vishnu becomes manifest, not just in the major Avatars, but also in other Gods and Goddesses too. This is particularly true of Hanuman, important in even later developments of *Ramayana*.

Sita's Wedding
Rama and Sita are models of devotion – between husbands and wives and between humans and God.

THE SEVEN BOOKS OF RAMAYANA

Rama's adventures are told in the seven books of Ramayana:

ॐ **BALAKANDA**: Book 1 deals with the childhood of the four princes and tells how Rama and his brother Lakshmana defeat demons, and how Rama, by bending a bow that other suitors could not even lift, is given his beloved Sita as his bride.

ॐ **AYODHYAKANDA**: This describes how Rama is supplanted as Dashartha's successor and is exiled to the forest with Lakshmana.

ॐ **ARANYAKANDA**: Book 3 deals with the forest exile and tells how the sister of Ravana, the demon king of Lanka, desires Rama. When Rama spurns her, she sees Sita as the obstacle and gets Ravana to abduct Sita – to the poignantly described grief of Rama, who searches for his beloved in vain.

ॐ **KISKHINDHAKANDA**: This tells how Rama assists Sugriva, the king of the monkeys (i.e., all the native forest dwellers), who in return sends Hanuman to find Sita.

ॐ **SUNDARAKANDA**: This describes how Hanuman finds Sita and frustrates Ravana.

ॐ **YUDDHAKANDA**: Book 6 tells of the battle between Rama and Ravana. Sita proves her innocence of any contact with Ravana by throwing herself onto the trial fire, which does not burn her. She is vindicated by Agni (p.63), after which Rama is crowned king.

ॐ **UTTARAKANDA**: The final book collects many supplementary stories, culminating in the death of Sita, the abandonment by Rama of his body, and their reunion in heaven.

Hanuman

The Monkey God

Monkey God
An 18th-century bronze plaque of Hanuman. For worshippers, he is the model of a servant in relation to a master, embodying strength and loyalty.

How does the Indian imagination see its much-loved Hanuman? It sees him:

"as a small monkey figure kneeling with joined hands beside Rama and his half brother Lakshmana and his consort Sita, sometimes tearing his chest open to show Rama's image in his heart, other times flying through the sky with a Himalayan peak in his hand, long-haired, occasionally five-headed, hands in the fear-removing (abhaya) *and wish-granting* (mudra) *gestures, carrying club, bow, and thunderbolt..., devoted and providing devotion, compassionate yet fierce, protector and remover of obstacles, giver of prosperity and destroyer of evil... all these are Hanuman"*

(Ludvik, p.1)

OF ALL THE MANIFESTATIONS OF GOD IN ANIMAL FORM, Hanuman, the monkey or ape, is among the most widely revered, especially in North India. Hanuman is Mahavira, the great hero of Hindu devotion, the son of Vayu, the wind, and the friend and servant of Rama.

He is best known in *Ramayana* (pp.78f) where he comes to the aid of Rama in rescuing Sita from Ravana, the evil king of Lanka. Hanuman gets into the kingdom by leaping across the ocean, but once there he is captured and dragged before Ravana. Ravana sits on a high, proud throne, but that does not bother Hanuman. He coils his long tail and rises up through the air until he is higher than Ravana. In fury, Ravana orders his throne to be raised on blocks, but Hanuman simply puts a few more coils in his tail and rises always higher than human pride – a vivid illustration of the phrase, *Deus semper maior*, "God is always greater".

Even more furious, Ravana orders, for a punishment, that Hanuman's insolent tail should be set on fire. But Hanuman runs faster than the wind, whose son indeed he is: the fire cannot possibly catch up with him. As Hanuman runs, the fire destroys all of Ravana's palaces, possessions, and crops.

During the great battle with Ravana that follows, Lakshmana, Rama's brother, is mortally wounded, so Hanuman is sent to get the only possible cure, a herb that grows on one of the Himalaya mountains. Off flies Hanuman, but when he reaches the mountain, he has completely forgotten which herb it is, so at once he uproots the whole mountain and carries it to Lanka. After the conquest of Ravana, Hanuman returns with Rama to Ayodhya, where he is rewarded with the gift of eternal youth – or, if not eternal, at least of a million years.

At one level, this is the common story of the hero who can bring good things to human beings only if he sets out on a journey that separates him from the known and familiar world, if he encounters and conquers evil forces, and if he returns assisted by the corresponding and countervailing forces of good. It is, for example, the story told of Jesus and of his testing in the wilderness, at the start of his ministry (p.238). The stories point far beyond themselves to the One who is the pioneer of the journeys through life of all humans, and who, as their helper, is worthy of worship and praise.

So it was with Tulsi Das (c.1532–1632CE; the name means "servant of the *tulsi*", a plant sacred to Vishnu). In Hindi, not in the sacred language of Sanskrit, he wrote *Ramcaritmanas*, "The Holy Lake of the Acts of Rama". This is a retelling of *Ramayana* in language accessible to ordinary people, and it has become for many their most deeply loved and treasured access to God. It has been called "the Bible of Northern India" (Macfie, p.vii). It introduces different narrators, including Shiva who is devoted to Rama – an attempt to unify the divergent traditions of God. It continues the emphasis on Dharma (pp.68, 78), but it stresses that Dharma is made possible by the presence of Rama dwelling in the lives of those who are devoted to him.

Tulsi Das was particularly devoted to Hanuman, turning to him always in times of need. Once the ruler in Delhi demanded that Tulsi Das should prove the truth of his faith by performing a miracle, and when Tulsi Das refused, the ruler threw him into prison. When Tulsi Das called on Hanuman, a great army of monkeys began to destroy Delhi, and the ruler at once begged forgiveness and released him. His praise of Hanuman (see box, right) is found in his collection of poems, *Vinaya-patrika* ("The Letter of Humble Petition" to Rama).

Hanuman is greatly loved, but there are myriad other forms in which God or Goddess becomes manifest. The stories of many of them are told in the Puranas.

"Hail, mine of fortune, dispeller of earth's load, Purari's form manifest in monkey guise,

Destroyer of the demons as though they were but moths, through Ram's wrath in the form of fire-flame-garlands!...

Hail, Son of Wind, of famous victories, vast arms, great strength and lengthy tail...,

Hail, face like the rising sun, ruddy eyes, with a knot of bristling grey hair,

With arching brows, with diamond teeth and claws, like a lion for the enemies maddened like elephants,...

Queller of agricultural calamities, great fear, ill-planets, spirits, thieves, fire, disease, great epidemics and afflictions!...

Of none other can this praise be told, that he makes the impossible possible and the possible impossible.

By remembering his image, abode of delight, a person is freed from sorrow and affliction"

(Allchin, pp.100, 102)

Humble Servant
Hanuman worshipping Rama, while Sita and Lakshmana look on. The birthday of Hanuman (Hanuman Jayanti) is celebrated especially in South India and Delhi.

The Puranas

Accounts of Ancient Times

THE PURANAS ARE WORKS in which Indian understandings of God are given paramount expression. They were called *purana* ("ancient"), partly because they were believed to be very old, but partly also because they collect accounts of ancient times – myths, ritual practices, cosmologies, and genealogies of Gods and kings. They began to be compiled in the time of the Guptas (c.320–500CE), but additions, editing, and some composition continued until about the 16th century.

Traditionally, a Purana must deal with five topics:

❖ The bringing into appearance of a universe (its creation)
❖ The destruction and subsequent re-creation of the universe
❖ Genealogies
❖ The reigns of the 14 Manus, the first ancestors of humans, each of whom rules over an aeon (*manvantara*)
❖ The dynasties and history of the solar and lunar rulers from whom all human kings are descended

Just as most of the Puranas deal with a much wider array of Gods and Goddesses than those with whom they are formally associated, so also they may fail to deal with the prescribed main topics. They certainly include much additional material, and by gathering so much information concerned with the Gods and Goddesses and the rituals through which they should be approached, the Puranas gave authority to the ways in which Brahmanic religion developed: in contrast to the large public sacrifices, the Puranas endorsed home-based rituals and therefore made access to God and Goddess possible for ordinary people. The Brahmans who endorsed this God-centred way of

Purana Scene
Bhagavata Purana *tells the story of how the God Vishnu, incarnate as Varaha the Boar, defeated the demon Hiranyaksha.*

THE GREAT AND LESSER PURANAS

Sacred texts on the Indian way of worship.

The Puranas are of immense size. They are traditionally divided into 18 Great Puranas (Mahapuranas) and 18 Lesser (Upapuranas), though the lists of the 18 may vary. The Mahapuranas are then divided into groups of six, each of which is associated with one of the three fundamental constituents of existence as seen, for example, in Samkhya: *sattva, rajas,* and *tamas* (p.76). Each of the three was then linked to the form of God dealt with in those six Puranas:

❧ Rajas/Brahma: Bhavishya; Brahma; Brahmanda; Brahmavaivarta; Markandeya; Vamana.
❧ Sattva/Vishnu: Bhagavata; Garuda; Naradiya; Padma; Varaha; Vishnu.
❧ Tamas/Shiva: Agni; Kurma; Linga; Matsya; Shiva; Skanda.

VISHNU

living were known as Smartas (because they followed Smriti, or supportive scriptures, cf Shruti, p.60) or as Pauranikas (exponents of the Puranas). The forms of worship and belief were in fact diverse, but they were at least theoretically drawn together in their acknowledgment and worship of five manifestations of God: Vishnu, Shiva, Ganesha (Shiva's son), Surya (the Sun), and Mahadevi (the Great Goddess).

The theoretical framework of the worship of the Five Deities (*pancayatana puja*) is important in the arguments (often in the form of stories) against the critiques of God (pp.68–77). *Vishnu Purana*, for example, rejects strongly those whom it calls Nagnas and Pasandas, who include Buddhists and Jains and any others who reject the efficacy of approaching God through ritual. In contrast, the Puranas unfold the worth and the ways of worshipping God. They played a major part in drawing diverse cults into coalitions focused on one particular manifestation of God, whether of Shiva and his consorts, or of Vishnu and his Avatars (incarnations), of whom Krishna is the most important (pp.92ff).

In any one Purana, there may be attempts to rank Gods and Goddesses according to its own focus of devotion – thus, *Vishnu Purana* 5.34.29 records how Krishna defeated Shiva. But the overriding consideration is that despite the critiques of God, God is not dead. There may be many forms through which God is worshipped, but they are all ways in which the One who is God (increasingly identified as Narayana, pp.90, 104) wills to become known (see box, right).

The Puranas, therefore, reflect the way in which the worship of many Gods and Goddesses began to coalesce and flow together into the two major movements in India: the Vaishnavites devoted to Vishnu and his Avatars; and the Shaivites, devoted to Shiva. Both these were divided into many movements of very different kinds, and yet in themselves and between each other there was no embittered rivalry.

This was helped by the belief of both Vaishnavites and Shaivites that Narayana (originally more associated with Vishnu) is the One who is God from whom all creation and all manifestations of God and Goddess come. Through the Gods and Goddesses as agents of Narayana, the whole process of the universe is kept in being. They are not, as a quick reading of the Vedas might suggest, *personifications* of nature, because that would give them distinct and separate identities – a genuine polytheism, i.e., a collection of many Gods and Goddesses. No doubt there were (and maybe still are) Indians who regard them in that way. But even within the Vedas themselves (i.e., at the time of the earliest records), attempts were made to express a very different view, that Gods and Goddesses are *manifestations* of the One source and origin of all reality. The quest for the One became paramount in the Upanishads.

"Just as rivers come from many sources, yet all become one with the ocean, so all the Vedas, all sacred writings, all truth, though they are different in the way they come into being, all come home to God"

(*Bhagavata Pur.* 8.1)

The Attack on Sacrifices
"The Nagnas say: All commands leading to the injury of animals are wrong; to claim that throwing butter into the sacred fire brings reward is to speak like an infant; if Indra, who is supposed to be a God, is sustained by the wood that is used as fuel on the sacred fire, then he is lower than the animals who at least feed on the leaves."
(*Vishnu Pur.* 3.18.25)

The Upanishads

Sacred Texts Seeking the One

THE UPANISHADS ARE SACRED TEXTS (about 200 altogether: the number depends on classification) that come from a long period (c.600BCE to the Middle Ages), but the later texts are extensions and commentaries on the earlier. *Muktika Upanishad* lists 108, but many of these come from a time well after the end of the Vedic period. The Upanishads that are closely connected to the Vedas and form the authoritative Vedanta (end or culmination of the Vedas) are usually reckoned at about 13–18 in number.

The Upanishads continue the quest for the inner meaning of the hymns and rituals addressed to the Gods (in the Vedas themselves Goddesses are not common), and above all they take further the belief that behind the many manifestations of God there is ultimately the One who is the source of all appearance including the Gods themselves (see box, left).

The Vedic religion had emphasized rituals and sacrifices as the way in which humans can bring the power and goodwill of the Gods into the world. The Upanishads seek the One universal reality that brings into being and sustains all that is, including each of the Gods.

But who or what is the One? Yajnavalkya (left) answered "Brahman", but what is Brahman? In early usage (see box, right), *brahman* is ritual power, and the word refers also to those in charge of it, in other words, the Brahmans/Brahmins. But by the time of the Brahmanas (pp.60f) and the Upanishads, the whole emphasis changes. The quest is no longer for power but for insight and knowledge of a kind that will set people free.

The characteristic prayer of the Upanishads is actually put into the mouth of the sacrificing priest, illustrating what sacrifices are really about:

One of the most renowned teachers in the Upanishads is Yajnavalkya. One day he was asked:

"How many Gods are there?" He answered that there are 3,306 (the number invoked in a hymn to all the Gods). "Yes", said his questioner, "But how many are there really?"

"He answered, 'Thirty three' [cf. p.63].
'Yes, but how many are there?'
'Six.'
'Yes, but how many are there?'
'Three.'
'Yes, but how many are there?'
'Two.'
'Yes, but how many are there?'
'One and a half.'
'Yes, but how many are there?'
'One...'
'Which is the One?'
'The Breath. He is Brahman.
They call him That [tat]'"

(*Brihadaranyaka Up.* 3.9.1,9)

Here in essence is the way in which the Upanishads changed the Indian story of God.

> *"From the unreal, lead me to the real; from darkness, lead me to light; from death, lead me to immortality"*

(*Brihadaranyaka Up.* 1.3.28)

Ritual may in fact be a serious impediment, because it moves people *into the world* and into the attempted control of this world, instead of *into themselves* in order to find out who they are and what they can become on the basis of that knowledge.

In *Shatapata Brahmana*, and then in the Upanishads, the word Brahman took on a different meaning. It came to mean the source of power, and therefore the impersonal, Supreme One that alone truly is, who (or "which") creates, supports, and rules the whole universe. According to the elliptical *Brahmasutra* 8.3, "*aksharam brahma paramam*", "Brahman is the Supreme One that does not change [or 'perish']."

Brahman is thus the Supreme Lord (Parameshvara, *para*, "supreme" + *ishvara* "Lord") of all things including the Gods. Brahman brings all things into being through the power known as *maya*, which means that all things reveal what Brahman is. People do not usually see Brahman directly because they impose their own interpretations on what they see. In that way, *maya* is also a cloak that prevents the realization of Brahman as the only truth, the reality of all that is: people may look at a piece of rope on a path and superimpose on it the belief that it is a snake. The way of salvation and release is to learn how to see what is actually the case (the way of knowledge, *jnana*) and also how to live in such a way that one realizes the truth in one's own person (the way of yoga).

In these ways one eventually comes to realize that one has always been whatever Brahman is, because there is not (nor ever has been) anything else but that – or That (*tat*; see box, left). This realization is summed up in the Mahavakyas (Great Sayings of the Upanishads) – "You are That (*tat-tvam-asi*), I am Brahman, All this is Brahman, This Self is Brahman, Pure Consciousness is Brahman".

Brahman is without attributes (*nirguna*) and cannot be described but only attained. Of Brahman one can only say what Brahman is not, *neti, neti*, "not this, not this". If, then, Brahman is the unproduced Producer of all that is, including the Goddesses and Gods, the question immediately arises: what is the relationship between Brahman and God and Goddess? To that question the great Indian philosophers turned their attention.

WHAT IS BRAHMAN?

In origin, Brahman is connected with power:

The word *brahman* comes perhaps from a root meaning "to grow great", "to increase", "to strengthen". It seems initially to have referred to the way in which sacrifices and rituals act almost magically to increase the power of those who offer them. In the earliest use of the word in the Vedas, and especially in Atharva Veda, the meaning of Brahman is the mysterious force behind a magical formula. It is also the sacred utterance or chant (*mantra*, p.129) through which rituals become effective, and the heavenly beings (*devas*) become great. Only later is it the Source of all that is.

Brahmans
Brahmans (often in English Brahmins) were custodians of ritual and intermediaries between God and the world.

Philosophers

Shankara

Ishvara
The three-headed form of God, Ishvara, in one of Shankara's temples reflects the Trimurti (p.90) action of God in the universe. But God is God only to those still in ignorance: to know Brahman is to know that God is only a form of appearance.

IN *CHANDOGYA UPANISHAD*, Uddalaka teaches his son, Shvetaketu, about the way in which all manifestation is an expression of Brahman: "In the beginning, dear one, this was Being (*sat*) alone, one only, without a second. True, some people say, 'In the beginning this was non-being (*asat*) alone, one only, without a second [i.e., essence without contingent existence; cf. pp.268f]: from that non-being, being was produced.' But in truth, dear one, how could this be? How could being be produced from non-being? On the contrary, dear one, this in the beginning was Being alone, one only, without a second. It thought, Would that I were many! Let me extend myself. It sent forth fire, and the fire thought, Would that I were many! Let me extend myself" (6.2.1–3; the sequence extends itself into the creation of all things).

It follows that all appearance is not different from Brahman: fire sends forth many sparks that seem individual, but they are all expressions of fire. This means that the essential nature of what a person is (the inner self or soul, known as Atman) is not different from Brahman. Atman *is* Brahman. To think otherwise is to impose on our self a wrong idea, as Gaudapada (8th century CE) put it in his commentary on *Mundaka Upanishad* (see box, top right).

According to tradition, Gaudapada was the teacher of the great philosopher, Shankara (788–822CE). Shankara developed this non-dualistic way of understanding Brahman and appearance, in which there is no duality between the two except that which is superimposed by false perception. This philosophy is therefore known as Advaita (*a-dvaita*, non-dualism). For Shankara, Brahman is Absolute Being without any attributes or qualities (nirguna Brahman), in which no distinctions between subject and object exist, and of which nothing can be said. When Brahman extends itself into manifest appearance, clearly some

---

SAT-CIT-ANANDA

Absolute Being, Pure Consciousness, Complete Bliss.

Sat-cit-ananda characterizes the essence of Brahman as known (incompletely) in human experience. *Sat*, "being" or "truth", emphasizes the unchanging nature of Brahman as pure unqualified existence preceding all other existence and experience, so that (following Samkhya, p.77) the effect must necessarily be carried within the preceding cause. *Cit*, "consciousness", emphasizes the conscious nature of Brahman experience: Brahman is the ultimate way of knowing, the self-luminous essence of knowing which makes possible all other derivative experience. *Ananda*, "bliss", emphasizes the sublime value of the experience of Brahman.

things can be said from a limited perspective. Brahman as characterized in a provisional and incomplete way is known as saguna Brahman (Brahman with characteristics): it can be said, for example, that Brahman is absolute Being (*sat*), pure Consciousness (*cit*) and complete Bliss (*ananda*), i.e., *sat-cit-ananda*, or *sacchidananda* (see box, below left).

To come to the knowledge and experience of Brahman is to transcend ignorance and misperception and to see things for what they truly are – i.e., not other than Brahman. Advaita therefore emphasizes *jnana-yoga* (the way of knowledge, p.92) as the supreme way to *moksha* (release from endless rebirth), but that knowledge is not an abstract intellectual assent. It is to realize for oneself the union that has always (because Atman is Brahman) been the case but is now grasped as a personal truth. The result of that union is ecstatic joy, since it brings into conscious awareness that one is not other than Being itself, whose nature is bliss. As salt put in water is absorbed and is indistinguishable from it, so Atman is absorbed in Brahman (*Chandogya Upanishad* 4.13.1–3).

Does this account eliminate God? Shankara thought not. He argued that, strictly speaking, it is not *Brahman* of whom one says *Sat-cit-ananda*, because if Brahman really is beyond language and description, to say anything about Brahman is to speak about less than Brahman. Shankara therefore distinguished between para-Brahman (Supreme Brahman) and apara-Brahman (saguna Brahman as above, Brahman perceived in provisional and approximate ways).

S hankara then identified apara-Brahman with Ishvara (from *ish,* "to have power"), the Indian word for Lord or God. Ishvara is Brahman as Brahman extends its Being creatively into appearance through the power of *maya* (p.85), and Ishvara thus allows Brahman to be reflected (experienced directly but not immediately, p.20) through the veil of *maya*. Ishvara or God is the Lord of Maya, immanent in the universe which he governs from within – and as the inner ruler receives the name Antaryamin. But Ishvara is also transcendent, because as Brahman, however much conditioned and reflected obliquely in our perception, Ishvara necessarily transcends all things.

In relation to the world, Ishvara is the One who creates, sustains, then destroys the universe (see caption, top left). Because Ishvara is accessible and is our only access to Brahman, Ishvara is the object of worship, devotion, and praise, and the guide to good and moral life. Not surprisingly, therefore, Shankara did much towards the end of his short life to restore temples and monasteries. According to tradition, his last act was to move closer to God: at the age of 32 he left Kedarnath in the Himalayas, set out for Kailasa, the abode of Shiva (pp.106f), and was seen no more. Even so, there were others who thought that the non-duality of Shankara's system had reduced God too far, and they offered different interpretations of Vedanta.

"A rope not clearly seen in the dark is imagined to be things like a snake or a trickle of water. The Self is misperceived in the same way. But when the rope is seen for what it is, false perceptions are dissolved, and consciousness becomes aware of non-duality with the recognition, 'This is only a rope'. So it is with the discernment of what the Self is"

(*Mandukyakarika* 2.17f)

Many Waves
All appearance is not different from Brahman: the ocean sustains many waves of different size and appearance, but they are all identical with the ocean that brought them into being and sustains them.

Philosophers

◇

Ramanuja and Madhva

Portable Worship
*Vishnu the Pervader is
worshipped in all places.
Small shrines which can be
carried about mean that he
is present to be worshipped
everywhere.*

SHANKARA DID NOT DENY the importance of devotion to God:
he came from South India where Bhakti flourished (p.95).
Even so, Ramanuja (11th–12th centuries CE), also from
South India, believed that Shankara had given too little status to
God. As a philosopher, he pressed home the logic of Shankara's
arguments about Brahman.

He agreed that Brahman is real and indeed is the only reality
there is. But, in that case, the conclusion that Brahman is Sat-cit-ananda
cannot be a conclusion about less than Brahman, because there is no
"less" to be. To posit apara-Brahman (p.87) is a clumsy way of saying that
any statement about Brahman is approximate, corrigible, and fallible (cf.
pp.16f). Ramanuja argued that it is nevertheless an approximate and
corrigible statement about *Brahman* – not something less than Brahman.

Ramanuja also agreed that Brahman is the unproduced Producer of all
that is, in whom effects are always contained in their causes, and that
consequently there cannot be anything that does not come from Brahman.
This means that matter and conscious selves are inseparable from Brahman
and cannot exist apart from Brahman. The inseparability of this relationship
he called *aprithak-siddhi* – but the relationship is not one of complete
identity. Just as consciousness relates to a body and is inseparable from it,
and yet is not identical with it, so Brahman relates to selves and their bodies
by being inseparable from them and yet not identical with them.

Just as a person is a self (Atman) with its body, so Brahman has the
world as its body, inseparable but not identical. Brahman is not an
unqualified identity but is, rather, an organic unity made up of identity-
in-difference, an identity in which one part predominates, controlling and
sustaining the other. So when the Upanishads declare, "There is no
multiplicity here", Ramanuja took that to mean not that the multiplicity
of apparent objects is in fact illusory (as in Advaita where there is no
duality), but that the multiplicity of objects (i.e., of creation) is real but
would be unable to exist apart from Brahman.

By arguing that Brahman is present in the universe as its body,
Ramanuja qualified the non-dualism of Shankara, so that his own system
is known as Vishishtadvaita, qualified non-dualism. As with Shankara,
Ishvara (Brahman as God) is the creator, sustainer, and destroyer of all
universes, but for Ramanuja, Brahman is realistically present in the form
of God (not present in a partial and reflected way). This means that for
Ramanuja the knowledge and worship of God gain even greater
importance, because they are the knowledge and worship of Brahman,
not of apara-Brahman. Not only is *jnana* (knowledge) a way to release
(*moksha*), so too is devotion or Bhakti, along with total surrender to God

(called by his followers *prapatti*). It leads to what Ramanuja called *darshana-samanakara-jnana*, a direct sensing of the reality of God.

Even further than that, Ramanuja claimed, on the basis of the widely reported experience of Bhakti, that Bhakti is rooted not in the effort of people to worship God, but in the purpose of God to make Bhakti possible. It is by the grace of God that people see and worship God. This means that the approach to God is not limited, as in Brahmanic religion, to the three higher castes: it is possible for all who receive and welcome the grace of God.

Madhva (1197–1276CE), a Brahman also from South India, started at the opposite end and took the fact of diversity and of difference to be the most fundamental fact of all that can be observed in the universe. Brahman cannot be identical with the universe, not even at one remove, since otherwise Brahman would rise and fall, wax and wane with the coming and going of this and any subsequent universe. The truth for Madhva is that Brahman *is* God, and God is identified with Vishnu (pp.91ff). God is distinct and different from all that has been created, so that the way to *moksha* (release) and the attainment of God must begin with detachment from the world and attachment to God.

The will and determination to take this basic step come most easily from study of what God has revealed, namely the Vedas. From the realization of the nature and immensity of God, the next step is devotion to God, and that implies doing all things (including one's worship) without any concern for the consequences – except that this is done for God. Instead of desiring *moksha*, one desires God. By realizing that God is wholly other and different, a relationship becomes possible, one that pervades every moment and every aspect of life. At the final stage, God removes the veil of misperception altogether, and the one who worships is left alone with the One.

Devotion
For Ramanuja and Madhva, worship was all-important. Here, worshippers wait to enter the Temple of Kali (p.117) at Dakshineshwar.

All these philosophers were interpreting the Upanishads (pp.84f), but since each of them arrived at different (and in some respects logically incompatible) results, it is obvious that the Upanishads do not contain a coherent system of philosophy. As with virtually all Indian religion, their purpose is to prompt and support those who seek release from the captivity of this world. The major enemy is ignorance, so the most important thing is to know the truth – to know, in other words, what is truly real. It is then supremely important to live the truth in the practice of life, and that includes recognizing and worshipping God in one of the many forms in which God becomes manifest in India. Two major forms of God are Shiva (worshipped especially by Shaivites) and Vishnu (worshipped especially by Vaishnaivites).

Vishnu

Sustainer of All Things

BOTH RAMANUJA AND MADHVA identified God as Vishnu, whose name means "the One who pervades all things". Vishnu is therefore the One who sustains all things and keeps them in being: according to the myth, he covered the entire universe in three strides; when Vishnu sleeps, the universe dissolves into a formless state as of an ocean without features; such remnants of being that there are form themselves into the coiled serpent, Shesha, and on Shesha the sleeping Vishnu rests.

In that state Vishnu is known as Narayana (moving on the waters) and is (another meaning of "Narayana") the final abode of human beings. In this way Narayana, who seems originally to have been a Dravidian (pp.58, 59) God and who was therefore relatively unimportant in the Vedas, was integrated into the cult of Vishnu – a cult that has become one of the major religious movements in India, that of the Vaishnavites.

Vishnu was also integrated into other Indian religious movements by becoming one of the "three forms", or Trimurti, of God manifest in all life: creation, sustenance, and dissolution. The Three are Brahma who creates, Vishnu who sustains, and Shiva who destroys. Brahma is worshipped now in relatively few temples, mainly in North India, but Vishnu and Shiva are the root and foundation of the most popular ways of devotion to God – so much so that each of them alone takes on those three necessary conditions of existence; creating, sustaining, and destroying. Vishnu is Ishvara, the Lord and God who is accessible to all.

Innumerable Forms
A gold ornament showing some of the many incarnations of Vishnu. "The Divine Being is not incapable of taking innumerable forms because he is beyond all form in his essence, nor by assuming them does he lose his divinity, but pours out rather in them the delight of his being and the glories of his godhead; thus gold does not cease to be gold because it shapes itself into all kinds of ornaments"
(Aurobindo, p.765).

THE FIVE FORMS OF VISHNU

Although Vishnu's attributes are many, he manifests himself in five main forms:

ॐ **PARA**: (Supreme), and therefore identical with para-Brahman (p.87).

ॐ **VYUHA**: Four powers, represented by the four arms of Vishnu, from which come forth all that is needed for existence. They appear in manifestations that can be approached and worshipped in their own right, such as Samkarshana who brings knowledge and strength, or Aniruddha who brings power (*shakti*) and glory.

ॐ **VIBHAVA**: The ability to come into the world as an *avatara* (incarnation).

ॐ **ANTARYAMIN**: The inner controller, Vishnu as guide and friend (cf. Shankara, pp.86f).

ॐ **ARCAVATARA**: Becoming present in the visible forms of temple, temple carvings, and images (see further, p.87), frequently of supreme beauty and power, in which Vishnu is welcomed, often through his attributes.

SYMBOL OF VISHNU

He is the cause of all effects who has everything, except his own being and consciousness, as his body. He is normally seen to exist in five main forms (see box, left) but his manifestations can be both vast and elaborate. The most important of Vishnu's many manifestations are summarized in the 24 icons of Vishnu, each of which carries Vishnu's four symbols in a different relationship to each other. These are the conch, representing the origin of existence; the wheel, representing the eternal Mind; the lotus, representing the unfolding universe; and the mace, representing the power of knowledge and the power of time.

Vishnu becomes present not only in temple and image but also, even more dramatically, in his Avatars (*avatara*). The word means "descent", and it is the nearest equivalent to what in English might be called "incarnation". But it is a special kind of incarnation, through which the source of all appearance becomes manifest within appearance.

This may be in any aspect of the created order – in rivers or trees, in the dawn or in the dusk. But supremely it came to be believed that Vishnu, the great controller and pervader of the universe, becomes manifest on earth in particular forms as a matter of free choice. In other words, Vishnu does not become manifest because karma, the law of moral conduct (p.92), has *compelled* him to become present: "The cause for the descent of an Avatar is only the free choice of Ishvara, not the necessary law of karma. Its purpose is the protection of the good and the destruction of the evil." According to the great text of the incarnate Vishnu, *Bhagavadgita* ("The Song of the Lord", pp.92f), God says:

> *"Whenever Dharma [ordered and orderly existence] breaks down, and Adharma [the opposite] flourishes, I create myself; I take on existence from age to age, for the rescue of the good and the destruction of the evil, in order to re-establish Dharma"* (4.8)

God is not in any way diminished or made less by the descent into manifest form, because all things are equally the manifestation of God (see caption, top left). The Avatars, therefore, become the focus of devotion to Vishnu, and that is supremely true of Krishna.

Vishnu's Avatars
The number of Avatars varies in different lists from 10 to 39. They begin in the natural order with Matsya, the fish, and Kurma, the tortoise, because any aspect of creation can manifest the presence of its creator; they include the great figures of Rama and Krishna – and also the Buddha, another way of assimilating a radically divergent tradition; and they culminate in Kalki, who will appear at the end of this universe to destroy evil-doers and to establish a final age of order: "In the twilight of this age, when all rulers are thieves, the Lord of the Universe will be born as Kalki" (Bhagavata Pur. 1.3.26).

 બીમ   નકુળ   સહદેવ   અર્જુન   યુધિષ્ઠિર

Family Conflict
The five hero brothers of the
Pandava family in carved
and painted stone, from the
Surya Temple in Bombay.

Vishnu

Mahabharata and Gita

IN INDIA, THE TWO GREAT EPICS, *Mahabharata* and *Ramayana* (pp.78f), are widely known and loved, providing an introduction for many to God. *Mahabharata* continued to grow over many centuries (c.400BCE–400CE) until it became a vast work of more than 100,000 rhyming couplets in 18 Books telling the story of a family conflict between the Pandavas and the Kauravas, culminating in the 18-day battle of Kurukshetra. Within the many plots and sub-plots of the story, a constant theme is the unfolding of Dharma (moral and appropriate conduct) guiding the Pandavas, and of Adharma (immoral conduct) guiding the Kauravas: "From Dharma come profit and pleasure; people gain everything by Dharma, because it is Dharma that is the essence and strength of the world" (3.9.30).

The Pandavas are supported by their cousin, Krishna, who is the Avatar (incarnation) of Vishnu. From Krishna's instruction of the chariot-driver Arjuna comes one of the supreme texts of India, *Bhagavadgita*, "The Song of the Lord".

The Gita forms part of Book 6 of *Mahabharata*, and in 18 sections of 700 verses, it explores first Arjuna's crisis of conscience: opposed in battle by members of his own family, should he attack and perhaps kill them? Offered the assistance of Krishna, he receives instruction on

THE THREE PATHS

In Mahabharata, Krishna points Arjuna to three paths known as Marga and Yoga:

ॐ **ACTION** (*karma-marga*): Karma is the impersonal law (like gravity) causing the consequences of all actions. Initially, it was the ritual action of sacrifice, then the power of Brahman brought into focus through the rituals; Karma in the Gita sustains both Gods and humans, but must be undertaken for its own sake, not for personal gain: "All the world is in bondage to the *karman* of action, except action for sacrifice; therefore engage in action for that purpose, disinterestedly" (3.9).

ॐ **KNOWLEDGE** (*jnana-marga*): Jnana is not "knowledge in general", but the insight that enables people to understand how they should act selflessly; this insight is *buddhi*, so that

buddhi-yoga actually combines both Karma and *jnana*: it is the effort to act with a mental attitude that is non-attached to the acting and its consequences in one's own case: "The enlightened who are armed with this singleness of purpose rid themselves of the fruits that follow upon acts, and, set free from the bondage of rebirth, go onto a state of bliss" (3.52).

ॐ **DEVOTION TO GOD** (*bhakti-marga*): God is the One behind all the manifestations of God, the source and sustenance of all being (10.20–42), but humans cannot worship an abstraction; they therefore recognize and worship God under different forms, but it is still *God* to whom they join themselves in devotion and love.

appropriate conduct and attitudes. In part, the advice is pragmatic. Since the soul survives the body's death (2.16–30), it follows that:

❖ a war justly fought opens the door to heaven (2.32)
❖ it is Arjuna's Dharma as a warrior to fight (2.33)
❖ if he does not do so, he will lose status (2.34)

But Krishna then offers teaching far beyond this. In order to achieve union with God, he points Arjuna to three paths or ways (*marga, see box, left*), known also as Yoga (the effort needed to reach a goal).

Arjuna asks Krishna which is the best way to find him, by devotion (Bhakti) or by "seeking out the imperishable that is not in itself manifest?" (12.1ff). Krishna answers: "Those who fix their minds on me in complete faith are the most adept at yoga", but those who, with great effort, seek "the unmanifest, eternal, everywhere present but nowhere visible, will reach me too... Those who follow the death-destroying way of devotion, revering me with constant faith as the supreme end, those devotees [*bhaktas*] are by far the dearest to me" (12.20).

The way of Bhakti (devotion to God) is supremely important in the Gita. The Gita seems to address the situation resulting from criticisms of the costly rituals of Brahmanic religion – the situation in which God had been marginalized in the development of Buddhism and Jainism as separate religions, and in the emergence of Samkhya (pp.68–77).

In contrast, the Gita argues the value of the three main ways of approaching God and of seeking *moksha* (release). The Gita can thus be read as articulating (and endorsing) virtually *all* Indian ways of progress towards the goal, whether of later Advaita, Vishishtadvaita, or Dvaita (pp.86–9). It attempts to reconcile diverging opinions and to hold the line against further schism.

Are all the options equally valid? The question has been much debated but, in the end, the Gita seems to hold that Bhakti is the highest possible way, because it is both inspired and helped by the grace (*prasada*) of God. According to tradition, the teaching of the Gita is summed up in a culminating verse (*caramashloka*): "Abandon all the considerations of Dharma [acting with an eye to the consequences] and instead seek shelter with me alone. Be unconcerned, I will set you free from all that is evil" (18.66).

Epic Battle
The chariot fight between the Pandavas and the Kauravas, at the outset of which Krishna offers the teaching to Arjuna that now forms Bhagavadgita.

Venugopala
When Krishna played his flute, animals and birds, as well as humans, were entranced by his music. As the cowherd with flute he is known as Venugopala.

Krishna

The Avatar of Vishnu

KRISHNA IS KNOWN NOT SIMPLY from *Bhagavadgita* but from a wide range of other texts and from an even wider range of practices through which people have expressed their devotion and love. This means that Krishna has unified different traditions (as happens repeatedly in India, pp.58f, p.83) and has connected them all to Vishnu. Some traces of these different traditions can still be discerned.

Krishna may well have been a historical character later recognized as God. His tribe of the Yadavas united with the Vrishnis whose God, Vasudeva, is mentioned in the Gita when Krishna says: "Among the Vrishnis I am Vasudeva, among the Pandavas Arjuna,... the wisdom of the wise" (10.37). The fusion of tribes is reflected in the fusion of Gods (cf. Yahweh and El, pp.178, 183). By at least the 2nd century BCE, Vasudeva-Krishna was known as Bhagavan ("worshipful Being") and his devotees as *bhagavatas*.

When Vasudeva-Krishna was linked to the cult of Vishnu as Avatar (incarnation), some (e.g., the Shrivaishnavas) took that to imply that he was subordinate – a form through which Vishnu becomes manifest. But for others (e.g., Gaudiya Vaishnavas) it implied the opposite: because Krishna was already active in the world, he supplied the opportunity for Vishnu to do through Krishna what he otherwise could not have done, so

PUJA

In an analysis of puja, *Lawrence Babb identified three constituent parts:*

❧ **CLEANSING**: The need to be clean or pure before approaching Goddess/God – hence the importance of water near places of worship. This was already evident in the Indus Valley (pp.60f), and equally apparent in the power of rivers, above all Ganga/the Ganges, to cleanse and to be the presence of the Deity, and thus to bring worshippers close.

❧ **PROSTRATION**: The act of prostrating oneself before the feet of Goddess or God (*pranam*) to honour them with accompanying acts: in human relations now, touching the feet of an honoured person has usually been translated into the practice of *namaste*, of showing respect to another by bringing one's hands together and raising them to one's face

while bowing slightly. A comparable but more dramatic respect is shown to the Deity in gestures like bowing or prostration, offering garlands or signs in red or yellow powder, singing hymns (*bhajans*) and *mantras* (chants, p.129), raising fire (*arti*) before them, and walking around the God/Goddess in whatever form they are present. These marks of honour are then reinforced by gifts of the kind requested by Krishna.

❧ **SHARING FOOD (*PRASAD*)**: The food offered is consumed spiritually by the Deity and transformed so that it bears power and grace: it is then offered back as *prasada*, to be consumed in turn by the worshippers in an act that unites them to the Deity.

that Krishna is Supreme. In what other ways was Krishna active? Among the Abhiras, he was known as the herdsman, the protector of cattle, Gopala. In stories that may well reflect the importance of God for securing fertility, the Abhiras told stories of Krishna/Gopala patrolling the forest of Vrindavana (Brindavan, still an immensely important centre of devotion to Krishna): he destroyed demons, and he danced and made love with the women guarding the cattle, the Gopis. There were more than 16,000 of them, but each thought that she alone was the love of Krishna. The way in which Krishna loves all as though each is unique, and becomes the universal love of all, formed the foundation of the outpouring of ecstatic devotion to Krishna known as Bhakti.

Bhakti (from *bhaj*, "to share", "to be loyal") was not originally a matter of ecstatic emotion or passion. It meant first "to like something" or "to be loyal", and in the Gita it implies an exclusively loyal concentration of all one's mental faculties on Krishna alone. But how is that loyalty to be shown? The Gita answers, by demonstrating this rightly directed concentration in offerings of love (see box, right). This seemingly simple statement is in fact a dramatic summary of the way in which devotion to God as Krishna moved away from the sacrifices of Brahmanism into *puja*.

The word *puja* may be derived from the early Dravidian word for "flower" + "offer". Certainly in practice, *puja* is the widespread Indian way, not least in village religion, of approaching Gods and Goddesses with offerings and gifts, exactly as if they were revered and honoured visitors and guests (see box, left). In *puja*, it is obvious that the Deity is present before the worshipper in the image, and much of the initiating ritual is designed to bring the Deity into the image; indeed, one of the forms of Avatar is *arcavatara*, the descent of Vishnu into the carved temple image, whether stone (*mula*) or metal (*utsava-vigraha*).

This means that worship is literally seeing, or viewing with respect (*darshana*), the Deity through the image. It is not that the image *is* the Deity, but that the Deity can be seen through the image (in other words, Goddess or God is seen directly but not immediately). So in villages, a simple image may be made from clay for the purpose of *puja*, and may then afterwards be simply thrown away.

When *puja* was linked to Bhakti, and Bhakti was transformed into the love of Krishna, a tide of ecstatic and emotional devotion was brought into the centre of the Indian story of God.

> "If any devoted person [bhaktya] offers to me – with love – a leaf, a flower, fruit or water, I accept that offering of love. Whatever you do, or eat, or offer, or give, or mortify,... make it an offering to me, and I will undo the bonds of karma, the good and evil fruits... Even a hardened criminal, who loves me and no other, is to be reckoned a saint [sadhu], because he becomes immersed in Dharma (p.68) and finds peace forever"
>
> (*Bhagavadgita*, 10.26ff)

Offerings of Love
Flowers are a better offering than sacrifices because the death of an animal is not involved (pp.112f).

Krishna and Radha

The Meaning of Love

Dance of Love
The love shared by Krishna and Radha represents the reality of the love that sustains the universe and every detail in it.

"She buries her cheek
In her palm,
Her cheek pallid
As the crescent moon at evening.

Destined to die
Through the unbearable pain
of separation
She moans, chanting
passionately 'Hari, Hari'
Hoping to attain you in the
next life…

She thinks of you and your
coming only.
She contemplates
Your soothing limbs

And so survives"

(Gitagovinda 4.916f, 21)

AMONG THE GOPIS, Krishna's favourite consort by far was Radha (earlier texts speak of Pinnai or Satya as the favourite, but at least by the 14th century CE Radha has become supreme). Their ecstatic love is the epitome of the love that is possible between humans and God. That love is made up of two major themes – separation and union – which are found repeatedly in the poetry of Bhakti (pp.93, 95). In the poetry of absence or of separation (*virahadukkha*; see box, left), God seems to be in hiding, or to have withdrawn, and the poets express their anguish and their longing for the return of God – in the absence of Krishna, Radha "suffers from the pain of being parted from you". In the poetry of passion and union (see box, right), love is expressed in vivid and physical terms.

Gitagovinda, one of the greatest expressions in poetry of these two themes of Bhakti, was written in the 12th century CE by Jayadeva to celebrate the supreme bliss of the union of the soul with God. It is made up of 24 songs. The first praises Krishna for his ten incarnations (p.91; Krishna is here taken to be Vishnu); the second relates to Krishna as Hari (Hari means "the tawny one" or "the destroyer of pain"; it is a common way of addressing the Avatars of Vishnu, and especially Krishna). The songs then tell of Radha's humiliation and anguish because she sees Krishna "making love to any maiden without distinction" (2.1), and "delighting in the embrace of many maidens, eager for rapturous love" (1.3.39). The songs are then divided between the themes of absence and separation (3–16), reconciliation and forgiveness (17–21), and union (22–24). The purpose of the songs is to awaken exactly the same love of God in those who read or hear the words:

"Let this compassionate song of Jayadeva
adorn your heart, and let
this song distil the essence
of devotion to the feet of Hari
destroying the several agonies
of this sinful dark aeon of Kali"

[the last of the four ages before all is dissolved and destroyed]

(Gitagovinda 12.24.24)

Indian Lovers
*In later developments,
particularly in the teaching
and tradition of Caitanya
(pp.136f), love as the union
between Krishna and Radha
becomes the interior
meaning of Brahman's
nature – i.e, one without
differentiation.*

The perfect union between Krishna and Radha is exactly what Brahman (p.85) is. The formula *sat-cit-ananda* (p.86) is made manifest in their union, with Radha as the embodiment of bliss, the *hladini-shakti* of Krishna: the relationship is non-dual (*advaita*; cf. p.86), and yet it is a unity constituted in the relationship of love (cf. the way in which Christians felt compelled to speak about God as Trinity, p.247).

To enter into this divine nature of union-in-relatedness became the goal of devotion. Rupa (16th century CE) showed how, within the confines of the physical body, a spiritual body can be developed in which it is possible to enter into the divine "play" (*lila*), which is the nature of God and the source of all appearance in the universe. His contemporary, Krishnadasa Kaviraja, wrote *Govindalilamrita* to show how the old discipline of visualization (pp.72f) can be adapted so that worshippers, after long and careful training, can lose themselves in the love of Radha and Krishna (in other words, can lose their own selves in God). It takes them far beyond the Vedic imagination of the Gods, even beyond the Creator, Brahma: "I surrender in astonishment to Shri Krishna Caitanya, the compassionate one who has cured the world of the madness of ignorance and then maddened it again with the nectar of the treasure of sacred love for himself. The ultimate goal of spiritual development, the loving service of the lotus-like feet of the friend of the heart of Radha, though unattainable by Brahma, Ananta [the cosmic snake on which Vishnu rests] and others, is achieved only through intense longing by those absorbed in his activities in Vraja [the pastures where Radha and Krishna met]" (Delmonico, p.248).

It was this yearning for God, seen on earth in Krishna, that brought into being the poets known collectively as the Alvars.

*"So the encounter in
love began,
when the shuddering of
bodies
hindered firm embrace;
where the joy of contemplating
one another
with searching looks
was interrupted by blinkings;
where the mutual sipping
of the honey of each other's lips
was impeded by the utterances
of small love-cries.
Yet even these seeming
hindrances
enhanced the delight in
love-play...
Though entwined in her arms
though crushed by the weight
of her breasts
though smitten by her fingernails
though bitten on the lips by
her small teeth
though overwhelmed by the
thirst of her thighs
his locks seized by her hands
inebriated with the nectar of
her lips
he drew immense pleasure from
such sweet torments.
Strange indeed are the
ways of love!"*

(*Gitagovinda* 12.23.10f)

Vishnu and Krishna

The Alvars

Butter Thief
Krishna dancing with lumps of butter he is said to have stolen. When Nammalvar sang of the episode, he fell unconscious at the pain of Krishna being punished – tied, for human fault, with a cord to a stone mortar.

*"He is beyond our knowledge,
He is this and not this,
He comes in the form those seek
who truly turn
to him,
And yet that may not be his
form"*

(Tiruvaymoli 2.5.9)

*"God, the infinite mystery,
Who on that distant day
measured the world with
his stride,
This day has come to me.
How? I do not know;
But life is swooning in
sweetness"*

(Periya Tiruvandadi 56)

SOME TIME IN ABOUT the 8th century CE, a boy called Maran was born in Tirukkuruhur in South India. The story goes that his parents saw something unusual in him, so they took him to the local temple dedicated to Vishnu. He was placed in the courtyard under a tamarind tree (the tamarind being the *avatara*/incarnation form of the snake on which Vishnu rests, p.90), and there he remained for the next 16 years in a state of deep meditation and trance. He was woken when Madurakavi (later his disciple) asked him a question: "When that which is little is born among the dead, what will it eat and where will it lie?" Maran answered, "It will eat the dead and lie on it."

At that moment, Maran awoke and began to sing the hymns that have become known as "the Tamil Veda" (by some, all four of his works are regarded as the Tamil Veda, by others it is *Tiruvaymoli* alone).

Maran became known as Nammalvar ("our immersed-in-God"), and is the most revered of the 12 Tamil Alvars, the group who put into superb poetry the understanding of God that Ramanuja (pp.88f) expressed in philosophy: Nammalvar is the body, the others are his limbs.

"Alvar" means "one who is immersed" in the love of God. For the 12, God is Narayana (the unproduced Producer and origin of all things), Vishnu (God manifest in creation and especially in Avatar/incarnation), and Antaryamin (God guiding within) – the three being necessarily only the One that they are.

The 12 Tamil Alvars lived between the 5th and 8th centuries, when Jains and Buddhists, still numerous in South India, were allowing space for the worship of God, but only in a form that those on their way towards enlightenment and nirvana would learn to leave behind.

For the Alvars, that was to trivialize God and negate the profound and life-changing love of God that humans can experience. They and the Nayanars (devoted to Shiva, see pp.110f) led the way in a revival of God-centred devotion.

In Nammalvar's poems, Narayana (Tirumal for the Tamils) is God beyond anything that can be said, the One who is the source of Goddesses and Gods as humans know them, greater than words can tell (see box, above left).

But God as Vishnu pervades the universe, as in the famous description of Vishnu covering the universe in three strides; and since "he is as much within as without" (*Tiruvaymoli* 1.3.2), he is always close (see box, left). That "closeness" takes visible form when Vishnu becomes incarnate for human rescue:

"The Lord taking birth as a human
Accepts this life with all its sorrow,
Coming here within our grasp
To raise us through suffering
To his Being as God"

(Tiruvaymoli 3.10.6)

The stories of Krishna's love of all the Gopis express both his love for all people and the joy of union with him (*samshlesha*, the Bhakti of union). The pain of his parting from them becomes the poetry of absence (*viraha*, the Bhakti of yearning and desire). Nammalvar's hymns express both conditions, as part of the victory of God:

"Glory be! Glory be! Glory be!
The dark weight in life is lifted,
Decay is decayed, hell is harrowed:
There is no space here for death.
Even the age of Kali will end.
Look! You can see the servants of the Lord...
Running, racing everywhere in crowds over the earth,
Dancing and singing his praise"

(Tiruvaymoli 5.2.1)

This reunion party with God is the free gift of God. All that is required of humans is to desire God, not for the sake of reward, but simply for the sake of God: "Lord measureless in glory [see box, right], the only treasure I desire is not to forget you".

"O Lord, measureless in
your glory,
I have grown and lost myself in
your grace:
Do not change, I beg you!
I do not desire to be set free
from rebirth,
I do not desire to be your servant
in heaven.
The only treasure I desire is
Not to forget you"

(Periya Tiruvandadi 58)

NAMMALVAR'S POEMS

Nammalvar is the avatara of Senai Mudaliar, the leader of the servants of God. He wrote four works:

❈ **TIRUVIRUTTAM**: ("God-filled"or "good" verse), 100 four-line verses express the longing of the soul for God, beginning:
"To deliver us from ignorance, and from evil and pollution in the body,
To save us from being born again and again,
To do all this and to give us life
You, Lord of those beyond death,
Came down here, taking birth in many wombs and taking many forms:
Accept, O Lord, my submission, made from my heart."

❈ **TIRUVACIRIYAM**: (*aciriyappa* is the metre), seven poems arising from a number of different stories told about God.

❈ **PERIYA TIRUVANDADI**: (*Periya* means "great", *andadi* is a style in which the last word of one verse becomes the first of the next).

❈ **TIRUVAYMOLI**: ("The Divine Word"), 1,102 poems exploring the five major themes of Vishishtadvaita (pp.88f) philosophy: the nature of Brahman as God; the soul seeking God; the means (*sadhana*) of attaining God; the goal to be attained; and the impediments on the way.

Krishna and Devotion

Mirabai

THE BHAKTI POETS OF DEVOTION TO GOD make it clear that their love for God is without reserve of any kind. Those in love forget all else and race to God, much as a woman may drop the conventions of society and rush to the one she loves:

> *"I dropped the veils of thought*
> *and ran and fled*
> *and took shelter*
> *at his feet"*

(Futehally, p.83)

The poem (left) shows the love that one of the greatest Bhakti poets had for God. Hari is the Lord Krishna, and Mira, who wrote that poem, is Mirabai, the Rajput princess who, in the 16th century, renounced family and convention and became a wandering singer of devotional songs to Krishna her Lord. From her poured forth the most powerful poetry of delight in the presence of God. But she also knew the absence of God:

> *"Says Meera,*
> *I count the stars, I wait*
> *For one pin of light"*

(Futehally, p.93)

Does absence make the heart grow fonder? Certainly it leads to a yearning for God that would not be felt in the same way without the gap – or sometimes the abyss – of absence:

> *"Piercing is my pain*
> *Through the absence of this night:*
> *When will gently rise again*
> *Shafts of dawning light?*
> *The moonlight – O deceiving foil –*
> *Brings no comfort to my heart;*
> *If I sleep, I wake in turmoil*
> *Anguished while from you apart:*
> *Lord of mercy, Lord of grace,*
> *Glimpse me blessings from your face"*

> *"I hear*
> *his whispered step*
> *and climb*
> *hill forts to seek*
> *his sight.*
>
> *It's the time*
> *frogs croak and peacocks call,*
> *the koel cries, the cuckoo shrills.*
>
> *Indra exults,*
> *calls down the clouds*
> *on all four*
> *sides, lightning stops*
> *being shy.*
>
> *The earth is*
> *newly dressed,*
> *awaits*
> *her meeting with the sky*
> *wants to look*
>
> *Unready,*
> *like any other*
> *bride*
> *and Meera says to Hari*
> *'Why can't you arrive?'"*

(Futehally, pp.89f)

But once experienced, even if literally only once, there can be no forgetting the power and quality of the love with God, however long the wait may subsequently be (see box, top right).

Mira's devotion to Krishna began, so the story goes, when she was young. A wandering holy man came by and showed her a little image of Krishna. She longed for it so much that after he had gone, she could not eat or drink anything. Warned in a dream, the holy man returned to her home and gave the image to Mira and, as she touched it, she passed into an ecstatic state. The image never left her. When she was married, she was so distant from her husband that he suspected her of adultery: bursting into her room one night, expecting to find her with a lover, he found her lost to the world in worship before the image.

When the tide of the world (see box, below right) did indeed come close, Mira preferred Krishna to the world and was lost in him forever. She was driven out of her home state, which then fell on bad times. A deputation was sent to her at the temple at Dwaraka, where Krishna had ruled on earth during his last years, and where Mira was now living, immersed in worship and love. The deputation begged her to return home, but she refused. In despair at her reply, the people said that they would starve themselves – to death if necessary – until she changed her mind. Mira knew she would be responsible for their deaths, and yet she could not leave her Lord. She turned to him in the temple, in desperate appeal. It was then that she poured out the song, *Hari, te hariya jan ro bhir*, "Lord, you remove the burdens of those who worship you", the song which became the inspiration for Mahatma Gandhi (p.138) in his own times of trouble.

Mira threw herself on the image of Krishna – and the image opened and absorbed her into itself. When the brahmans entered the temple, all they found was Mira's sari wrapped around the image.

That is poetry of a very real Bhakti indeed.

"What is this thing
they call
a meeting?

The night goes
in wait, the day is spent
in waiting

When he peeps
in my yard, I'm asleep
to the truth of things

Says Meera:
Is there a soul else
gives a glimpse
of himself, leaves inner
flames leaping?"

(Futehally, p.111)

"What is my native shore
but him?

What swims
in my heart
but his name?

My boat
when it breaks
where call I
but to him, time
after time, then again?

Let me hide,
Meera says,
in these folds.
The tide of the world
comes close"

(Futehally, p.113)

Mirabai
The chanting of hymns (bhajans) to God is an important part of worship, especially for wanderers who rely on alms, as depicted in this statue of Mirabai.

Sex and Tantra

The Warp on a Loom

THE STORY OF KRISHNA AND RADHA, especially as it was treated by Jayadeva (p.96), raised questions: what had become of Dharma, the way of acting appropriately, on which Krishna had insisted to Arjuna (p.93)? How did that accord with Krishna making love promiscuously, or choosing a married woman? Many answers were given – for example, that the story is an allegory of the nature of God as love, in which people are invited to participate, and was not intended as a model of everyday behaviour: Krishna's love of *all* the Gopis depicts the love of God for all beings; his love of a married woman shows how the love of God transcends all other considerations.

These explanations resemble the way in which Jews and Christians turned the biblical book *The Song of Songs* (another poem celebrating the longing of lovers and the joy of their union) into an allegory of God's love for the covenant people, or of Christ's love for the Church. But the Indian explanations do not marginalize the importance of sexual passions and acts, since it is in the reality of these emotions and activities that humans can discern something of God. God is known directly, though not immediately, since the "glimpse" of God is mediated through the union of sexual love.

For this reason sculptures on Indian temples often portray Gods and Goddesses in sexual union (*maithuna*). In *Brihadaranyaka Upanishad*, the act of sexual union is used as a metaphor of union with God (see box, left) but the same Upanishad makes it clear that sexual union in relation to God is much more than a metaphor: 6.4.20 states that in the sexual act to produce a son, the couple become identified with the cosmic process of life, the man with breath and heaven, the woman with sound/speech and earth. In 6.4.3, the woman in sex becomes the altar and the place of sacrifice, where humans and God are brought together.

The power of sexuality to unite human beings with God received its fullest expression in Tantra. Tantra (Sanskrit, "extension" or "the warp on a loom") is found in all Indian religions, in so many different forms, practices, and texts (known as Tantras or Agamas, dating from c.600CE onwards) that it is virtually a religion in itself.

Most, if not all, forms of Tantra have in common a fundamental recognition of the feminine/masculine bipolarity, and teaching practices (known as *sadhana*) that will release the divine feminine energy (Shakti, often in the form of the Goddess Kundalini) and that will unite the bipolar opposites in a way that leads to release (*moksha*). Tantric Sadhana consists of initiation (*diksha*), worship (*puja*), and yoga, in which the body is immensely important. The body holds the soul captive, and yet it

> "As a man when in the embrace of the woman he loves knows nothing of the outside or inside, so does the person know nothing of the outside or inside when in the embrace of the intelligent self [atman *which is Brahman*]"
>
> (*Brihadaranyaka Up.* 4.3.21)

can also be the gate to freedom and perfection. That is so because the human body contains within itself a miniature or compressed version of the entire cosmos, and it is made up of centres of energy (*chakras*) connected with each other by channels (*nadi*). This anatomy is visualized by the yogin and the energies within are brought to life. From the union between the feminine Shakti (divine energy and power) and the male Lord, the cosmos comes into being: through union of the male worshipper with the divine female energy, the whole process of creation is recapitulated in the body.

In this way, Tantra brings worshippers into contact with the power of the divine understood as the primordial energy from which (or "from whom") all life and all manifestation are derived. Tantric ritual purifies the body by symbolically destroying it and then recreating it as the body of Goddess or God through *mantra* (chant, p.129) and visualization. In this state, the power of God or Goddess is received and absorbed, and the highest form of *puja* becomes possible, because there is no distinction between the worshipper and God; and Tantric sects preserve the forms that that worship must take.

Tantric sects, however, differ in the ways they implement the practices of Sadhana. The major division is between right-hand (*dakshinacara*), which stays closer to the norms of Indian practice, and left-hand (*vamacara*), which seeks the power of God or Goddess in places and practices that Dharma-observant Indians abhor. The Kapalikas ("skull-wearers") live in cremation areas, cover themselves in the ashes of the dead, and use skulls as their cups; they meditate seated on the bodies of the dead and eat the flesh of corpses. This form of Tantra enters into the worst and lowest forms of life and finds the power of God or Goddess there. It is this form of Tantra that includes engagement in the "five Ms" (*panca-makara*) five rituals (normally avoided) whose first letter is M:

❖ Madya: Intoxicating liquor
❖ Mamsa: Meat
❖ Matsya: Fish
❖ Mudra: Parched grain
❖ Maithuna: Sexual intercourse with prostitutes, women who are menstruating, or dead

In all of these rituals, especially the last, the purpose is to overcome revulsion and retain control. Great power is thought to derive from retaining semen. As one Tantra (*Jnanasiddhi*) put it, "By the same acts that cause some to be reborn in hell for a thousand years, the yogin gains eternal salvation."

Tantra is an approach to God/Goddess that draws divine power into the body from all circumstances, but only by keeping all circumstances in control. Sexuality becomes a form of asceticism. For that reason, Shiva, the God often associated with the feminine Shakti, has been called "the erotic ascetic" (O'Flaherty). Even more widely than in Tantra alone, Shiva is the focus of much Indian devotion.

Shiva and Shakti
In Tantra the immense power of sexual union embodies the creative powers that bring the universe into being – it is the "imitation of God and Goddess", particularly of Shiva and Shakti, but it requires total control, especially in the retention of semen, for the power to be generated.

Shiva

The Many and the One

NAMMALVAR (P.98) IDENTIFIED GOD as Narayana, God simply as God is, beyond word or imagination. How then can anyone worship God or come to experience God directly? According to Nammalvar, only because Narayana becomes accessible in many forms, summarized in the Trinity of Narayana, Vishnu, and Antaryamin (p.90), and extended through Vishnu to other Gods and Goddesses who come from Narayana as the source and origin of all appearance:

"Narayana, the origin of all the Gods,
Made his own form come forth
As all the many different Gods"

(*Tiruvaymoli* 5.2.8)

It follows that all the Gods and Goddesses are essentially one, so that Narayana can equally be said to be the more traditional Trinity (Trimurti, p.90) of Vishnu, Shiva, and Brahma, who are "the Lord's form dispersed through all the worlds" – as are all the Gods (see box, left). In India this has become a way of understanding how the many Gods and Goddesses are related to the One that God must be, the absolute and unconditioned source of all things, the unproduced Producer of all that is. What looks superficially like polytheism (the recognition of many Gods/Goddesses) is a way in which monotheism becomes practical and practised in Indian life (see box, far right). This has not always been put into practice, and conflicts have occurred. Even so, it is this fundamental understanding of God that allows any particular form of God to attract to itself other forms of God in a kind of coalescence of imagination. It has allowed also the "migration" of the forms of God, in the process described on pp.58–9.

This means that some forms of God's appearance may fade in significance (some Gods prominent in the Vedas, such as Indra and Varuna, later become less so), while other Gods gain immensely in importance, gathering to themselves beliefs, legends, and practices that belonged initially to other Gods.

Theoretically, therefore, it should be possible to write a brief history of any one of the major Indian Gods or Goddesses, but in practice this is extremely difficult to do, because often the

Dancing Shiva
Shiva as Nataraja, Lord of the Dance, sustains and destroys the universe: the drum in one hand summons the universe into being, the flame in the other destroys it.

"You have made all the many forms of worship
And, through the fruitfulness of human imagination,
All the many forms of religion –
in conflict though they are –
And all the many Gods in all of them. And so
In countless forms you have extended yourself,
O you who have none other near or nearer you,
You who have none to compare with you:
It is for you that I yearn in my desire"

(*Tiruviruttam* 96)

earliest stages and the component parts have been so absorbed into the major figure that they cannot any longer be completely disentangled. Supremely this is true of Shiva.

Shiva scarcely appears in the Vedas, except as a word describing Rudra, meaning "the auspicious one" (later, Rudra becomes an epithet of Shiva, when Shiva has become the more important). Rudra is the power of destruction, the fire that burns, the water that drowns, the wind that destroys, the one who kills. Yet all these have an auspicious use, and Rudra is also the one who receives sacrifices and brings prosperity to humans and their herds. He has a hundred heads and a thousand eyes, so that nothing escapes his notice, and as a result he is the one who brings punishment and "gives to those who do wrong the pains of hell". Yet equally "the God who kills" (*Atharva Veda* 1.19.3) is the one who brings strength to those who deserve it.

All this duality was carried over into Shiva, but Shiva is not a simple development of the Vedic Rudra. Shiva may be found as early as the Indus Valley seals, if that interpretation (pp.60–61) is correct. In any case, Shiva absorbs many other forms of God, and the dual aspects of Rudra made that process easy.

Alain Daniélou spent a lifetime studying Indian religions. Here he describes the relationship between the Many and the One in this way:

"In the polytheistic religion [of India] each individual worshipper has a chosen deity (ishtadevata) and does not usually worship other gods in the same way as his own, as the one he feels nearer to himself. Yet he acknowledges other gods. The Hindu, whether he be a worshipper of the Pervader (Vishnu), the Destroyer (Shiva), Energy (Shakti), or the Sun (Surya), is always ready to acknowledge the equivalence of these deities as the manifestations of distinct powers springing from an unknowable 'Immensity'. He knows that ultimate Being or non-Being is ever beyond his grasp, beyond existence, and in no way can be worshipped or prayed to. Since he realizes that other deities are but other aspects of the one he worships, he is basically tolerant and must be ready to accept every form of knowledge or belief as potentially valid. Persecution or proselytisation of other religious groups, however strange their beliefs may seem to him, can never be a defensible attitude from the point of view of the Hindu"

(Daniélou, p.9)

Threefold Nature
The lines on Shiva's forehead represent his threefold nature – male, female, androgynous; creator, preserver, destroyer. For the symbol on his hand, see p.128.

Shiva

The three faces of Shiva representing the different ways in which he is present are depicted here on a painted wooden panel from Dandan-Oilig, Khotan.

Shiva

Lord and Origin of All Things

SHIVA IS, FOR MANY MILLIONS, the form and focus of God in worship and life. That has happened, in part, because Shiva absorbed into himself other Gods and attracted to himself, as his consorts, many Goddesses. That process was made easier because he carried with him the dualities that were found in Rudra. This meant that conflicting images and imaginations of Shiva could be affirmed together.

The apparent contradictions in Shiva's many manifestations (see box, below) are not in fact so, because they simply express the Indian realization that all appearance is fraught with *maya* (pp.85, 87), and that reality can be seen only in partial glimpses, never as a whole.

For that reason, Shiva is often portrayed, not least in sculpture, with three faces, in which two opposites are held together by a reconciling third – as, for example, creator, destroyer, and preserver; male, female, and androgynous (Ardhanavishvara; the three horizontal lines that Shaivites mark on their foreheads represent the threefold nature of Shiva). Shiva is also depicted with five faces, controlling the five senses, or surveying the four quarters and the whole of heaven.

In this way, Shiva becomes the One who contains all the pluralities that make up the experience of life, the One who brings them into being, sustains them, and destroys them – thereby combining in himself the three functions distributed elsewhere between the three Gods (p.90). This way of seeing Shiva as the One who is the source and origin of all things, including the other forms of God, resulted in the hymn of

THE MANY FACES OF SHIVA

The God Shiva can take many forms. These include:

❈ **THE ASCETIC**: His restraint generates the heat and power (*tapas*) that would otherwise be lost; yet he is also the erotic, fervent lover.

❈ **THE LOVER**: The model of conjugal love with his consorts Parvati or Amba; yet his lovers Kali, Candika, and Durga are fierce and destructive, and they transmit to him the power to destroy.

❈ **THE ALL-POWERFUL LORD**: The source of creation; yet without the female energy known as Shakti (p.116), he is powerless: he is often shown lying dead beneath her feet.

❈ **THE HUNTER**: He slays and skins his prey and dances in the still-bloody skin; yet he is the

world-escaping ascetic, who burns to ashes Kama, the God of desire and erotic love, with a single glance from his truth-discerning third eye.

❈ **THE WORLD-RENOUNCER**: The world-renouncing *samnyasin* (the fourth stage of Dharma-observant lives), he appears smeared with the white ashes of the cremation fire and holding a skull in acceptance of death (and wearing also a necklace of skulls), and he welcomes natural enemies, so that a snake coils itself around his body; he is also Pashupati, Lord of the animals; yet at the end of the age, he will dance the universe to destruction.

SHIVA

Shetashvetara Upanishad (see box, right). Shiva is the
unproduced Producer of all that is, and yet is equally present in
the universe, not least as the One who, through his dance of five
gestures (pancakritya), turns the wheel of creation and
destruction. Shiva has absorbed and become the figure of
Nataraja, the Lord of the dance. He also dances the Tandava
dance in cremation grounds, and the dance of the Gods on
Mount Kailasa in the Himalayas.

His dance summarizes the divine lila, or fun/sport/play: he
veils himself in the maya (pp.85, 87) of creation in order to draw
others into his dance and thereby to deliver them, in union with
himself, from rebirth. He dances at the centre of the universe, at
Chidambaram (originally Tillai) in South India, in a temple well
known to the Nayanars (pp.110f) and still "the home of dancing
Śivan" (the title of Paul Younger's study).

Shiva comes even closer to earth in Varanasi (Banaras) or in
its older name, Kashi, the City of Light. Here, Shiva is united
with his beloved Ganga (the Ganges, the flowing form of Shakti,
female energy): he originally caught her as she fell to earth and
tamed her wild turbulence by pouring her through the locks of
his hair and then allowing her to flow over the earth in life-giving
power. In Kashi, which Shiva chose from the beginning of
creation as his home, Ganga and Shiva meet, and worshippers
meet them – and hope to die in their embrace. For those who
die in Kashi, Shiva removes the burden of karma (past deeds) that might
otherwise lead to rebirth: he himself whispers the Taraka (ferryboat)
mantra in their ears, and carries them over the flood. Faith leads
immediately to freedom:

"Here in Kashi the gift is simple:
Give up the body to the fire.
Even the yogin with a mind controlled
Who wanders on from life to life
Will here in Kashi
reach the goal
Simply by dying"

(Kashi Khanda 60.55ff)

"He who is One, without any
colour but by the manifold
exercise of his power distributes
many colours in his hidden
purpose, and into whom in the
beginning and at the end the
universe is gathered, may he
endow us with a clear
understanding.

That indeed is Agni, that is
Aditya, that is Vayu, and that is
the moon. That indeed is the
pure. That is Brahma. That is
the waters. That is Prajapati.

You are woman. You are man.
You are the youth and the
maiden too. You, as an old man,
totter along with a staff.
Being born, you become facing
in every direction"

(Shetashvetara Up. 4.1–3)

Indra's Heaven
The River Ganges at
Varanasi: those who bathe in
the Ganga or leave part of
themselves (hair, bone, etc.)
on the left bank will attain
Indra's heaven.

Shiva's Sons

Ganesha and Kumara

A̲N IMPORTANT WAY IN WHICH THE CULT of other Gods/Goddesses was united with that of Shiva was by associating them with him as his offspring (or, in the case of Goddesses, as his consorts). Of these, two are widely recognized and worshipped in India – Ganapati (better known as Ganesha) and Kumara (also known as Skanda).

Ganesha is the elephant-headed God who brings wisdom and good fortune. Many different stories are told of how he lost his original head and received an elephant head instead: his head was lost because of the envy of Gods or of demons, or due to a glance from Shani (the planet Saturn), or by the blow of Shiva himself, and the first head that came to hand as a replacement was that of an elephant. *Shiva Purana* records a popular version: when Ganapati/Ganesha was born to Parvati and Shiva (p.116f), he was so protective of his mother that he even tried to prevent Shiva from approaching her; Shiva sent his servants to teach him better manners, but in the ensuing battle Ganesha's head was cut off; when Shiva saw the grief of Parvati, he replaced the severed head with the first alternative that came to hand, that of an elephant.

This union is now understood as the embodiment of a fundamental truth in Indian religion, that the human form contains within itself a compressed version of the energies of the entire cosmos (cf. Tantra, pp.102f): the insignificantly small human (the body) is joined to the immensely large cosmos (the elephant) through God as Ganesha.

The word "elephant", *gaja*, was taken to be made up of *ga*, "end" or "goal", and *ja*, "source" or "origin", so that Ganesha is Brahman (pp.84f). In one of the many texts written in imitation of the Upanishads (as also *Ganeshagita* in which Ganesha replaces Krishna of the *Bhagavadgita*) *Ganapati Upanishad* 2 states simply, "You are the visible form of That" (cf. the Mahavakyas, p.85). The cult of the elephant-headed God may well be very old, especially in villages, but in his present form he has become widely revered, and increasingly so, since the period of the Epics. Although Ganesha has few temples dedicated solely to him, his image, sculpted or hand-painted, is found everywhere, in homes, in shops, under trees, because he is known as the remover of obstacles, the embodiment of success, good-living, peace, and wisdom. He is invoked before all undertakings, from religious ceremonies (though not funerals) to written compositions, and before the worship of other deities.

Elephant Head
Ganesha is one of the most popular and widely revered Indian Gods because he is thought to bring success, peace, and wisdom to those who worship him.

Although the Ganapatyas make him the focus of their worship, he does not belong to one sect, but to all who need his help.

Shiva's other offspring, Kumara, is the ever-chaste youth who was born miraculously without the help of a woman. When the Gods were being harassed by Taraka, their enemy, Indra led a deputation to Brahma, the Creator, to ask for help. He told them that only a son of Shiva would be strong enough to defeat this powerful foe. To waken Shiva from meditation proved difficult (p.117), but once he was aroused, nothing, not even Agni (Fire), could bear the heat of his seed, until the Ganges took it to a thicket known as "the forest of arrows", and there Skanda, "the one who jumps" spontaneously from semen, was born. He was also given the name Kumara, because he remains chaste and young forever.

He was suckled by the six Pleiades (Krittikas), developing six faces for the purpose, and among many other names he is known also as Karttikeya. The six faces of Karttikeya are identified with the six subtle channels (*chakras*) through which the energy of the cosmos and the power of Goddess and God are brought to life in the human body (p.103). As Kumara, the chaste youth, he is important in yoga, because by concentration on Kumara yogis gain control over sexual activity, whether deliberate or involuntary. Yogis who gain this control, even in sleep, can use the energies of sexuality for attaining God, and they become the living image of Shiva.

Shiva also has many attendants, who again represent a way in which more local cults can be integrated into the sense that God is manifest in many forms. Of particular importance are the Gods and Goddesses who protect villages, *grama-devata* and *grama-kali*. Village deities are not related to the vast issues of the cosmos, but to more local events – the rites of passage from birth to death, and to emergencies that threaten to disrupt or destroy that process – disease, famine, and flood. They have, in the past, been far more commonly approached through animal sacrifice, and, since they are the source and sustenance of life, they are more likely to be Goddesses than Gods.

Greetings from Ganesha
A Diwali greeting card featuring the elephant-headed God, Ganesha. Images of Ganesha, often hand-painted, are found throughout India, in shops, homes, and offices.

Village shrines are usually extremely simple and almost entirely independent of temples and the Brahmanic cult. Even so, some village cults have made a deliberate attempt to integrate themselves into the wider Indian acknowledgment of God. For example, according to Sachinanand (*Culture Change in Tribal Bihar*), the Oraons in central India had begun by the 1960s to address Devi through their rituals, and to adopt Kabir (pp.120f) as guardian. Jatru Bhagat made an attempt to unify, or pull together, villagers in a common devotion, and since the word "pull" (*tano*) appears often in their Bhakti hymns, they have become known as Tana Bhagats.

In general, village religion does not need to be made a coherent part of a larger Indian devotion, nor is it organized or unified. It deals with the immediate events of life, and with the spirits of the ancestors. For that reason, it was easy to attach all the village Gods to Shiva as his attendants. For a Shaivite, however, it is the devotion to Shiva that matters.

Devotion to Shiva

◇

Nalvar and Nayanars

Shiva and Ganga
*Ganga/the River Ganges
came from the feet of Vishnu
and then flowed through
Shiva's hair to give life to
India. There is also a Ganga
in the sky (the Milky Way)
and in the underworld
(Patalaganga).*

BETWEEN THE 6TH AND 8TH CENTURIES CE, poets wandered through South India visiting temples and shrines devoted to Shiva, where they encouraged others to join them in singing their Tamil hymns of praise and love.

The three major poets involved were Campantar, Appar, and Cuntarar, and they are honoured as *muvar mutalikal*, "the first three saints". Later, a fourth, Manikkavacakar (c.9th century), was added to make up Nalvar, "the Four". They in turn inspired others, of whom (with them) 63 are known as Nayanars ("leaders", "guides").

Seven hundred and ninety six of the hymns of "the first three saints" are collected in the first seven books of *Tevaram*, a work also called *Tirumurai*, "sacred tradition", and regarded by Tamils as revealed scripture, the equivalent of the Vedas (p.60). Their hymns are the foundation and expression of Bhakti devotion to Shiva, greatly valued by each of the many different movements making up the Shaivites – and comparable to the hymns of the Alvars (pp.98f) in relation to Krishna and Vishnu, equally valued by the Vaishnavites.

In all, "the first three saints" visited 274 temples, which is a reminder of their commitment to ritual as a way of showing devotion to Shiva – it was only later that some Bhakti poets rejected ritual in favour of a direct and personal devotion to God (p.113). "The first three saints" saw the rituals of Temple and of Tantra as practical ways in which people can honour God. In sculpture, Appar is often shown carrying a farmer's hoe with which he cleared out weeds and undergrowth from the Temple areas, a symbol of his desire to open up a path to God:

*"Hands, join in worship,
strew fragrant flowers
on the Lord who binds
the hooded snake round his waist!
Hands, join in worship!*

*Of what use is the body
that never walked around
the temple of Siva,
offering him flowers in the worship rite?
Of what use is this body?"*

(Peterson, p.256)

Just as the Vedic hymns and many of the later Sanskrit poems of praise (*stotras*) were sung in the context of sacrifice, so the Tamil hymns became part of the offerings of *puja* (worship, p.94f). The hymns were offered like the garlands of flowers:

> *"Flowers make ornaments,*
> *and so does gold;*
> *yet if our Lord who sweetly abides in Arur*
> *were to desire an ornament for himself,*
> *simple heart, let us honour him*
> *with the ornament of Tamil song!"*

(Peterson, p.265)

The hymns celebrate Shiva's appearance and deeds, and often recite his names and attributes, much as the poet and dramatist Kalidasa had done two centuries earlier. But now the myths and images were linked both to the local shrines and to the individual worshippers, to bring Shiva closer to them. A hymn by Campantar makes this transition from the general attributes of Shiva (androgynous, matted-haired, riding a bull) to the local person and place:

> *"They praise him, calling him the Lord who is*
> *half woman,*
> *Lord with the matted hair, god who rides the bull.*
> *He is the thief who stole my heart.*
> *He is the Lord who lives in Piramapuram,*
> *Famed as the shrine which once floated*
> *On the dark ocean's cosmic flood"*

(Peterson, p.247)

As images in temples help worshippers to see God directly, even though mediated through the form of the image, so the hymns are designed to help worshippers to see Shiva directly, even though mediated through the words and music. They are intended to reach the emotions directly, with the intellectual reflection left, for the moment, on one side (cf. p.40). According to a popular saying, "No words can move those who do not melt when they hear these hymns."

So often did this happen that a new kind of Bhakti poetry developed, one in which the connection with Temple and ritual was deliberately abandoned.

Shiva is not a remote king:

> *"He came to us singing songs in*
> *varied rhythms,*
> *and took us by force.*
> *He shot the arrows of his eyes at*
> *us;*
> *with speeches that stir up*
> *passion*
> *he skillfully seduced us, made us*
> *sick with love.*
> *The skullbearer god [p.106 box]*
> *has mounted his swift bull;*
> *wearing a skin, his body covered*
> *with white ash,*
> *a sacred thread adorning his form,*
> *come, see the Master as he goes*
> *riding where all can see him.*
> *The Lord of Amattur is a*
> *handsome man, indeed!"*

(Peterson, p.210)

The love is passionately returned:

> *"My heart melts with love*
> *for the handsome god*
> *who bears the river [Ganges] in*
> *his hair...*
> *sweeter than sweet fruit, raw*
> *cane sugar,*
> *lovely women with fresh flowers*
> *in their hair,*
> *sweeter than sole dominion over*
> *vast lands*
> *is Itaimarutu's Lord*
> *to those who reach him"*

(Peterson, p.210)

Darshana
To come before the
representation of the Deity
is called darshana,
("seeing"). The worshipper
comes into the real presence
of God through the image,
not that the image is
identified with God.

Devotion to Shiva

Kannappar

T HE "FIRST THREE SAINTS" had Manikkavacakar added to them as another of the greatest poets of Bhakti devotion to Shiva. Yet Manikkavacakar knew of an even greater love than his own. A Tamil proverb says, 'True love is the love of Kannappar", and with that in mind, Manikkavacakar wrote:

"There was no love in me like that of Kannappar.
When he, my Lord, saw this, then me, poor
Beyond compare, he made by grace his own.
He spoke the word and bid me come to him.
Adorned, he shines with heavenly grace;
He wears white ashes and the dust of gold.
To him, of mercy made without a bound,
Go, go; and breathe his praise, O humming bee"

(Periya Purinam)

So who was Kannappar, this man whose love became proverbial and exceeded that of even the most enraptured saints? He was a low-caste hunter who therefore could not keep the rules of ritual purity if he wished to make an offering to Shiva. Instead, he used to bring gifts of wild flowers and scraps of (ritually forbidden) meat – anything that he could find. One day the Brahman in charge of the temple was shocked by the filthy appearance of Shiva's image, defiled, as it clearly was from his point of view, by the unclean objects brought by Kannappar. He started to clean the image, and conduct the more orthodox ritual. But that night Shiva appeared to the Brahman in a dream and said:

"That which worried you, to me is precious beyond price. The man who did these things is a wild man of the forest. He does not know the Vedas or the Shaiva texts. He does not know the rituals of worship. But do not think of him; think of the spirit and the intention of what he does. His rough and stumbling body is vivid with love for me, his only knowledge is knowledge of me. The food he offers to me, so polluting to you, is pure love. He loves me utterly. And tomorrow I will give you proof of his love: come, and see"

"Nine hounds unleashed
on a hare,
the body's lusts
cry out:
Let go!
Let go!
Let go! Let go!
cry the lusts
of the mind.
Will my heart reach you,
O Lord of the meeting rivers,
before the sensual bitches
touch and overtake?"

(Ramanujan, p.69)

The vacana poets reject the idea that sacrifice, ritual, or even effort can bring people to Shiva:

"The sacrificial lamb brought for the festival
ate up the green leaf brought for the decorations.

Not knowing a thing about the kill,
It wants only to fill its belly:
Born that day, to die that day.

But tell me:
Did the killers survive,
O lord of the meeting rivers?"

(Ramanujan, p.76)

So the next day, the Brahman went to the temple and saw Kannappar arrive. At that moment, Shiva caused blood to trickle from the right eye of his image. Without hesitation, Kannappar seized an arrow and gouged out his own right eye and laid it on the image, and at once the bleeding stopped. Was that enough to prove his devotion? Shiva immediately made the left eye of the image weep blood; and Kannappar prepared to do the same again. This time, Shiva held him back, because now the Brahman understood what true devotion is.

Kannappar became one of the Nayanars (pp.110f), but he was already indicating the way in which temple ritual became for some devotees of Shiva far less important than the union of utter commitment and love. Spokesmen for these were the brilliant *vacana* poets of the 10th to 12th centuries CE, writing in the Dravidian language of Kannada. *Vacana* means "a saying", "something said", so these poems are a kind of free, though tightly controlled, composition (see box, left). Among more than 300 *vacana* poets, four stand out: Allama, Basavanna, Dasimayya, and Mahadeviyakka. Basavanna worshipped Shiva at Kappadisangama, where three rivers meet: their meeting became for Basavanna a symbol of the way in which Shiva flows into, and becomes one with, those who are devoted to "the Lord of the meeting rivers" (see box, top left).

The *vacana* poets do not pretend that the way of union with God is easy. The poetry of absence, common in all Bhakti poetry, is sharpened even further to become the poetry of the apparent harshness of God:

"He'll grind you till you're fine and small.
He'll file you till your colour shows.
If your grain grows fine
in the grinding,
if you show colour
in the filing,
then our Lord of the meeting rivers
will love you
and look after you"

(Ramanujan, p.86)

But the experience of absence and of harshness does not last. Shiva reaches in all ways those who seek him. Mahadeviyakka worshipped Shiva in the temple at Udutadi, where he was known as Lord white as jasmine (see box, top right).

The *vacana* poets were not isolated in regarding the union with Shiva as far more important than the proper performance of long-established rituals in the temple. They were at the heart of a movement known as Virashaivites, "heroes of Shiva". They were also known as Lingayats, since for them the Linga was the most important vehicle of Shiva's presence.

"Sunlight made visible
the whole length of a sky,
movement of wind,
leaf, flower, all six colours
on tree, bush and creeper:
all this
is the day's worship.

The light of moon, star and fire,
lightnings and all things
that go by the name of light
are the night's worship.

Night and day in your worship
I forget myself
O lord white as jasmine"

(Ramanujan, p.130)

Simple Gifts
Hindu offerings to God or Goddess may be extremely simple, as here beside Ganga/the Ganges, and do not have to be made in a temple.

Devotion to Shiva

The Linga and the Lingayats

Mahadeviyakka was a female follower of Shiva:

"Like other bhaktas, her struggle was with her condition, as body, as woman, as social being tyrannized by social roles, as a human confined to a place and time. Through these shackles she burst, defiant in her quest for ecstasy

Like a silkworm weaving her house with love from her marrow, and dying in her body's threads winding tight, round and round, I burn Desiring what the heart desires.

Cut through, O lord, my heart's greed, and show me your way out O lord white as jasmine"

(Ramanujan, p.116)

S THE UNIVERSE DREW TO THE END of an era, Brahma and Vishnu were arguing about which of them was its creator and the greatest God. Suddenly, a brilliant and vivid column of light appeared. The two Gods agreed that the one who first succeeded in finding either the base or the top of the column would be accepted by the other as the supreme God.

Vishnu took the form of a boar (one of his classic forms of incarnation, *avatara*, p.91) in order to dig deep into the earth, and Brahma took the form of a wild goose and flew up into the air. The more they searched, the further the column of light extended beyond them, and they accepted that neither of them was as great as they had thought. At that moment, the light was revealed as Shiva in the form of the cosmic linga: he then stepped out of the light and revealed himself as Maheshvara ("supreme God"), with five faces (p.106) and ten arms, and Brahma and Vishnu immediately bowed down before Shiva, acknowledging his supremacy.

This story is told in *Shiva Purana* 2.1.6–9, showing the way in which Shaivites made Shiva supreme over all other Gods. But it shows also the supreme form through which Shiva makes himself manifest, the *jyotir-linga*, the pillar of endless light. The linga in general is the penis, the male organ of generation, and it is often found in temples in association with the yoni, the female counterpart. Together they are the fundamental power that brings all things into being.

The word *linga* means "symbol", and the linga is therefore the quintessential symbol of Shiva that does not represent his appearance in an icon or image – in other words, it is *aniconic*. Iconic symbols are those which portray Gods or Goddesses in some aspect of their being or power. The linga is the focus of worship in many temples, and it became the basic symbol of a group known as the Lingayats or Virashaivites (heroes of Shiva). The Lingayats came into being under the inspiration and guidance of Basavanna (p.113). At the "place of the meeting rivers", he began to worship Shiva in the temple, until in a dream Shiva commanded him to leave and serve a

Linga Worship
A devotee bathing a linga in milk in a temple devoted to Shiva.

distant king. Basavanna cried out against the cruelty of Shiva in banishing him from his beloved temple – "pulling away the earth from under a man falling from the sky, and cutting the throat of the faithful." The next night, in another dream, Shiva told Basavanna to come to the sacred bull in the temple the next day, and when he did so, Shiva appeared from the mouth of the bull bearing a linga which he bestowed on Basavanna. Carrying the linga, Basavanna knew that Shiva would be with him in all places, and from that moment he was set free from dependence on rituals and temples.

As word of Basavanna's passionate devotion to Shiva spread, a community of followers gathered round him, and these became the new Virashaivites – called also Lingayats because their only ritual symbol is a linga worn constantly round the neck: no other focus or reminder of God is necessary. Its loss is the equivalent of spiritual death, a reminder that the body is the true temple.

The new community regarded all as equal before Shiva, and its members abandoned caste and ritual other than its own. They banned child marriage, and approved of widows remarrying. Women and men came to be regarded as equal, and the former were no longer regarded as unclean at the time of menstruation. Because the one who worships Shiva in this way is believed to be united with him at the moment of death, Virashaivites do not even follow the rituals of cremation and of commitment of the dead to the ancestors. Instead, they bury the corpse.

A follower of Shiva in this way was Mahadeviyakka. She threw off convention (see box, left) and delighted in Shiva's association with Shakti, female energy in the form of Goddess (see box, right). In a brief life of great struggles, she cut herself off from the world and its conventions in order to be one with God:

Symbols of Shiva
Linga and Yoni represent the creative power of Shiva and Shakti as the source of life, as seen here in a 15th-century image in Java.

"Why do I need this dummy
of a dying world?
Illusion's chamberpot,
Hasty passion's whorehouse,
This crackpot
And leaky basement?"

(Ramanujan, p.133)

"Locks of shining red hair
a crown of diamonds
small beautiful teeth
and eyes in a laughing face
that light up fourteen worlds –
I saw his glory
And seeing, I quell today
The famine in my eyes...
I saw the Great One
who plays at love
with Shakti,
original to the world,
I saw his stance
and began to live"

(Ramanujan, p.120)

For millions of Indians it is Shakti in the forms of Mahadevi, the Great Goddess, who is the focus of their devotion.

Goddess and Shakti

Divine Female Energy

THE LINGA AND THE YONI are the male and the female counterparts in the creation and origin of life. They are, consequently, supreme symbols of God/Goddess understood as the "One without second" from whom all creation comes. The One, the source of all being, may be identified by different names (Brahman, Brahma, Narayana, Vishnu, Shiva, etc.), but it is recognized that the essential nature of the One lies far beyond names and words. Even so, humans can only approach the One beyond words in the ways in which the One becomes accessible to human feelings and thought.

Given the mutual dependence of male and female for the initiation of life, the One in accessible form may be either female or male (or a fusion of both, as in the androgynous form of Shiva, p.105). From the absolute Source of all being, however identified, come the many manifestations of Goddess and God.

The female source of energy is known in general as Shakti, and those who worship Goddess as Shakti are known as Shaktas. Shakti becomes manifest in nature itself (*prakriti*, p.76), in the restless power within natural phenomena to create, sustain, and destroy (those three functions associated with the Trimurti and individually with several Gods, e.g., Shiva, pp.90, 106). Shakti is therefore the power used by Gods such as Brahma, Vishnu, and Shiva to bring anything into being or effect. But Shakti herself can be approached in worship through the forms of Bhagavati (supreme Goddess) or Mahadevi (great Goddess).

Shakti/Mahadevi then becomes manifest in the form of many Goddesses who exercise particular aspects of power in the universe – powers that express the two ways in which the forces of nature work, either to create or to destroy. The two apparent opposites are in fact aspects of the one reality, and both require each other. Both come from, and are united in, Mahadevi and Shakti.

Of the creative and benign manifestations in the form of Goddess, two important examples are:

❖ Lakshmi: she is the power of Vishnu and bringer of good fortune: she is therefore known as Sri (Shri, auspicious; see caption, left).
❖ Parvati: she is the daughter of the mountain, Himalaya, from whom sustenance and strength flow forth. She became the wife of Shiva when he was mourning the death of his immolated wife Sati, of whom Parvati is a reincarnation. According to *Matsya Purana* 154, 289–92, Shiva withdrew to meditate on Mount Kailasa, and the demon Taraka took advantage of his absence to terrorize the world. Brahma then sent the god of love, Kama, to stir up in Shiva love for Parvati in order that

Lakshmi
Lakshmi accompanies Vishnu in all of his incarnations (Avatars) and brings good fortune to those who worship her – this includes Shiva according to the Vaishnavites, because he bowed before her and acknowledged her power. She is widely worshipped in India, not so much in temples as in homes.

a son might be born who would destroy the demon. But Shiva, having renounced the world in asceticism (*tapas*), destroyed Kama with a ray from his third eye and scorned the dark complexion of Parvati. She then took on the asceticism in order to win his love, and she succeeded. Their son Kumara (also known as Skanda or Karttikeya, p.109) then destroyed Taraka; and later the elephant-headed god Ganesha (p.108) was born to them.

On the opposite side are the fierce and destructive forms of Goddess, who are embodied statements of the fact that death, fear, and pain are as much the product of nature as everything that is benign and pleasing, and that Goddess can be found in the midst of them: the terrifying is made into a holy terror.

Of these, particularly revered is Kali. Kali is linked with Kala, time, and represents its all-powerful, devouring nature. She is depicted as having a terrifying appearance, naked or wearing a tiger skin, emaciated, with fang-like teeth, dishevelled hair, and eyes rolling with intoxication. She is garlanded with human heads, sometimes girdled with severed arms; laughing and howling, she dances, wild and frenzied, in the cremation grounds with a sword and noose or skull upon a staff.

Human sacrifices were made to Kali in the past (e.g., *Kalikapurana* 71), though in more recent times goats are usually substituted, and such sacrifices are made at the main temple of her cult, Kalighata (Calcutta). Devotees of Kali, were known as Thugs. They offered worship to Kali before committing murderous theft.

A widely told story relates how the Gods were unable to defeat a host of demons and asked her to do so. In the version recorded in *Devimahatmya*, she became angry, and Camunda leapt from her brow, crushing the demons in her jaws and decapitating the demon heroes Canda and Munda, taking their heads back to Mahadevi as a gift. Kali also defeated Raktabija – thought to be invincible because if he was wounded, exact replicas of himself sprang from each drop of blood; Kali simply devoured each one as it appeared.

Kali is worshipped as the One who has already embodied and defeated the worst that time and nature can produce. Those who worship Kali share in her victory over the dark and the terrifying that she so graphically, in story and sculpture, embodies. The same is true of Durga.

Fearsome Kali
As the terrifying aspect of Shakti, Kali is usually depicted as black, with four arms – two of which hold severed, bleeding heads, while the other two brandish a dagger and a sword. A necklace of skulls festoons her neck, and her tongue, dripping with the blood of those she has cannibalistically consumed, hangs from her mouth. She is even shown holding her own head and drinking her own blood as it spurts from a neck-wound.

Goddess and God

Uniting the Cults

Powerful Durga
The name Durga means "the one who is difficult to find" or "who deals with adversity". She rode on a lion in order to defeat Mahisha. Her seed mantra (p.129) is DUM.

OF ALL THE DEMONS, the most dangerous was Mahisha (the buffalo demon), or Mahishasura (*asuras* are opponents of the Gods/Goddesses). He was considered invincible because Brahma had promised that he would never be killed by a human, nor even by a God. The story goes that when Mahisha had subdued the world, he decided to conquer Heaven as well and sent out a challenge to Indra. Indra gave battle, but was routed and fled to Brahma for protection, then to Shiva, finally to Vishnu – all in vain because of Brahma's promise.

In terror and rage the Gods generated the strongest energy and power from themselves, and that brought into being Shakti in the form of Mahadevi, who for this crisis took the form of Durga, the fiercest form of Goddess. Each God gave her his special weapon, and, recognizing their own impotence compared with her, they surrounded her with shouts of encouragement and triumph.

When Mahisha heard this, he sent messengers to find out what was going on, and they returned with news of the most accomplished and beautiful woman they had ever seen. Mahisha sent them again to propose marriage, but Durga, having confused them with her enticing beauty, killed them all. Mahisha then took human form and proposed marriage himself, but Durga told him that since she must always protect the righteous, he must either go back to hell or fight. Confident of Brahma's promise, Mahisha attacked her in the form of different animals, but in vain. He was slaughtered by a Goddess, not by a God, and in this way Brahma's promise remained true.

This story makes clear the superiority of Goddess over God. But that is not the only way in which the relationship between the two has been expressed. At one extreme, the power of Goddess is brought under control by God: the Goddess is believed to be fierce and wild until she becomes a consort of a God, when she becomes a model of the submissive but beneficent Indian wife. Even Parvati (pp.116f) has a fierce form until she becomes the wife of Shiva. From this "marriage of Goddess and God", cults that were once separate became united. Vishnu came to have as his consort Shri (the auspicious one), though originally she was not connected with Vishnu. Once the cults were united, Shri became inseparable from Vishnu, who now wears on his body the mark of Shri (*shrivatsa*), and Shri became identified with Radha (pp.96f). The Shrivaishnavites became numerous in South India, where they valued the hymns and traditions of the Alvars so much that they were known as "the people of the two scriptures", i.e., Vedanta and the Alvar hymns.

At the other extreme, God depends totally on Goddess for power: Goddess remains the source of Shakti without whom Gods are powerless. Mahadevi, known as the Mother of the World (*jagad-ambika*), is portrayed seated on a throne as Bhuvaneshvari, Ruler of the Universe: the four legs of the throne are made up of the lifeless bodies of Brahma, Vishnu, Rudra, and Ishana (the last two being forms of Shiva), and the seat of the throne is the corpse of another form of Shiva, Sadashiva; the throne is known as *panca-pretasana*, seat of the five corpses.

Linking the two extremes is Tantra (pp.102f), in which the union of female and male is fundamental. In Tantra, Kali is the consort of Shiva as his Shakti, and they dance madly together in cremation grounds in a dance that threatens to destroy the cosmos until Kali is subdued by Shiva. But Kali also dances on the ithyphallic corpse of Shiva, in a way that expresses the union of passive consciousness (*purusha*) and dynamic energy (*prakriti*), which together make up the universe.

Shakta tantrism has many forms. One that has spread widely through India is Shrividya (Auspicious Wisdom). The name of the Goddess in this cult is Lalita, also known as Shri. But in contrast to Shri of the Shrivaishnavites, she does not become "auspicious" (*shri*) as a result of her union with Vishnu or any other God. She is auspicious in her own right, and although she is united with Shiva, she is not dependent on him. She has the power to change the created order in any way she wants, and those who worship her do so to bring that power into being for specific needs and occasions.

Lalita is thus an important step toward the understanding of Goddess as far above all Gods (and other manifestations of Goddess), an understanding that came to see her as identical with Brahman (p.85), the absolute and supreme, the unproduced Producer of all that is. The major expression of this is in *Devi Gita*, a text written as a deliberate counterpart to *Bhagavadgita* (pp.92f).

Devi Gita is a work of 507 verses appearing as chapters 31–40 of Book 7 of *Devi-Bhagavata Purana*, written some time after the 11th century CE. Many imitations of *Bhagavadgita* were written, but *Devi Gita* is remarkable for the way in which it sees Mahadevi Bhuvaneshavari as Brahman in terms of Advaita (see box, above right).

But Brahman as Mahadevi is in essence Goddess, and therefore *Devi Gita* strongly emphasizes Bhakti (7.11–27). It is only through devotion that the nature of Goddess is found to be one's own.

> "In me this whole world is woven in all directions...
>
> I am the Lord and the Cosmic Soul [the identity of Brahman and Atman, p.86]; I am myself the Cosmic Body.
>
> I am Brahma, Vishnu, and Rudra, as well as Gauri, Brahmi, and Vaishnavi...
>
> There is nothing at all, moving or unmoving, that is devoid of me;
>
> For if it were, it would be a nonentity, like the son of a barren woman.
>
> Just as a single rope may appear variously as a serpent or wreath,
>
> So also I may appear in the form of the Lord and the like"
>
> (Brown, p.118)

Durga in Combat
Durga fighting with the almost-invincible buffalo demon Mahishasura.

Kabir

Finding God Everywhere

Constant Attention
*"As the kingfisher gazes at
the fish,
As the goldsmith intently
fixes the gold while carving it,
As the debauched man stares
intently at another man's
wife,
As the gambler intently fixes
the dice as he throws them,
In such a way, wherever I
look, I see nothing but you,
O Ram!
For ever Nam meditates at
the feet of God."*

THE PASSIONATE DEVOTION TO GOD in Bhakti (pp.93, 95), whether addressed to Goddess or God, produced in India people known as Sants. Sants, basically, are holy and dedicated religious people, but by the 15th and 16th centuries CE, they had become organized in schools of training and learning. They emphasized that God lies far beyond human words and descriptions (cf. nirguna Brahman, p.86, Brahman without attributes). They believed that devotion to God can be direct, requiring no intermediary, not even the Avatar (incarnation) of God, nor such things as ritual, pilgrimage, and sacrifice:

*"Pilgrimages and sacrifices are a poisonous Creeper
which has spread all over the world –
Kabir has pulled it up by the roots
Lest people drink the poison"*

(Vaudeville, p.206)

Even asceticism and celibacy can get in the way of union in love with God (cf. the issue between Hasidim and Mitnaggedim, p.223). The way to this union is open to all, and therefore low-caste people and women can be Sants. All that is needed, according to the Sant Namdev is constant attention to God (see caption, above left). Among many great Sants, such as Namdev and Ravi Das, the best-known is Kabir (15th century CE), a low-caste weaver of North India. A Muslim by birth (though later sources claim that he was born of a Brahman widow and adopted by Muslim parents), Kabir found God everywhere, as much among Hindus as among Muslims: "Banaras is to the East, Mecca to the West; but go into your own heart and you will find both Rama and Allah are there." Kabir usually spoke of God as Hari, the Lord (Vaudeville, p.178):

*"When I was, Hari was not,
now Hari is and I am no more:
All darkness vanished
When I found the Lamp within my heart"*

But the Lord bears many names for those who love God – Ram, Allah, Karim, Rahim (the Merciful One). What matters is to realize the presence of God in the pulse of life at every moment:

*"Hari dwells in the East, they say,
and Allah resides in the west [i.e., Mecca],*

*"A saint retains his holiness
in the midst of ungodly crowds,
As the malaya tree retains
its coolness
in the embrace of a
poisonous snake.*

*Horses, elephants in plenty,
royal canopies and fluttering
banners:
Rather beggarliness than such
abundance,
if the beggar never ceases
invoking Hari!"*

(Vaudeville, p.173)

Search for Him in your heart, in the heart of your heart:
There He dwells, Rahim-Ram.
All men and women ever born
Are nothing but forms of Yourself:
Kabir is the child of Allah-Ram:
He is my Guru and my Pir"

The pir in Islam is the spiritual guide, the equivalent of the guru. Kabir knew well that his only guide and guru was God – God who races into the depth of the souls of those who yearn in love, and who certainly does not stand at the door checking the religious credentials of those who arrive in faith before they are allowed to enter in (see box, right).

In India, the *sati* is a widow who in devotion to truth expressed as duty, or Dharma, sacrifices herself by throwing herself onto the funeral pyre of her husband. According to Kabir, the true *satis* are those who sacrifice everything in life in order to throw themselves onto God and become as a drop of water which is lost in the vast ocean of God. That is a common image in India – and far beyond (cf. Eckhart, p.274) – for what it means for the soul to be truly united with God. But Kabir knew God well enough to know that the opposite is also true: "Everyone knows that the drop merges into the ocean, very few realize that when that happens, the ocean merges into the drop." In this way Kabir was the poet of complete devotion to God, finding God in the texture and toil of the world (see box, left). Kabir died as he had lived, adhering to God and not to one religion rather than another:

"Repeating 'You, You', I became who You are:
In myself no 'I' remains.
Offering myself into your Name,
Wherever I look, there is: You"

Kabir's Hindu and Muslim followers, true to human type, started quarrelling over his corpse: should it be buried as Muslim or burned as Hindu? In their struggle, they pulled off the cloth that covered the body, and they found nothing but flowers. Half were cremated and half were buried. And that might seem to be the end of the story – but there was more to come.

"Even if you be a Pandit,
knowing all scriptures
and all sciences and grammars,
And if you know all treatises and
spells and herb-balms
in the end, die you must…

And if you be a Yogi, a Yati, a
Tapi or a Samnyasi,
going on endless pilgrimages –
With shaven head or plucked
hair, a silent One or One with
matted locks,
in the end, die you must.

Says Kabir, I've thought and
pondered, watching the whole
world:
none has ever escaped –
So I have taken refuge in You:
Free me from that round of birth
and death!"

(Vaudeville, p.241)

The Ocean and the Wave
"Whisper the name of Hari
and all your sins will go.
You are I, and I am You,
without difference, as are
gold and the bracelet, the
ocean and the wave"
(Adi Granth).

Sikhs

Guru Nanak

Guru Nanak
Guru Nanak's life is told in reverent accounts called Janam-Sakhis. He is shown in clothes of a holy man, in a rural setting to emphasize the many years spent as a wandering ascetic.

BECAUSE KABIR FOUND GOD surely and most securely in the depth of his own life, he therefore became critical of the external rituals and rivalries of religion:

*"The Lord God is like sugar spilled in the sand:
An elephant rages around and cannot pick it up.
Says Kabir: The guru gave me the hint:
Become an ant and eat it!"*

This way of understanding God left him with an uncertain religious future of his own. His followers organized themselves into a group (the Kabir Panth) that continued to express, both his passion for God in the heart rather than in the institutions, and his social protests, but they were never a large movement. Yet in fact Kabir contributed to a very extensive religious consequence, because his views were among those which influenced a young Punjabi, Nanak (1469–1539CE), later Guru Nanak, the first human Guru of what became the Sikh religion. How *directly* Kabir influenced Nanak is unknown. Stories exist about the two men meeting, but these seem to have been told later in order to exalt Nanak by having Kabir acknowledge Nanak as greater than himself.

Leaving aside the issue of influence, it is clear that they had much in common. First and foremost, they shared an overwhelming sense of God as the source and foundation of all appearance, of this or of any other universe. That is clear in the Mul Mantra (see box, below).

As with Kabir and others in the Sant tradition (p.120), Nanak believed that God can be directly known. It is true that God is far above all human thought and far beyond words, the One who brings creation into being with a single word, the One who decides what to make or unmake (AG p.413). God may be regarded as the gardener, tending the plants and

THE MUL MANTRA

The composition that became the foundation mantra of the Adi Granth:

The Mul Mantra was one of Guru Nanak's first compositions. It stands at the head of the *Adi Granth* (*The First* or *The Primordial Book*, also known as *Guru Granth Sahib*, p.126), the collection of the words inspired by God which was gathered together by the fifth Guru, Arjan, and which includes 226 *shabads* (songs) by Kabir himself. The Mul Mantra is impossible to translate, but means roughly: "There is One Being, whose Name is Truth, Source, and Creator, without fear, without hostility, timeless in form, unborn, self-existent, the grace of the Guru."

caring for what is growing (*AG* p.765), but God is not to be confused with the garden: "He is completely other, and he is outside time: it is his light which shines in creation, and that light is in everyone and everything" (*AG* p.579):

"You alone are the Creator,
All that exists comes from you,
Without you, nothing else could exist:
Ever creating, you see and know all things.
Says Nanak the slave, Through the Guru
You are revealed"

(Evening Prayer, *Rahiras*)

Despite this absolute transcendence, God wills to be known and is known. The Word of God creates all things, and therefore creation mediates the nature (or Name, p.124) of God: "All that he makes is the expression of his Name. There is nothing in any part of creation that is not that self-expression" (*AG* p.4). This means that God can be encountered and discerned everywhere:

"You are the ocean, embracing all, knowing and seeing all.
How can I, a fish in the ocean, ever perceive the limit of
what you are?
Wherever I look, there you are.
If I leave you, I gasp and die"

(*AG* p.25)

Guru Nanak had come to know the truth of this by direct experience. At Sultanpur, in about 1499CE, he was bathing in the River Bein, and disappeared beneath the water for three days. When he emerged, he spent a further day in silent meditation, and then proclaimed, "There is no Hindu, there is no Muslim", meaning, probably, not that there is one universal religion, but that there are none who live their faith completely. A biography of Nanak written at a later date records how he received a direct commission from God (see box, top right).

Guru Nanak gave away his possessions and spent the next 24 years travelling through India and beyond, pointing to the truth of God. In this simple way, discarding such things as caste and sacrifice, the Sikh religion began, and the story of God took a new turn.

"As the Primal Being willed, the devotee was ushered into the Divine Presence. Then a cup of amrit [the drink of immortality, fundamental in Sikh rituals] was given him with the command, 'Nanak, this is the cup of Name-adoration. Drink it: I am with you, and I bless and exalt you. Whoever remembers you will have my favour. Go, rejoice, in my name and teach others to do so... I have bestowed upon you the gift of my Name. Let this be your calling.' Nanak offered his salutations and stood up"

(Bhai Vir Singh, p.16)

Sikh Practice
In contrast to Kabir, Guru Nanak did organize his followers. When he settled eventually in Kartapur he and they observed a daily routine of bathing, hymn-singing, and eating together.

Sikhs

The Name Of God

For Sikhs, the supreme symbol of God, shown on the left, is Ik Onkar, or Ikk Oan Kar. It is the first line of the Mul Mantra (p.122). This is made up of:

❖ the numeral 1
❖ the sign for Oan ("that which truly is", the Sanskrit Aum, p.128)
❖ the word kar, "syllable".

It means literally "the syllable Oan [is] One", emphasizing the absolute and uncompromised Oneness of God. It summarizes (and, when spoken, *is*) the reality of God.

The next line of the Mul Mantra is Sat Naam, "True Name". For Sikhs, as for Indian religion in general, the realization of God comes through the sound and the sounding of the Name: the dynamic nature of God is carried through the sacred sound of mantras (p.129). For Sikhs, therefore, concentration and meditation on Nam, the Name (*Nam simaran*), are fundamental. The Sikh religion is sometimes called Nam Yoga, because it is in this way that Sikhs meet the self-revelation of God:

"Meditate on the name of God and through the Name enter the state of supreme bliss"

(AG p.26)

That which is truly real has been given many names (God, Rama, Allah, Vishnu, Shiva), and these all manifest in some way what God is, but Nam, the essence (essential nature and being) of God lies far beyond these approximate names and words (see box, below left).

Nam simaran is not simply a matter of reciting the name of God. Guru Nanak said: "Anyone can speak the name of God, but speaking is not realization. It is only when God settles within, by the Guru's grace, that one gathers the fruit... Why are you shouting God's name aloud in a frenzy, when those who have attained God have God hidden in the heart?"

Guru Gobind Singh gave the same warning: it is not reciting the words that counts, but realization of the power within them: "You cry aloud to God five times; so does the wolf in winter. If you could attain God by repeating 'Thou, Thou', over and over again, well! the birds are singing that cry all the time."

Nam, the Name, is the point of contact for humans with the One who is otherwise far beyond knowledge, but who is found already deep within their own nature. To make the connection

Ik Onkar
This is the fundamental summary of Sikh belief that God is One, the source of all that is. It contrasts with (though is not in ultimate conflict with) the wider Indian understanding of God becoming manifest in different forms, such as the Trimurti (p.90).

"How can Nam be known? Nam is within us, yet how can Nam be reached? Nam is at work everywhere, permeating the whole of space. The perfect guru [Granth Sahib] awakens you to the vision of Nam. It is by the grace of God that one comes to this enlightenment"

(AG p.1242)

with God, neither mediator (like an *avatara* or incarnation) nor external ritual is needed – though Sikhs often make use of a *mala*, similar to what is called in Christianity a rosary. Music and dance are regarded with suspicion: they do indeed create states of trance and joy (cf. pp.40f), but they may well distract from God:

> *"It is the mind that should dance itself into the state of devotion so that the mind, through the Guru's word, meets with the Name. Those who shout and scream and gyrate the body are gathering illusion and pain within"*

(MajhM.3)

The offering of oneself to God is the only ritual or sacrifice required. "The comings and goings of the mind cease, and one lives in a perpetual state of the dawn of Bliss." As Guru Amar Das put it, "When you close your nine doors [of the senses], and your interactions with the world cease, you come to rest within the tenth door, your real home. Here, without end, you hear the Guru's word although it is unuttered." This does not in any way mean the rejection of the world: it means recognizing God in all places and therefore living in the world with responsibility and delight.

The union of the self with God is like the union of lovers. The soul, therefore, must rid itself of lies and deceit. As a Sikh writer comments, "The Bride who seeks to be abed with God must dress herself in the utter nakedness of the soul" (Gopal Singh, p.34). The Gurus frequently speak from the point of view of the woman, the bride, awaiting her lover:

Delhi Bank
The Reserve Bank of India. Guru Ram Das, when he was asked by a man what he should do to be saved, answered, "Go and open a bank in Delhi, and pray for your customers."

> *"My mind and body yearn*
> *but my lover is far away in foreign lands.*
> *The Beloved does not come home, I am sighing to death,*
> *and the lightning strikes fear in me.*
> *I lie alone on the bed, tormented;*
> *mother, pain is like death to me.*
> *Without the Divine One how can there be sleep or hunger?*
> *What clothing can soothe the skin?*
> *Nanak says, the bride is truly wed*
> *when she is embraced by her Beloved"*

(Barah Maha 3)

The pain of absence increases the yearning for God (cf. *viraha* Bhakti, p.95), and, in the end, God will always receive those who come in trust, as Guru Amar Das said: "The world is on fire: save it, O God, through whatever door people come to you."

Sikhs

Guru Granth Sahib

"Without the Word one is
condemned to wander on a sea
uncharted. The things of this
world drag us down into the
depth. Think, apply your
understanding to the Word,
and you will sail safely over
into God"

(Kaur Singh, p.19)

IN 1603CE, GURU ARJAN, the fifth Sikh Guru, realized that the
Sikh community (the Panth) was spreading rapidly, so he
decided that the revelations coming from God through Guru
Nanak and his successors must be collected together. He knew
that the growing community, the Khalsa, needed guidance, but it
was clear that people could no longer come physically to one
place to consult a single human Guru. He was concerned also
that spurious words might be claimed as revelation.

The hymns and poems were organized into 31 sections,
sorted by their musical measures, and then, within each of the
31 sections, ordered also according to the date, in succession, of
the Gurus. The collection was called simply Granth ("book"), but
because it contains the self-revealing of God through his new Guru, it
became known as the Guru itself, worthy of respect (*sahib*), hence the
full name Guru Granth Sahib. It is called also the first or the primordial
book, Adi Granth. When the tenth Guru, Gobind Singh, died (in
October 1708CE) he left instructions that there would be no further
human successors as Gurus, but that this Book would be in future the
living Guru. Each day in their prayers Sikhs say: "Acknowledge the Guru
Granth as the visible body of the Gurus."

When the collecting was complete, there were great celebrations,
compared at the time to those of a splendid wedding. On 16 August
1604CE, the Guru Granth was installed with great ceremony in the inner
sanctuary of the Temple in Amritsar – known later as the Golden Temple.

That reverence for the Guru Granth continues to the present day.
Each Sikh community has a place where it can assemble, and this
place is known as "the gateway to the Guru", Guru-dwara ("door"),
or, as it is more often spelt, the Gurdwara. Here the Guru Granth
Sahib is enshrined. There are no sculptures or images
representing God, nor, usually, are there any chairs. The people
sit humbly before the living Guru, which is always placed on a
higher platform above them, and it is treated with the
reverence that Hindus express in their own temples
before the images of God. Sikhs bow in the presence
of the book, with heads covered and shoes removed.
Each day at dawn, there is a ceremony known as
prakash karna, making the light manifest. The
book is richly clothed and protected by a
canopy, with a whisk (*chauri*) waved over
it as a mark of respect and to keep
insects from alighting on it. The Ardas

God's Word
*Many Sikhs keep the living
Guru in their own homes,
often in a separate room,
and treat it with extreme
reverence, going to it for
guidance. It is God
speaking directly to
the believer.*

("Petition") is then recited, interspersed with the cry "Vahiguru", ending with the words: "To the praiseworthy Lord Guru belongs the Khalsa, to the praiseworthy Lord Guru belongs victory." The cry "Vahiguru" means "praise to the Guru", but it has come to be a name for God. Then the Guru Granth is opened at random, and the passage at the top of the left-hand page is read aloud. The passage is called *vak* or *hukam*, the word or order for the day, and this practice is known as *vak lao*, "taking the Word". At the end of the day comes a ritual called Sukhasan, "to sit comfortably" – after a further reading and prayers, the book is carefully closed.

Through the Guru Granth Sahib, God as Word is present in the midst of the community and of the world (see box, left). There may be no need for intermediaries or incarnations, but the Guru Granth Sahib is a direct equivalent (see caption, left).

There was a time, between the two World Wars, when large numbers of Hindu outcastes in the Punjab were becoming Sikhs (or, in some cases, Christians) to break out of their wretched condition. There was a problem: Guru Nanak had condemned caste, but Sikhs have found it difficult to give it up, especially in the case of marriage. The problem was that in the Gurdwara the sharing of food as *prasad* (cf. p.94) is a fundamental duty: but could it be shared, at least in centre of Sikh life at Amritsar, with those who had been outcastes? It was decided to consult the living Guru through *vak lao*. The book was opened at the passage shown above right. Whatever the feelings of Sikhs about outcastes might be, it was clear that the Guru Granth Sahib had accepted them.

"Upon the least worthy, if they offer themselves in service, the True Guru bestows grace. Raised above all things is the service of the True Guru in remembering the divine Name. It is God who offers grace and union. All of us, as sinners, are among the least worthy, but the True Guru has drawn us into that union of bliss"

(AG 638.3)

Golden Temple
The Golden Temple was built in 1601CE, and was called Harimandir Sahib ("honoured temple of God") or Darbar Sahib ("honoured royal court"). It became "golden" when gilded copper sheets were added in the early 19th century.

Sound

The Expression of God

FOR SIKHS, SOUND AND WORD (*Shabad*) are profoundly related. Without Sound formed into Word humans could not communicate with each other, or with God. Through the Word, God becomes known: "God has no form, no colour, no material identity, and yet is revealed through the true Word" (AG 597).

But if Shabad (the Word) expresses that inner nature of God, it follows that behind or preceding Shabad is the unspoken or "unsounded" sound, the soundless sound (*anahad shabad*), and that is the essence of God. To repeat the Name (*Nam*, p.124) of God is to tune oneself to that unsounded sound, to feel it and nothing else vibrating in one's own being, and in this way to attain complete union with God: "By means of Shabad, Nam is enthroned in one's heart" (AG 1242).

This understanding of Sound, Word, and Name is important in India in general, where Shabad appears as Shabda. As early as the Vedas, sound was revered as the self-being and self-expression of God. Vac ("speech") is Goddess embodying sound and creating speech. Probably a folk Goddess, she was integrated into Aryan (p.60) belief because of the emphasis on the correct reciting of the Vedic chants and hymns through which alone the power of ritual and sacrifice is released.

The creative power of Vac is shared by humans: when humans make words they become creators of truth and reality that previously had not

Om or Aum
The eternal Hindu symbol said or sung before and after prayers is made up of three component parts pointing to the Trimurti (p.90), with the silence at the end being a fourth expressing the attainment of God/Brahman. This symbol is on the hand of Shiva (p.105).

SOUND AND MEANING

It is Vac who converts meaningless noise into the various ways in which sound is the bearer of meaning:

ॐ **SPHOTA**: The fundamental capacity of meaning to break forth (as when a boil is lanced) from noise: it is this capacity that relates Shabda to the inner nature of God or Brahman as the source of all order and meaning: "The eternal Word called *sphota* is without division and is the cause of the world – and is in truth Brahman" (*Sarvadarshana-samgraha* 13.6).

ॐ **NADA**: the constant, undivided "sounding of sound" with potential for meaning, but as yet

simply the expression of the inner nature of God/Brahman, perceptible only to those trained (above all through yoga) and attuned to it – as, e.g., the rishis who sense the Vedas (p.60).

ॐ **ANAHATA**: Sound as potential meaning but not yet expressed, e.g., a thought

ॐ **AHATA**: Expressed sound of all kinds, whether or not humans can hear it or understand it – e.g., the sound of a forest or jungle at night in which animals, birds, and insects participate in the creativity of God.

existed. Vac is therefore to be worshipped as the one who will enable humans to use that borrowed power to good and not evil effect:

"When humans, by name-giving,
Brought forth the first sounds of Vac,
Things that were excellent in them, that were pure,
Secrets hidden deep, through love were brought to light.
When they created language with wisdom,
As if winnowing flour through a sieve,
Friends acknowledged the signs of friendship,
And their speech retained its touch...
Many who see do not see Vac,
Many who hear do not hear her.
But to another she reveals her beauty
Like a radiant bride yielding to her husband...
Those who move neither forward nor backward,
Are not brahmans, do not offer libations,
They are ineffective craftsmen, misusing Vac,
Ignorant, they spin out a useless thread for themselves"

(*RV* 10.71)

> *"A name may be regarded as equivalent to what is named ... Both name and form are the shadows of the Lord, who, rightly understood, is unspeakable and uncreated ... The form is of less importance than the name, for without the name you cannot come to a knowledge of the form, but meditate on the name without seeing the form, and your soul is filled with devotion. The name acts as an interpreter between the material and immaterial forms of the deity, and is a guide and an interpreter to both"*
>
> (Tulsi Das in Growse, p.17)

The repeating of God's Name is important because Shabda *is* God, both in essence and manifestation: to sound (repeat) the Name of God is to come into union with God (see box, right). The link with God through sound is expressed through mantra ("instrument of thought"). Mantras (at least as early as the Vedas) are a verse, syllable, or series of syllables used in ritual to express the nature of God. There are three kinds:

❖ those that have meaning, such as *namah Shivaya*, "praise to Shiva", or the Gayatri mantra, repeated by the twice-born daily: *Om, bhur, bhuva, sva, tat savitur varenyam bhargo devasya dhimahi dhiyo yo nah pracodayat*; "Om, earth, space, sky; we meditate on the brilliant light of Savitri, worshipful God; may he illuminate our minds"
❖ those that have no meaning, including the supremely important Om or Aum, known as *pranava*, "reverberation" (see caption, left)
❖ *Bija* or "seed" mantras compress the essence into the simplest form; thus *krim* is the essence of Krishna; Om is the *bija* of all mantras

Because repetition of a mantra, silently or aloud, leads to union with God, so it can only be imparted and learned from a guru. The right way of concentration leads to the consciousness of the worshipper taking on the form of the Deity. A text of the Kashmir Shaivites says: "Those who attain the supreme Brahman are steeped in the sound of God (*shabdabrahman*), the unstruck sound [*nada*], vibrating without contact, that can be heard by the ear made competent by the guidance of a guru, the unbroken sound rushing like a river" (*Vijnanabhairava* 38).

Drum of Shiva
The double-sided drum of Shiva (p.104) sustains the rhythms of life, and it summons new creations into being. It contrasts with the flame of destruction held in Shiva's other hand.

Mandala and Yantra

The Essence of God

GOD BECOMES MANIFEST IN and through sound, and equally in space, where the encounter with God is created through mandalas (Sanskrit, "circle") and yantras ("instrument for supporting something"). These are symbolic representations or pictures of the entire cosmos: just as mantras compress God's essence into sound, so mandalas compress the essence of God encountered in the universe.

Mandalas are diagrams painted on walls, on scrolls, or on consecrated ground. Their shape is basically that of a circle, indicating the way in which God surrounds and includes everything. The outer circle is often a ring of flames, indicating God's protective power; and as yogins visualize their entry into the mandala, their impurities are symbolically burned. A second circle consists of a ring of weapons (e.g., *vajras*, or thunderbolts), symbolizing the indestructible quality of union with God.

For Buddhists, this is the indestructible quality of enlightenment, and for them, especially in mandalas of wrathful deities (pp.72f), there is a third circle of eight cemeteries in which die the eight superficial and distracting modes of consciousness: a final ring of lotus petals signifies the purity of the land they now enter.

Having in their visualization crossed these borders, the yogins stand outside a "pure palace" (*vimana*) which, by representing the four directions in its four walls (adorned with auspicious symbols) and its four open gateways (*dvara*), includes within itself the whole external world. Its own centre is the centre of the world, the *axis mundi*.

By visualizing themselves in the mandala, and by identifying with the central deity, the yogins enter into union with God or Goddess, or, in the case of Buddhists, into enlightenment.

Mandalas are particularly important in Tantra (pp.102f), and are carefully described in Tantric texts. For example, *Lakshmi Tantra* (37.3–19) describes the mandala of nine lotuses. This is made up of a series of squares with nine lotuses within the central square, upon which various deities are situated, particularly Narayana (p.98) with Lakshmi (p.116) in the central lotus, surrounded by the manifestations of God (the *vyuhas* of Vishnu, p.90) and other deities on the petals. Other manifestations of Shakti (pp.116f) are placed on the other lotuses. This creates an entire picture of the cosmos and of the energies that bring it into being and sustain it. The worshipper, by entering into the mandala, enters into those energies and becomes one with their manifestation in the form of God or Goddess. In worship (*puja*, p.94), a mandala is the

Chandra

Chandra, the moon, is the offering of Soma (pp.62f), the sustenance of the sun and the end to which all creation moves. The sun and the moon together make up the entire cosmic sacrifice, the way of exchange between life and death (p.62), to which the mandala offers access.

sacred place where a form of God or Goddess is invoked by mantra. The placing of mantras on the mandala (*nyasa*) gives it life, and the mandala is then regarded, like mantra, as the Deity itself, and not as a mere representation. *Nyasa* is also the ritual placing of mantras or sacred signs on the body as a mark of one's intention to destroy the mundane body and replace it with the body of the Deity, often – especially in Tantra – identified with Shakti (p.116f). It is part of the ritual known as *bhutasuddhi*, a preliminary rite in virtually all forms of Tantric puja.

Bhutasuddhi ("purification of the elements") is the ritual dissolution of the five gross elements of the body (earth, water, fire, air, space) in order to prepare it for the realization of God or Goddess. Through visualization and mantra, each element is systematically dissolved. Each element is associated with a particular area of the body (though correspondences vary in different texts): earth from the feet to the knees, water from the knees to the navel, fire from the navel to the heart, air from the heart to between the eyes, and space from between the eyes upwards. So beginning with the feet and working upwards, those seeking union (*sadhakas*) dissolve the gross body, replacing it with Shakti, realized in the form of the seed (*bija*) mantra (p.129). In the next stage of this *puja*, they draw the divine mantra body of the Deity into their own through *nyasa*. Their bodies become the Deity's body and the Deity possesses them, at which point true worship becomes possible, since only God can worship God in an equal sharing of delight. *Sadhakas* enter into the inner being of God which brings pure joy.

Yantras are, like mandalas, geometrical designs compressing the cosmos and enabling worshippers to enter from the outer edges of the world to the being of God or Goddess in the centre. Unlike mandalas, they may be constructed in three dimensions out of stone or metal plates. They often have a seed mantra inscribed on them, investing them with the power of the Deity, and they are the focus of meditation since they embody the real presence of God.

There are different yantras for various purposes, such as protection, fulfilling desires, controlling others, or killing an enemy. Embracing them all is the Shriyantra, important especially to Shrividya (p.119), but to many others as well. It is made up of nine intersecting triangles, five "female" triangles (representing Shakti) pointing downwards and four "male" triangles (representing Shiva) pointing upwards – though sometimes the order is reversed. The triangles represent the interpenetration of Shiva and Shakti, the male-female polarity of the entire cosmos, from which all existence is derived. Surrounding the triangles are five circles, the innermost circle being embellished with eight lotus petals, the next with 16. Beyond the circles are three concentric rectangles with four gates. A dot (*bindu*) in the centre represents the source of manifestation, Goddess as Brahman. Mandalas are visual equivalents of mantras. They also underlie the presence of God or Goddess in another form – that of the temple.

Painted Yogi

Yoga (Sanskrit yuj, "yoke together") is the uniting of the whole person into a state far beyond the ordinary possibilities of consciousness, mind, and body. A yogi follows one of the many paths that lead to this "giving up of all conditions of existence". In Patanjali's "royal yoga" (Yogadarshanam 1.24), God is that condition of freedom.

Temples of India

God's Presence on Earth

Linking Heaven and Earth
This temple, from Mataram in Indonesia, shows the shikhara (see text) linking heaven and earth. Temples may be dedicated to a particular Deity, but Hindus can, without disloyalty, visit temples that are not dedicated to the Deity of their own devotion. Geoffrey Moorhouse described the temples of South India: "Every Hindu coming to Madurai was intent on acknowledging Shiva's omnipotence. Each might have a personal deity – the benign elephant Ganesh [p.108], the terrible blood-stained Kali [p.117], Hanuman the monkey [pp.80f], Garuda the celestial bird [p.316]... to be adored daily, petitioned regularly, invoked at all times and in all places. But every true pilgrimage to the Sri Meenakshi Temple would above all else involve humble prostration before the linga [pp.114f] ... of Lord Shiva."

LIKE MANDALAS, TEMPLES are the vehicle of the presence of God or Goddess on earth – so much so that temples are built on the foundation and plan of particular mandalas. Early and common is the *vastu-purusha mandala*, a square on to which the figure of Purusha, the unmoved Mover, is mapped (p.76). The entire square is divided into smaller squares, of which the central one is the abode of Brahma the Creator. The next inner squares are occupied by the major Deities, with an outer set of 32 squares for the 32 Deities (p.63). The Deities at the four cardinal points and at the corners guard the sacred space from irreverence or contamination, send the power of the Deities out to the "four corners of the earth", and invite worshippers to approach from wherever they are. For that reason, this mandala also underlies the layout of some towns, as, for example, at Jaipur.

Other mandalas, more common in South India, are *padmagarbha mandala*, which again has Brahma at the centre, surrounded first by Deities, then by humans, then by asuras (p.118), and *sthandila mandala*, with an even larger field of 60 squares, giving place to more Deities and therefore allowing even greater resemblance to God's kingdom on earth as it is in heaven.

The architecture and groundplan of temples are carefully laid down in texts of authority (*vastu-shastras*), and while different styles developed, especially between the so-called *nagara* styles of the North and *dravida* of the South, there are basic features in common. At the centre is the "womb" or womb-chamber (*garbha-griha*) in which the image of the major Deity (or, in the case of Shiva, the aniconic Linga, pp.114f) is placed. Dark and mysterious, it is the centre of the world, the *axis mundi*, since even if God or Goddess becomes present in other temples, there is only one Deity on whom the world turns and depends.

Directly above the *garbha-griha* is the *shikhara*, the tower or pillar resembling Mount Meru, the bridge between earth and heaven. Through the *shikhara*, the presence and power of the Deity is drawn into the image in the innermost shrine.

Immediately outside the *garbha-griha* are one or more halls or porches (*mandapa*): these are stages on which people honour the Deity in various ways – in dance, in recitation of texts, in hymns and songs, and in processions. Beyond these will be an outer fence or wall, or in large temples a series of passages, around which people can circumambulate in honour of the Deity. Beyond the outer wall may be a further area where the ordinary commerce of life continues – but close to the presence of God. From the *garbha-griha* the power of the Deity surges forth into the creation of the consequence of God and Goddess in prolific carvings and sculptures on almost any available surface. They carry the power of Gods and Goddesses into the world and into the lives of worshippers. As well as the Deities and the symbols of their particular power, other auspicious symbols are carved to bring to the worshippers whatever they need – such things as sons, crops, or rain. Fundamentally, therefore, people go to temples, not because there are set times or services when they are expected to go there, but because they want or need to see God or Goddess.

The word for "seeing" the Deity is *darshana*, a basic word for worship because Indian temples bring God or Goddess into a visible, even tangible, presence. Much of the ritual in any temple consists, therefore, in ceremonies through which the Deity is welcomed, or through which the Deity is woken each day and put to rest at night. Beyond that, there are many individual acts of worship (*puja*, p.94) that may be controlled by custom and tradition, but which are not prescribed in an agreed or compulsory liturgy. Even so, there are common and communal occasions in the festivals associated with any temple. It has been said that India has a major religious festival for every day of the year, but that is a serious underestimate. Festivals do not have to be attached to temples but they may be. It is in such festivals that differences between village religion and Brahmanic religion may in practice dissolve, since festivals are open to anyone who wishes to celebrate.

Of this, the cult and festivals of Jagannatha (at Puri in Orissa) are an example, well-known throughout India and beyond, because 19th-century observers saw the vast image dragged in procession with, as they thought, people throwing themselves under the wheels and dying in religious fervour: they transliterated Jagannatha as Juggernaut. Jagannatha ("Lord of the Universe") is now the local name for Vishnu/Krishna, but the worship of Vishnu arrived relatively late in that part of Orissa – c.7th century CE in the area of Puri. Inside the temple are three images made of wood in an abstract, geometrical style, typical of tribal art. Once again, therefore, a local cult has been, not destroyed by, but assimilated into, the invading religion.

The present temple (begun in the 12th century CE) attracts pilgrims from all over India. In its festivals, the wooden images are carried in procession on huge carts (up to 20 m [66 ft] high), requiring 4,000 or more men to pull them. Accidents happen and people are caught under the wheels, but it is unlikely that this is religious suicide. Even so, the enthusiasm and the huge crowds illustrate the importance of the visible presence of God on earth in the temple images. To see (i.e., worship) them is worth a journey. That journey is often a pilgrimage.

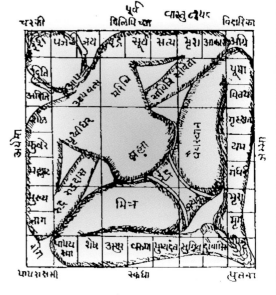

Vastu-purusha
On this mandala Klostermaier comments: "In India, 'the person is the measure of all things': the figure of a person enclosed by a square is the basic pattern from which all temple architecture develops...The centre square (equal to 3 x 3 small squares) is occupied by Brahma, who gave shape to the world."

Pilgrimage

Seeking the Ford

Bathing in the Ganges
Supreme among places of pilgrimage is Ganga (p.110), whose water cleanses the family of a living person for the previous seven generations, and purifies the ashes of the dead so that their souls are preserved in heaven.

THE INDIAN JOURNEY IN SEARCH OF GOD or Goddess becomes literal when it takes the form of pilgrimage. The places of pilgrimage are known as *tirtha*, "ford" (cf. the Jain name for "the ford-makers", p.71), the place where a way is opened up that leads to the goal. Pilgrimage is therefore known as *tirtha-yatra*, "making one's way to the river ford".

Because Deities are manifest, and can be encountered in almost limitless ways in India, there are many places and people serving as "ways across to the Godhead". As a result, there are many places of pilgrimage. Some of these are literally rivers, or places sited on rivers.

Of the many holy sites on the River Ganges, three (*tristhali*) are of all places on earth the closest by way of access to God: Prayaga (renamed Allahabad by the Muslims) where the River Yamuna joins Ganga; Gaya (sacred also to Buddhists under the name Bodhgaya as the place where the Buddha entered into enlightenment); and Kashi/Varanasi (p.107).

The *tristhali,* however, are far from being alone as centres of pilgrimage. At four places – Hardwar, Nasik, Prayaga/Allahabad, and Ujjain – the story goes that the food of immortality dropped inadvertently to earth during a conflict in heaven. Every three years, a *kumbhamela* is held at each in turn, attracting many millions of pilgrims: at Prayaga/Allahabad in 1989, it was estimated that there were about 12 million, in 2001 a staggering 70 million.

Not all places of pilgrimage are on such a large scale; some indeed come down to visiting a holy person in a particular place. The point is that God or Goddess can become manifest anywhere, and for that reason *Mahabharata* (p.92) regards the whole of India as a place of pilgrimage. S.M. Bhardwaj's analysis of the placenames mentioned in the Tirtha-Yatra section of *Mahabharata* suggests that the epic envisaged a clockwise circular pilgrimage of India.

The virtue of pilgrimage is expressed powerfully in *Aitareya Brahmana* 7.15, where pilgrims are likened to a flower which, as it grows, rises above the dust and dirt of the earth: "All their sins fall away, slain by the labour of their journeying." That journeying can take place without the pilgrim moving a single step. Because God or Goddess can be encountered anywhere, that encounter can take place in the interior life or soul of those who visualize the seven sacred cities (Ayodhya, birthplace of Rama, Mathura, Gaya, Kashi, Kanci, Ujjain, and Dvaraka) and the Deity that they encounter there. The point is obvious: "seeking the ford" is to seek the best way in which one can attain union with God – the point of so many different religious practices. The feeling of that union is known as *rasa* ("relish", "passion"), the experience of spiritual ecstasy in union with the divine. *Rasa* is in fact analyzed into eight different emotions (including, for example, anger), so that the emotion of union with Deity is recognized as distinct. But equally, all emotional experience can be converted to God or Goddess, especially when it arises in drama, music, dance, sculpture, and art. As M.L. Varapande puts it, "*Rasa* is the aesthetic experience culminating into bliss". One important way in which this can happen was advocated by Abhinavagupta (c.11th century CE): observers of any of those aesthetic ways (above) of expressing the nature of God or Goddess train themselves to pass into the characters and thus into the emotions being expressed: in that way they re-enact in themselves the union being displayed. For example, a dance or drama enacting the love of the Gopis for Krishna (p.95) offers the opportunity to become one of their number and to experience Krishna's love. For that reason it can be said of Krishna, *raso vai sah*, "he truly is Rasa". It is through the emotions that people catch their first glimpse of God.

The state to which *rasa* leads is *samadhi* ("putting together", "union"). *Samadhi* is a state in which ordinary consciousness is absorbed and disappears, and in which any distinction between subject and object is gone. If the "object" (i.e., the goal of the exercises leading to *samadhi*) is God or Goddess, then the state is one of union or absorption. *Samadhi* is therefore the consequence of meditation or other exercise, rather than the act of meditation itself.

Samadhi is common in Indian religions (including Buddhism, though there it is not experienced in relation to God), but it is particularly important in Yoga, where various levels of *samadhi* are described, along with the ways of attaining them. They lead to liberation (*kaivalya*) from rebirth. *Yoga Sutra* 1.41 describes *samadhi* as the state of a flawless jewel, translucent and transparent. In Yoga, *samadhi* can be attained in relation to three objects of meditation: God or Goddess, the self (*atman*; but since *atman* is Brahman, p.86, this is another route to the same end), and *prakriti* (p.76), through which Purusha is discerned.

Ayodhya
Ayodhya ("Invincible") is regarded as the birthplace of Rama (p.78), one of the seven sacred cities that are equally sacred to Jains and Buddhists. After the Muslim conquest of Uttar Pradesh, a mosque was built on the site of the temple dedicated to Rama. The destruction of the mosque in 1992 led to communal conflict.

Knowledge and Love

Teaching by Example

J
UST AS DEVOTION TO SHIVA DEVELOPED and deepened
throughout the centuries (pp.110–15), so also the same
happened in relation to Vishnu/Krishna. Among philosophers
devoted to Vishnu/Krishna was Nimbarka (dates unknown),
founder of the Sanakas. He argued for a dualism within a non-dual
understanding of Brahman as God (*dvaitadvaita* or *bhedabheda*).
The universe is not identical with God who would in that case
suffer all its imperfections; it participates in God as the wave
participates in the ocean but is not identical with it; *jnana*
(knowledge, p.92) enables the wave to realize its relation to the
ocean (not identical with it but partaking of the same essence),
and Bhakti feels that relationship and delights in it. Another
philosopher, Vallabha (1479–1531), founder of the Rudras,
produced Shuddhadvaita Vedanta (pure non-duality vedanta),
mediating between Shankara and Ramanuja (pp.86–9). Vallabha
maintained the goodness and purity of both world and self as parts
of what truly is, the creation produced by God out of sheer delight
and joy (*lila*). This in itself is unaffected by the misperceptions of
maya (p.87), although *maya* rapidly distorts human perceptions
through ignorance. Even so, the bliss-relation of self to God, or of
atman to Brahman, cannot be subverted by *maya*, and Bhakti is
the realization of this: Bhakti is the true path to *moksha* (release).
Among poets devoted to Vishnu/Krishna, Surdas (born c.1478)
became a follower of Vallabha; he was a brilliant musician and
singer of hymns (*kirtan*) who used the drama of abrupt and
arresting musical chords in introducing his poems: the box
(top left) is an example of *viraha* (p.96) Bhakti.

Tukaram (c.1607–49) was another singer and dancer of
kirtans who became so caught up in the love of Krishna that his
poems poured forth in continuous lines (*abhanga*) filled not only
with praise but with practical advice – though his own
foundation is simple: "Sit quietly and repeat the Name [of God,
p.128] and you will, I promise you, come to God." In one poem,
he foresaw his own death (see box, bottom left).

Two teachers were of such outstanding inspiration that they
left behind them strong movements (*sampradayas*) to preserve
and continue their teaching: Caitanya (1485–1533), founder of
the Caitanya or Gaudiya Sampradaya, was originally a brilliant
scholar, but on pilgrimage to Gaya when he was 22, he had a
powerful experience of religious love, and he was initiated into
the worship of Krishna. When he returned, he stood before his

"Nobody ever became happy
loving.
The moth loved the fire,
it burnt itself.
Nobody ever became happy
loving.
The bee loved the lotus,
the petals became his prison.
Nobody ever became happy
loving…

We, who loved the Honeyed
One,

were struck dumb when he was
leaving.
Nobody ever became happy
loving.
O Surdas, without our Lord we
suffer,
our tears are always streaming.
Nobody ever became happy
loving"

(Surdas, p.35)

"I saw my death with my own
eyes –
Superbly glorious it was:
The whole universe shook with
joy…
Death and birth are no more,
And I am free from the pettiness
of 'me' and 'mine'.
God has set me in his place to
live,
And in his world I am setting
him forth"

(Minstrels of God)

pupils and told them he could no longer teach them because all he could now see was the young Krishna playing on his flute; and he burst into a chant (*kirtan*) praising the name of God that is sung by his followers to this day. His life passed into three moods, between which he would move: *samadhi* (p.135); dancing in trance (in the world but unable to speak); and able to speak, but still almost all the time singing the praise of God. He went on pilgrimage to Puri (p.133) where he stayed and eventually died, walking into the temple and never being seen again. He was believed by his followers to be an Avatar (incarnation, p.91) of the joint figure of Krishna and Radha, so that he was later depicted in cult images as fair (like Radha) and not dark (like Krishna).

Ramakrishna (1836–86), born Gadadhar Chattopadhyaya, was walking through a field, carrying rice. He was about seven years old. Suddenly he saw a flock of white cranes flying against dark clouds and was so overwhelmed by beauty that he fell down unconscious. From that moment he sought the final and unending beauty in God. He became a devotee of Kali (p.117) in a temple near Calcutta, and moved into prolonged states of *samadhi*. Married by his family to a five-year old bride (in the hope of bringing him back to earth), he simply discerned in her (when he first met her) the form of Mahadevi, the great Mother (pp.118f), to whom he was completely devoted. In states of union with God, he began to see visions of teachers in other religions – Buddha, Jesus, Muhammad – and tried to practise their teachings. From this he concluded that all religions are at heart the same. This was taken even further by his best-known disciple, Vivekananda (1863–1902) who helped to found the Ramakrishna Mission, and who made Ramakrishna's gospel known through the first World's Parliament of Religions in Chicago in 1893. Teaching by example, these and others showed how union with God can be attained as much in the present as in the past. However, the present began to challenge traditional understandings of God in India as well as elsewhere.

Hare Krishna
Caitanya's ecstatic, even wild, forms of dance were later thought to have been his participation in the divine lila, *or play, the source of creativity itself. His emphasis on chanting the name of Krishna and on dancing in delight became familiar outside India through the Hare Krishna movement (International Society for Krishna Consciousness).*

From Tagore to Gandhi

Giving New Life to Old Traditions

THE IMPACT OF EUROPEAN colonizing powers faced India with a challenge, at least in terms of technology – Karl Marx once observed that the only enduring consequence of the British Raj was likely to be its railways. But Europeans raised questions also about such things as the caste system and the self-immolation of a widow (*sati*) on her deceased husband's funeral pyre. Some Indians responded by calling for reform of Indian society, and that necessarily meant the reform of Indian religion, since the two are one. Ram Mohan Roy (1772–1833) was a nationalist who believed that the recovery of India depended on the death of superstition, and for that reason he founded Brahmo Sabha in 1828, to encourage the worship of one God, true and formless (akin, therefore, to Brahman) without the use of images. This led to a reorganized reforming movement, Brahmo Samaj, brought together in 1843 by Debendrenath Tagore. His son Rabindranath (1861–1941) made more widely known, through his writings, this Indian version of love leading to the unity of all things – which is God. He won the Nobel prize (1913) for *Gitanjali*, verses that, like much of his prolific writing, draw loosely on Indian tradition (see box, right). Others made attempts to reformulate the tradition in terms that recognize the achievements of science from the 19th century onwards. One such was Sri Aurobindo (1872–1950), who strongly opposed the claim of Advaita (pp.86f) that appearances are deceptive because, through *maya* (p.87), we impose misperceptions on them: "Individual salvation can have no real sense if existence in the cosmos is itself an illusion". He believed, therefore, that the Absolute manifests itself in a series of grades of reality, in a way that is coherent with evolution, and that the aim of Yoga is not to seek to escape from reality/illusion in order to attain Brahman, but to find one's place in this completely integrated nature of reality: it is there that Brahman already is. He called his system *purna-yoga*, Integral Yoga. These attempts to restate the tradition were extremely important during the time when many Indians were seeking an Indian foundation in which they could take pride, and on which they could build their claim to independence. But one man who was well aware of these endeavours believed that the actual tradition, however much reformed, must be retained and given new life. That man was Mahatma Gandhi (1869–1948). Gandhi knew the world outside India well, having trained as a lawyer in London

Satyagraha
Gandhi's fundamental belief in Satyagraha came into being before the name was invented. He then recalled finding the name: "I could not for the life of me find out a new name, and therefore offered a nominal prize through Indian Opinion... As a result Maganlal Gandhi coined the word "Sadagraha" (Sat = Truth, Agraha = Firmness) and won the prize. But in order to make it clearer I changed the word to "Satyagraha" which has since become current in Gujarati as a designation for the struggle."
(Gandhi pp.153–4)

and practised as a barrister in South Africa. He was influenced by *Bhagavadgita* (pp.92f), but also by writings such as the Sermon on the Mount in the Christian New Testament, Tolstoy's *The Kingdom of God is Within You*, Thoreau's *Civil Disobedience*, and Ruskin's *Unto This Last*. He learned from a Jain, Shrimad Rajachandra (1867–1901) to value *ahimsa*, non-violence, and from a Christian, C.F. Andrewes, that "to turn the other cheek" is not to show weakness but strength.

But however strong the influences were, they were related to traditional beliefs and practices – as, for example, when Gandhi revived *brahmacharya* (the recognized period of chastity in Indian life) in order to generate *tapas* (the power of ascetics including Shiva, pp.78, 117), and linked it to the strength of non-resistance and *satya-graha* ("truth-insistence"; see caption, left). He emphasized the symbols of India's interior strength, since against these, the weapons of the British were futile: revering the cow, the ancient symbol of the abundant fruitfulness of the earth, was more powerful than relying on a tank. Although people talk about "sacred cows", cows were not personified in India as Goddess or God. In the Vedas (p.60), Aditi and Vac (pp.128f) are likened to cows because they are themselves so generous (*RV* 8.89.11; 8.90.15). The cow was for Gandhi a uniquely Indian reminder that we cannot rescue ourselves. We require the graciousness of the mother, Earth, to live from one day to another (see caption, right). The cow is the constant, ever-present reminder that all things are the word spoken by Brahman/God: "From God", says the Mundaka Upanishad, "All things are born, the heavens, humans, cattle, birds, our breathing in and our breathing out, rice and barley, restraint, faith, truth and chastity, and all the laws of our being" (2.1.7).

Gandhi had a total commitment to truth:

> *"My uniform experience has convinced me that there is no other God than Truth"*

But truth is not an abstraction: it is secured in the immovable guarantee of God, in whom alone there is no change or variation. God may be known under many names, but it is God who is being named. When Gandhi was assassinated by fellow-Hindus who believed that he had made too many concessions to the embryonic Pakistan, he died murmuring the Name of God, "Ram, Ram".

"When I go from hence let this be my parting word, that what I have seen is unsurpassable. I have tasted of the hidden honey of this lotus that expands on the ocean of light, and thus am I blessed – let this be my parting word. In this playhouse of infinite forms I have had my play and here I have caught sight of him that is formless. My whole body and my limbs have thrilled with his touch who is beyond touch; and if the end comes here, let it come – let this be my parting word"

(Gitanjali)

Sacred Cows

The cow was valued in India because it is the source of so much that is essential for life, the pancagavya, *the five products: milk, curds, ghi, urine, and dung. Cows became associated with ritual because they are the most valuable gifts to give to the Brahmans, the ritual and sacrifice experts, and in that way cows became sacrificial animals.*

李老君

斗七星

朱衣

東嶽

孩童

電丹

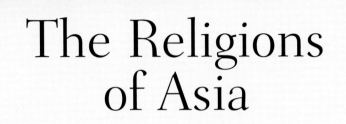

The Religions of Asia

◇

How God is understood in the countries of China, Korea, and Japan.

THE RELIGIONS OF ASIA

GEOGRAPHY HAS MEANT that the religions of China, Korea, and Japan are closely related; often, the religions of China have been (in adapted forms) the religions of those other countries. Even so, Korea and Japan have indigenous religions that precede the arrival of imports from China.

Chinese religion is made up of many different religions and philosophies. Three are known as San-jiao, the three "ways", themselves made up of many different strands. Of the San-jiao, one is the "way" of Confucius (p.148). Confucianism does not emphasize God and revelation, but teaches a kind of humanism open to an agent or principle of moral order known as Tian, Heaven (p.146). Recognition of Tian as the source and guarantor of order gives stability to human society. Rulers could claim to be exercising the Mandate of Heaven. The second "way" is Daoism. Dao means "the way". The Dao is the

"unproduced Producer of all that is" the source and guarantee of all that there is. The "way" of Dao means going with the flow and not struggling against the tide. In religious Daoism, called Dao-jiao, the quest for immortality is important; popular Daoism offers help, especially through Deities, in daily life.

The third "way" is Buddhism. It entered China at about the beginning of the Christian era, reaching its height during the Tang dynasty (618–907CE). Offering to the Chinese an analysis of the transitory and suffering nature of life, it also offered a way of release – but introducing the possibility that the ancestors were being tormented in hell. Schools of devotion and meditation appeared, notably Pure Land and Chan/Zen. Pure Land says that all beings, no matter how depraved or wicked, can attain the salvation of the Western Paradise by simple and complete faith in the help of

Amitabha/Amida, the Buddha who rules over this Paradise (p.158).

A fourth "way" is the popular religion of daily life, with dramatic festivals, spirit-worlds, techniques of magic, and care of the dead and the ancestors. Chinese people do not feel that they must choose only one religion. They choose whatever seems most suitable or helpful – whether at home, in public life, or for one of their rites of passage.

ASIA TIMELINE

Mountains
In China, mountains "embody the basic principle of fertility that renews and sustains the world" (Bernbaum, p.24).

Chinese dynasties are in **bold**

Xia · Oracle bones	c.2205– c.1600
Shang · Zhou Xin defeated	c.1600– 1122
Zhou · King Wu · Laozi? · King Li inscription · Confucius · Zhuangzi · Mozi · Warring States · Xunzi	1122–255
Han · Confucianism enters Korea & Japan · Buddhism enters China	206BCE– 220CE
Wei-jin · Buddhism strong in Korea	220– 420
Southern & Northern · Wang Wei · Imperial line begins in Japan · Paekche kingdom · Buddhism enters Japan	386–581
Sui-Tang · Discovery of block printin · Horyu-ji · Nara period in Japan (710–94) · Yomei · Shotoku · Taika reform · Temmu · Taiho Code · Kojiki & Nihongi · Heian period in Japan (794–1191) · Koryo dynasty in Korea (935–1329)	581–907
Song · Confucian revival	960–1279
Yuan · Civil service exams based on Confucius	1260–1368
Ming · Christian missions in Japan & China · Xavier & Ricci · Yi dynasty in Korea (1392–1910) · Urabe Kanetome	1368–1644
Qing · Kokugaku (National Learning) · Motoori Norinaga · Hirata Atsutane · Taiping rebellion · Meiji period in Japan (1868–1912) · Yasukuni Shrine	1644–1911
Republic of China (1911) · People's Republic of China (1949)	1911– PRESENT

Oracle Bones

Shang Di and Tian

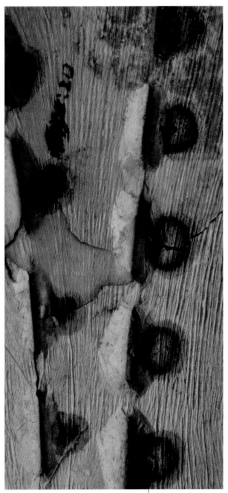

Divination
Close-up of a bone burned by Shang rulers with hot iron rods to get answers to questions asked of ancestral Deities in Anyang, Henan, China. Occasionally, the outcome of the divination was recorded.

THE BEGINNINGS (at least, so far as evidence has survived) of the story of God in China are scratched on the shoulder-bones of oxen and on the shells of turtles and tortoises. These are the Oracle Bones, found from the end of the 19th century onwards at Anyang, the capital of the Shang dynasty (c.1766–1122BCE). The bones were used in divination, being cracked in fire to yield answers, with the outcome being inscribed on the bones.

The form of writing is that of pictographs, of which about 4,000 survive. About half of these are connected with the later development of Chinese characters. Among these are pictographs representing *Di*, Lord, or *Shang Di*, High Lord (*Ti* or *Shang Ti* in the older, Wade-Giles transliteration of the Chinese). Di, in the pictograms, may represent a tablet relating to the spirits, or a bundle of wood for fire in sacrifice, linking the living with the dead, and may thus have been regarded as the supreme ancestor of the royal house; or it may represent a flower, seen as the source of growth and fertility. Both make sense, since Di was closely related to the worship and sacrifices offered by the ruler, and since Di is described as controlling storms and other natural phenomena.

In those early times, Shang Di is known also from two written works, *The Book of History (Shijing)* and *The Book of Odes (Shujing)*. Together these portray Shang Di as one who is a source of goodness and blessing, but not as the creator. He works through lesser agents (cf. the council of El, pp.178, 183) who do his work in controlling both natural phenomena and the affairs of the ruler on earth.

Among those agents were the spirits of former rulers who, when they died, had gone to be with Shang Di and thus to influence him in his control of affairs on earth. For that reason, on earth only the living ruler could approach Shang Di in sacrifice, worship, and divination. It therefore became extremely important that the rulers should, on behalf of the peace and wellbeing of the nation, maintain the connection with Shang Di through the correct rituals, and through a proper respect for the ancestors who were acting as Shang Di's advisors. Only those rulers who were in Shang Di's good favour could bring prosperity to the people.

What if that favour were withdrawn? Then natural disasters like flood or famine might strike, or the state might be overrun by enemies. That is how the Shang dynasty had replaced the Xia ("The Way of Heaven is to bless the good and make the wicked wretched, therefore it sent disasters on Xia and made its guilt manifest to all. For that reason, I, a little child, did not dare to show mercy" (*History*, 'The Announcement of Tang'), and that is how the Zhou interpreted their own success in overthrowing the Shang in 1122: Wu, the ruler of the Zhou, accused the Shang ruler of failing to serve Shang Di, so that he, Wu, had to conquer the Shang in order to "help Shang Di and to restore peace to the four quarters" (*History*, 'The Great Declaration').

On that basis, we might expect the God of the conquering people to displace Shang Di, the High Lord of the conquered Shang; and at first glance that seems to have happened, since the Zhou gave worship and reverence to Tian/T'ien, and Tian certainly became more important than Shang Di during the long reign of the Zhou dynasties (1122–255BCE). Tian, often translated as Heaven, or even simply as God, became of paramount importance in Chinese thought and belief.

Early Script
The pictographs used in the earliest inscriptions do not seem at first sight to resemble the characters of later Chinese writing, the standard script of which was established in the 3rd century BCE. However, careful study shows that there are connections between them.

I t is, however, too simple to say that Tian invaded the territory of Shang Di and took it over, since the two were *already*, and remained afterwards, much more closely related than that: Zhou had been a state within the Shang domain, and Tian appears on the Oracle Bones – though its meaning there is uncertain. The pictograph may represent a great man (i.e., high god) who, for the Zhou, came to represent the greatest man, or in other words their ancestral rulers; in that case, Tian was originally connected with royal ancestral worship. Or Tian may be represented in a pictogram of an altar on which human sacrifices were offered, so that Tian would then be the god of the sky to whom the offerings were made (hence the later connection with Heaven). Or, making the same connection with Heaven, Tian may be the sky as the destination to which the smoke and ashes of cremated victims go.

On any of those understandings, Tian was already known under the Shang. Although Tian became more prominent under the Zhou, Shang Di and Tian continued to be worshipped together throughout Chinese history (even though Tian took on many additional meanings), and there are important continuities of practice and belief between the two.

Tian

The Mandate of Heaven

URING THE TIME OF THE ZHOU (1122–255BCE), Tian became the paramount reality under whom, or under which, the world and its rulers were ordered and judged. The uncertainty of "whom" or "which" arises because it is uncertain whether Tian was understood as a personal agent, or as the impersonal process of the natural order. In fact, it seems as though both meanings were held to be true, with each being brought into play according to different circumstances – and this made *both* meanings available later, in the long history of Chinese thought and belief, with major consequences for both.

Under the Zhou, it seems clear that the personal meaning of Tian as God was the dominant one but, even so, its meanings were diverse. Tian was certainly regarded as all-powerful, the one who could guarantee peace and justice, the one also who could bring punishment by way of disaster. Tian would support the rulers while they themselves maintained order and justice, but if they did otherwise, Tian would withdraw all support. This supervision, giving or taking away support, was known as Tian Ming, the Mandate of Heaven (see box, left).

This means that the ruler was the vital link between the people and Tian. Under the Zhou, only the ruler approached Tian through ritual and sacrifice. Those who were not members of the royal house did not even pray to Tian, let alone offer sacrifice. Eventually, the ruler was regarded as virtually identical with Tian: he was known as Tian-zi, the Son of Heaven, and was seen as Tian's presence on the earth. This relationship of harmony and inter-reliance is expressed in an inscription from the time of King Li, c.850BCE:

> *"When the Shang lost the Mandate of Heaven, we, the Zhou, received it. But I cannot venture to say beyond doubt that our inheritance will stay always on the side of prosperity... The Mandate of Heaven is not easily preserved, because it is so difficult to discern. Those who lost the Mandate of Heaven did so because they did not practise the splendid ways of the ancestors. As for the present, it is not possible for me, a little child, to correct the king. My way of guiding him would be to make it possible to bring the splendour of the ancestors to help the young king"*
>
> (The Book of History)

"The King said, I am only a small child, but without ceasing, by day and by night, I act in harmony with the kings [who ruled] before me in order to be worthy of majestic Tian. I make this food container for sacrifice..., in order to sustain those mighty exemplars, my splendid ancestors. May it draw down those exemplary men of old who are now servants in the court of Di and who execute the marvellous Mandate of Heaven"

This meant that the ruler had to take great care to maintain rituals both to Tian and to the ancestors. He did this, not just for his own benefit, but for the benefit of the people. It meant also that the palace and the ceremonial sites became an increasingly magnetic centre for people at large, especially when the funeral rites of the rulers took place there, since through their death they were strengthening the links with Tian. Throughout the world, it was this recognition of the indispensable importance of common and corporate ritual in relation to God (in this case Tian) that drew people to a common centre and led to the formation of cities, so many of which were planned, originally, on the lines that ritual and ceremony required (cf p.169).

Reverence for Tian was greatly enhanced during the Han dynasty, when speculation about the origins and nature of the cosmos was paramount. Tian, earth, and humans are a unity in triadic (cf Trinity, pp.97, 246) form: they are interdependent and interact with each other, so that Tian is not an independent Creator who remains separate from creation. Maintaining the harmony of this triad is the foundation of life: "In all things, one must not violate the way of Tian, nor disrupt the principles of earth, nor confuse the laws governing humans" (*The Spring and Autumn of Lu*). Tian, although not an independent Creator, nevertheless is the producer of all people, so that they are all equally related to Tian, and on that basis the reverence of children for parents (*xiao*, "filial piety") is entirely natural.

The link between Tian and the ruler made sense while the kingdom prospered, and it made sense also if the ruler was evil and disaster struck. But what if disaster struck a ruler who was evidently attempting to rule justly and in accordance with the Mandate of Heaven? That question became obvious and urgent (see box, right). While the human king was strong and prosperous, Tian could be regarded as wise and just. But once evil people began to prosper and justice ceased to prevail, Tian became nothing better than the old sky god, unjust and blind. If Tian could not be relied on to produce consistent consequence in the events of history, what purpose, if any, did Tian serve? That question was increasingly asked.

This poem from the *Book of Odes* (194/1) raises the question of what happens when a just ruler is struck by disaster beyond his control:

"Bright Tian so vast prolongs not its grace,
Hurls misery and famine, beheading the states.
Bright Tian rises awesome, unthinking, unplanning,
Lets the guilty go free; they have paid for their crimes –
And the guiltless must join them, all drowning as one"

Temple of Heaven, Beijing
Emperors received here the Mandate of Heaven and offered annual sacrifices.

Confucius

The Servant of Heaven

ON THE 27TH DAY of the eighth month of the Chinese calendar, the anniversary of the birthday of Confucius (b.552BCE?) is celebrated (though not in mainland China) with a holiday for teachers and pupils. It is a recognition of what teachers contribute to society, remembering the part Confucius played in establishing education in China. Confucius is the Western form of Kongfuzi (Wade-Giles K'ung Fu-tzu), Master Kong. His teachings, or sayings, were gathered in *The Analects* (*Lunyu*, the Conversations of Confucius) years after his death. They, along with the classic texts associated with Confucius, became the foundation of Chinese public life for more than 2,000 years.

At first sight, Confucius seems to have little to contribute to the Chinese story of God. His sayings on matters of religion are cautious (e.g., see box, left).

He valued sacrifice greatly, but was sceptical about those who claimed to know its meaning: "Someone asked Confucius to explain the meaning of the sacrifice to the Ancestor of the Dynasty. The Master said: 'How could I know? Whoever knew that would master the world as if he had it in the palm of his hand.' And he put his finger in his hand" (*Analects* 3.11).

A reason why Confucius remained aloof from these questions was because, in his own estimation, he was a practical man of action who spent his working life seeking (unsuccessfully) a state or kingdom willing to put his ideas into practice. He had no ambition to be what British poet Hilaire Belloc (1870–1953) was to call in another tradition "a remote and ineffectual don". Confucius lived at a time of political confusion and conflict as the Zhou empire began to break up, raising those questions about Tian (p.147). Confucius refused to discuss them in the abstract. He asked (and answered) the question how in practice the condition of peace, harmony, and justice (the will of Tian) could be brought into being.

For that reason, Confucius placed great emphasis on *li*. *Li* is usually translated as "ritual", and its ideogram is made up of a religious classifier and a vessel used in offerings to the ancestors. So *li* is rooted in religious ritual, but it came to mean much

Confucius on Himself
"At 15 I took to learning, at 30 to standing firm, at 40 I ceased to doubt, at 50 I knew the will of Heaven, at 60 my ear understood, at 70 I did as I desired and broke no rule" (Analects 2.4).

more than that. *Li* is more like "customs" and "manners": it is made up of those acts that create an ordered pattern of life and draw into harmony the many constituents of life in family, society, and the worlds of spirits and of nature. *Li* brings into being and puts into action the will or the mandate of Tian (Heaven). For that reason, Confucius regarded sacrifice as necessary and good. When he was asked the meaning of *xiao*, the bond between children and parents, he said: "When your parents are alive, serve them according to the ritual. When they die, bury them according to the ritual, make sacrifices to them according to the ritual" (*Analects* 2.5). This cannot be a matter of outward form only: "Sacrifice implies presence. One should sacrifice to the gods as if they were present. The Master said: 'If I do not sacrifice with my whole heart, I might as well not sacrifice'" (*Analects* 3.12). Not surprisingly, the early Confucians were masters of ritual, described as:

"dressed in colourful robes, playing zithers or beating drums, chanting, dancing, and living their lives through an eccentric form of ritual playacting suggestive, perhaps, of nothing as much as Peking Opera. They performed this intricate choreography surrounded by the scorn of a society that viewed them as hopelessly out of step with the times — but for these first Confucians, their dance was part of an eternal pattern; it was the times that were out of step"

(Eno, p.1)

Learning and practising the way of Tian was thus important for Confucius (*Analects* 2.4) because Tian acts as a background, or domain assumption: it is the true foundation on which a good life, a life of *ren* (humaneness), can be built with unshakeable confidence. When Confucius was threatened by Huan Tui, he observed: "Tian vested me with moral power. What do I have to fear from Huan Tui?" (7.25). The ideal person (*junzi*) always respects Tian (see box, right), so there is no mistaking the importance to Confucius of Tian. But what did Tian mean? Confucius was not much help: "Zigong said: 'Our Master's views on culture can be gathered, but it is not possible to hear his views on the nature of things and on the Way of Tian'" (*Analects* 5.13).

It was a major question for those who followed.

Birthday Celebrations
Confucians have traditionally honoured Confucius on his birthday in colourful ways. They are taught that "humans have their mission in the world [which] cannot be fulfilled unless men and women have done their best to fulfill their ethical and moral duties" (Yao p.46).

"The junzi fears three things: the will of Tian, great men and the words of the wise. The opposite [to the junzi] do not fear the will of Tian, because they do not know it. They despise those who are great and mock the words of the wise"

(*Analects* 16.8)

Nature and God

The Teachings of Xun Kuang and Mozi

THE UNWILLINGNESS OF CONFUCIUS to discuss whether Tian should be understood as God or as Nature left open either possibility among his successors. At one extreme, on the side of Nature, was a work called *Xunzi*, attributed to Xun Kuang (*Xunzi* means Master Xun). He lived at a time when the Zhou dynasty was disintegrating among warring states (3rd century BCE). He admired Confucius greatly, but criticized his followers, known as Ru, for their obsessive emphasis on ritual. He took the view that human nature is evil, or at least that its natural inclination is to put its own self-centred interests first, and that goodness has to be acquired – or instilled. Confucius, he believed, was right in saying that humans can be brought to good behaviour through education, example, and control, so for him, *li* (pp.148f) is made up of rules of conduct whereby metal can be made into a sharp knife and a block of wood can be shaped in different ways (see box, left).

Xun Kuang strongly rejected popular beliefs in ghosts and spirits and refused to allow that there are supernatural causes of events. He therefore included a chapter (17) in *Xunzi* in which he rejected the view that Tian is like a personal agent who rewards or punishes human behaviour. Tian is the impersonal process of nature, far beyond human comprehension, but not for that reason to be turned into an enigmatic Person. He regarded ritual as important for society, although prayer and sacrifice have no effect: "If people pray for rain and it rains, how is that? I would say: nothing in particular. Just as when people do not pray for rain, it also rains" (de Bary, p.103).

At the opposite extreme was Mozi. He lived in the 5th century BCE, not long after Confucius, so for him also the time was one of conflict and violence. However, in contrast to Xun Kuang, he believed that human nature is capable of great goodness – indeed, of mutual love (*ai*). He recognized that humans once lived in selfish conflict with each other, but he argued that that would still be the case unless humans had decided to live together in a better way. There was nothing inevitable about this: it required acts of will to work out a more harmonious way to live. But in searching for a better way to live, the question at once arises: against what can "better" or "worse" be measured? It cannot be a matter of human opinion, for in that case those who (like Xun Kuang) argued that behaviour is simply an expression of natural dispositions might well be right, and there would be no reason (at least for many people) to change those dispositions. Mozi believed that Tian provides, and in fact is, that absolute definition and source of goodness. As a carpenter's tools,

> "Straight wood to be straight does not require the carpenter's tools. Crooked wood needs to undergo steaming and bending by the carpenter's tools and then only will it be made straight... As the nature of man is evil, it must be submitted to the government of the sage-kings and the reforming influence of the rules of decorum and righteousness; then only will everyone issue forth in orderliness and be in accordance with goodness"
>
> (de Bary, p.107)

a compass or a square, measure what is round or straight, so the will of Tian measures what is right and wrong (*Mozi* 26). Why is goodness good, and better than evil? Because it searches for, and produces for all people, that which they recognize as beneficial and pleasing. Tian brings that goodness into being in the world, especially through those who seek the goodness of Tian through the communication of prayer and sacrifice. Life becomes the imitation of God (cf. p.211) in acts of selfless love (see box, right). Confucius had impressed on his followers the conviction that people can be educated or coerced into a wise way of life, even though he had left open the possibility of radically different understandings of human nature and of Tian. But those differences were not trivial, and the question began to be raised whether the exploration of God and nature might be better approached in another way. That "way" was the Dao.

"Mozi said: Partiality should be replaced by universality. But how can partiality be replaced by universality? …If men were to regard the families of others as they regard their own, then who would raise up his family to overthrow that of another? It would be like overthrowing his own…

When we inquire into the cause of such benefits, what do we find has produced them? Do they come about from hating others and trying to injure them? Surely not! They come rather from loving others and trying to benefit them. And when we set out to classify and describe those who love and benefit others, shall we say that their actions are motivated by partiality or by universality? Surely we must answer, by universality, and it is this universality in their dealings with one another that gives rise to all the great benefits in the world. Therefore Mozi has said that universality is right"

(Watson, p.40)

Mountain and Stream
Shan-shui, "mountain and stream", are two of the eight elements of the universe: "The wise find joy on the water, the good find joy in the mountains" (*Analects* 6.23).

Daode jing

The Foundation of Daoism

> "You look at it, but it is not to be seen; Its name is Formless. You listen to it, but it is not to be heard; Its name is Soundless. You grasp it, but it is not to be held; Its name is Bodiless. These three elude all scrutiny, And hence they blend and become the Supreme One"
>
> (Daode jing 14)

Laozi
Laozi appeared to Zhang Dao-ling in the 2nd century CE in the form of god and gave him the revelations that led to the revival of Daoism in the tradition of Wutoumidao.

ACCORDING TO TRADITION, Confucius once met a wise man before whom he was full of respect – so much so that he even asked him questions about li. The man was Laozi, and other stories told of him travelling to India to become the teacher of the Buddha (p.69). He was held up at the border by a customs official who asked him to declare what he had with him of value. When he declared his wisdom, the official insisted that Laozi should write his wisdom down before he could pass. So Laozi wrote down the *Daode jing*, in 81 short sections of about 5,000 Chinese characters. Then, mounting a bull (a very common picture all over East Asia, see left), he disappeared to the West.

It is unlikely that such stories describe events that actually happened, but *Daode jing* certainly contains profound wisdom. It became, along with *Zhuangzi* (c.4th century BCE), the foundation of Daoism (Taoism). Dao (Tao) is the Way, the source and goal of all life. It is obvious to all and yet cannot be contained in sight or words (see box, left). It is self-defeating to ask what the "It" is, because an answer to that question would have to be wrong:

> "The Dao that can be described as Dao is not the eternal Dao. The name that can be named is not the eternal name. Nameless, it is the origin of earth and heaven; Able to be named, it is the mother of all things"

Those are the opening words of *Daode jing*, a deep well of living water for Chinese thought and life – obscurely so, at first sight: for how can people draw inspiration from that of which they cannot speak? "Whereof one cannot speak", observed Wittgenstein, "thereof one must be silent". But since the Dao is the source, the unproduced Producer, of all that is – the reason why anything exists at all – the Dao is not wholly indiscernible. Through *de*, the potency in all things to become something rather than nothing, all appearances are brought into being, so that the Maker can be discerned in the effects. All that exists is a consequence of Dao, almost, as we might say, of primordial energy, of particles and atoms hurtling into new architectures of appearance – plants and planets, stars and suns. The Dao, the Source, cannot be found as one object among other objects in the universe; rather, it supplies the possibility of all nature and of all individual appearances; but those are the Dao as it becomes nameable:

> *"Always non-existent,*
> *that we may apprehend its inner secret,*
> *Always existent,*
> *that we may discern its outer manifestations:*
> *These two are the same;*
> *Only as they manifest themselves do they receive*
> *different names"*

(Daode jing 1)

T he outer appearance of things, though often beautiful and fair, is only the surface of truth: to look *at* it is to stand in a doorway and admire the timber and its construction, while never passing through the doorway into life. The purpose of Daoism is to help people to enter into the Way, to realize that they themselves are a part of the unfolding nature of Dao.

Before all things, the Dao is. In order to produce from itself, it becomes concentrated energy, *qi*, and is called the Supreme One, the initiating singularity (later it was called at this stage *taiji*, the Supreme Ultimate). It brings forth the two contrasting energies, the yin and the yang, the boundary condition within which manifold and varied appearance becomes possible. The yin and the yang (see caption, right) are visible in the contrasts of the universe – female and male, heavy and light, cold and hot. If there is a harmony between them, it is sought through contest and conflict: summer is attacked and overcome by winter, but then winter is overcome by summer. All life is caught up in the dualism of yin and yang, and human wisdom lies not in struggling to discipline those dualities, but in going with them as they unfold the Dao, so that every action can also be called "inaction"; and that is *wu-wei* – acting without effort in accordance with the unfolding of Dao.

That sounds like *Xunzi's* "impersonal nature" (p.150). But the Two gave birth to the Three (see box, right); and with the Three, Daoism opened the way to the discernment of God in the world.

Is Dao God? To ask that is to fall into the trap of supposing that Dao can be captured in the net of human words. All that can be known of Dao are the effects of Dao in bringing into being and sustaining all that is:

"Dao gave birth to One; One gave birth to Two; Two gave birth to Three; Three gave birth to all the myriad things. The myriad things carry the yin on their backs and hold the yang in their embrace, and derive their harmony from the permeation of these forces"

(Daode jing 42)

Yin and Yang
The yin and yang are the opposite and often conflicting energies in the universe. This symbol represents their interaction.

Three from One

The Gods of Daoism

THE TWO, ACCORDING TO LAOZI, gave birth to Three, and the Three gave birth to all the myriad things. The Three, therefore, are decisive agents in bringing the manifest world into being: the Three are the One (the Dao) at work. But who are the Three?

There have been several different identifications by Daoists. In Shangqing Daoism, for example, the Three are the three levels that sustain appearances; heaven, earth, and humanity. But more often, the Three are personal, and they offer a way in which humans can interact and communicate with the Dao. The Dao remains the unproduced Producer of all that is (including the Three, who nevertheless are the Dao since they share its nature), the unmoved Mover. But as the philosopher A.N. Whitehead (p.317) observed of Aristotle's comparable proposition of God as the unmoved Mover, this did not produce a God available for the purposes of prayer, worship, and devotion. So the Three were more often identified as Sanqing, the Three Pure Ones (see box, below) who were the lords of life, life being concentrated in *qi* (breath). Of these, Daode Tianzun was connected with Laozi.

Laozi was regarded as the incarnation of Dao at least as early as *Laozi ming*, the Laozi Inscription of September, 165CE. This records his earthly career as adviser to the Zhou rulers, and then describes him at the centre of the universe and the beginning of time, worshipped by the emperor Huan after a dream. The author, Bian Shou, expresses his own view that Laozi was a hermit whose perfection evoked reverence and then worship, and finally he records the power of Laozi who holds the sun and stars and other constellations in their places.

This "promotion" of mortals into the ranks of the Gods or the immortals is known as Euhemerism, from the Greek philosopher Euhemerus (c.320BCE), who argued that the Greek Gods were originally

THE THREE PURE ONES

The Lords of the Sanqing are:

- **YUANSHI TIANZUN**: The Heavenly One of Primeval Origins, the first consequence of yin and yang, the one who orders and governs the universe – or did so, according to *Feng-shen Yan-yi* (p.156) until he despaired at human evil and resigned in favour of the Jade Emperor (p.156).
- **LINGBAO TIANZUN**: The Heavenly One of the Spiritual Treasure, who mediates between Heaven and Earth and ensures that yin and yang (p.153) keep the rules.
- **DAODE TIANZUN**: The Dao-with-De (p.153) Heavenly One, who brings the Dao into manifest effect in the world, and is often identified with Laozi.

human beings who had lived heroic lives, and who, being revered, became in the course of time Gods. In Daoism, this process created beings who could help people to achieve the goals of Daoism, one of which is immortality. The character for *xian*, immortal, is made up of the pictographs for "a man" and "a mountain". To attain this state, the understanding and control of *qi*, breath and breathing, is vital, because it brings one into alignment with the unfolding of Dao, and thus eventually into union with Dao; and mastery of *qi* remains central to Daoism.

Another form of the character suggests someone dancing with flying sleeves, pointing to those who take off and transcend the limits of human life. Journeys to the realms of the immortals, based perhaps on belief in shamans (p.160), became important, since these, like breathing, are possible for all, and not just for an élite.

On this basis, heavenly figures, like the Ba Xian, the Eight Immortals, are not regarded as Gods who condescend to humans, but as humans who have followed successfully the way of Dao and who can help others in the same direction. Philosophical Daoists might argue that the Gods of the Daoist pantheon are mental constructions with no real existence beyond that, but popular Daoism holds the Gods to be both real and important, because they demonstrate what is possible for those still living on earth. There are five different levels of that attainment:

❖ Kui-shen: Spirits who are still seeking a place of rest
❖ Ren-shen: Those who have overcome the weaknesses of human life
❖ Di-shen: Those who have attained immortality on this earth
❖ Shen-xian: Those who have reached the land of the immortals
❖ Tian-xian: Those who have attained immortality in Heaven

Any of the Tian-xian might be approached as God. Equally, any of the Gods or important figures of Chinese tradition outside Daoism could be brought into this system. In this way, Daoism was not at odds with other Chinese beliefs.

Even when Buddhism arrived in China, Daoists worked out effective ways of relating the two traditions. It meant also that the most popular images of God could be affirmed and not contested.

The Heavens of Sanqing
The Sanqing are associated with the three heavens of Pure Jade, of Purity, and of Highest Purity. The offerings made to them are called jiao.

The Investiture of the Gods

Feng-shen Yan-yi

TOWARDS THE END OF THE MING DYNASTY, in the late 16th century, a long epic was written called *Feng-shen Yan-yi,* The Investiture of the Gods. Its purpose was to show how the quest for immortality, or for personal advance, fits into the whole story of struggle (the unending contest of yin and yang, p.153) in the cosmic process. It therefore gathers together (as Daoist life gathers together) stories of the major Gods, of their origins in Chinese history or legend, and of how they came to hold the place they do in the hierarchy of Gods and is one of the few attempts to classify them all in a systematic mythology.

It begins with the legendary kings who established the lands that eventually became China, and then turns to long descriptions of the campaigns of Wu, the ruler of the Zhou (p.145), that resulted in the overthrow of Zhou Xin, ruler of the Shang. At the end of these wars, the chief minister of Wu, Jiang Zi-ya, received from Yuanshi tianzun (the first of the Three Pure Ones, p.154) the mandate to appoint the spirits of the dead heroes (from the vanquished as well as from the victors) to various posts in the hierarchy of Heaven.

Many of the Deities that were appointed had in fact been known and worshipped long before even the time of the Shang, but they became integrated into this more organized mythology. Thus Jiang Zi-ya, worshipped widely today as the commander of all the forces of Heaven and as the one who protects shops and homes, was believed originally to have been a Daoist hermit seeking immortality in the mountains. To help restore order in the world, he was commanded to assist Wen Wang, the first of the Zhou rulers, and he became chief adviser (with the title Tai-gong) first to Wen Wang and then to his victorious son Wu. At the investiture of the Gods, he intended to become the Jade Emperor, the most important of the Gods, himself. But when he was offered the post, he paused, with conventional modesty, saying, *"Deng lai"* ("Wait a moment"). At once Zhang Deng-lai sprang forward saying, "Here am I", and thanking Jiang Zi-ya for making him the Jade Emperor. Jiang could not withdraw what he had said, but he cursed the posterity of Zhang Deng-lai in ways that reverberate down to the present.

The story is coherent, but in fact the Jade Emperor long preceded the fall of the Shang dynasty. He is Yu Huang Shang-Di, the Jade Emperor Lord on High, also known as Tian Gong or Tian Wang, the Lord of Heaven. He is a major form of God in China, the ruler of the heavenly realms in parallel to the human emperor who rules on earth. The worship of Yu Huang became widespread in China in the 11th century after a

Yuanshi tianzun
Yuanshi tianzun dwells in the Heaven of Pure Jade. He created heaven and earth, bringing all wild and chaotic disorder into order. He is without beginning, and sends to humans instruction in the way of Dao.

GODS OF *FENG-SHEN YAN-YI*

Feng-shen Yan-yi integrates many other Gods with important cults, including the Three Rulers:

- **TAI SUI:** The ruler of time and of the year is Tai Sui. He was born Yin Jiao as a lump of flesh without form and was discarded by his father outside the city wall. But the flesh was split open and he was recognized within as one of the Immortals (p.155). He is worshipped as Lord of Time in order to divert the movement of time away from disaster, but the occasions when worship takes place are likely to be infrequent for fear of setting time in motion in some other undesirable direction.

- **ER LANG SHEN**: The "Second Born" is Er Lang Shen, nephew of the Jade Emperor, and the most resourceful of the Gods. It is he who leads the armies of the Gods when all others have failed, and he alone was able to outwit Monkey – though Guan Yin (p.158) did succeed in placing a circlet round Monkey's head which compresses his head if he starts getting into mischief. The story of Monkey, Sun Hou-zi, is told in the marvellous satire of the 16th century, *Xiyou ji, The Journey to the West.*

- **LI NA-ZHA**: The Third Prince, Li Na-zha (Na-zha Tai-zi), deals with demons and evil spirits. He may exorcise them, but his dealings with them are often more ambiguous, adopting their powers of destruction (hence the worship of him that involves self-mutilation).

Sung emperor justified an unpopular treaty he had signed by claiming that he had received his orders direct from Yu Huang in a dream.

Yu Huang is widely revered, supreme above all other Deities. He is so far above human thought and imagination that often no image of him is made. Instead, a tablet bearing his name and titles is placed on the altar – if that: in Fukien, he is believed to reside in the ash of the incense fire, and not even a tablet is allowed. He is believed to be the final judge of human conduct, and is approached in worship with great care lest he be offended.

As well as the Three Rulers (see box, above) many other gods are drawn together into a coherent account by *Feng-shen Yan-yi.* Not all the gods, however, could be included. There are many others of great importance, not just in the past, but in the lives of Chinese people today.

Place of Sacrifice
The great stele on the summit of Taishan, where emperors performed feng *and* shan *sacrifices to the Heavens and Earth. The inscription was composed by Tang Emperor Xuan Zong at the time of the* feng *sacrifice in 726.*

Buddhas and Bodhisattvas

Helpers on High

THE CHINESE ARE, in their imagination of God, generous – and generous in two senses: they are prolific and they are hospitable. They believe that their many Gods and Goddesses are part of the worlds in which people live, so if additional Deities appear with newly arrived religions they are easily assimilated. New religions like Christianity and Buddhism have come under severe persecution at various times, but this is generally for political rather than than theological reasons.

That generosity to the Gods of strangers might seem unlikely in the case of Buddhists arriving in China from about the beginning of the Christian era, because God is not a prominent part of the Buddhist missionary message. However, Buddhists brought with them many figures who would seem to the Chinese to be exactly like their own inhabitants of the heavenly worlds. The Buddhist heavens are filled with countless Buddhas and Bodhisattvas (p.71) who became the centre of devotional worship and prayer, especially in their capacity to act as saviours.

Of the many Buddhas, one of the most important is Amitabha ("Light without Limit") who became known in China as O-mi-tuo Fu from Skt. Amita (Amida in Japan); he is also known as Amitayus ("Life without Limit"). He is the saviour of the Pure Land tradition, which claims that devotion to Amitabha, and trust of a simple kind, will lead to rebirth in the Pure Land (pp.74f).

Of the Bodhisattvas, widely revered is Avalokiteshvara, one of the two helpers of Amitabha. Avalokiteshvara mediates the compassion of Amitabha into the world, and he is seen as the incarnation of that compassion, inspiring other Bodhisattvas to the same works of mercy. He has made a vow that he will remain a Bodhisattva until all sentient beings have been rescued from suffering.

When Avalokiteshvara moved to China, "he" became "she", because the qualities of compassion and mercy were associated in China with women more than with men. She became Guan Yin Pu-sa or Guan Shi-yin, "Hearer of the Cries of the World" (from the different Sanskrit word *Avalokitashvara*).

Many of these Buddhist figures offered to the Chinese ways of salvation, and that was particularly true of Mi-lo Fu, the Bodhisattva known in Sanskrit as Maitreya, the One who is waiting to come in the future as the next Buddha. In China, he is sent by Wu-sheng lao-mu, the

The Chinese Pantheon
The Chinese pantheon is as hierarchical as Chinese society, which means also that the Chinese imperial system reflects the pantheon. At the summit is enthroned the Jade Emperor (p.156).

Eternal and Revered Mother, to rescue those who are lost. That "rescue" was sometimes enacted in the secret societies that undertook revolutionary warfare against evil or corrupt authorities. Mi-lo Fu is the Saviour of the poor and oppressed.

Buddhism, therefore, brought to China many figures who were easily adopted into the ranks of the existing Gods, of whom there were already a vast number. Through their belief in Gods and Goddesses, Chinese people are connected to a vast "Internet" , through which they can express their hopes and fears, purchase (with symbolic goods or money) what they need for a successful life, and receive information and advice. The crucial point is not the ontological status of these beings, i.e. "do they exist or not?" (the unwillingness of Confucius to be drawn on such matters has left a very relaxed legacy about such things): the crux of the matter is what this "Internet" has helped Chinese people to be in their daily lives, not least when they have been threatened or invaded by outsiders.

CHINESE GODS

In China, Gods and Goddesses are accessible to help people throughout their lives and in every aspect of daily life:

- **BIRTH**: Jin-hua Fu-ren (among many others) brings fertility and looks after sick or ailing children.
- **PASSING EXAMS**: Wen Zhang Di-jun helps students to achieve success in their examinations and is incarnate on earth about once every hundred years in the form of a major scholar.
- **MARRIAGE**: Yue Lao Xing-jun arranges marriages.
- **CONDUCTING A SUCCESSFUL BUSINESS**: Cai Shen is a collective name for those who bring prosperity – or simply ward off starvation; two merry twins, He He Er Xian, overcome the obstructions of bureaucracy; and there are patron Gods of every business. Supremely important is Guan-di: where Kongfuzi (Confucius, p.148) was revered as the one who assists in matters of intellect, Guan-di was revered as the one who assists in practical matters, especially warfare.
- **AGRICULTURE AND WEATHER**: Tu-di Gong and Di-mu Niang-niang are known together as Tu-di and control the forces of nature; Feng Shen is the God of wind, Lei Gong is the God of thunder, Yu Shen is the God of rain.
- **HEALTH**: There are Gods who make up a virtual National Health Service. In the bureaucracy that this requires, the top level is run by the founders of Chinese medicine, Fu Xi (who also invented the eight trigrams through which works such as the *Yi Jing* are able to diagnose and divine the unknown), Shen Nung (who invented agriculture and brought to humans the healing power of herbs), and Huang Di, a pioneer in the quest for immortality.
- **DEATH**: Because care for ancestors is vital, many Gods are concerned with their fate. Dong-yue Da-Di rules over the underworld.

Avalokiteshvara
Avalokiteshvara is one of the most popular heavenly figures and appears on many Chinese altars, in homes as well as in temples. She is the protector of children, travellers, and those working on the land. She also looks after the spirits of the dead, and Daoists call on her during death rituals to rescue the spirit from the ten courts of judgement in the underworld. Her succour extends to animals, so that meat is seldom offered to her: instead, tea, fruit, or money is offered, or tiny shoes as a thanksgiving for the birth of a son.

Korea

Mudangs and Shamans

WRITING IN THE 1ST CENTURY CE, the historian Sima Tan (died c.110) observed that the Chinese had developed six different ways of seeking good government and a stable society, and he quoted a commentary on the *Yi Jing/I Ching* (*The Book of Changes*, p.168) to explain why: "There is one moving force, but from it a hundred thoughts and schemes arise; all have the same objective though their ways are different" (*Shiji* in de Bary, pp.189f).

The six ways he referred to were Daoism and different forms of Confucianism, and Sima Tan himself favoured Daoism: "Daoists teach people to live with spiritual focus and to act in harmony with the unseen: their teaching covers all that is necessary" (*op. cit.*, p.190). In terms of "spiritual focus", the six ways were extended greatly by the arrival of Buddhism; and they were in any case even more diverse at the level not of political theory, but of folk religion.

A major consequence of this is that in general the Chinese have never felt under pressure to belong to only one religion or philosophy (see box, left). This ability not just to tolerate, but to involve whatever seems of value in new religions or philosophies was immensely important when the Chinese spread into Korea and Japan. They took with them not just political theory and social practice, but also their many inventions, including writing.

Far from displacing already existing religious beliefs and practices, they found ways of living with them that reproduced the creative coexistence of so many differences in China. Often there was serious conflict when the indigenous beliefs reasserted themselves, but even then the underlying theme was to find new ways of coexisting. Religions like Christianity and Islam, not given to coexisting with other religions, gained adherents but could not attract a more substantial following; in the case of Christianity, its exclusiveness led at times to persecution.

In Korea, a common (though not the only) form of native belief and practice is "shamanism". The word "shaman" is now used of many different kinds of trained, gifted, or possessed people. The word was associated first with the Tungu in Siberia, where shamans are common, but it came to be used more widely of those in many parts of the world who, in general, go into trance or ecstatic states (p.40f), often using techniques that override or suppress ordinary senses (for example, using hallucinogens, or going into the total darkness of a cave, or dancing to the rhythm from drums). They may report visions, or they may become an animal or bird. They make journeys to the spirit world, and they

> "The Chinese who ask deeper questions than how to behave as a filial son and as a loyal minister, and who require a mystical philosophy or a religion, turn to Daoism or [often 'and'] Buddhism. This does not mean that they cease to be 'Confucians' ... This condition will seem surprising if one imagines that it is like being a Christian and a Muslim at the same time; but it is much more like being both a Christian and a gentleman"
>
> (Graham, p.365)

incorporate (take into their own bodies) the spirits, or the causes, of distress or evil, so that they can control and thus overcome the *dis-ease*. The skill of shamans is to incorporate the spirits at will, thereby bringing them under their own control. In their trance states, shamans are protected by spirits, and therefore are capable of feats that fill those who watch them with awe and wonder: they can walk on sharp knives, dance on hot coals, or inflict flesh wounds on themselves without bleeding.

In Korea, shamans, known as *paksu* (men) and *mudang* (women) are basic to the well-being of society. Even now, when traditional beliefs are no longer insulated from a changing world, there are at least 10,000 shamans in South Korea. Some are hereditary (*sesupmu*), who learn their skills from their ancestors. Others (*kangsinmu, mansin*) become shamans through being possessed by a spirit descending into them (*sinnaerim*). They suffer a painful physical and spiritual illness, or they may have endured a traumatic experience. They then go through an arduous ceremony known as *naerim-gut*, in which the spirit possessing them is named, the reasons why it is possessing them are established, and then it is banished. If they choose to continue as shamans, they learn from an instructor how to bring the spirits under control at will, and they then exercise that control for the benefit of those around them, often through rituals known as *kut* – not only religious rituals, but "the music, dance, and drama integrated into those rituals", from which "many theatricals have stemmed" (Huhm, p.9). *Kut* serve three main purposes: bringing good fortune, calming and guiding the souls of the dead, and curing illnesses. In these, the *mudangs* relate to the relevant Gods and spirits, often by singing songs (*muga*) and dancing before them.

During the long periods when Buddhism or Confucianism was dominant in Korea, the way of the *mudangs* was influenced but never destroyed. The same proved equally true of the way of the Kami in Japan.

Fire Walking
Shamans demonstrate the power of the spirits they embody in many ways, including fire-walking. In Korea, they also dance barefoot on sharp knives (chaktu) used for cutting grain or grass.

KOREAN GODS

Mudangs approach the Gods via ritual for the good of the whole society. Among the major Gods are:

- **PUJONGNIM**: This God has the power to remove all uncleanness.
- **SANSIN OR SAN-MANURA**: A God inhabiting mountains and mediating between heaven and earth.
- **PYOLSANG KORI AND KUNUNG KORI**: Warriors and kings who have been deified.

Other Gods were added to the original number of Korean Gods from those of the Chinese Buddhists when they arrived (e.g., Chonwang chung t'aryong are the Heavenly Kings of Buddhism who guard Dharma), and one, Chesok kori, the God who guards birth, is the Buddhist adaptation of a form of the Indian God Indra.

Korea and Japan

The Meeting of Ways

U NDER THE KORYO DYNASTY in Korea (935–1392CE), the Buddhism imported from China attained its greatest influence. After Yi Songye established the Yi dynasty (1392–1910CE), Buddhism was blamed for the failures of the Koryo dynasty, and it was reduced from many sects to two – Sun (i.e., Ch'an/Zen) and Kyo (active in the world). Even then, Confucian thought was endorsed.

But the long duration of Chinese dominance did not dislodge the indigenous beliefs focused on the *mudang*. Some have argued that Buddhist ideas and stories created the modern forms of *muga* (ritual songs), but recent research points the other way: "The only conclusion that can be drawn from our survey is that the evidence of influences from the Chinese… on the *muga* is meagre. This is not to say that the *muga* do not contain many Buddhist elements – they most certainly do – but it is difficult to prove that the origin of narrative *muga* is in Buddhist literature and that the modern *muga* go back in a straight line to the older forms of Buddhist tales" (Mulraven, pp.104f).

The tenacity of old and indigenous beliefs when new arrivals become politically and culturally dominant is as clear in Korea as it is India (e.g., the relation between Tamil and Aryan/Brahmanic beliefs, pp.58f), although the ways of resistance, coexistence, and assimilation were different in each case. Exactly the same is true of Japan. The indigenous form of Japanese religion is known as Kami-no-michi or in Chinese Shen-tao (hence Shinto), "the Way of the Kami" ("spiritual powers": on the meaning of kami, see pp.164–67). This clearly pre-existed the arrival of Buddhism, Confucianism, and Daoism from Korea and from China, and it was affected by them, but it was not displaced; and it therefore became the means for Japanese at different times to reassert the greater value of the native Japanese tradition – Shinto, "the Way of the Kami".

In the 6th century CE, the powerful clan or family of Yamoto established a line of rulers and emperors that has continued unbroken (even when others such as the Shoguns were exercising actual power) down to the present day. One of their earliest acts was to make an alliance with the king of Paekche (South-west Korea) who, in 552, sealed the alliance with the gift of "an image of the Buddha Shakyamuni ["the wise one of the Shakya clan"] in gilded bronze with several banners and canopies and a number of scrolls of sacred texts."

The Buddha
Section from a temple hanging showing the Buddha before enlightenment. He sits on a meditation throne in the shape of a lotus, the palms of his hands and soles of his feet painted red with henna, a traditional mark of beauty.

"Harmony is to be valued, and an avoidance of wanton opposition is to be honoured… Where those above are harmonious and those below are friendly, and there is concord in the discussion of business, right views of things spontaneously gain acceptance. Then what is there that cannot be accomplished?"

(Tsunoda, p.48)

The influence of Buddhism and of Chinese thought and beliefs increased steadily until Buddhism was formally recognized by Shotoku (prince regent 593–622) in his 17 Article Constitution (604), and in the building of Horyuji, a complex of shrines and temples containing some of the oldest wooden buildings in the world (see caption, below right). The first of the 17 Articles sets the tone for much of Japan's subsequent policy towards different religions and philosophies (see box, below left).

The opening clause reflects *The Analects* of Confucius 1.12, which continues in a way that was also deeply influential on Japan (see box, right). As in China, so even more in Japan, the correct ordering of ritual, from the highest to the simplest level, became the means through which the coherence of society was achieved. Individual and personal beliefs might vary greatly, but the rituals of Shinto were expected to be common to all.

"Master You said: 'When practising the ritual, what matters most is harmony. This is what made the beauty of the way of the ancient kings; it inspired their every move, great or small. Yet they knew where to stop: harmony cannot be sought for its own sake, it must always be subordinated to the ritual; otherwise it would not do"

One result of the quest for harmony, exemplified and enacted in ritual, was the more formal ordering of "the Way of the Kami". *Nihongi* 21 records that Yomei (emperor 586–87) "believed in the teaching of Buddhism and revered *shin-do*", the earliest surviving use of the name. Buddhism was originally called Butsu-do, "the way of the Buddha", but later was called Bukkyo – *kyo* meaning "teaching", which implies that the belief-system came from a founding teacher, like Kirsitukyo (Christ-teaching) – whereas Shinto has no human origin but is eternal truth.

This formal ordering of Shinto was advanced through the Taika reform (645–46) when land was attached to the Great Shrine of Ise. Festivals were organized and attempts were made (in works now lost) to draw together the many myths and legends into a more coherent narrative of the origins of creation and of Japan. This was reinforced in the Taiho Code (701–02), in which the many Shinto shrines (*jinja*) were recognized as places of importance in Japanese life. There are now about 80,000 Shinto shrines in Japan, influenced by Chinese and Buddhist architecture but in function quite distinct from Buddhist temples (*tera*).

The shrines are built for the particular kami associated with them. The kamis are so numerous that each shrine will be largely independent and different from any other. But they will, in general, share the same mythology, an achievement that goes back to these early days.

Horyuji
The Kondo or Main Hall of the ancient temple complex, which stands near its centre. Completed in 607, the original buildings burnt down in 670 and were rebuilt shortly after.

Japan

The Powers of the Kami

"In general, the word kami *refers to, first of all, the various* kami *of heaven and earth spoken of in the classics, and the spirits [mitama] enshrined in their shrines, and it goes without saying that it also refers to people, and even birds and beasts and grass and trees, ocean and mountains – and anything else which has superior and extraordinary power, provoking awe. Here, "superb" means not only superior in nobility and goodness, but also awe-inspiring things of great evil and weirdness, anything which provokes a high degree of wonder...*

Kami *of course include the most exalted lineage of emperors, who are called 'distant* kami' *since they are so far removed from the ordinary person, and worthy of reverence. Then there are the human* kami, *who existed long ago and also at present; a certain number of human* kami *exist in each province, village, and house, each in accord with his or her station...In this way,* kami *are of manifold varieties, some noble and some base, some strong and some weak, some good and some evil, each being immediately in accord with its own mind and behaviour"*

(Havens, pp.234ff)

WHEN TEMMU SEIZED THE THRONE as emperor in 672CE, he was guided by the Buddhist text *The Sutra of the Sovereign Kings of the Golden Light Ray* (*Konko myo saisho o gyo*), and he marked his success by showing his devotion to Buddhism – demanding, for example, that there should be a shrine to the Buddha in every house.

But he remembered the fundamental principle of harmony (p.162), and he therefore also initiated the compilation of a record of the origins of Japan and of the imperial family. In his view, the genealogies, myths, legends, and song sequences passed on by word of mouth in individual families contained errors. In his decree issued in 681CE, he stated that a correct account of these matters is "the foundation of the state, the great foundation of the imperial influence."

The result, completed in 712CE, was Kojiki, "The Records of Ancient Matters". It was supplemented by Nihongi, "Chronicles of Japan", completed in 720CE. Where the early mythology is concerned, the two works cover much of the same ground, but not in exactly the same way. Both works begin with the separation of heaven and earth (not with their creation). They then tell of the generations of the kami, including the Male-who-invites, Izanagi-no-mikoto, and the Female-who-invites, Izanami-no-mikoto. A complex sequence of myths tells how they create the islands of Japan, and how Amaterasu is born from them.

As ancestor of the imperial family, Amaterasu was enshrined in the central shrine of Shinto at Ise. Originally, worship at the Inner Shrine was confined to the imperial family alone, but with the building of further shrines, Ise has become a place where everyone can worship Amaterasu, seek her help in times of trouble, and appeal to her for her life-giving power of renewal.

None of this prevented the influence of Buddhism from increasing during the Nara period (710–94CE), when Shomu (701–56CE) in particular became an enthusiastic supporter. Even so, an attempt was made to keep both Buddhism and Shinto in balance, so when Shomu commissioned a vast bronze figure of the Buddha to act as guardian of the nation, and it was found that the difficulties of casting the figure were too great, prayer was made to the kami Hachiman who came in response to Nara in the form of a priestess. He promised, "I will lead the kami of heaven and earth, and will without fail bring the great Buddha to completion" (Shoku Nihongi 1.12.27).

Hachiman ("eight banners") became a highly visible symbol of the way in which Buddhist and Shinto worlds are connected. He seems originally to have been the kami protector of rulers in ancient Japan who were especially associated with conquering Korea and thus with military victory. Although he remained linked with the military (bushi) classes, he became popular with all classes across the whole of Japan, especially in times of military conflict. But to make the connection with Buddhism, he was also identified as Hachiman Daibosatsu, the Great Bodhisattva, and the incarnate form Amida (p.158).

This way of linking Buddhas/Bodhisattvas and kami became known formally as *honji-suijaku*, literally "original essence, descended manifestation": the original essence of the Buddhas/Bodhisattvas found its attainable manifestation in the kami, and correspondences between the two were drawn up.

This was challenged by those who thought that it demeaned or diminished Shinto too much, first by Urabe Kanetome (1435–1511) and later by the Kokugaku or National Learning Movement, among whom leading figures were Motoori Norinaga (1730–1801) and Hirata Atsutane (1776–1843). For them it became imperative to define the kami in a way that did not subordinate them to Chinese or Indian figures, but gave them independent Japanese status. This definition was achieved by Motoori Norinaga. Motoori's definition of the kami (see box, left) identified them as the cause of the emotions and feelings people have of great power – feelings that arise from experiencing the world in particularly profound ways.

Motoori's definition of the kami recognized that they are sacred powers venerated by the Japanese, but in a way that cannot easily be equated with (or translated as) "God". Hirata Atsutane (above) made some moves in that direction, arguing that one particular kami (Ame-no-minaka-nushi-o-kami) pre-existed heaven and earth and could therefore be the creator of both. But in

Amaterasu

Amaterasu-o-Mikami (Heavenly Shining Kami) is the major and unifying kami, associated with the sun and with the imperial family. According to Kojiki and Nihongi, she was the daughter of Izanagi and Izanami, and became ruler of "the high heavenly plain" where the heavenly kami dwell. Subsequently, she sent her grandson, Ninigi, to rule the islands of Japan. Out of this process the earthly kami were subjugated to the heavenly kami, and the imperial line came into being.

general the kami have continued to be regarded as the cause of human emotions, not as manifestations of God who brings them into being. They are therefore countless in number, far beyond the possibility of any systematic record. According to the traditional phrase *yaoyorozu no kami*, "vast myriads of kami", the entire universe is full of kami. They are commonly divided into two kinds – heavenly kami (*amatsukami*) and earthly kami (*kunitsukami*), the most important of whom are recorded in *Kojikii* and *Nihongi* (p.164).

The kami are not previously existent gods who create and thus transcend the world, nor does one of them stand over all creation and the other kami. Indeed, kami are born and die. Rather, the kami are the powers through which life is generated and grows: they maintain harmony in the cosmos and in human existence.

There are, nevertheless, distinctions of rank among them, in terms of their contribution to human wellbeing and happiness. Amaterasu-o-Mikami (pp.164–165) is usually recognized as supreme, but her position is not absolute or exclusive, for she pays her respects to other kami, and ordinary people worship other kami as well as her.

Amaterasu is of paramount importance for the emperor, whose ancestor she is and with whom he is united in the Daijosai accession ritual. Was this contradicted when the Emperor formally denied his divinity at the end of World War II? Most Japanese think not, because the kami are not God: "God" in Christian Bibles was translated Tenshu, Lord of Heaven, though some 19th-century translations did use the word kami. The Emperor simply denied what he had never been. The kami, therefore, bring into human life and society the power, lying within both people and things, that moves and inspires them.

The word *kami* became familiar outside Japan in the form *kamikaze*, the name given to the "suicide-bombers" of World War II (see caption, right). After death, the spirits of the *kamikaze* pilots were thought to return to the Yasukuni shrine. This shrine was founded in 1879 as the Tokyo Shokon Jinja (shrine). Originally the spirits of all who died in battle returned to Yasukuni, since all who died for the emperor were reckoned to be followers of Shinto. Since 1945, only those who had themselves adhered to Shinto have been included, hence the strong resistance among some Japanese to formal state ceremonies honouring the war dead being held at the shrine, since those of other religions (especially Buddhists and Christians) resist the *post mortem* conversion of their ancestors; other countries (e.g., Korea) have objected to the enshrinement of war criminals.

The conflict underlines how far removed the kami are from understandings of God outside Japan. Nevertheless, they are worshipped in the many shrines in ways very like the worship of God. The kami of the shrines are often those mentioned in the Shinto mythologies, but they are also ancestors of emperors and famous clans, kami of food and

Shime Nawa
Rope is hung across the main gate of the Shinto shrine, Heian Jingu. The rope, known as a "shime nawa" and the paper strips, "gohei", designate sacred places where Shinto spirits called kami reside.

productivity, kami of land and professions, and historical figures who have made striking contributions to human society. The power of the kami at a particular shrine can be divided and sent to another dependent shrine without the kami being in any way diminished – and in that way "daughter-shrines" are established.

Worshipping the kami includes rituals of purification, offerings of food (*shinsen*), the chanting of prayers (*norito*), dance, and music – the latter especially in the many shrine festivals (*matsuri*, "attending to" or "entertaining" the kami). Not all kami are worshipped at shrines. Their presence is felt everywhere. Thus when work on a house is about to begin, a ceremony called *jichin-sai* is performed on the construction site to conciliate the kami of the area through offerings of rice, sake, lengths of cloth, or money. In ordinary houses, a *kamidana* or kami shelf becomes, in effect, a personal shrine where worship and gifts are offered to the kami, not least those who need to be appeased and pacified. Kami with destructive powers (e.g., *magatsuhi-no-kami*) are the source of uncleanness and calamities, but ultimately they too are manifestations of a power of life that requires reverence and worship.

The kami are therefore sacred power that may be threatening, but more often provides happiness. There is a strong connection between the Kami and human life, with humans as well as nature seen as children of the Kami, blood relatives in an *oya-ko* ("parent–child") relationship. In worshipping the Kami, humans come into contact with life-power that is infinite and good, both for the enhancing of life in this world and for the protection of ancestors. In the shrines, the Japanese make space for that which transcends and yet affects human life; and in that way they resemble the Chinese, who also build temples and shrines with a kind of reverent enthusiasm.

Kamikaze Pilots

The word kamikaze means "Divine Wind", so-called after the strong winds that dispersed two Mongol invasions in 1274 and 1281. The name was adopted by Japanese pilots during World War II who volunteered to undertake missions against enemy targets in which they and their aircraft were "flying bombs", and from which, therefore, they could not expect to return alive. They were first used at Leyte Gulf in October 1944, and extensively at Okinawa. They wore white scarves and a white cloth, taken from the hachimaki, the cloths worn by samurai warriors. In Japanese belief, the spirits of warriors who die in obedience to the emperor return to Japan, and in particular to the Yasukuni (Country of Peace) shrine in Tokyo (hence the ironic words of soldiers before battle, "See you in Yasukuni"), where remembrance of them is made.

Temples and Ritual

Honouring the Gods

SHAO YONG WAS A MATHEMATICIAN and philosopher who died in 1077CE. Nearly 400 years later (in 1455), two farmers were ploughing a field near his home town, Lo-yang, when they turned up a large stone with an inscription on it. One farmer claimed it, saying that he had found it, but the other also claimed it, saying that the field was his. Since neither would give way, they took their dispute to the local magistrate (You Ting Shi), who read the inscription. It said:

"In the year of Jing Dai [the blue pig, 1455], and under the Ming dynasty, magistrate You Ting Shi will rebuild my home and build a temple in my honour"

Recognizing the amazing accuracy of the prediction, the magistrate erected a temple in honour of Shao Yong.

Honouring those who are worthy of respect in visible and spatial terms is a characteristic Chinese response. That is why altars and temples are found, not just in places of spectacular importance, but beside roads and in even the humblest houses. To honour Shao Yong in that way was particularly appropriate, because it was he who had brought new order and precision into *Yi Jing* (*I Ching*, the famous *Book of Changes* used for analysis of the present and prediction of the future). He had also produced a spatial map showing the trigramic hexagrams that make up the book. For the Chinese, care of space is not just a matter of town and country planning: it is a matter of sensitivity, of respecting the nature of a place and of not violating it. That sensitivity is perhaps most familiar in the practice of *feng shui* ("wind and water"), or geomancy, in which human habitations, as much for the dead as for the living, are sited in places that will gather the circulating currents of vital and empowering breath (*qi*, pp.153–155). The principles of *feng shui* were important in the placing and the architecture of temples and may even have affected the layout of cities, at least metaphorically (Meyer, p.44).

Among spectacular examples of these are the Altar of Heaven and the Altar of Earth. The Altar of Heaven was built south of the inner-city of Beijing, slightly east of the north-south axis. Eventually a complex of impressive buildings surrounded it, but the Altar of Heaven remained the focus. It was a structure without a roof, with a three-tier circular platform constructed of concentric circles of stone, the sizes of which were controlled by the important numbers of the yang – three, five, and nine. Here the emperors offered, once a year, in the pre-dawn darkness of the winter solstice, the sacrifice to Shang Di on behalf of the whole empire. The Altar of Earth was built north of Beijing to honour the earth spirits (see caption, left).

As the Gods and the beliefs about them are so numerous and varied in China, there is no single plan or style for temples. Nevertheless, some features recur (see box, below), even though temples may be basically Daoist or Buddhist or simply of popular devotion: people do not have to be exclusive in their beliefs and practices.

CHINESE TEMPLES

With many varied beliefs in China, temples of many different styles and sizes exist:

- **BUILDING STYLE**: Temples are built in local materials and to some extent in local style, but there is a tendency to repeat traditional motifs. Roofs are likely to have curved ridges topped by five legendary birds and animals, protectors against evil.
- **CUSTODIANS**: Larger temples have custodians (Buddhist temples may also have monks attached to them).
- **ENTRANCE**: At the entrance stand protector guardians, or their image is painted on the door posts. Through the entrance is an open court, containing the sacrificial altar or incinerator in which symbolic offerings to the Gods (paper money or other objects) are burnt, especially on behalf of the dead.
- **SIZE**: Temples may be as small and simple as a single room, but they may also be large complexes of buildings.
- **IMAGES OF MANY GODS**: They are likely to have within them the images and symbols of many Gods, or of God expressed in many images and symbols: worshippers, while they may have their own particular focus of devotion, are likely to respect all the others as well, at least with a simple bow.
- **LAYOUT**: Around the perimeter are shrines to particular Deities, and in the centre the main Hall. Here again the images proliferate, even though one, or a single group, may have the most important place. Ceremonies focus on personal dedication, vows, offerings, although at the time of particular festivals the ceremony is more ordered and public.

Mountains

The Link Between Heaven and Earth

THE TRIADIC UNION BETWEEN HEAVEN, humans, and earth (p.154) means that, while temples are important, the truth of reality – including God for those who think in those terms – can be found everywhere. For that reason, mountains and water are an opportunity of revelation and attainment. *Li Ji* (*Record of Rituals*) states that "mountains, forests, rivers, and valleys wreathe with clouds and produce storms and rain, and people see in them mysterious things", and it concludes that they must be the home of Deities.

Those Deities may have a personal association with a particular mountain. Thus Dongyue Da Di (the Great God of the Eastern Peak) was one of the judges of people after death, and was revered as the One who protects communities from disorder and who secures them in peace. After the defeat of the Taiping rebellion (1850–64), an imperial edict ordered sacrifices and names of honour to be given to the Gods of mountains and rivers throughout China since it was "through the blessing and help of the Gods of mountains and rivers that the campaign against the rebels achieved success."

Often, though, these more-than-human realities may simply be the spirit of the mountain in question, Shan Shen, and may not be thought of in such personal terms. That impersonal sense of the spirit pervading places such as mountains lent itself to the Daoist pursuit of union with the Dao that pervades all things (see box, left).

Wang Wei, who in the 5th century did much to unify the arts of poetry and painting in China, drew his inspiration from mountains and streams (see box, left). Of all the many mountains in China, the Kun-lun, the Mountains of the Immortals in the West, play a particularly important part in the Chinese story of God – and of Goddess; for this is the abode of Jin-mu, the Golden Mother, better known as Xi Wang-mu, the Queen Mother of the West, who is sometimes believed to be the wife of the Jade Emperor (p.156), and sometimes an independent and original Goddess.

The Queen Mother presides over the many thousands who have attained immortality, sending them out to help others to attain the same goal; and there she grows the peaches of immortality which ripen once every 3,000 years – the peaches that Monkey (p.157) stole. As the One who bestows immortality, she is often portrayed with a peach in her hand, and she is among the most widely revered and worshipped, both by Daoists and in popular religion.

"Wave-break of ridge and peak
From near or far,
from foot or summit,
The form flows.
The Lu mountains have no face
Available for recognition,
Once we ourselves
Are drowned in their depth"

(Su Tongpo, *In Xi-lin Temple*)

"Since the days of my middle life
I was deeply devoted to Dao.
Recently I came to live
In the mountains of Zhong-nan.
Often, with joy in my heart,
I wander alone from here to here.
It is a wonderful thing
To know myself as I am.
When the streams end my journey
I settle down and catch
The moment of rising mists"

(Wang Wei)

The quest for immortality pervades Chinese religion and takes many different forms. The Ba Xian, the Eight Immortals, are a particular encouragement because, although they are now surrounded by legend and story, at least some of them are connected with historical people. Promoted in a euhemeristic (p.154) way, they demonstrate how the eight conditions of life (youth, age, poverty, wealth, high rank, low or no rank, feminine, masculine) can all equally be transcended, and how, therefore, from any condition, immortality can be attained.

The way of attaining immortality can be assisted by Gods and Goddesses in their many forms, but in the end they too are a part of the triadic unity of heaven, humans, and earth. Mountains are a visible form of that unity, stretching from earth to heaven: the natural place to find the meaning of life:

"Lately I became aware of the meaning of still peace.
Day after day I stayed away from the crowd.
I cleaned my cottage and prepared it for the visit of a monk
Who came to me from the distant mountains.
He descended from the cloud-hidden peaks
To see me in my thatched house.

Sitting on the grass we shared the resin of the pine;
Burning incense, we read the words of Dao.
When the day was over, we lit our lamp.
The temple bells announced the beginning of the evening.
In a moment I realized the still peace which is most certain joy,
And I felt that my life has infinite space"

(Wang Wei)

Between Heaven
and Earth
"This chapter is closed now,
not one word more
until we meet some day
and the voices rising to the
window take wing and fly...
And just as you came into
life surprised
you go out again, lifted,
cloud-hidden
from one unknown to
another
and fall and turn
and appear again in the
mountains"
(Whyte, Cloud-Hidden).

The Religions of Abraham

Judaism, Christianity, and Islam.

JUDAISM

GENESIS 12.1 RECORDS two words (in Hebrew) that mark a decisive moment in the human search for God – and of God's search for humans. They are the command to Abram (later called Abraham and in Arabic Ibrahim), *Lek leka*, "Arise and go". Abram is told to go to a new land where he will be made founder of a great nation and a blessing to others. By his obedience and faith, Abraham became the father of those who commit themselves to God, not just the Jews, but also Christians who believe that they, along with the Jews, inherit the promises ("Those who believe are the descendants of Abraham", Galatians 3.7) and Muslims who believe that they truly live the religion of Ibrahim (Quran 2.130/136).

The Jews were called into a Covenant with God, and their response and understanding unfolds in the Bible, texts that were written and gathered over a period of about 1,000 years. But with no agreed interpretation of how the Covenant should be implemented, different forms of Judaism emerged, of which in origin Christianity was one.

When the Romans defeated two rebellions (66–70, 132–5) and destroyed the Temple, Jews were scattered into a wide dispersion (Diaspora). This led to two major communities, the Ashkenazim, who lived mainly in Europe (many now also in the US), and the Sephardim in Spain and around the Mediterranean.

After the fall of Jerusalem, the rabbis (teachers) rebuilt Judaism, based on family and synagogue, by showing how life should now be lived. Their interpretations were collected in Mishnah and Talmuds, which were later organized in codes, of which the code of Maimonides (pp.218–22) and of Joseph Caro

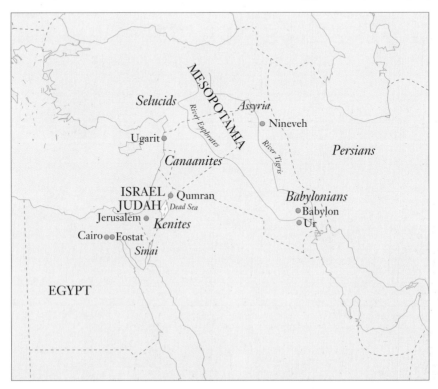

(1488–1575), known as Shulchan Arukh, are paramount. Jews also went deeper into the love and worship of God in Kabbalah (pp.216–17) and in Hasidism (pp.222–23). In the 19th century, the Zionist movement sought the return of the Jews to Jerusalem. Not all Jews agree, because they believe that only the Messiah can restore Jerusalem. Jews are divided on other issues: important forms of Judaism are Orthodox, Conservative, Reform, and Liberal. But the fundamental vocation remains: to be God's people, bearing the weight of holiness in an unholy and often cruel world.

JUDAISM TIMELINE

Western Wall
The base of the Western Wall retains stones from a wall adjacent to the Jerusalem Temple and is a sacred place of prayer.

Abraham · Exodus · Moses · Settlement in Canaan	2000–1000
David · Capture of Jerusalem · Solomon · Building of the Temple · Divided kingdoms, Israel and Judah · Ahab & Elijah · Amos · Micah · Hosea · Isaiah	1000–750
Fall of N. Kingdom · Nahum · Habakkuk · Jeremiah · Fall of Jerusalem · Babylonian Exile · Ezekiel · Zoroaster · Cyrus · Ezra & Nehemiah	750–500
Development of Temple & priests	500–250
Wisdom literature · Antiochus Epiphanes · Maccabean revolt · Hasmonaean independence · Hakamim · Pompey & Rome · Herod · Development of Qumran	250–0
HaTefillah · 1st Jewish revolt · Founding of rabbinic Judaism · 2nd Jewish revolt · Akiba · Synagogues, liturgy, & Piyyutim · Mishnah	0–250
Babylonian Talmuds	250–500
Masoretes	500–750
Maimonides	750–1000
Moses of Leon & Zohar · Kabbalah	1250–1500
Isaac of Luria · Spinoza · Israel ben Eliezer (the Besht) · Hasidism · Moses Mendelsohn · Solomon Maimon	1500–1750
Buber · Heschel · Rise of Nazis · Shoah (the Holocaust)	1750–PRESENT

The Bible and God

The Foundations of Belief and Understanding

THE BEGINNING OF THE JEWISH story of God is bound up with the beginning of the Jewish people. "A wandering Aramean was my ancestor" (Deuteronomy 26.5), say the Jewish people, each time they bring the offering of the first fruits to God. How a group of nomadic herdsmen came to believe that God had called them to specific work and responsibilities in the world is the story told in the Bible.

The Bible story in briefest form is this: God is the One who has created all things. The Bible begins "in the beginning God created…" (Genesis 1.1). Genesis goes on to show how the goodness of all creation is disturbed by humans deciding to pursue knowledge and make their own decisions. The opening chapters of Genesis portray the progressive break-up of relationships – between husband and wife, humans and God, humans and the natural order, town and country, the God-fearing and those who are not, and between different nations, culminating in the confusion of languages after the building of the Tower of Babel (Genesis 11.1–9).

The Bible as a whole then shows how God begins the work of repair, bringing healing and renewal. This process is focused in a series of agreements known as covenants, made at first with individuals, such as Noah and Abraham, and then, through Moses, with the whole nation descended from Abraham, Isaac, and Jacob. Thus the people of Israel exist to be the instrument of God's work of repair in the world, and they do this not just for their own sake, but so that all people may learn to recognize who and what God is (see, e.g., Habakkuk 2.14, Zechariah 8.20–3).

God takes the initiative in calling Israelites to do this work and in helping them to do it. When they are in slavery in Egypt, God rescues them dramatically in the Exodus, leading them into the wilderness and on to the Promised Land of Canaan, whose people they are told to conquer. In the wilderness God gives them, through Moses, the laws in the Torah that become the basic conditions of the new and enduring covenant (Torah means "guidance": it applies to the whole of the first five books of the Bible, and indeed to the whole of scripture, but it may also apply to the specific laws). Fundamental to the covenant agreement is the recognition

Ten Commandments
The giving of the Ten Words (Aseret haDibrot) is told of in Exodus 34.27f, where they are to become the heart of the Covenant. There are two versions, in Exodus 20.2–14 and Deuteronomy 5.6–18.

that God is truly God, the only one who is God, in contrast to the many claimed gods and goddesses in the world around. The most profound statement of Jewish faith is found in Deuteronomy 6.4: "Hear [Hebrew *shema'*, hence the name Shema given to the basic Jewish statement of faith that begins with this verse], O Israel, the Lord your God the Lord is One."

The people, however, by no means always keep to the terms of the covenant agreement. They continue, often, to invest their gifts, sacrifices, worship, and allegiance in the local gods. Even when it seems necessary, because of threats from neighbouring countries and invading Philistines, to draw the people together under a single leader as king, this is seen as a failure of trust in the sovereignty of God. But God endorses David as their king and, after David captures Jerusalem, makes a new covenant with him and his descendants as *mashiach* ("messiah" or "anointed one"). Solomon, David's son, builds the Temple, but after his death, the kingdom is split, and the period of kings proves to be another failure.

In protest against the many betrayals of God, prophets emerge speaking directly in the name of God and challenging the people with the words, "Thus says the Lord…". The prophets are not opposed to the covenant and its laws: although they seldom mention them directly, they are urging the people to live justly in the way that God demands. Their appeals are in vain, and God summons first the Assyrians in the 8th century BCE to destroy the northern kingdom, and then the Babylonians in the 6th century BCE to destroy Jerusalem and the Temple and take the people into Exile. After the Exile, the people return, the Temple is rebuilt, and the priests become dominant in deciding matters of faith and practice: since God has given Torah to Israel, its teachings must be followed if the people are to prosper. It becomes vital, therefore, to show what Torah means in daily life.

After the Biblical period, it seems for a while that they are prospering under God. During the rule of a family known as the Hasmonaeans (142–63BCE), the people live in an independent state, and even though that independence is removed by the Romans, the Herods reinforce the prosperity of Jerusalem. Two further attempts at independence from Rome end in disaster: in the years 70 and 135CE, the rebellions are defeated, Jerusalem is captured, and the Temple is once more destroyed.

Throughout this story, God is portrayed in vivid and dramatic terms. But all this is a simplified picture from a faith community trying to understand itself, its dealings with God and the nature of the One with whom they are involved. The Bible is an anthology of writings from more than 1,000 years. It reveals not only that simple picture, but also a process of change and correction, of truth leading to transformation, in the understanding of the name and nature of God. The Jewish understanding of God is deeply embedded in history: that history is by no means easy to recover, but it, too, belongs to the Jewish story of God.

Frontispiece of Genesis
The central word above is bereshith, *meaning "in the beginning". It is the first word of the Book of Genesis (and of the Bible), and therefore the Jewish name of this book. For the association of this word with Wisdom, see pp.204–5.*

Hazor
Cities like Hazor show the
skill of the Canaanites. From
them the Israelites gained
much, including an alphabet
to write their records.

Marduk
Among thousands of
Babylonian gods,
Nebuchadnezzar I (ruled
1125–1104BCE) gave
prominence to Marduk as
sharilani, king of the gods,
who threatened Yahweh at
the time of the Exile, p.194.

God and Lord

The Only God There Is

THE COMMAND THAT BRINGS Israel into being is the Shema. It is read aloud in the form, *Shema Israel Adonai Eloheynu Adonai Ehad* (Deuteronomy 6.4). Translated word for word, that means, "Hear, O Israel, my Lord our God my Lord One". The words sound strange, but they hold the all-important key that unlocks the Jewish understanding of God. "*Adonai*" means "my Lord", but that word does not actually appear in the Hebrew text. Written in the text are the four letters YHWH (known, from the Greek for "four-lettered", as the Tetragrammaton). YHWH was the name revealed by God to Moses (p.180), but because it shared in the holiness of God, it was pronounced by no one except the high priest on the Day of Atonement. Many Jews prefer to say instead *haShem*, the Name, translating it perhaps as "the Eternal"; and wherever the letters YHWH occur in the text of scripture, the vowels of Adonai are inserted, to remind the reader not to try to pronounce the name, but to say instead Adonai. That is why, in English translations of what Christians call the Old Testament, the name of God is translated as "the LORD". Older translations made a mistaken attempt to transliterate the name, putting the vowels of Adonai into YHWH and producing the impossible form, Jehovah. In academic scholarship, it has become conventional to represent this name of God as Yahweh. Already, therefore, this reveals something important about the self-revelation of God: God's holiness extends even to God's name, which must be treated with due reverence.

The word *eloheynu* is the word *elohim*, God, with a pronoun added to its end, so that it means "our God". So the sentence means "Yahweh is our God, Yahweh is One"; or "Yahweh our God, Yahweh is One"; or "Yahweh is our God, Yahweh alone". Even though the meaning is uncertain, this tells us much about the beginnings of the Jewish understanding of God. El was the name of the supreme God in the world of the Middle East in which the nomad tribes became the people of Israel. In early Canaanite myths, El is the God above gods, the father of the gods, the head of the council of gods. El is so far above the world that he employs lesser gods to do his work, or to represent him in a particular place. That is why, in the Bible, we find terms like El Bethel (God of Bethel), or El Olam (God who endures), El Roi (God who sees), El Elyon (God supreme), and El Berith (God of the covenant).

The lesser gods who do the work of the supreme El are the Elohim: *elohim* is often translated in the Bible as God, although it is in fact a plural word, and can mean, quite straightforwardly, "gods", as it does in Genesis 31.30, Judges 17.5, Daniel 11.8, and even

*"This is my sentence: elohim
you may be,
Sons of Elyon all of you may be,
But like mortal beings
you will die:
The strongest princes fall,
without exception,
and so will you"*

(Psalm 82.6f)

more often when the so-called gods (*elohim*) of other nations are denounced as not being God at all. In Psalm 96.5 they are derided, by a play on words, as *elilim*, nonentities, not-gods at all. In Psalm 82, God appears in court as the prosecuting counsel against the gods, the *elohim*, and mocks them: if you are the gods you say you are, let the weak and the orphan have justice, be fair to the wretched and destitute, rescue the needy and save them from the grasp of the wicked. But they cannot do it: they are completely without power, and therefore God pronounces sentence against them (see box, top left).

Throughout the Bible, the same picture unfolds. It is a picture of conflict, of contest between Israel's God and the so-called gods of the other nations. For example, in the Canaanite myths, it is clear that the authority of El is being challenged and his territory invaded by a more boisterous god, Baal-hadad, the god of the storm.

Passover
The festival of Passover is a major observance in Jewish homes. Unleavened bread (matzah) indicates total trust in God, since nothing, not even leaven, comes from the previous year.

The invasion of one god's territory by another probably reflects events that were happening on the ground, the attack and defeat of one tribe or nation by another. This was extremely important for the Israelites, because when they invaded Canaanite territory, their own God, Yahweh, had to attack and defeat the Canaanite god, El, as well as all the lesser gods, the Baals, the owners of land and fertility. If there is only one God (*ehad*, One), then all other so-called gods must be thrown out as false pretenders to the throne.

That is the conflict described in the Bible. It is all the more remarkable because there was a time when the ancestors of the people of Israel worshipped many gods (*elohim*). Joshua assembled the people, after they had begun to conquer the Promised Land, in order to renew their covenant agreement with God. He began by reminding them, "Thus says Yahweh the Elohim [God] of Israel: long ago your ancestors – Terah and his sons Abraham and Nahor – lived beyond the river Euphrates and served other gods (*elohim aheyrim*)" (Joshua 24.2). How did they move from worshipping many gods to worshipping Yahweh, and to affirming that Yahweh is the only God that there is?

"God [Elohim] spoke to Moses and said to him: 'I am the Lord [Yhwh]. I appeared to Abraham, Isaac and Jacob as God Almighty [El Shaddai], but by my name Yahweh I did not make myself known to them"

(Exodus 6.30)

According to Exodus 6.3, God first made his name known as Yahweh to Moses (see box, left). That seems to be contradicted by the preceding book of Genesis, in which the name Yahweh is used from the beginning. Genesis 4.26 says that it was at that time (just after the murder of Abel by Cain) that people began to call on the name of Yahweh. Later Jewish exegesis recognized the contradiction, and suggested that the word "began" was in fact a different Hebrew word meaning "rebel". In other words, they took the verse to mean, in the context of Cain's crime, that people began to use the name Yahweh offensively and trivially, and that is why the name was not known generally until later. This contradiction was the first clue that made the French scholar Astruc realize, in the 18th century, that the Pentateuch (the first five books in the Bible) is made up of different earlier works, combined later into a single work. These earlier works carry with them their own understanding of the nature and character of God. A source known as J uses the name J/YHWH from the outset, E uses Elohim until the revelation to Moses.

The nature (and even existence) of these sources has been questioned, but the Pentateuch itself states that it draws on pre-existing traditions and sources, from which attempts are made by historians to answer the question, how did Yahweh become Israel's God? Too little evidence now survives to be sure. Yau/Yah is known in the Middle East as the name of a god, so perhaps Yah was the god of one of the tribes. Another possibility notes that the children of Israel (the Bene Israel) were originally family groups loosely related by kinship. The different parts of this kinship group followed different histories, although they supported each other in crises. At a time of famine, some of them went to Egypt seeking food, but they had to work as slaves to get it. One of them, Moses, was driven out and took refuge with a tribe known as the Kenites. He later married the daughter of Jethro, a priest of that tribe, and first encountered God as Yahweh in a dramatic episode that established the character of God beyond doubt as holy; as a historical force (compelling the Pharaoh of Egypt by a mighty hand) to bring the people of Israel to where they are meant to be; and also, as one with whom Moses (and later many others in the Bible) can argue (Exodus 3–4). God has always been God, but only now is known as Yahweh, and in the name and strength of God whose name and nature have been revealed, Moses delivers the people from Egypt in the Exodus.

The Exodus becomes the supreme example of God's power to act. Each year, the Jews celebrate Passover, commemorating the way in which God smote the dwellings of the Egyptians, but passed over those of the Israelites (see box, right). When the people returned to Canaan, they linked up with other parts of the kinship group, and Joshua 24 reflects the way in which the whole group, the Bene Jacob/Israel (descendants of Jacob/Israel), accepted Yahweh as their God. It is Yahweh, not those "other gods", who initiated their history together by taking Abraham from beyond the River Euphrates, and by giving to him and to his descendants Canaan as a new land. They took over much of the Canaanite understanding of El as the supreme God. In the end, however, the issue was clear: if Yahweh is to be their God, other gods must be driven out, just as the inhabitants of the land must be defeated if Israel is to make it its own. That contest became a dramatic part of the Jewish story of God.

The celebration of Passover is one of the most important of Jewish festivals. At the beginning of the celebration, at the moment when the unleavened bread is uncovered, those assembled say these words from an old text, the *Passover Haggadah*:

"We were slaves to Pharaoh in Egypt, and the Eternal [Yahweh] our Elohim brought us out from there with a mighty hand and an outstretched arm. And if the Holy One, blessed be He, had not brought forth our ancestors from Egypt, we and our children and our children's children would still have continued as slaves to the Pharaohs in Egypt. All of us are wise, all of us are people of experience, all of us know the Torah, yet it is an obligation upon us to recite the going forth from Egypt, and all those who make much of the account of the going forth from Egypt are to be praised"

Passover Foods
Bitter herbs (symbolizing the bitterness of slavery), an egg commemorating festival sacrifice, and a shank bone to represent the sacrificial lamb are among foods eaten at Passover, along with unleavened bread.

Defeat of the gods

Yahweh Alone

Y AHWEH'S CONFLICT WITH OTHER GODS is summed up in an episode that took place about 100 years after David had captured Jerusalem (c.1000BCE) and Solomon had built the Temple as a centre for all the tribes to give their allegiance to Yahweh (pp.190–91). A king called Ahab was ruling over Israel (the northern kingdom). Where God was concerned, Ahab was hedging his bets. Yes, he and all the people were supposed to be serving Yahweh alone, but what if the local gods, the Baals (*ba'alim*), had not been driven out? Maybe they were still in business, and maybe they were still essential for the crops and for fertility. To be on the safe side, "he went and served Baal and worshipped him; he erected an altar for Baal in the house of Baal, which he built in Samaria" (I Kings 16.31f).

He was immediately challenged by a spokesman (a prophet) of Yahweh called Elijah, and they agreed to a showdown between the Baals and Yahweh. Elijah and the prophets of the Baals met at Mount Carmel. Each side built an altar on which each in turn was to call down fire to demonstrate which God was able to bring fire on earth (see box, left). Then Elijah made his own preparations, and prayed to God:

"'O Yahweh, Elohim of Abraham, Isaac, and Israel, let it be known this day that you are God in Israel, that I am your servant, and that I have done all these things at your bidding. Answer me, O Lord, answer me so that this people may know that you, O Yahweh, are El, and that you have turned their hearts back.' Then the fire of Yahweh fell and consumed the burnt-offering, the wood, the stones, and the dust, and even licked up the water that was in the trench. When all the people saw it, they fell on their faces and said, 'Yahweh indeed is Elohim, Yahweh indeed is Elohim'"

(I Kings 18. 36–9)

Here, in miniature, is the conflict that can be traced throughout the Bible, between Yahweh and all other claimed gods. Repeatedly prophets of Yahweh call the people back from the worship of other gods, which they liken to adultery or even to prostitution (see, for example, Hosea 2.4–15). The literal war on earth to conquer the Promised Land is reflected in a war in heaven, as Yahweh invades the domain of El, the supreme high God, and takes over his functions until, in the end, they are so indistinguishable that El simply becomes a name for what Yahweh is – the One who is God. This was a major change. To begin with, Yahweh had simply been one of the many gods under El, looking after one particular area, exactly as Deuteronomy 32.8 (in its original text) says. The supreme God divides up the nations of the world according to the number of lesser gods (*elohim*), and gives one nation to each (see box, below left).

The writers of the later and official (Masoretic) text were so shocked at the apparent recognition of other gods that they changed the words to read, "…according to the number of the children of Israel", but the original text captures the early understanding of God and gods very accurately. Psalm 82, quoted on p.180, in which Yahweh denounces the other gods, reveals this early relationship between Yahweh and El with equal clarity. The first verse reads very oddly. Literally, it says, "Elohim takes his stand in the council of El, to deliver a judgement among the Elohim" (Psalm 82.1). But this Psalm comes from a part of the whole Psalter in which the name Yahweh has been removed (out of reverence, p.178) and replaced with Elohim. So the verse *originally* read, "Yahweh takes his stand in the council of El, to deliver judgement among the *elohim* [the other gods]".

The Bible as a whole shows how Yahweh not only invaded the domain of El and of the other gods but took it over completely. Yahweh becomes all that the gods can be. To represent gods in carved or pictorial form was condemned repeatedly and fiercely as idolatry – the worship, not of God, but of dead and useless idols, who cannot do anything (see, for example, Psalm 115.3–8, Isaiah 46.1ff).

The Shema (p.178) then makes absolute sense: Yahweh our Elohim is Yahweh alone. The God of life rises from the death of gods. This was a huge and embattled revolution in human vision and imagination. It was not easily achieved. But once begun, it made certain that God would be worthy of human adoration and praise.

Elijah
This illuminated manuscript of the 13th century CE shows scenes from the life of the prophet Elijah, including the futile attempt of King Ahaziah to silence him: the first party of soldiers sent to kill him are destroyed by fire, the second are spared after begging for mercy
(2 Kings 1).

The Anger of God

A Devouring Fire

"As for the towns of these peoples that the Lord [Yahweh] your God [Elohim] is giving you as an inheritance, you must not let anything that breathes remain alive. You shall annihilate them – the Hittites and the Amorites, the Canaanites and the Perizzites, the Hivites and the Jebusites – just as the Lord your God has commanded, so that they may not teach you to do all the abhorrent things that they do for their gods, and you thus sin against the Lord your God"

(Deuteronomy 20.16)

To serve other gods epitomizes the failure that evokes the anger of God, a characteristic note in Deuteronomy, as in chapter 29 (note verse 27, and see also 6.15; 11.16ff.), and also in Hosea (5.10-15), who sees the betrayal as adultery and prostitution. It is the same image in Ezekiel, who begins a passage describing the anger of God: "And therefore, O whore, hear the word of the Lord" (16.35ff.). The anger of God culminates in the Day of the Lord:

"On that day, says the Lord God, I will make the sun go down at noon, and darken the earth in broad daylight. I will turn your feasts into mourning, and all your songs into lamentation; I will bring sackcloth on all loins, and baldness on every head; I will make it like the mourning for an only son, and the end of it like a bitter day"

(Amos 8.9f)

THE WAR IN HEAVEN was very much reflected in the war on earth. Approaching the Promised Land, God commands the people to annihilate all living things (see box, top left). In the chapters in the book of Joshua (5.13–12.24) describing the conquest, God appears as an angry predator who destroys all who stand in the way. The wrath of God appears widely in the Bible. The Hebrew words for anger are mainly physical (blowing violently, heating up, bursting out, overflowing), and they are used far more frequently of God than they are of human beings.

God's anger takes many different forms: the prophet Isaiah seems to be searching for ever-more powerful metaphors through which to describe it:

"See, the name of the Lord comes from far away, burning with anger, and in thick and rising smoke; his lips are full of indignation, and his tongue is like a devouring fire; his breath is like an overflowing stream that reaches up to the neck – to sift the nations with the sieve of destruction, and to place on the jaws of the peoples a bridle that leads them astray"

(Isaiah 30. 27f)

This anger is no mild irritation. It brings death: when Korah, Nathan, and Abiram rejected Moses, Moses was angry but so also was God: the three were swallowed up by the earth, and when others complained about the severity of this, they were struck by plague (Numbers 16). God's anger brings destruction to the people, as in the successive disasters of Isaiah 9.8–21 (cf. Ezekiel 5.13–7), with the recurrent refrain, "for all this, his anger has not turned away; his hand is stretched out still." It brings misery to individuals, as can be seen in the Psalms (see, for example, 88.16; 90.7–10; 102.9–12).

What makes God angry? Occasionally, there seems to be no reason. After David buried Saul, it is said that "God heeded supplications for the land" (2 Samuel 21.14); but in 24.1, "again the anger of the Lord was kindled against Israel", although nothing has happened in the meantime. More often it is for evil behaviour, as with the Philistines in Ezekiel 25.15–17:

"Thus says the Lord God: Because with unending hostilities the Philistines acted in vengeance, and with malice of heart took revenge in destruction; therefore thus says the Lord God, I will stretch out my hand against the Philistines, cut off the Cherethites, and destroy the rest of the sea coast. I will execute great vengeance on them with wrathful punishments. Then they shall know that I am the Lord, when I lay my vengeance upon them"

But if justice is involved, anger is all the more likely to fall on Israel itself, because they have been called to live in holiness and to do God's work in the world, and they have been given the covenant with its conditions to help them to do this. The prophets (the spokesmen of God) repeatedly threaten exactly this judgement of God (see box, bottom left). Despite this, there is even more emphasis on the patience of God, and on the willingness of God to find a way through the obstinacy of human beings. It is true that the anger of God may be immediate: on one occasion, "while the meat was still between their teeth, before it was consumed, the anger of the Lord was kindled against the people, and the Lord struck the people with a very great plague" (Numbers 11.33). But far more often it is said that God is slow to anger, as in Psalm 103, which recognizes that "the Lord is merciful and gracious, slow to anger and abounding in steadfast love. He will not always accuse, nor will he keep his anger for ever" (Psalm 103.8f; see also Exodus 34.6; Isaiah 48.).

This means that God is always open to prayer and intercessions on behalf of those who have done wrong, as when Abraham intercedes on behalf of Sodom (Genesis 18.16–33), or Moses when he speaks for the unfaithful people (Exodus 32.11,31f; Numbers 11.1f; 14.11f); or Amos for Israel (Amos 7.2,5); or Jeremiah for Judah (Jeremiah 14.7ff; 18.2); or Job for his friends (Job 42.7f). There is, throughout the Bible, realism about what sin and rebellion deserve. But against this is set an entirely different character of God, one of faithful perseverance.

Fighting the Amalekites
Exodus 17.8–16 tells how Joshua fought the Amalekites and "whenever he held up his hand, Israel prevailed, and whenever he lowered his hand, Amalek prevailed", but as he grew weary, Aaron and Hur held up his hands.

The Love of God

A Mother and Child

It is the enduring, unshakeable commitment of *hesed* that underlies the great metaphors of relationship in Israel's experience of God: of husband and wife, of shepherd and flock, of mother and child:

"O Lord, my heart is not proud, nor are my eyes haughty. I do not busy myself in great matters, or in things too wonderful for me. But I have calmed and quieted my soul like a weaned child upon its mother's breast, like a child on its mother's breast is my soul within me. O Israel, trust in the Lord from this time forward and for ever"

(Psalm 131)

God's Love as Mother
"As a mother comforts her child, so I will comfort you; you shall be comforted in Jerusalem" (Isaiah 66.9; cf. 49.15).

I T IS EASY TO CONSTRUCT from the Bible a picture of God as a Mafia boss – a literal God-Father: he has his own family and protects it fiercely, especially where marriage is concerned; he has his own territory and protects that also; he expects certain, very specific, standards of behaviour (eventually, in this case, written down, but for a long time an unwritten code); he engages, if necessary, in war with rivals; and deals with offenders in a brutal and conclusive way. Like Mario Puzo's Godfather, God makes offers to the Israelites that they can't refuse.

But that is not the only or the whole picture. The covenant implies obligation on the part of Israel but it involves obligation also from God. As the Israelites found that obligation unfailing, so they began to characterize God as utterly trustworthy. This trustworthiness they summarized in the word *hesed*.

That word is basically a legal term, and it sums up the quality of complete reliability that makes a legal agreement possible. When Solomon dedicated the Temple (see caption, right), his prayer began: "O Lord, God of Israel, there is no God like you in heaven above or on earth beneath, keeping covenant and *hesed* for your servants who walk before you with all their heart, the covenant that you kept for your servant my father David as you declared to him" (I Kings 8.22ff; covenant and *hesed* are combined also, e.g., in Deuteronomy 7.2, 9, 12; 2 Chronicles 6.14; Nehemiah 1.5; 9.32; Daniel 9.4; and Psalm 50.5, 36; 89.29, 34).

The word *hesed* carries with it a sense of the power and strength to do things, since an impotent partner in a covenant is useless. So *hesed* is frequently used to mean the same as strength, as in Psalm 144 (see box, top right). For the people of Israel, however, *hesed* moves far beyond the legal commitments of a stronger partner, becoming a quality that they experience in God of one who longs to bring into being all that the covenant promises, not least the wellbeing of all the people, rich and poor alike. When Moses cut the tablets of stone, the words establishing the covenant begin:

"The Lord, the Lord, a God merciful and gracious, slow to anger, and abounding in steadfast love [hesed] and faithfulness, keeping steadfast love for the thousandth generation, forgiving iniquities and transgression and sin" (Exodus 34.6f)

True, the text goes on to say that the guilty are still under judgement. But the faithful commitment of Yahweh, summarized in *hesed*, is the basis on which the Israelites can know that even when they have sinned, they will always be received with forgiveness when they turn back to God:

"Do not fear, for you will not be ashamed; do not be discouraged, for you will not suffer disgrace; for you will forget the shame of your youth, and the disgrace of your widowhood you will remember no more. For your Maker is your husband, the Lord of hosts is his name; the Holy One of Israel is your Redeemer, the God of the whole earth he is called. For the Lord has called you like a wife forsaken and grieved in spirit, like the wife of a man's youth when she is cast off, says your God.
For a brief moment I abandoned you, but with great compassion I will gather you. In overflowing wrath for a moment I hid my face from you, but with everlasting love [hesed] I will have compassion on you, says the Lord, your Redeemer"

(Isaiah 54.4–8)

Israel may once have hoped, occasionally feared, that God was a gangland boss, dealing with their rivals in a ruthless way. But they came to know God as one who, while expecting much, also loves much (see box, left). Love increasingly takes over as the basic characteristic of God, and Jeremiah even uses words of physical passion to express that desire:

"Thus says the Lord: the people who survived the sword found grace in the wilderness; when Israel sought for rest, the Lord would appear to him from far away. I have loved you with an everlasting love; therefore I have continued my faithfulness [hesed] to you. Again I will build you, and you shall be built O virgin Israel!"

(Jeremiah 31.2–4)

"Blessed be the Lord, my rock, who trains my hands for war, and my fingers for battle; my hesed *and my fortress, my stronghold and my deliverer, my shield, in whom I take refuge, who subdues the peoples under me"*

(Ps. 144, vss.1–2; cf. Ps. 62.11f.: "Once God has spoken; twice have I heard this: that power belongs to God, and *hesed* belongs to you, O Lord")

Solomon's Prayer
Solomon prays that if the people sin and are carried away into captivity, they will continue to pray towards Jerusalem and will be forgiven, "for you have separated them from among all the peoples of the earth, to be your heritage" (I Kings 8.53).

The Holiness of God

Separation from All that is Unclean

WHEN DAVID FINALLY DEFEATED the Philistines (p.177), he went with 30,000 chosen men to rescue the Ark of the Covenant that the Philistines had captured. The Ark had been constructed to contain the covenant (Exodus 25), and it represented the presence of Yahweh in Israel. It was, therefore, the holiest of all possible things. As the oxen pulled the cart, the Ark slipped, and Uzzah put out his hand to steady it. Immediately, "the anger of the Lord was kindled against him, and God struck him there because he reached out his hand to the Ark, and he died there beside the Ark of God" (2 Samuel 6.6f). To touch something holy in a casual way is to invite death.

Holiness is a quality that belongs to God alone, and it can be extremely dangerous. The word for "holy" is *qadosh*. In Hebrew and other languages like it, that word means, basically, to be cut off or separate. God is utterly different from anything that might corrupt or contaminate: God is the source of all life and power, and anything that is brought close to God that is unclean or casual is burnt up by that holiness. The sons of Aaron, Nadab and Abihu, "offered unholy fire before the Lord, such as he had not commanded them; and fire came out from the presence of the Lord and consumed them, and they died before the Lord" (Leviticus 10.1f). Moses immediately commented: "This is what the Lord meant

On Holy Ground
"Moses was keeping the flock of his father-in-law, Jethro, the priest of Midian; he led his flock beyond the wilderness, and came to Horeb, the mountain of God. There the angel of the Lord appeared to him in a flame of fire out of a bush; he looked, and the bush was blazing, yet it was not consumed" (Exodus 3.1f). He then took off his sandals because he knew he was standing on holy ground.

when he said, Through those who are near me I will show myself holy, and before all people I will be glorified" (vs.3).

God is called many things in the Bible (wise, mighty, merciful, loving, etc), but only holiness describes God's own nature – what God essentially is. That is why, characteristically, God is called the Holy One of Israel. Not surprisingly, therefore, it is impossible to see God and survive the experience. Even Moses was allowed to glimpse only God's back (Exodus 33.17–23; cf. Judges 13.19–23).

Because holiness belongs to the essential nature of God alone, things and people become holy only when they are brought into relationship with God. Thus the altar for sacrifice and all its utensils were holy (Exodus 29.37, 30.28f.), as were the priests and their vestments (29.1; 28.4); the bread of the Presence was holy bread (I Samuel 21.6); and places became holy because of their association with God: when Moses was summoned to recognize God in the burning bush (caption, left), God said to him, "Come no closer! Remove the sandals from your feet, for the place on which you are standing is holy ground" (Exodus 3.5). Even more extensively, the whole of the mountain in Sinai is set apart, following the command of God, "Set limits around the mountain and keep it holy" (Exodus 19.23).

From the holiness of God follows inevitably the holiness of the people of Israel, because they, out of all the peoples of the world, have been brought closest to God in order to live with God in a covenant of faith and trust (hesed, p.186). At that same time when the mountain was made off-limits because of its holiness, Yahweh said to Moses:

"Now therefore, if you obey my voice and keep my covenant, you shall be my treasured possession out of all the peoples. Indeed, the whole earth is mine, but you shall be for me a priestly kingdom and a holy nation"

(Deuteronomy 19.5f; cf.26.19)

"Thus says the Lord: I remember the devotion of your youth, your love as a bride, how you followed me in the wilderness, in a land not sown. Israel was holy to the Lord, the first fruits of his harvest. All who ate of it were held guilty; disaster came upon them, says the Lord"

(Jeremiah 2.3)

"The Lord spoke to Moses saying: speak to all the congregation of the people of Israel and say to them: you shall be holy, for I the Lord your God am holy"

(Leviticus 19.2)

Israel is like the offering of first fruits to God, and any other nation that attacks them is in danger from the holiness of God (see box, above right). It is the fundamental vocation of the people of Israel, the reason for being Jewish, to offer themselves to God in that condition of holiness (see box, bottom right). That is an extremely dangerous condition to live in. Holiness is a magnificently creative power, but wrongly approached it is death-dealingly destructive. It is not unlike a nuclear reactor: if wisely used, its power provides energy for a whole society, but if it is treated carelessly or casually, the consequences can be disastrous. So how can anyone live with the holiness of God? As with a nuclear reactor, only by maintaining proper procedures and by having teams of trained technicians who understand what they are doing. In the priesthood, that is exactly what Israel produced.

Temple, Holiness, and Priests

The Majesty and Otherness of God

Herod's Temple
When Herod the Great (37–4BCE) rebuilt the Second Temple in splendid style, people were protected from approaching the holiness of God unawares. There were walls and courts through which only those who were prepared and purified could pass.

"Rise up, O Lord, and go to your resting-place, you and the Ark of your might… For the Lord has chosen Zion; he has desired it for his habitation: this is my resting-place forever; here I will reside, for I have desired it"

(Psalm 132.8,13)

I N THE YEAR THAT KING UZZIAH DIED (some time in the 8th century BCE), the prophet Isaiah saw in the Temple an overwhelming and majestic vision of God, "sitting on a throne, high and lofty, and the hem of his robe filled the temple" (Isaiah 6.1). He was not the only prophet to see a vision of God beside an altar: so also had Amos (9.1) and Micaiah ben Imlah (I Kings 22.19), but Isaiah alone left a record of his reaction. He said, "Woe is me! I am lost, for I am a man of unclean lips [not in a condition of holiness], and I live among a people of unclean lips; yet my eyes have seen the King, the Lord of Hosts" (Isaiah 6.5). The holiness of God burns up all that is unclean, and Isaiah had to be cleansed with a live coal on his lips for his uncleanness to be purged.

The holiness of God is a way of saying that God cannot be approached casually: those who come near must do so in a state of ritual purity. Sacrifices are a formal way in which God can be approached, but these too must be carefully regulated. That was difficult to achieve when each community, and sometimes each family, had its own altar and ritual. After David had made Jerusalem a new capital in order to draw the families of the kinship group into a closer alliance with each other and with Yahweh as their God, the next logical step was for Solomon to build a Temple as a focus for the common service and worship of God. Other shrines and temples continued, but Jerusalem and Mount Zion became, in Jewish imagination, the centre, not just of their own loyalty, but of the entire world. Priests mediated between heaven and earth (see box, below).

The first Temple housed the Ark, the symbol of God's presence. Psalm 132 celebrates the occasion when the Ark was brought to Jerusalem (see box, left). When the first Temple (that

PRIESTS

The organization of priests as the technicians of holiness took centuries to develop:

Priests gradually became technicians of holiness, overseeing the sacrifices that were made in the Temple. Their purpose was to ensure that the people would approach God only in a condition of holiness, and that the sacrifices would be carefully regulated. Looking back on the Wilderness period,

Leviticus was written to show how the whole encampment of the Israelites and its sanctuary were meant to prevent what is impure coming into contact with what is holy, and its regulations anticipate the way in which this was to be achieved through the Temple.

of Solomon) was destroyed by the Babylonians in the 6th century BCE (p.194), the "lost Ark of the Covenant" was far more probably not lost but destroyed. When rebuilt (see caption, left) the Holy of Holies, the central shrine in the very heart of the Temple, was left almost entirely empty. Here, no one entered except the high priest once a year on the Day of Atonement.

God's presence was by no means confined to the Temple. The people had known God's presence in the Exodus and in the Wilderness, and they had worshipped God in many temples before the Temple of Solomon had been built. Indeed, there were those who protested strongly against the building of the Jerusalem Temple, on the grounds that God had never needed a house to live in before.

Even when the Temple had been built, not all the people worshipped there. The northern tribes did not recognize the house of David, and they had their own Temple in Samaria. But increasingly in the south, the Temple in Jerusalem became the point of connection between the people and God, until King Josiah, just before the Exile, made a deliberate attempt to abolish other shrines and make Jerusalem the centre of the pilgrimage festivals and of worship in general.

The Temple, therefore, stated strongly in stone and rich ornament that the holiness of God is not to be taken lightly, and that the worship of God requires the best that can be offered. In return, all the people (not just Isaiah in his vision) can know that the glory of God touches the earth in this place (see box, right).

"Great is the Lord and greatly to be praised in the city of our God. His holy mountain, beautiful in elevation, is the joy all the earth, Mount Zion, in the far north, the city of the great King. Within its citadels God has shown himself a sure defence"

(Psalm 48.1–3)

Bringing Up the Ark
On one occasion, during the long conflicts with the Philistines, the Philistines captured the Ark (I Samuel 5). The celebrations when it was recaptured are described in 2 Samuel 6. At this time, the Temple had not yet been built.

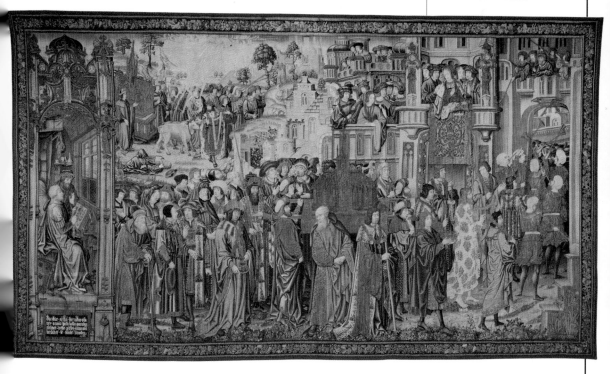

Sacrifice and Psalms

Praise and Protest

Day of Atonement
The large letters on the scroll in this synagogue window read Yom Kippur, *the Day of Atonement, the most solemn and holy day of the Jewish year. Observed once in the Temple, it is now observed in synagogues and homes.*

THE STORY OF GOD was told repeatedly in the Temple, where the agricultural festivals of field and flock were linked to the great events of rescue in the Exodus and of sustenance in the Wilderness, to produce Pesach (Passover; for the *Passover Haggadah* see p.181) and Sukkot (Booths or Tabernacles). Other sacrifices, and above all the Day of Atonement, sought to repair the damage done when the terms of the covenant had been broken, or when individuals had failed God. Day by day and year by year these occasions articulated in the midst of Israel's life the great works that God has done and continues to do.

The regulations for sacrifice are found mainly in Leviticus 1–7 (see also Leviticus 14.10–32; 22.17–30; 27; Numbers 18–19), but these passages give no account of what the sacrifices actually meant to the people involved. In contrast, the book of Psalms contains many hymns that in origin probably belonged to festivals or other cultic occasions, especially in the Temple. In this case the meaning is clear, but there is no text or rubric saying to what liturgical occasion they belong. Psalm 45, for example, seems to have belonged to a king's wedding, Psalm 110 to a coronation. The Psalms, however, contain much more than hymns for temple services. More than any other collection of texts, they illustrate the meaning of God for the people of the Biblical period. Indeed, some of them challenge as sharply as did the prophets the worth of sacrifice if sacrifice becomes a substitute for life lived as God desires it. Isaiah drew a contrast between people who, God says, "trample my courts", bringing futile offerings: "Your new moons and your appointed festivals my soul hates; they have become a burden to me, I am weary of bearing them" (Isaiah 1.12–1).

In contrast, God demands,

*"Wash yourselves; make yourselves clean;
remove the evil of your doings from before my eyes; cease to
do evil, learn to do good; seek justice, rescue the oppressed,
defend the orphan, plead for the widow"*

(Isaiah 1.16f)

The same contrast was drawn by Micah:

"Will the Lord be pleased with thousands of rams, with tens of thousands of rivers of oil? Shall I give my first-born for my transgression, the fruit of my body for the sin of my soul? He has told you, O mortal, what is good; and what does the Lord require of you but to do justice, and to love kindness, and to walk humbly with your God?"

(Micah 6.7f)

Psalm 51.15–7 makes exactly that commitment:

*"O Lord, open my lips, and my mouth will declare your praise.
For you have no delight in sacrifice;
if I were to give a burnt-offering, you would not be pleased.
The sacrifice acceptable to God is a broken spirit;
A broken and contrite heart, O God, you will not despise"*

*"How long, O Lord?
Will you forget me forever?
How long will you hide your face from me?
How long must I bear pain in my soul,
and have sorrow in my heart all day long?
How long shall my enemy be exalted over me?"*

(Psalm 13.1f; see also Psalms 4, 6, 12, 22, 35, 38–44, 55, 60, 69, 74, 77, 79, 83, 88, 102, 109, 137, 140–43)

*"Where can I go from your spirit?
Or where can I flee from your presence?
If I ascend to heaven, you are there;
if I make my bed in Sheol [the grave], you are there.
If I take the wings of the morning
and settle at the farthest limits of the sea,
even there your hand shall lead me,
and your right hand shall hold me fast.
If I say, 'Surely the darkness shall cover me,
and the light around me become night',
even the darkness is not dark to you;
the night is as bright as the day,
for darkness is as light to you"*

(Psalm 139.7–12)

Many of the Psalms express directly and eloquently the profound struggle that went on among the people of Israel to understand the meaning of God in their lives as individuals and as a nation. There is praise and adoration, certainly, but there is argument also, as people try to understand why God seems, on so many occasions, to be absent ("Truly, you are a God who hides himself", Isaiah 45.15; see box, top right).

There is, in the Psalms, exultation over the defeat and destruction of enemies, not least in the drowning of the Egyptian riders and their horses in the Exodus (Exodus 15.1; see Psalms 78, 135, 136). But there is also profound recognition, based clearly on experience, that the hand of God is stretched out in mercy and renewal over all the nations and over the whole of creation (see, for example, Psalms 8, 29, 67, 104, 113, 148).

The ways of God may seem, on occasion, hard to decipher, and God may seem often to be absent. However, all the great metaphors of relationship are there in the Psalms, and come, clearly, from an experience lived and known to be true: shepherd (Psalm 23), mother (Psalm 131), shelter (Psalm 91), and guide (Psalm 31). Many of the Psalms are a welcoming feather bed of huge reassurance and comfort. But, wrote Thomas More, we do not get to heaven on a feather bed. Other Psalms are more like sleeping rough on the streets. Even there, "your hand shall lead me, and your right hand shall hold me fast" (see box, right).

The Exile

Suffering and Renewal

THE FAITH EXPRESSED in Psalm 139 (see box, p.193) is profound indeed. But in the 6th century BCE, this faith was shaken. Babylon had been gaining power, and that inevitably brought it into conflict with Egypt, because both were seeking control of the Mediterranean coast. Judah was caught between the two, and backed Egypt the loser.

Two attempts to resist the Babylonians ended in failure, and in 587/6 the Babylonians destroyed Jerusalem and its Temple, and took many of the inhabitants into Exile.

This was a major disaster. Jeremiah, a prophet at the time, had warned the people that to put their trust in human allies like the Egyptians, and not in God, would lead to catastrophe, and he had been proved right. Did this mean that Yahweh had abandoned Israel?

"Will the Lord spurn forever, and never again be favourable? Has his steadfast love ceased forever? Are his promises at an end for all time? Has God forgotten to be gracious? Has he in anger shut up his compassion?"

(Psalm 77.7–9)

On the old understanding (p.180; and caption, left), if the people had been defeated so too had their gods. It led some to wonder, might it therefore be prudent to switch allegiance and to worship the gods of Babylon?

It was at this time of deep depression and despair that the most extraordinary affirmations of Israel's faith were made. Chapters 40–55 of Isaiah deal with the Exile and, in powerful poetry, they remind the people that Yahweh is the only God there is. The so-called gods of the Babylonians are mocked as they are carried past in a procession:

"Bel bows down, Nebo stoops, their idols are on beasts and cattle; these things you carry are loaded as burdens on weary animals. They stoop, they bow down together; they cannot save the burden, but themselves go into captivity"

(Isaiah 46.1f)

Shamash

Shamash (the name means Sun) was a Sumerian God (Utu) taken over by the Assyrians when they conquered the Sumerians, and then by the Babylonians when they conquered the Assyrians. That process did not happen with Yahweh.

In contrast, the prophet reminds the exiles of the consistency and faithfulness of God in their history – in the promises to the ancestors, during the Exodus, throughout the settlement of the land, and in the covenant with the house of David. They know the power of God beyond question in the creation of the world and the control of all the nations (Isaiah 40.12–31). The prophet therefore assures the people that God will use their wretched condition in captivity to demonstrate his far greater power as Redeemer, building the equivalent of a motorway in order bring the people home to Jerusalem, with all the nations in grandstands on each side of the road watching this demonstration of God's control over the affairs of the world (Isaiah 40.1ff.). Yes, the people are at present suffering, but they bear the suffering so that others will receive healing and peace (Isaiah 42.1–4; 49.1–6; 50.4–9; 52.13–53.1).

Babylonian Empire
Hammurapi (1792–1750BCE) laid the foundations for the mighty Babylonian Empire, and produced a famous law-code that has parallels with the later Biblical laws. This bas-relief sculpture depicts Hammurapi receiving the law from Shamash, the sun god.

On the basis of that confident knowledge of what God had done in the past, the prophet managed to interpret the career of Cyrus (who was leading a successful campaign against Babylon) as being that of God's Shepherd and even as the Messiah (Isaiah 44.28–45.7). Another prophet in the Exile, Ezekiel, also had absolute faith that the Exile was a necessary punishment, but that God would restore the Temple even more splendidly than before. Many of those in the Exile were quoting a proverb in order to put the blame for the Exile on to their parents: "The parents have eaten sour grapes, and the children's teeth are set on edge" (Jeremiah 31.29; Ezekiel 18.1). Ezekiel insists that they, not their parents, are to blame, and in graphic language details the sins that have brought about the punishment:

"She [Jerusalem] increased her whorings, remembering the days of her youth, when she played the whore in the land of Egypt and lusted after her paramours there, whose members were like those of donkeys, and whose emission was like that of stallions. Thus you longed for the lewdness of your youth, when the Egyptians fondled your bosom and caressed your young breasts"

(Ezekiel 23.19–21)

Ezekiel is sure that God will rescue the people and restore them (see box, right). But if the Israelites are to keep the statutes so carefully that they will not be punished in this way again, then God must surely find a way to make sure that they understand what is required of them. That is why the last chapters of Ezekiel (40–48) are a vision of a rebuilt Temple in Jerusalem in which the priests will be prominent. So began a new stage in the Jewish story of God.

"A new heart I will give you, and a new spirit I will put within you, and I will remove from your body the heart of stone and give you a heart of flesh. I will put my spirit within you, and make you follow my statutes and be careful to observe my ordinances. Then you shall live in the land that I gave to your ancestors; and you shall be my people, and I will be your God"

(Ezekiel 36.26–8)

Zoroaster

Iranian Prophet

Zoroastrian Deity
*This symbol is carved on the
wall of a ruined temple at
Persepolis (in Iran), the
former capital of Persia. It
represents Ahura Mazda as
the guardian of all who put
their trust in him, and thus
also the guardian spirit
known as fravashi. The solar
disk in the centre is Ahura
Mazda as creator of Light.*

WHILE THEY WERE IN EXILE, the Jews met more in the way
of other gods than just Bel and Nebo. At least some of
them encountered the religion of the Iranian prophet
Zoroaster, often spelt Zarathustra. The time at which he lived is
uncertain: it may have been as early as the 12th or as late as the
6th century BCE. Not many words of his own teaching have been
preserved: they survive in 17 hymns known as *Gathas*, and shows
connections with early Indian religion. His own distinctive
understanding of God began with his conviction that he had seen
God in a vision, and had been given a personal mission to make God
known in the world. God he called Ahura Mazda, meaning either the Wise
Lord or the Lord Wisdom. God is the source of all order and goodness. In
one of his hymns, Zoroaster asks who created all that is good in the universe
(see box, left). Zoroaster answers that it is the Father of Order, God.

Who, then, created evil and disorder? Zoroaster lived at a time when
there were many wars and raids, and he saw in the merciless cruelty of
conflict an example in miniature of warfare on a cosmic scale. Zoroaster
believed that there co-existed with Ahura Mazda a creator of evil and
destruction whom he called Angra Mainyu, the destructive spirit, known
in Pahlavi as Ahriman. Angra Mainyu is the source of everything that is
evil – of pollution, misery, suffering, and death – and of anything like
mould or rust that eats into things that are otherwise good. There is a
constant conflict between Ahura Mazda and Angra Mainyu, and both
created armies to assist them in this conflict. The assistants of Ahura
Mazda are known as Amesa Spentas. Those of Angra Mainyu are
the daevas (the devas of Indian religion, where they are on the
side of good) and also the khrafstras, creatures such as snakes,
rats, flies, and lions who "prowl about seeking whom they may
devour" (I Peter 5.8). The world is therefore a battleground
between good and evil – an example of what is known as
"dualism". But since evil is only real in the world when it gains
possession of material things, the human body becomes the
focus of this conflict. Humans are at the forefront of the battle
against evil, which means that Zoroastrianism is a deeply moral
religion, not least because the final outcome of human destiny
depends on the balance between good and evil deeds. Humans
are assisted in their conflict by the Amesa Spentas, who mediate
between humans and God, carrying prayers and worship in one
direction and blessings and strength in the other.

The religion of the Zoroastrians became, through much
change, struggle, and persecution, the religion of the Parsis

*"Who established the course of
the sun and stars? Through
whom does the moon wax and
wane? Who has upheld the earth
from below, and the heavens
from falling? Who sustains the
waters and plants? Who
harnessed swift steeds to wind
and clouds? What craftsman
created light and darkness? What
craftsman created both sleep and
activity? Through whom exist
dawn, noon and eve?"*

(Yasna 44.3–6)

(those from Persia). It may also have influenced the story of God far beyond its own tradition. When the Jews in Exile welcomed the Persian king Cyrus in his successful campaigns against the Babylonians (p.195), they may also have welcomed some of these Persian ideas, as of Satan (see caption, right) or of the Amesa Spentas, the good spirits, who perhaps gave a new form to the angels and archangels who mediate between heaven and earth, and who bring the help of God to humans in their struggles.

Above all, the moral character of God, so strongly emphasized in both the Torah and the Prophets, was powerfully reinforced. God's moral consistency, according to Zoroaster, is absolute and unvarying. In Israel, this moral consistency led to the combining of goodness with wisdom (p.204), and God therefore often reverses the more established values and expectations of human beings and turns the world upside down. Zoroastrians understand God as One who enters the contest against evil. Songs in the Bible, like the Song of Hannah at the birth of Samuel (or the Song of Mary in Luke 1.46–55) express a similar understanding:

"The bows of the mighty are broken,
but the feeble gird on the strength.
Those who were full have hired themselves out for bread,
but those who were hungry are fat with spoil…
The Lord makes poor and makes rich;
he brings low, he also exalts.
He raises up the poor from the dust;
he lifts the needy from the ash heap,
to make them sit with princes
and inherit a seat of honour…
The Lord! His adversaries shall be shattered;
The Most High will thunder in heaven."

(I Samuel 2.4–10)

Satan
Satan is smitten by the Archangel Michael in a scene from Milton's Paradise Lost, *derived from Jude 9 and Revelations 12.7–9. Satan was originally one who tests humans, only becoming an opponent of God and humans after the Exile, ending up as the Devil. This development may (though some dispute this) be a consequence of Jews meeting in the Exile the dualism of the Zoroastrians.*

After the Exile

The Renewal of the Covenant

After the Exile, the role of priests as interpreters of religious law became increasingly important. Scribes were used to record their decisions. An early instance of this can be found in Zechariah 7.2.

PSALM 125.1 SAYS "THOSE WHO TRUST IN THE LORD are like Mount Zion, which cannot be shaken but endures forever". In the 6th century BCE, however, Zion *was* shaken and Jerusalem fell to the Babylonian armies. How could the worship and service of God be continued in a strange land, as the Psalmist asked, "by the rivers of Babylon" (Psalm 137)? In the prayer offered long before, at the dedication of the Temple, provision had been included for exactly this circumstance (1 Kings 8. 46–51, pp.186, 187): it now became an issue what that "faith in captivity" could be.

It helped greatly that people had usually worshipped God wherever they happened to live. The great drive by Josiah to centralize all worship in Jerusalem had taken place less than 40 years before the Exile, so that for most people faith in Yahweh did not depend on attendance at the Temple. During the Exile, family observances became vital, and emphasis was put on unmistakeable marks of allegiance such as circumcision, celebration of the Passover, and the keeping of the Sabbath (Ezekiel 20.12, 20; cf. Exodus 31. 13, 17). Adhering to laws of diet and purity offered another way of faithful observance.

In 539BCE, Cyrus, king of Persia, finally entered Babylon and deposed the ruler. In the following year, he decreed that the Temple of the Jews should be rebuilt and its stolen items returned. It was part of his policy of trying to win the goodwill of the people over whom he ruled, and as a result at least some Jews returned to Jerusalem. This was not quite the triumphant procession that the prophet had envisaged (p.195). There were some attempts to restore Israel's faith as it had been before the disaster – immediately after the Return, the prophets Haggai and Zechariah believed that the descendant of David should once again be made king and welcomed as God's messiah ("anointed one"). But even they recognized that the high priest would now have to be sitting on the same throne beside him (Zechariah 5.11–14), and before long the hopes were abandoned that had, in the past, been centred on their kings. The coming of the true Messiah was projected into the future, at a time when God would send him. Instead of the king as God's messiah, the high priest (also a messiah, because he too was an anointed figure) became all-important, along with the Temple when it was rebuilt. One vital question was to know how another catastrophe of the same magnitude could be avoided. If the prophets were right, and the Exile had been a deserved punishment (p.195), then the way to avoid punishment in the future would be to live their lives in an exemplary fashion.

At once it became vital that everyone should know and apply the conditions of the Covenant contained in Torah (p.200). The Temple priests became decisive in interpreting and applying God's word to changing circumstances of life – so much so that prophets, who had been for so long the spokesmen of God, became suspect and soon disappeared from mainstream religion: prophets cannot be controlled, because they claim direct inspiration from God; they might again, as they had in the past, challenge the Temple and its cult (p.190) with the dramatic words, "Thus says the Lord." It came to be believed that the Holy Spirit who had inspired the prophets had been withdrawn by God as part of the punishment of the Exile.

Important though the Temple priests became as interpreters of Torah, not all Jews lived in or near Jerusalem. The Exile had proved that God could be worshipped without the Temple, even in Babylon, and many people chose to remain in Babylon when the return to Jerusalem became possible. Eventually, large communities of Jews were to be found in virtually every Mediterranean land, in what is known as the Diaspora, the Greek word for dispersion. Diaspora Jews were tied to Jerusalem by the pilgrimage feasts, by annual tribute to the Temple, and by the passionate loyalty expressed so often in the Psalms.

Even so, it was uncertain how such a wide scattering of people could be kept within the agreed boundary of the covenant. Ezra and Nehemiah, two leaders after the Exile, had drawn the people in Jerusalem into a renewed and solemn commitment to Torah (Nehemiah 8.1–6). But God had asked all the people, not just a few who lived in or near Jerusalem, to offer themselves in holiness (p.189). How could all the people be helped to live in this condition? It was the pressure of this issue that accelerated the creation of Scripture, and led to development of the synagogue.

THE BEGINNINGS OF SCRIPTURE

Gathering together a written history of the people of Israel and their relationship with God became of prime importance during the uncertain period of Exile.

During the Exile, a new sense developed of what it meant to belong to the people of Israel – a move from an identity fixed purely by geographical location and national institutions to one based on commitment to God made known through a long religious and cultural tradition. One major consequence of the Exile was the determination of the people to gather the records of that tradition into what eventually became Scripture, in which history as God's story played a prominent part. For the first time it begins to become possible to think of "Judaism" and of a "people of the Book".

Scripture

The Word of God in the Words of God

ABOUT 100 YEARS AFTER the Exile ended, the leaders, Ezra and Nehemiah, made an attempt to renew the commitment of the people in Jerusalem to Yahweh. On one all-important occasion, Ezra brought the book of the law before the assembled people. He opened the book in their sight and blessed the Lord. All the people answered, "Amen, Amen" (Nehemiah 8.6). Then the book was read and interpreted to all those present.

This formal commitment to Torah (see caption, left) marked a new departure in accepting God as guide to life. The Torah became the living word ofGod spoken to the people. The Torah was regarded as the eternal and unchanging word of God, but to it were added, over the course of many centuries, the words of the prophets (*Nebi'im*) and other writings (*Kethubim*), known collectively as *qabbalah* ("tradition"), and these three divisions make up Scripture. From the initial letters of Torah, Nebi'im, and Kethubim, the Jewish Bible is often known as Tanakh.

The gathering together of the writings that eventually were accepted as Scripture was dramatically important for the Jewish story of God. It meant that God had not only spoken to Moses and inspired the prophets and other writers long ago, but also continues to speak through the words of Tanakh in the present.

As the synagogue developed to gather the Jews in the Diaspora together (p.199), so Scripture was read aloud every week. Scripture was always read in Hebrew, the sacred language through which God had revealed the word, but since, as time went by, fewer people knew or understood Hebrew, an interpreter would then give a paraphrase of the text in the language of the people present. These Targums (*targumim*, "interpretations") were often extremely free, because the actual word of God had already been read. Thus the Targums in the synagogue conveyed not only the word of God but also the meaning of that word to make sure that it worked its way into understanding and life.

The study and interpretation of Torah became the most precious and valued of all occupations. The rabbis (teachers) argued, in the 2nd century CE, whether it was more important in the eyes of God to study Torah or to practise it. Rabbi Akiba won the

Torah

The word "torah" means basically guidance or instruction, but it came to refer particularly to the first five books of the Bible, the books associated with Moses (the Torah), and to the guidance and law that those books contain (Torah). Thus Torah is contained in the Torah, and eventually the term was extended to cover the whole of what eventually (in about the 3rd century CE) came to be accepted as Scripture.

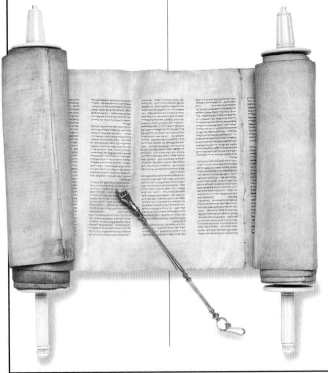

argument when he said that it is more important to study Torah, because study leads to practice. From this study developed Halakah and Haggadah (see box, below), which showed how the laws are to be applied in life, and what they mean.

The results of this search for the meaning and application of the original written laws (*Torah she bi ketabh*, "Torah which is written") were eventually gathered, first into the Mishnah, and then into the Talmuds, of which the Babylonian Talmud has continuing authority. It came to be believed that this orally transmitted law (*Torah she be 'al peh*, "Torah according to the mouth") was also revealed by God to Moses on Mount Sinai, to be transmitted not in writing but by word of mouth, to be given public expression later as circumstances demanded it.

The process of interpretation continues to the present day, with some rabbis becoming consummate authorities on such questions as whether it is possible to travel in a lift on the Sabbath (see box, below) if someone else presses the button. It used to be said of one of these authorities, Rabbi Mosheh Feinstein (1895–1986), that a newly ordained rabbi needed only two things: his ordination certificate and Rabbi Mosheh's telephone number.

The laws, however, are not the whole story. The Torah contains much more than law: it contains stories and wisdom, encouragement and guidance known as Haggadah ("narration", see box, below). This too was developed in order to bring God closer to the lives of the people, and is also to be found in the Talmud. Through the two Torahs (*Toroth*), written and oral, God is a constant and living reality in Jewish life.

In the best of times and in the worst of times, God, through these words, is an enduring and inviting presence.

The Talmud
The Talmud contains in the centre of each page the Mishnah *and the* Gemara *(commentary) on it, and is the fundamental authority, after* Tanakh (Scripture), *in Jewish life. Around it are printed later commentaries.*

HALAKAH AND HAGGADAH
Traditions helping people to walk and talk as the Torah decrees.

Halakah comes from the verb *halak*, meaning "he walked". Halakah shows how the law revealed to Moses is to be applied, and how, therefore, people are to walk through life with God as their guide, keeping the terms of the covenant. Haggadah comes from a word meaning narrative, or telling, and it refers to the stories and other material that exemplify the meaning of Torah. The original laws are often extremely brief or general, and questions have continually been raised about how they should be applied to new or changed circumstances. For example, it is forbidden to work on the Sabbath, but what counts as work? As the many answers and applications developed, it came to be said that the laws on the Sabbath are like a mountain hanging from a hair.

Change and Stability

How New Understandings of God Developed

T HE WRITINGS THAT CAME to make up Tanakh (Scripture) were composed over a period of a least 1,000 years. Once they were put into a Canon (agreed list) of the books making up Scripture, there was a tendency to make all parts of Scripture equally valid as the word of God, without much reference to the process of history in those thousand years. It was believed that Torah came directly from God through Moses, and that the prophets and the writings came from the initiative of God but with the co-operation of human agents; but all parts have authority. This means that in the Jewish quest for God in the words of God, any part can interpret any other part.

This can obscure the fact that the writings reveal an extraordinary process of change, correction, and growth in the understanding of God. This was dramatically clear in the way in which Yahweh invaded and took over the role and functions of El, becoming in the end the One who is El (pp.178, 183). It was shown also in the realization, reluctant on the part of some, that God is not a gangster who will always fight on Israel's side and defeat enemies (p.186).

In a way, those two changes belong together. If Yahweh is indeed the One who is God, then Yahweh is obviously the God of all nations (since the so-called gods of those nations are not gods at all) and not just of Israel. That is why God can deploy nations like Assyria and Babylonia to punish the Covenant people. In Amos (8th century BCE), God does indeed punish other nations for their transgressions, but does exactly the same to Israel and Judah.

Even beyond that was the realization that God is not simply the judge of all the nations but is their saviour as well. The prophet Nahum (7th century BCE) had breathed out vengeance against Assyria, the enemy that destroyed the northern kingdom and threatened Judah in the south. After the Exile, the book of Jonah was written to show how God condemns thoughts of destructive vengeance and rescues Nineveh, the Assyrian capital – "and also many animals" (the final words of the book that extended the new imagination of God even further).

Elijah

Elijah marks the transition from prophets who go into trance states and who provide guidance for kings and others, and those who become spokesmen for Yahweh even when it leads them into conflict with kings and others. In this scene (I Kings 17.1–7) Elijah trusts God and is fed by ravens.

This constant transformation of the way in which successive generations understood the nature of God is found throughout the whole of Scripture. Prophets, for example, were found elsewhere in the Ancient Near East, usually attached to cultic centres where they went into trances in order to answer questions and give oracles. That is how the prophets of Israel began, and the test of a true prophet was simply whether his answer or his prediction about a future event came true.

"You may say to yourself, 'How can we recognize the word that the Lord has not spoken?' If a prophet speaks in the name of the Lord but the thing does not take place or prove true, it is a word that the Lord has not spoken"

(Deuteronomy 18. 21)

"If prophets or those who divine by dreams appear among you and promise you omens or portents, and they take place, and they say, 'Let us follow other gods', you must not heed the words of those prophets..., for the Lord your God is testing you, to know whether you indeed love the Lord your God with all your heart and soul"

(Deuteronomy 13.1–3)

But in that case, no one knows who the true prophet is until after the event – when it is too late to matter! So what became decisive was whether a prophet's words were true to Yahweh (see box, above right). By this seemingly small shift, the prophets of Israel emerged as independent agents of God, utterly different from the prophets they originally resembled.

This brilliant transformation of what Israel found in the surrounding nations happened over and over again. For example, kings at that time were either regarded as gods, as in Egypt, or as representatives of God on earth, as in Mesopotamia. But the king in Israel could not possibly represent God on ritual occasions, let alone be God, because God was already known to be holy and far removed from the earth. In Israel, therefore, the king represented the people before God and became the link through whom prayers and blessings flow. From this, the idea of the future Messiah developed (see caption, right).

Historians and archaeologists have shown how much Israel shared in common with its neighbours, and how like them in many ways it was. The question then becomes obvious: why was Israel not *more* like them? What was it that made Israel take up the opportunities of belief and practice in the world around them and constantly make out of them something utterly different?

The answer is simple. It was God – or at least, it was what they, through many generations, had come to know of God as they lived with God, not just in easy times, but in times of suffering and disaster as well. They treasured their tradition because it taught them truth. Therefore they did not destroy or erase earlier parts of it as they came later to understand God more profoundly, even when those earlier parts showed them or their heroes (e.g., David) in a bad light. It was God who remained consistent even in the midst of change. This consistency led them to understand God as the source of wisdom and guarantee of truth.

David
When David captured Jerusalem from the Jebusites, he took over and adapted their ideas and rituals involving kings. To be God, or even to represent God, was impossible, but the king (the anointed one, or Messiah) could be the link between the people and God, and from this adaptation, the idea of the Messiah eventually developed.

Wisdom

God's Partner in Creation

The Natural Order
The Jews were deeply impressed by the way in which the natural order serves so many different purposes and is stable – it is reliable, even though great upheavals and disasters may occur. They recognized that this reliability is not a matter of chance but of purpose on the part of God – the One who, in their language, is Rock, Fortress, and Strength.

THE BIBLE EMPHASIZES GOD as Creator, in at least four different creation stories. It begins (Genesis 1.1) with the words *bereshith bara Elohim*, "in the beginning God created", but those words are slightly odd, in the sense that *reshith* looks like a Hebrew genitive, in which case it ought to mean "in the beginning of". In the beginning of what? The text does not say, and therefore early Jewish interpreters of the Bible took those words to mean something else and translated them, "by means of wisdom God created". That interpretation seems far from the original text, but the way they reached it points to a spectacular advance in the Biblical understanding of God: the association of wisdom with God.

A main word for wisdom, *hokmah*, has to do with human skill and the ability to do things, from making curtains (Exodus 36.8) to ruling as a king (I Kings 3.12, 28). The Hakamim are the wise, those who are well trained and possess the competence needed for the task in hand, and they are often the teachers of others. Qoheleth, the speaker in the book of Ecclesiastes, is defined as wise, and therefore "he taught the people knowledge, weighing and studying and arranging many proverbs; he sought to find accurate words, and he wrote words of truth plainly" (Ecclesiastes 12.9f.). Wisdom, however, is more than trained competence. Another word for wisdom is *binah*, from the preposition *ben*, "between", so that it means something like discrimination, insight, and understanding. It is often used in association with *hokmah*, as in Proverbs 7.4: "Say to wisdom, 'You are my sister', and call insight your intimate friend." Wisdom was also personified as the ideal wife, and the mother who nurtures her children and brings them to maturity (see box, below). Personifying Wisdom allowed her to be beside God as the

---

WISDOM AS MOTHER

The personification of Wisdom in the Bible allowed her to assist God in creation.

It may seem strange to speak of wisdom as a close member of the family, but as both of the Hebrew words for wisdom (*binah* and *hokmah*) are feminine, this allowed the Jews to personify Wisdom and portray her as a woman, often a mother, caring for the young and setting them on the right path. The book of Proverbs begins with the praise of Wisdom, displaying her indispensable purpose, and it sees her calling back the foolish

from their self-destructive ways:
"Wisdom cries out in the street; in the square she raises her voice…. My child, if you accept my words and treasure up my commandments within you, if you indeed cry out for insight, and raise your voice for understanding; if you seek it like silver, and search for it as for hidden treasures – then you will understand the fear of the Lord and find the knowledge of God" (Proverbs 1.20, 2.1–5)

necessary instrument of creation. It is here that the connection with Genesis 1.1 was made, because Proverbs 8.22–31 describes the part played by Wisdom in creation, and it begins: "The Lord possessed me the *reshith* [beginning] of his ways, the first of his acts of long ago." When God made all things, "then I was beside him, like a skilled worker; and I was daily a delight, rejoicing before him always, rejoicing in his inhabited world and delighting in the human race" (vss.30f.). *Reshith* was taken as a name for Wisdom, and so the first verse of Genesis was translated as "by means of Wisdom God created".

Wisdom (Greek, *Sofia*) thus became an independent figure assisting God. In Ecclesiasticus 24.2, Wisdom even enters the council of God, much as Yahweh entered the council of El long before (p.178, 183), and then becomes embedded in creation, and particularly among the descendants of Jacob. Wisdom is therefore equated with Torah (24.23). In the Book of Wisdom, Solomon prays for Wisdom, and Wisdom is described:

"Within her is a spirit intelligent, holy, unique, manifold, subtle, mobile, incisive, unsullied, lucid, invulnerable, benevolent, shrewd, irresistible, beneficent, friendly to human beings.... For wisdom is quicker to move than any motion; she is so pure, she pervades and permeates all things. She is a breath of the power of God, pure emanation of the glory of the Almighty; so nothing impure can find its way into her. For she is a reflection of the eternal light, an untarnished mirror of God's active power, and the image of his goodness"

(Wisdom 7.22–6)

The association of Wisdom with God had enormous consequences. Along with Greek rationality, it is the reason why science and civilization developed as they did in the West. The conviction that all things were created in wisdom, that all things are in consequence naturally good and not malicious, carried into the heart of the Western world the belief that the universe is consistent. Logic and reliability were built into it from the start: kettles boil, pigs do not fly. Life is not a tale told by an idiot signifying nothing. Creation is a work of wonder which humans have a chance of understanding. No wonder Solomon prays: "Despatch Wisdom from the holy heavens, send her forth from your throne of glory to help me and to toil with me and teach me what is pleasing to you" (Wisdom 9.10).

From Genes to Genesis
The mapping of the human genome depends on consistency in what is being mapped – it is not one thing today and another tomorrow. This consistency goes back to the idea of Creation, which means that there is something rather than nothing. "Nothing" is not what God makes things out of; it is the absence of anything and everything. Thus the Jews began to realize that the question, "Why is there something rather than nothing?" is fundamental (p.366).

Creation

The Contrast With Greek Myths

IN THE BEGINNING GOD CREATED: five words (three in Hebrew) that express with brief conviction the belief that God brings into being the whole created order and yet remains distinct from it: God is not a part of the cosmos or universe who lives within it, but is, rather, the One who brings into being this and all other universes, and remains whether they continue to exist or not.

It seems perhaps obvious, but that belief is in fact very different from the far more common understandings of creation which envisage the gods and goddesses emerging from a prior state – from chaos, for example, or from an egg, or from a primordial tree. According to *The Theogony* (Birth of the Gods) of Hesiod (8th century BCE in Greece) and other Greek myths, in the beginning was a chaotic void out of which emerged Ge or Gaia, "wide-bosomed earth", a foundation for Olympus, the abode of the goddesses and gods. Gaia gave birth to Ouranos (the Heavens), who produced Night, and who, being greater than Gaia, completely covered her. From that union came the first gods, the Titans, among whom were Oceanos, the one-eyed Cyclopes, and the fearsome Hyperion, Rhea, and Kronos.

Gaia enlisted Kronos and the other Titans to destroy Ouranos, and, with a sickle provided by her, Kronos castrated Ouranos. The drops of blood that fell on Gaia became the vengeful Furies, but the genitals, falling into the sea, produced a thick foam from which emerged the most beautiful of all women, Aphrodite, whose son (or follower) was Eros, Desire. Night meanwhile brought forth Death, Sleep, Dreams, and other works of darkness, such as Deceit, Old Age, and Strife.

Kronos then raped his sister Rhea, and from that union began the family of goddesses and gods who would later live on Mount Olympus (the Olympians), including the great Zeus, who, by overcoming Kronos, became the ruler of Olympus. Zeus married his sister, Hera, and from them came Hephaistos (controller of iron) and Ares (of war). Among Zeus' offspring by other unions were Athena (who according to some sprang fully armed from the head of Zeus), Hermes (the messenger of the gods), and Apollo, god of light, music, and youth.

The stories continue to the creation of humans, with gods and goddesses distinct from humans but involved in their affairs. Myths of this kind are an extremely powerful way in which people can think about the universe and about their own status and significance within it. The power of myth is that it offers a public and simple language of imagination that people have in common, not least because it can be told in stories. Myths are not true (nothing happened exactly like that), and

Aphrodite

Aphrodite (aphros, "foam"), called by the Romans Venus, was the goddess of desire and fertility. Her cult probably came from the cult of other similar goddesses of the Near East, especially Astarte or Ishtar. Other important gods and goddesses were Hestia (of the hearth), Dionysus (the vine god representing the wild side of human nature), Hades (of the underworld) and Poseidon (of the sea).

therefore they are able to convey the truth. The power of Greek myth is so great that it has remained the means through which artists, dramatists, and musicians have explored the meaning of God and nature until very recently. Only in the 20th century did the word "myth" become ill-used and corrupted (mainly by politicians and journalists) to mean the same as "false", and in that corruption, humans have done to their imagination exactly what Kronos did to Ouranos.

But for all the power of myth in human imagination, enabling it to explore worlds that remain otherwise inaccessible, the Jewish understanding of God and creation is entirely different. There is no theogony, no birth of God or the gods. God does not emerge from a pre-existing universe or chaos, but is the source and origin of everything that exists. There are several different creation stories in the Bible, and from these it is clear that the Jews knew of other creation myths and made use of them. But they made use of them to tell an entirely different story, one of the absolute difference between God and all that has been created. Thus in the Psalms (74.12–17, 89.9–13) and Job (ch.41) use is made of the myth of creation emerging out of chaos, but in the Biblical account it is God who takes on chaos and overcomes it to produce orderly life. In Genesis 1.1–2.25, two different accounts have been combined, one with its focus on orderly creation, the other on the creation of humans, but in both God precedes all that has been created and remains independent from it: God does not come to birth or die, does not have sexual desires in order to bring demi-gods into being, and has no need of "other gods" at all. This in part explains the passion with which other gods are so often denounced and derided in the Bible. There *is* no God except God (p.178, 183): there cannot be, since otherwise "God" would be less than the absolute sovereign Lord, the One who produces all things but is not produced from anything, the One who abides and endures even when heaven and earth pass away. No wonder the Psalmist cried out, "O Lord, how manifold are your works! In wisdom you have made them all" (Psalms 104.24). In that case, the question was bound to arise: why is there so much suffering and disorder in the world? That question was asked repeatedly throughout the whole of the Biblical period.

The Sea
The sea was widely regarded as fearsome but inviting. It contains rich resources but it can be violent and destructive. Poseidon, the sea god, was well known for his violent rages but Yahweh conquers the violence and dangers of the sea.

Suffering

Why?

The cause-and-effect explanation of suffering occurs throughout the Bible. It underlies the idea of the covenant, through which the people of Israel expressed their understanding of how, most fundamentally, they were related to God. A covenant depends on promise and threat, the outcome depending on the extent to which the conditions have been observed or broken. That belief was most fully worked out in the book Deuteronomy, and it was then applied to the early history of Israel in the way that the historical books were edited. It is an understanding of God expressed in Psalm 37:

"Do not fret because of the wicked;
do not be envious of wrongdoers,
for they will soon fade like the grass,
and wither like the green herb.
Trust in the Lord, and do good;
so you will live in the land, and
enjoy security.
Take delight in the Lord,
and he will give you the desires
of your heart."

GENESIS 1.31 SAYS "God saw everything that he had made, and indeed, it was very good". Why then is there so much in human experience that is not good? Why do some suffer and others do not? And why, in particular, is it so often the case that the good suffer while the wicked flourish like a bay tree (Psalm 37.35)? The early and common answer was to say that good people do *not* in fact suffer. Suffering shows that they are not good, because only the wicked are punished in this way:

"Tell the innocent how fortunate they are,
for they shall eat the fruit of their labours.
Woe to the guilty! How unfortunate they are,
for what their hands have done shall be done to them"

(Isaiah 3.10f)

Unfortunately, this idea of cause and effect (see box, left) was open to an important objection: it was not true. Even the most casual observation of life makes it clear that the wicked do not get cut off, and that the ruthless frequently prosper:

"The rain it raineth every day
Upon the just and unjust fellas,
But mainly on the just because
The unjust steal the justs' umbrellas"

(Anon)

Why is the distribution of suffering so unequal? Jeremiah raised the question (as did Abraham, Genesis 18.22–33) in almost despairing anger (see especially ch.12). Even more so did Job.

The book of Job is a dialogue between Job, who suffers greatly, and his three friends, Eliphaz, Bildad, and Zophar (and a fourth speaker, Elihu), who try to explain to him the reason for his suffering in classical terms (that suffering is a punishment for sin). The essential point about Job is that he is defined in the Prologue as being absolutely innocent, "a sound and honest man who feared God and shunned evil", and even in the worst of his afflictions he did not waver or cry out against God. That has to be so, since otherwise it would be open to his friends to say – as in fact they do say – that no one is totally innocent, and that all commit some offences that merit punishment from God. But Job is defined, artificially and completely, as innocent, so that the classical solution is ruled out. In the end, God answers Job directly from the storm – if answer is the right word. God simply states that suffering must be set in the context of creation, where it plays its part in the whole purpose of God. And that was how, supremely, Israel came to understand its own suffering. Through trust, and through acceptance of suffering, far greater good can be brought not just to Israel but to the whole world (see box, right). This trust, even in the most grievous suffering, forged the character of Israel as iron in fire:

> *"Though the fig tree does not blossom,*
> *and no fruit is on the vines;*
> *though the produce of the olive fails*
> *and the fields yield no food;*
> *though the flock is cut off from the fold*
> *and there is no herd in the stalls,*
> *yet I will rejoice in the Lord;*
> *I will exult in the God of my salvation.*
> *God, the Lord, is my strength;*
> *he makes my feet like the feet of a deer,*
> *and makes me tread upon the heights"*

(Habakkuk 3.17–19)

This complete trust in God was achieved without any belief that there will be life with God after death. Virtually the whole Bible, with its extraordinary openness to God, was written without any belief that there will be a worthwhile life with God after death (Job 19.25f. is a scene in a court of justice, not of life after death). Yet this did become a possibility at the very end of the Biblical period and thereafter. The martyrs of the Maccabean revolt (2nd century BCE) raised the issue acutely: here were people keeping faith with God, refusing to abandon Torah, yet they were slaughtered. Slowly it began to be realized that God, whom they had come to know so profoundly, will not abandon the faithful but will keep them safe even beyond death. How that will be was a matter of speculation. That it *will* be was not.

> *"Here is my servant, whom*
> *I uphold,*
> *my chosen, in whom my*
> *soul delights;*
> *I have put my spirit upon him;*
> *he will bring forth justice to*
> *the nations...*
> *He will not grow faint or*
> *be crushed*
> *until he has established justice*
> *in the earth..."*

(Isaiah 42.1–4)

Maccabean Martyrs
When the Seleucid Emperor Antiochus Epiphanes ("manifestation", perhaps of God) tried to impose Hellenistic (Greek-style) worship and practices, many Jews resisted and some rebelled. When they were approached by the Seleucid army on the Sabbath, they refused to fight on that day and so were slaughtered.

The Rabbis

Rebuilding Faith and Practice

IN THE YEAR 63BCE, the Roman general Pompey (106–48) entered Jerusalem and soon overcame the resistance in the Temple area. In the Temple itself, he admired the rich adornments, and he entered the Holy of Holies expecting to find the greatest treasure of all. To his great surprise he found it empty of riches and images of God. Here was an understanding of God that set the Godhead far above any human representation, and from this time on, Judaism was a powerful missionary religion in the Roman Empire, attracting young people in particular with its moral view of life and its understanding of God far removed from Greek and Roman myths (p.206). At the same time, however, Palestine came under Roman rule, even though that rule was delegated to others, including the Herods. After 100 years of independence, people had to work out their attitude to Roman authority. Some co-operated, but others rebelled, looking for God to help them by the sending of a Messiah. Two major rebellions ended in disaster, in 70 and 135CE, after which the Temple was destroyed and the Temple site ploughed with salt.

Before the first rebellion, the Sadducees accepted the Roman presence, believing that the Temple was still God's chosen place. Others passionately rejected what was going on in the Temple, and they took off as religious refugees to various places, building alternative temples (as at Leontopolis in Egypt) or establishing communities in remote parts where they could live in the holiness that God had commanded.

One such community was established at Qumran, where the scrolls they wrote and collected expressed this conservative understanding of God. They believed that their Teacher of Righteousness had been sent by God to establish a new covenant, and that they had been chosen by God to be members of this new community not simply by being born as Jews (as under the old covenant) but by making an individual decision. To continue in this way of holiness requires the direct help of God, and they believed that the Holy Spirit had been returned to them to help them walk in the ways of God. They foresaw a great war approaching between the sons of light and the sons of darkness. The "exiles of the desert" would march on Jerusalem and restore in the Temple the true worship that God desired.

Between a compromising Temple and sectarian extremists, a small group looked back to the Torah and asked how its guidance and laws could be brought into effect in the lives of all people, rich or poor, living in Jerusalem or in distant parts of the Roman Empire. By careful teaching and by word of mouth they transmitted their interpretations of Torah to show how, in practice, people could live faithfully in the

Jewish Coins

These two coins come from the time of the 2nd Jewish revolt against Rome under Bar Kochba (132–135). Bar Kochba began to rebuild the Temple, so the top coin shows a lulab *and* ethrog, *used in the Temple festival of Sukkot. The lower (a* tetradrachm *or* shekel), *inscribed Simon, shows the Temple containing the Ark.*

covenant before God: their interpretations were eventually collected in Mishnah and Talmuds (p.201).

These people were the predecessors of the rabbis (teachers), who emerged under that name from the 2nd century onwards. The historian Josephus called them the Pharisees, but the rabbis never referred to their predecessors by that name. They called them the Hakamim, the Wise (p.204). In fact, the rabbis attacked people they called Pharisees ("separatists") as fiercely as Jesus did, and for the same reason, as being people who had lost sight of God by concentrating only on the detail of law. The Hakamim, in contrast, were trying to help all people to offer their lives in holiness to God. Of course the conditions of the covenant were important, but only insofar as they led to life lived as the imitation of God (see box, right).

Even when Jerusalem and the Temple were destroyed, the rabbis showed how Israel could continue to keep faith with God, whose presence (Shekinah) was still among them and whose voice (Bath Qol) was still heard. Supremely, rabbinic Judaism continued to be lived under the command Shema (p.178). At the end of the second revolt against the Romans R. Akiba, the leading rabbi of his day, was arrested and put to death, his flesh ripped from his body with iron rakes. His eyes remained fixed on God and he seemed happy in his sufferings. The Roman commander asked him whether he was using magic. He answered, "No, but all my life I have said the words, 'You shall love the Lord your God with all your heart and with all your soul and with all your strength', and I have felt deeply sad. I have loved God with all my heart and with all my strength, but I did not understand how to love God with all my soul. Now that my soul is demanded and the time for reciting the Shema has come, and I am not wavering as I recite it, should I not laugh for joy?" As he died, he uttered the last word of the Shema, *ehad*, One.

The imitation of God goes back to the Creation account in Genesis which says that humans are made in God's image, and should "walk in all his ways" (Deuteronomy 10.12). R. Hana bar Hinena (3rd century CE) asked:

"How can a person walk in God's ways? What is meant is that one ought to walk according to the attributes of God. Just as the Lord clothed the naked, so you shall clothe the naked (Genesis 3.21). Just as the Lord visits the sick, so you should visit the sick (Genesis 18.1). Just as the Lord comforts mourners, so you shall comfort mourners (Leviticus 16.1). Just as the Lord buries the dead, so you shall bury the dead (Deuteronomy 34.6)"

Roman Triumph
Despite two rebellions and the burning of the Temple, Jews continued to live peacefully in all parts of the Empire, particularly Rome itself.

The Synagogue

Gathering Jewish Communities

The Ark

The Holy Ark was originally a chest that could be carried around, as it had been long ago in the Wilderness, and as it may still be in circumstances that demand it – for example, by chaplains on military service. However, far more often nowadays, the Holy Ark is a large, elaborately carved cabinet, which is often highly decorative, in order to give honour to the holy word of God. It may be covered by a beautifully wrought curtain, the parokhet, *derived from the veil that used to hang in the Jerusalem Temple.*

O NE OF THE MAJOR ACHIEVEMENTS of the rabbis was to develop synagogues as the centre of Jewish life. The word "synagogue" comes from a Greek word meaning "place of assembly", in Hebrew *bet kenesset*. The synagogue plays a crucial part in the Jewish story of God, because it makes it clear, in stone and glass and wood, that belief in God, and living with God, are not matters of individual preference or decision – they are matters that belong to the whole community in any place, just as much as they belong to each family. As a Yiddish proverb puts it:

"If there were only two Jews left in the world, one would be issuing the summons to the synagogue, and the other would be hurrying to attend it"

The synagogue is built primarily as a place where Jews can assemble to worship God and to celebrate the festivals, but it is also the school (perhaps in a separate building, Bet haMidrash), a library, and a place where hospitality can be given to strangers and travellers. Any ten Jews who have reached the age of maturity can form a congregation, a *minyan*. That word means simply "a number", but in effect it means the requisite number of ten.

There is no one style of architecture prescribed for synagogues, and they tend to follow the styles of any prevailing culture. They range from the simple wooden synagogues of Poland to the synagogues of India and China that resemble the local buildings. Wherever there are, they will be turned in the direction of Jerusalem, so that Jews are always facing the place where God established the Holy of Holies (p.191), the point of contact between heaven and earth. They should always have windows, partly to remind those present that they should look constantly to Heaven, and partly to remind them that they should remember the world around them, which also belongs to God. Often the windows will be 12 in number, as a reminder of the 12 tribes of Israel.

Inside the synagogue, the main focus is on the Holy Ark, *Aron Kodesh*, in which the scrolls of Torah are kept. Equally obvious in most synagogues will be the *Bimah*, which is a table on a platform for the Cantor and the person who reads the Torah. When the Temple was destroyed in 135CE, the synagogue took over many of its functions and services, particularly in relation to festivals. Thus the times of the Temple sacrifices became the times of the synagogue services. However, the Jews were warned that, as a sign of mourning for the last Temple, they should not copy anything that had belonged to it. For that reason, the Menorah, the seven-branched candlestick that used to stand in the Temple, may appear in synagogues with six or eight branches and the shield of David (the *Magen*, a six-pointed star that was the device on the shield of King David) in the centre (see also p.218).

The single feature that connects the Temple most closely to the synagogue is the desire of those who come there to draw near to the holiness of God, in worship, joy, penitence, and praise. For this reason, the objects in a synagogue have a ranking in holiness. Holiest of all is the Torah scroll itself, because it contains the name of God. The holiness of other objects depends on how close they are, in use and location, to the scroll of Torah. So, for example, if a particular Holy Ark grows old and falls into disuse, it may not be used to make the bench on which the scroll of Torah is placed; but, conversely, wood from the bench could be "promoted" to construct the Ark.

The synagogue, therefore, draws Jews together to become what they are meant to be, the holy people of God. A traveller to Eastern Europe, just before the Nazis set out to eradicate Jews from the earth, wrote home: "Mystery upon mystery! This is indeed a puzzle. I came to a city and it was empty. I entered the synagogue and it was full." And what were the people doing there? They were engaging in the service and worship of God known as Liturgy.

The Menorah
As a sign of mourning for the last Temple, this Menorah has eight branches and the Shield of David (the original Menorah had seven branches).

Modern Synagogue
The style of architecture for synagogues varies enormously from one country to another. This example, the Beth Yitzchak Synagogue in Jerusalem, is an imposing modern structure.

Liturgy

The Public Worship of God

THE JEWISH STORY OF GOD is told repeatedly through the prayer and worship of liturgy. The word "liturgy" comes from the Greek *leitourgia*, which meant originally any public service or work, but came to mean the public service of the gods, and hence the ordered and public worship of God.

For Jews, this is supremely important. Both in home and synagogue, opportunity is given to recognize God as one who pours out gifts on the world, who forgives and restores those that have gone wrong but have turned back in sorrow, and who continues in the present as in the past "to do mighty works" (*gevurot*). The Jewish liturgical year follows the acts of God in the past and prays for their continuance in the present. In this way, the Jewish liturgy makes central the recital of all that God has done: it focuses on Torah, and from Torah it derives prayers and blessings for every occasion.

God is therefore One who is in a constant and unending interaction with the world, with all people, and especially with the Jews in their vocation to offer themselves in holiness. Where sacrifices had been the outward sign of this in the Temple, prayers have now replaced the sacrifices. Central is the prayer called exactly that: *HaTefillah, The* Prayer. It is also known as *Amidah*, the standing prayer (from *'amadh*, "he stood"). In contrast to Muslims (p.348), Jews rarely kneel or prostrate themselves in prayer (except on the days of New Year and of Atonement): they obey the biblical command that the congregation should stand before God. *HaTefillah*, The Prayer, going back in parts to the 1st century CE, is also known as *Shemoneh Esreh*, Eighteen, because it consisted originally of 18 blessings, although now there are 19. *HaTefillah* varies according to the season and day on which it is said, but in structure it remains the same. It begins with the verse from Psalm 51, "O Lord, open my lips; and my mouth shall show forth your praise", and then moves immediately into that praise of God in the first three blessings (*shevah*). It introduces, and repeats often, the phrase that is so characteristic in the Jewish understanding of God, *Barukh Attah Adonai*, "Blessed are you, O Lord…" It is said that the Jews have a blessing for every occasion of life, even for those that might be regarded as a disaster.

The blessing for the ancestors begins: "Blessed are you, O Lord, our God, and God of our Fathers, God of Abraham, God of Isaac and God of Jacob, the great, the mighty, the awesome, God far beyond, generous in gifts of kindness and goodness, the One who possesses all things, remembers the faithful love of our ancestors, and who out of love rescues

Creation speaks through the poet to the glory of God:

"The One God on earth, the Holy One in Heaven, The mighty One on high: he receives a song from the sea, Praise from the deep, adoration from the lights, Speech from the days, songs from the nights, Fire blazes forth his name, the trees of the forest rejoice, The animals teach the strength of his awe-inspiring deeds"

(Yose ben Yose (4th/5th centuries CE), for the service on the Day of Atonement, Prologue in praise of God)

the generations who succeed them: king, helper, saviour and shield, blessed are you, O Lord." *HaTefillah* continues by acknowledging the God-entrusted competence of human beings to know and to understand: "You enrich each person with knowledge and every person with discrimination. Enrich us from yourself with knowledge, discrimination and discernment. Blessed are you, O Lord, you who enrich us with knowledge." This knowledge leads to a recognition of offence and of the need for forgiveness: "Forgive us, our Father, for we have sinned."

The prayer expresses dependence on God for protection and for healing, and asks for the continuing gifts of God in rain, food, and sustenance. It then prays for the restoration of God's people: "Sound the great Shofar [the horn sounded at the New Year festival] for our freedom: lift up the miracle-working standard to gather our exiles, and bring us together from the four corners of the earth." There is a plea for justice and for the overthrow of the wicked, and for tender mercy to be shown to the good. There is prayer for the restoration and the rebuilding of Jerusalem, and for the renewal of the house of David, followed by a general plea that God will hear and answer requests. The prayer ends with thanksgiving. So shall "everything that lives give thanks and praise your name in truth, O God, our salvation and our help. Blessed are you, O Lord: your name is good, and to you it is right to give thanks."

It is in prayer and liturgy that the Jewish understanding of the nature and character of God becomes most clear. God hears prayer and answers it, but the purpose of prayer is not to gain favours for oneself. It is to give thanks for all that God has given, freely and generously, as much in the past as in the present; and it is, therefore, to call down a blessing on God's name. All of this was expressed in heartfelt poems known as *piyyutim* (sing., *piyyut*). They were composed between the 1st and 18th centuries CE, and were originally intended to replace parts of the liturgy in order to add variety to it. Eventually they were incorporated into the liturgy itself to deepen and reinforce it (for an example, see box, left).

Western Wall
The Western Wall (HaKotel haMaaravi) has at its base stones from an outer wall of Herod's Temple (p.190). Prayers offered at the Wall are offered close to where the Holy of Holies used to be, and are believed to be particularly efficacious. They may be written on slips of paper and left in the Wall.

Kabbalah

God's Contact with the World

YHWH
The four letters
(Tetragrammaton, p.178) of
the name of God are the
large letters on each arm.
The emanations are sent
forth, with Keter, Hokmah,
and Binah *at the top.*

T HE JEWISH UNDERSTANDING of God stresses the holiness of
God, the complete separation of the Godhead from all
that might contaminate or corrupt (pp.188f). God is
utterly transcendent, that is, utterly different from all that has
been created. On the other hand, the Bible attributes to God
far more direct action and control in the world, and many
Jews know a direct contact with God in prayer and worship.
But how can this be? How can the Creator, so removed and
different from Creation, make contact with it?

A tradition began to develop explaining how this contact between the
Creator and the Created is made. The Jewish word for tradition is
qabbalah (p.200), and this word came to be used of this particular
tradition. Central to Kabbalah is a work known as the Zohar (*The Book of
Splendour*, from the word "brightness" in Daniel 12.3), an anthology of
works compiled by Moses of Leon in the 13th century, but thought by
many to be much earlier in origin.

Kabbalah tried to answer the question about God's contact with the
world by accepting that God's own nature and being are uniquely what
they are; indeed, the essential nature of God is so far beyond human
understanding that nothing can be known or said of it. In technical
language, this unknowable essence of God is known as the aseity of God,
from the Latin *a se*, "in himself".

The unknowable aseity of God is called in Kabbalah *En Sof* ("without
limit"), God utterly beyond human comprehension. But according to

THE SEFIROT

Ten manifestations come from En Sof; *the names vary, so a sample is given here:*

✡ **KETER**: The first to emerge is the *Keter*
(crown), the willingness of God to extend effect
from the *En Sof*, the unknowable essence.

✡ **HOKMAH AND BINAH**: The next are
Hokmah and *Binah,* wisdom and discrimination,
the will to create, not as an abstract proposition
but in detail and in particular. Even these are
too close to the divine essence for people to
approach, let alone comprehend.

✡ **HESED, GEVURAH, AND DIN**: From the
emanations of *Hokmah* and *Binah* come first

Hesed (love), then *Gevurah* (power), then *Din*
(judgement).

✡ **TIFERET, NETZAH, AND HOD**: From
Hesed, Gevurah, and *Din* emanate *Tiferet,
Netzah*, and *Hod* (beauty, majesty, and
splendour, exactly those features that give to
many their first realization that God exists).

✡ **YESOD AND MALKHUT**: These emanations
merge into *Yesod,* the foundation of all creation,
culminating in *Malkhut,* sovereignty, through
which God acts to govern the world.

Kabbalah, from the unknowable source come forth ten manifestations, like different rivers from an unknown and unknowable spring. In a sense, all the rivers are made up of the same water as the spring, but the water of the river estuary, while it comes from the spring, is not the same as the spring itself; nor can the nature of the spring be known from the water of the estuary. The water came from the spring, and in that way the spring reaches the sea and yet remains far removed and completely different from it. These emanations are known as the Sefirot (see box, below left), ten manifestations of power, corresponding to the ten words in Genesis through which all things were created.

The Kabbalistic beliefs became elaborated into a vast symbolic map of the relation of all creation to God – a kind of early Sci-fi – except that the fi(ction) is believed to be fact. The map is densely complicated and requires much study to understand it. The Bible is seen as a code to the hidden meanings.

Even so, the purpose of Kabbalah is not simply to solve an intellectual puzzle – how, if God is wholly other and utterly transcendent, can God and humans be in any contact with each other? It is to offer people a universe in their imagination through which they can fight against evil and draw close to God. And since Kabbalah offers that contact with God through the Sefirot, the powers of the Sefirot become available to those with understanding and faith.

The purpose of human life is then to engage in the work of repairing the world and human life within it, so that individuals and the whole world become receptacles, worthy once more to receive the outreach and presence of God. The Hebrew word *berakah* ("blessing") is regarded as a synonym of *beyrakah*, a pool or a receptacle: by making oneself a worthy receptacle, one is filled with the blessing of God.

All this became even more explicit in the work of Isaac Luria (1534–72). Since God is everywhere and everything, he believed that God must have made a contraction (*tsimtsum*) in order to make space for creation. Connection is made through the Sefirot, but the receptacles containing the emanation of light could not bear the weight of glory. Or perhaps they even rebelled against bearing it. In any case, they disintegrated and became contaminated.

Set against this disaster is the work of repair (*tikkun*), the particular responsibility of Adam. When Adam failed, God called the Jews to undertake this work of repair on behalf of the whole world. Jewish history is thus the history of that struggle, and each life is a particular contribution to it. By keeping the law, this work of repair is continued.

By keeping close to God through the Sefirot, the coming of the Messiah is brought nearer.

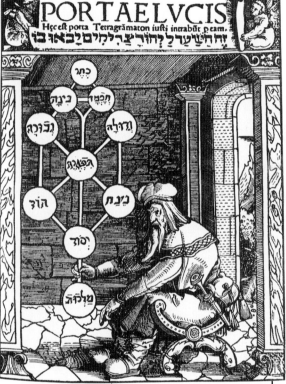

Sefirot
This is the title page of a Latin translation of a Spanish Kabbalist, Joseph Gikatilla. The Sefirot exist in a natural connection to each other, as in the parts of a tree growing from the earth. Because Kabbalah was believed to be the Gateway to Light, it was studied outside Judaism by Christians and others.

Maimonides

Faith and Reason in Harmony

IN ABOUT THE YEAR 1203CE, an old man was leaning exhausted against a wall in Fostat, a small town near Cairo. A scholar, Samuel ibn Tibbon, who was translating one of this man's books, had written to him requesting an interview, and he had replied: "God knows that in order to write this letter to you, I have escaped to a hidden place, where no one would think to find me, sometimes leaning against the wall for support, sometimes lying down because of my great weakness, because I am now old and feeble".

Who was this man, and what had so exhausted him? He was Moses b. Maimon, better known as Rambam, or in a Latin version as Maimonides (1135–1204CE). He was born in Spain, but when a Muslim dynasty, the Almohads, began to persecute those who were not Muslim, his family fled. After many years of wandering, they settled in Fostat, in Egypt.

What had exhausted him was a life of immensely hard work. He was a doctor (Court physician to the Sultan), but he was also a fine philosopher with a profound knowledge of Jewish life and law, who made a decisive contribution to the Jewish story of God. All Jewish life is founded on following the guidance of God in Torah, Mishnah, and Talmud (p.201). So Maimonides made it his major task to write a commentary on Mishnah, and to codify the laws (scattered as they are through so many sources) into his great work, *Mishneh Torah* (the Second Torah).

As a philosopher he was keen to show that the Jewish faith is fully supported by reason, so he also wrote *The Guide for the Perplexed*. Starting from the Bible, Maimonides argued that "the basic principle of all principles and the pillar of all sciences is to realize that there is a first Being who brought every existing thing into being" (*Fundamental Principles 2*). "Because there is One who exists absolutely, all other existence, dependent on that Being, becomes possible. That One Being is God, the life of the universe (*He ha'Olamim*)".

The difference, therefore, between God and ourselves is this: our existence is contingent (we happen to be here, but it is possible that we might not have existed at all) and we are made up of many different bits and pieces (such things as atoms, hair, bones, and skin). But God simply exists (there is no possibility that God might not have existed), and God is not made up of anything at all (God's essence is to be existent).

It is therefore nonsensical to think that we can know what, essentially, makes up, or constitutes, God: "God's existence is absolute, and is not composed of anything. Therefore we can know only the fact that God exists, not what God essentially [in essence] is" (*Guide* 1.59). That means, surely, that we cannot say what God is like. Maimonides agrees. "We cannot say that God is round or tall or wise or strong. We cannot

OPPOSITE:

The Menorah
The Menorah (see also p.213) is first described in Exodus 25.31–8 and 37.17–24. A carving of a seven-branched Menorah can be seen on the Arch of Titus, erected in Rome to celebrate the triumph of Titus in defeating the 1st Jewish revolt. It has not always been a central symbol for Jews, but it became so with the rise of the Zionist movement in the late 19th and 20th centuries.

Silence Before God

"This idea is best expressed in the Book of Psalms: 'Silence is praise to you' [65.2, understanding the Hebrew differently from most English translations]. It is a profound remark on the subject, because whatever we say with the intention of praising and extolling God contains something that cannot be applied to God, and must always be saying of God less than God is. It is therefore better by far to be silent and to be, simply, before God with the intention of your mind, as the Psalm again says: "Ponder upon your beds, and be silent" [Psalm 4.5]"

(*Guide* 1.59)

even say that God exists in addition to being essentially whatever that essence is: God's essence is simply and absolutely to exist."

In technical language, this means that we cannot give to God any positive attributes. That seems ridiculous as soon as you open the Bible, because the Bible is full of statements that attribute things to God: God stands and walks and is wise and strong. Maimonides answers that the Bible is written in simple and pictorial language so that all can begin to understand and approach God through it. He often quoted the statement of the rabbis, "The Torah speaks in the language of ordinary people" (B. Berakoth 31b). Wise people, using reason, realize that this language points to much deeper truth: to say "God stands" means that God is constant and unchanging.

When we attribute things to God, we are really trying to describe the effects that God brings into being in the world, since God can only be known through those effects. But those effects do not mean that God is identical with them, or that the essence of God (the whole essential nature of God) can be known in them. We know that fire may boil or burn or bleach or blacken or make things hard. These effects come from the essence of fire, but fire is not identical with them, nor, by observing them, do we know what that essential nature is. In the same way, human reason "enables a person to sew, to do carpentry, to weave, to build, to study, to understand geometry, and to govern a state", but reason brings these effects into being without the essential nature of reason being contained in any of them; nor do these many different actions describe the simple essence of reason.

This means that human reason cannot know *what* God is. "Human knowledge is limited: as long as the soul dwells in the body, it cannot know what is beyond matter" (*Responsum* to Hasdai haLevi). It follows that "the negative attributes of God are the true attributes" (*Guide* 1.59): we can say what God is not, but we can never say what God is *like*, because that would turn God into an object like any other object, in the very fact that

THE LOVE OF GOD

Maimonides was an eminent philosopher and physician with a profound knowledge of Jewish life and law. He believed that the wise live their lives deepening their love of God.

For Maimonides, the purpose of Jewish life and practice, and the right course for any reasonable person seeking the best way to live, is to draw close to God through Torah, and through worship, prayer, and praise: "Those who serve God out of love, occupy themselves with the study of Torah, keeping of the commandments and walking in the paths of wisdom. They are not driven by any external motive of any kind, being moved neither by fear of disaster, nor by the desire to obtain material benefits. Such people do what is truly right because it is truly right, and, ultimately, happiness comes to them as a result of the way they live." (*Fundamental Principles* 10).

Maimonides and Aristotle
This early illustration shows Maimonides in dialogue with Aristotle and other philosophers. The works of Aristotle had been preserved and used by Muslim philosophers (pp.352–59) writing in Arabic and Persian. Much of their translation into Latin was done in Spain where they were available to Jews, Muslims, and Christians.

the two are being compared: God would be wise *like* us, although God happens to be wiser, strong like us, although stronger.

This all sounds very academic, but it changes the whole way we live before God. It means that the majesty and transcendence of God always lie far beyond our words and ideas. It means also that prayer should never try to capture God in what it says about God, as, for example, when it uses a word like "Almighty", because a word like that brings God within the scope of human ideas and descriptions. To pray is to bring oneself before the majesty of God, lost in wonder, love, and praise (see box, top left).

So revelation and reason make it evident *that* God is, but human reason cannot comprehend *what* God is in essence (essential nature). "I have shown you that the intellect is the link that joins us to God. You have it in your power to strengthen that bond, if you choose to do so, or to weaken it gradually until it breaks if you prefer this. It will only become strong if you employ it in the love of God and seek that love" (*Guide* 3.51). Love is the purpose of life (see box, bottom left).

Maimonides' great achievement was the calm way in which he showed that faith is not opposed to reason, but is in harmony with reason and supported by it. His influence was immense, as much on Christians as on Jews. Among Jews, there were some who rejected what he had done, arguing that Judaism is a way of life and not a philosophy, a matter of practice rather than creed and dogma. But Maimonides has endured, because he showed that faith is rational, and that it is the wise, not the foolish, who live their lives deepening their love of God (see box, right).

"What is the love of God? It is to love the Eternal with a great and exceeding love, so strong that one's soul shall be knit up with the love of God, and one should be continually enraptured by it, like a love-sick individual, whose mind is at no time free from his passion for a particular woman: the thought of her fills his heart at all times, whether sitting down or rising up, whether eating or drinking. Even more intense should be the love of God in the hearts of those who long for God. And this love should continually possess them, even as God commanded us in the sentence "You shall love the Lord your God with all your heart, and with all your soul" [Deuteronomy 6.4]. This Solomon expressed in the sentence, "For I am sick with love" [Song of Songs 2.5]. The entire Song of Songs is indeed an allegory describing this love"

(Fundamental Principles 10)

The Hasidim

The Passionate Loving of God

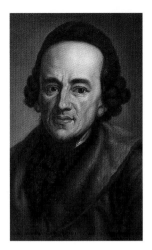

Moses Mendelssohn
Mendelssohn's philosophy was that there is only one God, but many ways of serving God. He believed that different religions should show mutual respect.

The Hasidim on Judgement

Before he died, Rabbi Zusya said,
"In the world to come, they will not ask me, why were you not Moses? They will ask me, why were you not Zusya?"

Rabbi Shneur Zalman once broke off his prayers and said,
"I do not want Your paradise. I do not want Your world to come. I want You, only You, and You only"

Rabbi Elimelekh said,
"When I am judged and asked if I acted, prayed, and studied well, I will have to say, No. The verdict will be, You have told the truth. For the sake of truth, enter the world to come"

MAIMONIDES (pp.218–221) HAD SHOWN that the intellect is the link that joins humans to God. Many others followed his lead, using reason to clarify Jewish belief. Notable were Spinoza (1632–77CE), and Solomon Maimon (1753–1800CE), who once shrewdly observed "God knows what God is", and of whom Kant said that no one understood his ideas as well as Maimon. Both of them were condemned and excommunicated for ideas that challenged or lay outside the boundary of revelation. Others stayed closer to the tradition:

❖ Moses Mendelssohn (1729–86CE) emphasized that while there are different ways of serving God, there can only be one God, and that religions should therefore respect each other (he was the model for Nathan in Lessing's famous play on this theme, *Nathan the Wise*)
❖ Martin Buber (1878–1965CE) drew on the way that early existentialists had emphasized the differences in our ways of relating to each other, either impersonally in I-It relationships, or with personal commitments, including love, of an I-Thou kind, and Buber argued that human relations with God must be of the latter kind
   ❖ Abraham Heschel (1907–72CE) argued that God has particular work for Jews in the long drama of redemption: the laws of Halakah (p.201) are the notes which make possible the music of a great symphony

Maimonides had also emphasized the love of God as paramount, and that led to a new development in the Jewish story of God from the 18th century onwards. This took place among the Hasidim, whose founder was Israel ben Eliezer (1700–60), known as Baal Shem Tov (Master of the Good Name) or, by abbreviation, Besht. The word *hasid* is derived from the same root as *hesed* (p.186), and in the Bible it means roughly "one who is devoted to God". The Hasidim were pupils gathered round inspired leaders known as Zaddikim (sing. *Zaddik*, "the Righteous") who set out to show what a true devotion to God must mean. They aimed to "cleave to God" (Deuteronomy 11.22) in a condition of total, often ecstatic, union known as *devekut* (Hebrew "cleaving"). This was the love of God for God's own sake, not for the sake of reward. The Besht once wondered whether he could ever be worthy to live with God in the world to come. But then he said to himself, "If I love God in this moment, what more could I possibly want?"

The Besht and his successors were much influenced by Kabbalah (p.216) and by the belief that God reaches into the world through Sefirot (emanations). There is, therefore, within each human being, the divine spark, the outpost of God in human life. The purpose of each life is to bring that divine spark into a consuming fire. The Zaddik's job is not to tell others how to do this, but to awaken in them the realization that this is what they can and should do, in their own way. Rabbi Mordecai of Neskhizh said that people go to a Zaddik for many different reasons – some to learn how to pray, others to learn how to study Torah, others to climb a little higher on the spiritual ladder. But they are the wrong reasons: all those ways of approaching God are easy to learn, and when they have been learnt, people think that they have succeeded and that nothing more is needed. In fact, the only true reason for seeking guidance from a Zaddik is to seek God; and to *that* journey there is, in this life, no end. A Zaddik can point people to God but cannot make the journey for them. For this reason, much of the teaching of the Zaddikim is by example or in splendid stories – often subversive – to destroy preconceptions about God that stand in the way of a direct relationship.

Among those preconceptions that get in the way will certainly be orthodox practice and belief if these have lost the spirit and become a matter of observance only. Not surprisingly, the Hasidim were bitterly opposed by the Orthodox (known as the *Mitnaggedim*, the Opponents). But the Hasidim continued to insist that the purpose of religious practice is to come into such a union with God that it permeates the whole of life. The consequence is inevitably an experience of overwhelming joy, indeed of trance (p.41). The Zaddikim are often described as having changed appearance in their prayer, glowing with visible light.

Great emphasis, in prayer, is placed on music, song, and dancing. Through these practices, all connection with the everyday world is banished. The aim of the one who dances in prayer is *bittul haYesh*, "the annihilation of that which is", or the obliteration of the world-anchored self so that only God is left. This is possible because the Divine Nature already lies within human nature: through annihilation of all else that surrounds it, the one is left with the One, and there is no distinction between them.

Other practices (for example, the repetitive and quiet reciting of the Shema, or the continuous chanting of *devekut niggun*, the attachment melody) achieve the same purpose: they cut off connection with the world and other distractions, both inside and outside the person involved, leading to a union of joy with God.

Rabbi Levi Yizhak of Berditchev used to sing a song that began: "Wherever I wander, I find You; whatever I think, I find You: You, only You, You again, always You… Sky is You, earth is You, You above, You below, always You – You, You, You."

Martin Buber
Deeply influenced by the Hasidim (he translated many of their stories), Buber believed that the Bible is the record of Israel's dialogue with God, the Eternal Thou. In that personal engagement with God, Buber did not exclude those of other religions and referred to Jesus as "my brother".

The Holocaust

The Destruction of Jews in Europe

T**HE CONFLICT BETWEEN** the Hasidim and the Mitnaggedim (p.223) was only a concentrated example of a far wider issue in the Jewish story of God. As the prophet Micah had said, "He has told you what is good; and what does the Lord require of you but to do justice, and to love kindness, and to walk humbly with your God?" (6.8).

What in practice does that mean? For the Orthodox, the 613 commands in Torah are the detailed way in which that requirement is to be put into effect: rabbis through the ages have shown how to apply those original commands to the unfolding and changing circumstances of life, so Jews can always "know what is required of them". It is through the appropriation of Torah into their lives that they know the way to walk (the underlying meaning of Halakah, p.201), and have the opportunity to offer themselves in holiness to God (Leviticus 19.2). But other Jews,

Persecution
In the face of the Nazi attempt to rid Europe of Jews (Judenrein) and therefore to destroy men, women, and children alike, the question of why God did nothing obvious to help those who prayed for help became inevitable.

Reform and Liberal, have seen the laws in Torah as a point of departure only, and, in the spirit of Micah's question, have sought to bring, not the laws to changing circumstances, but changing circumstances to the laws, so that the worship and service of God are not isolated in a distant past. There can be no reconciliation between the two extremes: the Orthodox feel that if Jews abandon Torah as unfolded in Halakah, they have abandoned God who entrusted to them this way of service. Others feel that to insist on the smallest detail of every law is to make life impossible for most Jews today.

These different ways of acknowledging God coexist wherever Jews have settled. In Europe, all ways of being Jewish were threatened and then extensively destroyed by the Nazis from 1933 onwards. The *Shoah* ("calamity") or *Hurban* ("destruction"), also known as the Holocaust, called the whole story of God into question.

It came as no surprise to Jews that they, yet again, were "despised and rejected by others, a people of suffering and acquainted with grief" (Isaiah 53.3), or that humans are often vicious and evil in what they do and think. But in the face of a determination to eradicate Jews from the earth (the policy of *Judenrein*), and in the midst of the ghettos and extermination camps where that policy was put into effect, where was God? Why did God not do something to help?

There have been many attempts to tell the story of God after Auschwitz. Some have brought the deep resources and experiences of Jewish history to bear. For example, in this third calamity (the others being the two destructions of the Temple, pp.194, 210), perhaps Hitler, like Cyrus before him, was the agent of an even more glorious restoration than the return after the Exile (p.198), and the establishing of the State of Israel has been regarded in that way.

Some have argued that God "becomes powerless so that history may happen": Israel is indeed the Suffering Servant (Isaiah 53): by accepting suffering, they become a moral challenge to the world to turn from evil and repent.

Others looked at the story of the Exodus and the Wilderness, and observed that God was present in different ways: in the Exodus as a saving presence, and in the Wilderness as a commanding presence. In the camps, God was present, not as a saving presence, but as a commanding one. For Berkowits, this became the 614th commandment: "Thou shalt survive." (see box, right)

But for Jews like R.J. Rubenstein, all this seemed too remote from the magnitude of the disaster and of God's failure to stop it. He concluded that the God of tradition and history was dead. People had once believed that God would intervene if prayed to in the right way, or with sufficient devotion. That God, said Rubenstein, is dead. But God as the focus of Jewish life and renewal is all the more important:

"Judaism is the way in which we share the decisive times and crises of life through the traditions of our inherited community. The need for sharing is not diminished in the time of the death of God. We no longer believe in the God who has the power to annul the tragic necessities of existence; the need to religiously share that existence remains"

Clearly, the story of God cannot continue "after Auschwitz" as though nothing has happened. Nor can the story of humanity be told as though it is making progress, and as though other evils of great magnitude will not happen – since they continue, steadily, to do so. In the Jewish story of God, the experience of God is not diminished, even though it is accepted that explanation is futile. The Orthodox continue

"They are commanded to survive as Jews, lest the Jewish people perish. They are commanded to remember the victims of Auschwitz, lest their memory perish. They are forbidden to despair of man and his world, lest they co-operate in delivering the world over to the forces of Auschwitz. Finally, they are forbidden to despair of the God of Israel, lest Judaism perish"

(Faith After the Holocaust)

God-given Identity
One of the first acts of the Nazis was to dehumanize their victims by taking away their clothes, their hair, and even their names – as the Japanese did with prisoners, calling them maruta, logs of wood. Neither the Japanese nor the Nazis could eradicate the unique identity conferred by God.

OPPOSITE:

Buchenwald
"This is the way in.
The words
Wrought in iron on
the gate:
JEDEM DAS SEINE.
Everybody gets what he
deserves.

The bare drab rubble of
the place.
The dull damp stone.
The rain.
The emptiness.
The human lack.
JEDEM DAS SEINE.
JEDEM DAS SEINE.
Everybody gets what he
deserves...
And it could happen again
And they could hang like
broken carcasses
And they could scream in
terror without light
And they could count the
strokes that split their skin
And they could smoulder
under cigarettes
And they could suffer and
bear every blow
And they could starve and
live for death
And they could live for
hope alone
And it could happen again.
Everybody gets what he
deserves...

This happened near the core
Of a world's culture. This
Occurred among higher
things.
This was a philosophical
conclusion.
Everybody gets what he
deserves.
The bare drab rubble of
the place.
The dull damp stone.
The rain.
The emptiness.
The human lack."

(Bold, pp.33–6)

to offer themselves in holiness to God on behalf of the whole world, and the Hasidim continue to dance and sing because God exists even in the midst of the concentration camps. In 1944, a 14-year old boy called Moshe was brought to Mauthausen. He had been a pupil of the great Hasidic rabbi of Bobov, Ben-Zion Halberstam. One day in December, one of the prisoners was missing. The other prisoners were stripped naked and ordered to assemble on the parade ground: "An hour passed. The naked people began to be covered with a thin layer of white frost; breathing became more and more difficult and people began to fall on the snow like frozen laundry dropping from a clothesline. The search for the missing man continued. The ranks of standing prisoners became sparse, while the rows of bodies on the trodden snow grew longer and longer. Young Moshe tried to move his feet and his hands, but his body no longer responded to his will. He felt that he too was slowly freezing into a pillar of ice, being drawn and pulled to the white snow on the ground beneath him. Suddenly he felt the Rabbi of Bobov supporting him. The rabbi's reassuring voice rang in his ears: 'Don't fall, my young friend, don't stumble! You must survive! A Hasid must sing, a Hasid must dance; it is the secret of our survival!' The rabbi's melody was burning in his head, ringing in his ears, but his frozen lips could not utter a single sound. Then slowly his lips began to move. A note forced its way through the colourless lips. It was followed by another and another, individual notes strung together into the rabbi's niggun, his melody. Like burning coals the tune scorched his lips and set his body aflame. One foot began to move, to free itself from its chains of frost. The ice crackled; one foot began to dance. The other foot tore itself away from the clinging ice. The snow became red as skin from the sole of Moshe's foot remained grafted to the ice. Bones, muscles, and sinews began to step in the snow, to dance to the rabbi's niggun. Moshe's heart warmed up, burning tears streamed down his face as his body and soul sang the Bobov melody.

The Zeilappell was over. The Mauthausen camp square was strewn with scores of bodies. But Moshe's red footprints burned the white snow with the glow of a Bobov melody" (Eliach, pp.219f).

Moshe survived to become a rabbi in New York. That is not "an answer". It is a realization, renewed in every generation, that this part of the Jewish story of God remains, for many Jews, forever true:

"But now thus says the Lord, he who created you, O Jacob, he who formed you, O Israel: do not fear, for I have redeemed you; I have called you by name, you are mine. When you pass through the waters, I will be with you; and through the rivers, they shall not overwhelm you; when you walk through fire you shall not be burned, and the flame shall not consume you. For I am the Lord your God, the Holy One of Israel, your saviour"

(Isaiah 43.1–3)

CHRISTIANITY

CHRISTIANITY BEGAN IN THE LIFE, ministry, death, resurrection, and ascension of Jesus, a Jewish man whom Christians believe to be the Son of God; but its roots lie further back in Judaism, with Christianity understanding itself as the New Covenant (or Testament) in relation to the Old. The New Testament writers recognize that God was speaking and acting in Jesus through his teaching, forgiveness of sins, and healing, and is offering the same salvation to all – hence the spread of Christianity throughout the world.

At first, Christianity was a small movement, confident because of its experience of God as Holy Spirit and its trust in Christ's resurrection. After the reign of Emperor Constantine (c.274–337), it became the religion of the Roman Empire, inheriting much from the Romans. This absorption is characteristic of Christianity wherever it has spread. In the early Church, the Body of Christ was a metaphor of many equal parts under one Head, but the metaphor changed to one of the Roman army, with strong authority and command, ending up, in Roman Catholicism, with a Pope as head of the Church. Other forms of Christianity, such as Presbyterianism and Congregationalism, tried to retain the earlier democratic model of the Body.

Christians have never agreed on faith and practice. In the early centuries, councils established creeds as passwords (minimal statements of true belief). But major divisions appeared, especially between Western and Eastern (or Orthodox) Christianity. Orthodox Christianity is made up principally of the Greek and Russian Churches. Western Christianity was

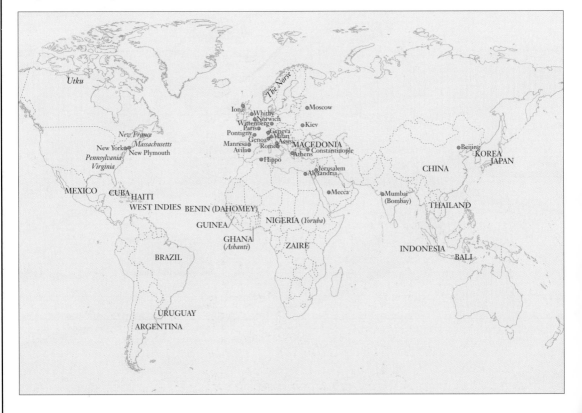

divided in the Reformation (pp.290–91), and the Reformed Churches have continued to divide, leading to such Churches as Lutheran, Baptist, and Methodist.

Monastic and religious orders have concentrated on God in prayer. The worship of God led to churches becoming centres of music, art, and architecture. The quest for holiness, and the desire to be "in touch" with holy things, made pilgrimage to shrines and relics popular. Preserving ancient learning led to schools and universities being established.

Commitment to the poor has brought education and healthcare to the world, in response to the only criterion of judgement: "Inasmuch as you have done it to the least of one of these, you have done it to me" (Matthew 25.40).

CHRISTIANITY TIMELINE

Crucifixion
The crucifixion of Jesus is not simply an event in the past: as the point of reconciliation with God, it enters every Christian life in the present, as in this painting (see p.284).

Plato • Euhemerus • Aristotle • Augustus & Virgil	400–0
Jesus • Paul • Completion of NT • Irenaeus • Athenagoras • Clement of Alexandria • Plotinus	0–250
Antony & Desert Fathers • Arius • Athanasius • Sabellius • Council of Nicaea • Cappadocian Fathers (Gregory & Basil) • Hesychastic prayer begins • Augustine • Council of Chalcedon • 1st church of San Clemente • Ps.-Dionysius	250–500
Cathedral of St Denis • Benedict • Iona founded: Celtic Christianity • Romanos & Kontakia • John Climacus	500–750
Iconoclastic controversies • 2nd Council of Nicaea • Vladimir of Kiev	750–1000
Council of Constantinople; East/West schism • Suger • Bernard of Clairvaux • Dominic • Francis	1000–1250
Aquinas • Dante • Eckhart • Giotto • English mystics • Gregory Palamas • Hesychastic controversy • Wycliffe • Botticelli & Grünewald • Erasmus • Luther & Calvin	1250–1500
Cranach • Teresa & John of the Cross • Ignatius & the Jesuits • The Metaphysicals • Puritans • Ricci & Valignano • Edict of Nantes • Calderon • Bradford & the Pilgrim Fathers • Pascal • John Bunyan • Penn & Quaker Settlements • Bach • Handel	1500–1750
John & Charles Wesley • Rites Controversy • Seraphim of Sarov • Wilberforce & abolition of slavery • Hegel • Wordsworth • Strauss • Kierkegaard • Dostoevsky • Hopkins • Rilke • Barth • Bonhoeffer • Process Theology • Taizé • Liberation Theology • Eliot, Auden, & Thomas • Martin Luther King	1750– PRESENT

The Background

The Worlds of Greece and Rome

The School of Athens
In Raphael's School of Athens *(fresco in the Vatican, 1509–11), Plato, pointing upwards to the Idea of the Good, stands next to Aristotle, who points down to the earth and natural phenomena. Beside Aristotle are such figures as Ptolemy and Euclid. Much Greek learning and philosophy was preserved by Muslims.*

I F YOU HAD ATTENDED THE EQUIVALENT of a university lecture in Athens during the 4th century BCE, you might well have passed through a door above which were inscribed the words, "Let no one enter here who is ignorant of mathematics". The door led into the Academy of Plato, to whose work A.N. Whitehead (see p.317) once claimed that all subsequent Western philosophy had been written as a footnote. Certainly Plato, along with his most famous pupil Aristotle, had a massive effect on the story of God as it came to be told in the three Semitic religions – Judaism, Christianity, and Islam – even though it is not clear exactly what Plato and Aristotle themselves believed about God.

What Plato certainly did believe is that the true philosopher can come to understand the "Form of the Good" as the greatest object of learning.

The "Form", or "Idea", of the Good exists far beyond particular instances of the good, the beautiful, or the true, because any particular examples can come and go, and in our human experience of them they are entangled in much that is evil, ugly, or false. Particular instances that we encounter are not eternal or ideal, and are therefore pale shadows of the ultimately good, real, and true.

Nevertheless, the beautiful can be discerned even in the midst of the ugliness and confusion of the world. Plato's great teacher, Socrates, was physically ugly, but within him could be seen great grace and truth. The point of life, or at least of the true philosopher, is to ascend from the ugly and the untrue to "the whole ocean of the beautiful".

Can we be sure that the ideal Form of the Good actually exists? Plato believed it does because it endures even when the contingent accidents (the particular circumstances) in which it is discerned – "in the order of the world around us and of the stars above us" – change or even disappear. We can discern it also within ourselves: our physical bodies come into being and pass away in death; they are always changing and are never perfect; nevertheless, there is within us that which does not change and which gives us our true identity, or permanent form, even in the midst of frailty, change, and death; and that is the soul.

Truth unaffected by time, the permanent and unchanging stability that lies behind all things and allows them to exist at all, was demonstrated for Plato particularly in mathematics. One apple or another may come and go, but one apple added to another always results in two.

So Plato argued that the Form of the Good exists quite apart from our perceptions of its manifestations, tangled up as they always are with the corrupt and the confused. The proper object of knowledge is not the transient object that appears before us, but the independent idea of what it is that enables us to identify it and say what it is an example of – a goat, for example, or a sheep. If we did not have some idea of what a sheep is we could never pick out examples of one. The Form of the Good enables the universe to exist but it remains completely separate from it: the sun causes cabbages to grow but does not create them.

Plato believed that there is a controller or demiurge able to bring into being in transient appearances souls that are expressions of the Form of the Good. The demiurge is like the master player of a game who uses the limited moves made by lesser players (for example, human beings) to bring the game to a wise conclusion. But is that demiurge God? Plato criticized the conventional gods of the Greeks: the pantheon dwelling on Olympus of whom entertaining but often scandalous stories were told (p.206). If that demiurge, bringing the Form of the Good to bear on the world, is God, it is God kept far (to avoid contamination) from the world in which the corruption of good is all too evident.

Aristotle's belief that truth exists in a proper understanding of nature (see caption, right) leads inevitably back to the source of nature, the beginning, or *arche* (p.246), of all things. This is the perfect knowledge

Aristotle
One of Plato's pupils was Aristotle, who admired his teacher but moved away from him in decisive ways. Aristotle thought that Plato was wrong in placing the ultimately true and good outside the world in which we live. In his view, truth must begin and end in a proper understanding of nature.

San Clemente
The basilica of San Clemente is built in layers: at the base is a temple of Mithras, whose altar is seen here. Above this, the first Christian church was built in the 4th century; above the ruins of this was built a new church in 1108; this was rebuilt in the 18th century. All these layers can still be seen and visited.

"If God is always in that good state in which we sometimes are, this compels our wonder; and if in a better state, this compels it yet more. And God is in a better state. And life also belongs to God; for the actuality of thought is life, and God is that actuality; and God's essential actuality is life most good and eternal. We say therefore that God is a living being, eternal, most good, so that life and duration continuous and eternal belong to God; for this is God"

(*Metaphysics* 12.1072b 12–29)

and understanding of why all things are as they are and of how and why they exist. All things have their own characteristic form – not the Form of the Good as Plato understood it, lying outside the world, but the form that makes each object characteristically what it is: particular sheep may come and go, but there is a characteristic form of sheep which is made up in part of their organized shape, but in part also of their purpose, what they are for. The form or soul of a knife is that it is made of metal in such a way that it has a sharp edge that is used for cutting. The form or soul of humans is that they have intelligence (*nous*) and that they use it to attain God.

For Aristotle, that meant that humans have a deep desire to know and understand truth. In searching for truth, they are participating in God, since God is the perfection of understanding that is called in Greek *nous* (intellect, intelligence). To aspire to God is to aspire to understanding.

All things, according to Aristotle, are striving, in a constant process of change, to attain the goal that belongs to their own nature. The goal of humans is to ascend through their knowledge of nature to the source and origin of all nature – to that pure act-and-being which enables all other acts and beings to exist. All other entities have something defective about them, not least in the sense that they are contingent: they happen to exist, but they might not have done so. Aristotle believed that the human soul overcomes contingency, even the defect of death, because it participates in that complete intelligence and truth which is God (*nous*).

That participation comes into the contemplation of complete truth, the state that God is always in, since *nous*, total intelligence, is always contemplating that which is the total truth (see box, left).

Intelligible truth or *nous* is the abiding source of all that is. Worlds may come and go, but this abides. In this way, God was regarded by Aristotle as the unmoved mover from whom (or which) all things derive their being, and to whom (or which) humans, if they are wise, strive to return, rising through their use of intelligence from the world of contingency to the source of all being. Reason, or Logos, is so much the supreme characteristic that the Stoics were later to speak of it as the seed sown by God within us (*spermatikos logos*) which, if we nurture it, will bring us naturally to the goal.

In the accounts of God given by Plato and Aristotle, the understanding of God is not developed, and many read them, now as in the past, in ways that leave "God" as a kind of shorthand for what is ultimately real and true. But in the centuries that immediately followed them, there were many who

THE ROMAN EMPIRE

The religious and philosophical world of the early Roman Empire was particularly varied:

✝ **PHILOSOPHIES**: Among philosophies there were Sceptics, Epicureans, Stoics, and Cynics. Cynics (from Greek *kunikos*, dog-like) were so called because they lived with a freedom from social convention not unlike that of dogs: they did not wash, dressed, if at all, in rags, had no possessions, saw no difference between yours and mine, public and private, raw and cooked.

✝ **RELIGIONS**: Among religions were mystery religions, which claimed to hold the secret (Greek, *musterion*) to salvation: they often coalesced round a Saviour, such as Isis and Osiris, or Mithras, who overcomes death, often in enacted form, by dying and rising again.

✝ **EMPEROR WORSHIP**: In the Roman Empire, loyalty to the Emperor was increasingly expressed by regarding him as the embodiment of all the gods who had hitherto ensured the success of Rome. The poet Virgil (cf. p.271) greeted the first emperor Augustus as the beginning of a splendid New Age.

sought to interpret them in ways that endorsed the human senses of God in worship and prayer. The Neoplatonists (i.e., the new Platonists, especially Plotinus, c.205–70) made a kind of fusion of Aristotle with Plato, emphasizing the striving for truth and the escape from evil and ignorance, and accepting that the ultimately true, the source of all being and the goal of the human quest, cannot be compromised in the frailty and contingency of this world. They produced a picture of the One who is absolutely transcendent and removed from this world. From the One emanates a hierarchy, or chain of being, each member of which participates in its immediate source and then gives rise to the next in succession. From this chain of being eventually arises the created world. The goal or purpose of life is then to work one's way back up the chain of being, or the ladder of perfection, until one returns to the One; and this, in Plotinus' famous phrase, is the flight of the alone to the Alone.

Much of that general understanding appears in other systems of thought. Gnosticism (from the Greek *gnosis*, "knowledge") is a term given to many that share certain characteristics. Some are philosophical, others mythological, others claim to be revealed by a Biblical figure or by Jesus. In general, Gnostic movements, from about the 1st century CE onwards, claimed to have preserved knowledge, or teaching, that is the key to salvation. A key text or teacher offers the knowledge or the wisdom (and Sofia, pp.204–5, is often the key figure) that will enable the wise or spirit-filled person to escape from this world and return to God.

As with Neoplatonism, the supreme Divine Being has not got entangled in the creating or the running of this world; that has been the work of an inferior demiurge who was powerful enough to create but not wise enough to see the limitations of what he was doing – hence the imperfections of the world and of this life, from which Gnosticism offers an escape. Among the dramatically diverse religions of the early Roman Empire, a man began to write letters giving news of yet another development in this varied religious world.

Augustus
Romans believed that the help of their gods was essential. Julius Caesar was associated with the gods, but after Augustus (27BCE–14CE) established the Empire, the emperors were believed to be gods. Virgil described in a famous poem (eclogue) the yearning for the coming of God: "The jarring nations he in peace will bind/ And with paternal virtues rule mankind."

Paul

Good News for the World

Saul's Conversion
Saul, as a Jew, engaged in Merkabah mysticism, in which visions were seen. On the road to Damascus, he was certain that Jesus was speaking directly to him (see Bowker, 1971).

SOME TIME JUST BEFORE or during the reign of the Roman Emperor Nero (54–68CE), a man in prison wrote a letter to his friends in Philippi, a Roman colony in Macedonia, making an appeal to them (see box, left). That amazing statement was written by Paul, a well-educated Jew who had come to believe that a man called Jesus was the promised Messiah or, in Greek, Christ – and it was for that belief that he was in prison. When Paul wrote those words, Jesus had been executed as a criminal on a cross only 20 or 30 years earlier – perhaps even less, because it looks as though that passage is a hymn that Paul was quoting. So within a few years of that abject death, people were already associating Jesus with God so closely that the adoration and worship due to God are due also to Jesus.

What is so extraordinary and stunning is that they and Paul, even though they believed that Jesus is Christ and Lord, continued to use his ordinary, human name. From the start of the Christian story, people knew that Jesus was not a mythological figure in some Gnostic system (p.233), nor was he a dying and rising God in a mystery religion (p.233): he was a man who had lived in Galilee and had died outside Jerusalem, and they continued to call him by his ordinary human name, Jesus.

From the very start, therefore, they knew that this human Jesus had brought God into their midst, and had done for them what they believed only God could do, above all in healing the ills of their bodies and minds. Paul made the even more astonishing claim that those who have been baptized have been transferred into Christ and with him have overcome

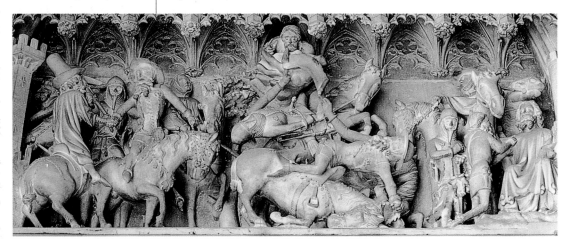

death. In some sense, they are made a part of him, as his body: where Christ is, in association with God, there they also are by their being taken into him, much as an abandoned child is made safe by being taken into a home and made part of the family (see box, right). The strong language of incorporation can also be found in Romans 16.7; I Corinthians 12.13; 15.22; 2 Corinthians 5.17; and Philippians 3.8f. The language of union between Christ and believers is equally strong in the Gospel according to John, but that was written later.

In Romans 8, the claims have gone even further: Jesus is the Son of God who was sent to deal with the destructive power of sin and death. Paul repeatedly claims that the death of Jesus on the cross was the decisive act that has brought the world and all people back into a healed relationship with God. What Paul and other New Testament writers realized (because they knew it from their own experience) was that just as Jesus had healed people whom he met and had forgiven their sins (very much the act of God), so, through the cross, that healing and forgiveness had been made universal: it is not just for a few in Galilee, but for all. They could say that with confidence, because they knew that death had not been the end of Jesus: they knew (again because for many of them it was a matter of their own experience) that in some way Jesus was as certainly alive after death as he had, most certainly, died. As a result, this man who had lived among them is the one who brings God to the world and the world to God in a new way of reconciliation and friendship:

"We declare to you what was from the beginning, what we have heard, what we have seen with our eyes, what we have looked at and touched with our hands, concerning the word of life – this life was revealed, and we have seen it and testify to it, and declare to you the eternal life that was with the Father but was revealed to us – we declare to you what we have seen and heard so that you also may have fellowship with us; and truly our fellowship is with the Father and with his Son Jesus Christ

(1 John 1.1–3)

These claims were not added on at a later date by people who were trying, like Euhemerus (pp.154f), to turn a simple teacher into God. The highest claims about Jesus are the earliest in the New Testament. Not surprisingly people began to ask, who was this Jesus, and why did he die? And for that reason, the Gospels were written.

"There is therefore now no condemnation for those who are in Christ Jesus. For the law of the Spirit of Life in Christ Jesus has set you free from the law of sin and death. For God has done what the law, weakened by the flesh, could not do: by sending his own Son…"

(Romans 8.1–3)

The Cross
The crucifixion became, as Paul put it, "a stumbling block to Jews and foolishness to Gentiles" (I Corinthians 1.23), because it was a criminal's death. Grünewald (c.1475–1530) brings home the hideous pain of this death in this painting, completed in 1501.

Jesus

Son of Man, Son of God

NOT ONLY PAUL, BUT ALSO OTHER NEW TESTAMENT WRITERS, linked Jesus with God so closely that, although they recognized a distinction between them (expressed in the language of that time as Father and Son), they also realized that in and through the human person of Jesus, God had acted decisively in the world:

*"In the beginning was the Word [Logos, p.232], and the
Word was with God, and the Word was God…
And the Word became flesh and lived among us, and
we have seen his glory, the glory as of the Father's only
Son, full of grace and truth"*

(John 1.1,14)

*"Blessed be the God and Father
of our Lord Jesus Christ, who
has blessed us in Christ with
every spiritual blessing in the
heavenly places, just as he chose
us in Christ before the
foundation of the world to be
holy and blameless before him in
love. He destined us for adoption
as his children through Jesus
Christ, according to the good
pleasure of his will, to the praise
of his glorious grace that he
freely bestowed on us in
the Beloved"*

(Ephesians 3.3–10)

With the same recognition of God in Christ, Paul wrote: "He is the image of the invisible God, the first-born of all creation; for in him all things in heaven and on earth were created, things visible and invisible, whether thrones or dominions or rulers or powers – all things have been created through him and for him. He himself is before things, and in him all things hold together…. For in him all the fullness of God was pleased to dwell, and through him God was pleased to reconcile to himself all things, whether on earth or in heaven, by making peace through the blood of his cross" (Colossians 1.15–20). These and other passages like them (see box, left) were written of a man who had lived among them and whose human name, Jesus, they continued to use. And yet he had died as a criminal executed on a cross. Why?

The Gospels were written (later than Paul but using earlier traditions) at least in part to answer that question. Although not full biographies in the modern sense, they resemble the style of some "lives" (*bioi*) of the ancient world. They are accounts of the last days of Jesus and of his death (Passion narratives), preceded by brief accounts of his ministry and teaching.

*"Long ago God spoke to our
ancestors in many and various
ways by the prophets, but in
these last days he has spoken to
us by a Son, whom he appointed
heir of all things, through whom
he also created the worlds. He is
the reflection of God's glory and
the exact imprint of God's very
being, and he sustains all things
by his powerful word"*

(Hebrews 1.1–3)

Three of the Gospels (those according to Matthew, Mark, and Luke, known as the Synoptics) are related to each other; the Fourth Gospel (the Gospel according to John) draws on different traditions, but is in the same pattern. The Gospel writers, even when they were quoting each other or the same sources, made no attempt to report the words or deeds of Jesus in an exactly identical way, but used the material to show why Jesus remains decisively important, and why those high claims about Jesus

Jesus and Caiaphas
This Byzantine book illumination shows Jesus brought before the High Priest, the highest authority among Jews at that time. This was not a trial but an investigation to see whether he accepted that authority or whether he would continue to "threaten the Temple".

are rightly made about this man who had lived among them: they are justified by what he taught, who he was, and even how he died.

The life and ministry of Jesus were formed by his conviction that God, whom he addressed as Father (in Aramaic, *Abba*, not an informal word like Daddy, but a term of respectful affection), was present to the world and at work through him. This was tested in the temptations (Matthew 4.1–11, Luke 4.1–13) and confirmed in his baptism by John (Matthew 3.13–17; Mark 1.9–11; Luke 3.21f; John 1.32–4). He insisted, often in lively stories or parables drawn from familiar, everyday life, that the activity of God (the kingdom of God or of Heaven) is truly at work, here and now. He also looked to its completion in the future, so that his teaching talks of the kingdom in both the present and the future.

The kingdom as Jesus taught and lived it demands a complete revolution in received attitudes, welcoming all as the children of God, especially those in need. Asked to identify the greatest command in Torah (p.200), Jesus replied, "Love God wholeheartedly, and love your neighbour as yourself" (Matthew 22.34–8; Mark 12.28–31; Luke 10.25–8). To the question, "And who *is* my neighbour?" Jesus gave a searching and demanding answer (Luke 10.29–37).

The meaning of that kingdom was not just taught: it was enacted, in the healing of those who were sick and in the forgiveness of those who were estranged from God and from each other. It was obvious to those who encountered this that the power (in Greek, *dunamis*, as in the English words dynamic or dynamite) of God was at work in the world. But how could this be? They knew that Jesus was one of themselves (see box, top right). From the answer to the three Greek words of that question (*pothen touto tauta*, lit., "whence to this man these things?") Christianity begins. Jesus insisted that the words and works of power came, not from himself, but from God. It was not as a special figure that he did those things – he was not an angel or a prophet or a Messiah: he called himself, quite simply, the son of man (see box, below). That was dramatically new and different teaching. But was it true? According to the Book of Deuteronomy 17.8–13, disputed or contested claims could

THE SON OF MAN

What did Jesus mean by referring to himself in this way?

This phrase was not a title. It was the way in which Jesus insisted that he was in every way human. In what was then becoming the Bible, it has two main meanings: in Psalms and Job it means a mortal human being, one who has to die. But in Daniel 7, the Son of Man represents the faithful who, after persecution, are vindicated by God beyond death. By calling himself "the son of man", Jesus meant that he spoke and did all these powerful things, not as a special creation on the part of God, but as one who, like all human beings, has to die, but as one who will be vindicated by God after death.

be resolved only by the highest authority of the time: at the time of Jesus, that was the high priest in Jerusalem. That is why Jesus insisted that he must go to Jerusalem: all the Gospels use the strongest possible Greek word (*dei*, it is necessary) of Jesus' perception that the son of man must suffer, and Matthew 16.21 adds that he *must* (*dei*) go to Jerusalem for this to happen.

When Jesus arrived there, he was challenged and tested on many key teaching issues until eventually he was brought to the high priest – not in a formal trial, but in an investigation. The issue was profoundly serious, because Deuteronomy requires that anyone who refuses to accept the judgement of the highest authority must be executed (17.12f). When Jesus was accused of threatening the Temple (Matthew 26.61; Mark 14.58) he remained silent. His teaching about the Kingdom and his part in it could be seen as a threat to Temple authority: but perhaps the private teaching could be justified because he was a prophet, directly inspired by God? They tried to test him, but Jesus again remained silent (Matthew 26.67; Mark 14.65; Luke 22.63–5); and for that reason he was handed over to the Romans for execution.

The cross demonstrated the truth of Jesus' claim that he was the son of man, the one who must die like all others. But what of the other biblical sense of that phrase in Daniel, the Son of Man (see box, left) who was vindicated beyond death? On the cross it seemed untrue: he cried, "My God, my God, why have you forsaken me?" (Matthew 27.46; Mark 15.34).

And yet, on the morning of the third day after his crucifixion, his disciples – the women first, who had not deserted him at the time of his crucifixion – became convinced that he was alive. The stories they told of how they encountered him reveal graphically the chaos and confusion it caused them. They knew that he had died, and yet they knew with equal certainty that in a real way he was now alive. It was so totally unexpected that they failed initially to recognize him, or to believe that it could possibly be true. He who came to them as they worked by a lake, or walked with them, was unmistakably Jesus, and yet the form in which he appeared to them was not exactly like a human body. It was the first step towards a new domain of life beyond death, into which Jesus invited them and others to enter. That is why Paul defined Christians as those who are already dead: "You are already dead, and your life is hidden with Christ in God" (Colossians 3.3). Christians are those who already live on the other side of death, and that is why, according to Jesus, they should live with a kind of reckless generosity to those around them: "Take therefore no thought for the morrow" (Matthew 6.34). Through the enacted sign of baptism they are brought into the risen body of Christ, and through the eucharist (the command of Christ at his last supper that they should take the bread as his body and the wine as the sign of the new covenant), they are kept in communion with Christ whose life becomes theirs.

"They said, 'Where did this man get all this? What is this wisdom that has been given to him? What deeds of power are being done by his hands! Is not this the carpenter, the son of Mary and brother of James and Joses and Judas and Simon, and are not his sisters here with us?'"

(Mark 6.2f)

Jesus Condemned
It was for his silent refusal to acknowledge the authority of the Temple that, according to Deuteronomy, Jesus had to be executed. There was no need of further witnesses (Mark 14.63) when Jesus agreed with the High Priest that he was "the Messiah, the son of the Blessed One", but not at all as the High Priest understood it – only in terms of the son of man (Matthew 26.64; Mark 14.62).

The New Testament

A Covenant With All Peoples

PAUL WAS TIRELESS IN SHARING with others his vision of God at work in Christ. When he preached in Athens, some Epicurean and Stoic philosophers (p.233; see caption, left) asked him, "May we know what this new teaching is that you are presenting?" (Acts 17.19).

It may have sounded new to the philosophers, because New Testament writers rarely expressed their ideas in philosophical terms (that was to come later). But it was not new to the Jewish people. The understanding of God in the New Testament is fundamentally that of the covenant people, the Jews, whom God had called into special obedience and service on behalf of the whole world. They in turn offered themselves in holiness to God (pp.188–9), with laws to help and guide them. The New Testament writers believed that God had now extended that covenant to include, on the basis of faith, non-Jews (Gentiles) as well: the vocation to holiness remained, but the laws were neither a necessary nor a sufficient condition of holiness.

The way, therefore, that God is portrayed in the New Testament is very like that of Jewish scripture. God is faithful, wise, and true; God is merciful and just, even in anger; God is the God of peace, of hope, of comfort, and of love. Above all, God seeks to bring healing and redemption to the whole world. It is never questioned or doubted that there is only one who is truly God (pp.178–9). Other so-called gods are foolish and dangerous inventions: to eat food offered to idols is to sit down at a meal prepared with poison. And yet, without compromising that absolute sovereignty and uniqueness of God, Jesus is related to God in an equally unique way. Particularly striking is the way that the New Testament writers claimed the Jewish Bible for Jesus, seeing him as the fulfilment of the purpose of God from the moment of creation onwards, as well as the fulfilment of specific texts. They did this sometimes without any reference to the original meaning of the text. Thus Matthew 1.23 quotes a text that referred originally to the birth of a royal child and may in the Hebrew have had no reference to a virginal conception, and 2.15 quotes a passage from Hosea that referred originally to the Exodus. But the point is not whether the New Testament writers imposed their own meaning on texts in the past, which at times they clearly did, but rather that in this way they could emphasize how exactly Jesus, in his life, death, and resurrection, was the continuation and fulfilment of the purpose of God throughout the whole Biblical period (see box, right).

But how can Jesus be so closely related to God and yet still be so unequivocally human? Seeing the relationship as one of Father and Son

Paul at Athens
This stained glass window depicts Paul preaching in Athens (Acts 17.22–34). He said: "Athenians, I see how extremely religious you are in every way. For as I went through the city and looked carefully at the objects of your worship, I found among them an altar with the inscription, 'To an unknown god'. What you worship as unknown, this I proclaim to you."

(as Jesus did himself) expressed the dynamic nature of that relationship. The New Testament also continues the Biblical portrayal of God present to people in the world as Holy Spirit: the Holy Spirit is God present to particular people inspiring and changing them in many ways. The word "spirit" meant originally "breath", and hence it came to express the way in which God breathes into and thus inspires (the Latin *inspiro* means "I breathe into") such people as prophets. The Jews believed that the Holy Spirit had been withdrawn, as part of the punishment, at the time of the Exile. But Christians believed that the Holy Spirit had been present to the life of Jesus and was continuing to inspire and change their own lives with gifts of love, joy, peace, patience, kindness, generosity, faithfulness, gentleness, and self-control (Galatians 5.22).

All this left two major questions:

❖ How can the nature of God and human nature be combined in the one person of Jesus? That is the question of Christology

❖ How can God be absolutely and uniquely one and yet be Father, Son, and Holy Spirit? That is the question of the Trinity, of what has to be said about the inner nature of God if justice is to be done to the evidence of Jesus and the Holy Spirit recorded in the New Testament

Those were to be major questions in the future. From the outset, it was the person of Christ, much more even than his teaching, that made the Christian story of God take off in such a radically new way. Far more than that, it remains the reason why Christians find their access to God in and through the risen and ascended Christ, as this prayer of devotion makes clear:

"Jesus, may all that is you flow into me.
May your body and blood unite me to yourself,
May your passion and death be my strength and life.
Jesus, with you by my side enough has been given.
May the shelter I seek be the shadow of your cross.
Let me not run from the love which you offer,
But hold me safe from the forces of evil.
On each of my dyings shed your light and your love.
Keep calling to me until that day comes,
When, with your saints, I may praise you for ever"

"It is on Jesus, as on no other figure in Jewish myth or history, that his followers found converging all the ideal qualities of a collective body of persons in a right relation with God; and if Paul speaks of the Church as the body of Christ (or as a body because incorporated in Christ [p.235]), that is partly because he has found in Christ all that the people of God were designed to be"

(Moule, p.131)

Last Supper
In his last supper with his disciples, Jesus pledged that even after his death he would be with them, "even to the end of the world". This pledge becomes true as often as his followers are united with him in his body and receive his blood as the sign of an entirely new covenant with God.

The Person of Christ

How Is Jesus Related to God?

Incarnation

The incarnation (Latin in carne, "in the body") means that Jesus was born at a particular moment of history in a particular family. But the effect of his life, death, and resurrection is offered to all people in all places. The story of Jesus is told in local ways, as in this Chinese painting, while the truth of the story remains universal.

IN ABOUT THE YEAR 318CE, the Bishop of Alexandria, Alexander, called his clergy together and gave them a lecture on God – or, more specifically, on the unity that exists in the Trinity in which all Three Persons are equally God. A presbyter present disagreed so profoundly with the Bishop that he stood up and said so:

"If we say that Jesus is the Son of the Father, it means that he was brought into being [begotten] at some point in time; from which it follows that there was a time when he did not exist [and is thus not equal to God]"

(Socrates, 1.5)

The presbyter who said these words was Arius, originator of the doctrine of Arianism. His view that the Son had not existed eternally in the Godhead was summarized in a Greek phrase *en pote hote ouk en*, "there was a time when he was not".

It seems a small point from a distant world, but in fact it was the beginning of a major uproar and conflict, the consequences of which have left their mark on the Christian understanding of God ever since. From the first, Christians had to account for the fact that Jesus was clearly a real human being and yet that he had brought into the world through his own person the effect and power of God, whom he called *Abba*, Father. He was therefore distinct from God and yet brought God to life in and through himself. How could the nature of God be united with human nature in the person of Jesus Christ in such a way that God was not compromised or diminished (like a genie stuffed into a bottle) and that the humanity of Jesus was not overwhelmed (like dry land submerged under a flood)?

All the different views held by people (see box, right) on who or what Jesus really was had in common the belief that it is simply impossible for God to be united with a human life and body. Their present-day equivalents are likely to believe that God does not even exist, so that the claim that Jesus was uniquely related to God is held to have arisen from mistaken early believers who wanted to give Jesus the highest possible honour after his death, rather like a posthumous prize or decoration.

The search for the best (or the least inadequate) way to understand God in relation to Jesus still goes on today. The challenge lies in the fact that all the views summarized in the box below are correct. But they are correct only up to a point – the "even so" in each of those sentences in the box. Jesus resembled many of the ways in which, at that time, it was believed that people could be God-related, and yet, crucially, he was unlike all of them. And the word "crucially" is literally meant. It comes from the Latin *crux*, "a cross": Jesus had died on a cross and yet was known to be alive. Through those events, the way for others to pass from death to life was opened up: "If the Spirit of him who raised Jesus from the dead dwells in you, he who raised Christ from the dead will give life to your mortal bodies also through his Spirit that dwells in you" (Romans 8.11). That could not be achieved by any human, no matter how gifted. It could be achieved only by God; and even then, not by God working at a distance, like a football manager on the bench, shouting and gesticulating while the players get on with the game. It could only be achieved (if it was achieved; and after the resurrection, Christians had no doubt that it *had* been achieved) by God becoming involved in the game and taking it to a different result. But it was exactly that which seemed impossible: how *could* God be involved in a human life and death without becoming less than God? That was the question raised by Arius.

The Cross
This African crucifixion (from Zaire) expresses as vividly as did Grünewald (on p.235), the pain and suffering of the cross – but in African, not medieval European, terms.

WHO WAS JESUS?

From the earliest days of Christianity, many answers to the question of how God could be united with a human life in the person of Christ were offered, some in the New Testament itself. Perhaps Jesus was:

✝ **A PROPHET**: In some ways Jesus spoke like a prophet, and in many ways he acted like one, especially at the Last Supper when he said of bread and wine, "This is myself and the sign of the new covenant"; even so, he was much more than a prophet, and no prophet had ever pledged to be with his followers after his death.

✝ **THE WISDOM OR LOGOS OF GOD** : Jesus was certainly described as being related to God in the way that the Bible relates wisdom to God (pp.204–5), especially in creating the world; even so, the humanity of Jesus extended the meaning of wisdom far beyond the ways in which it had hitherto been understood.

✝ **A NEW AGE PHILOSOPHER**: He may have looked like some kind of philosopher heralding the birth of a New Age; even so, his words and deeds were entirely different.

✝ **A MESSIAH** (p.203): Much of what he said and did suggested that he was a Messiah; even so, not all the signs of a Messiah were with him, and no Messiah suffered and died as he did.

✝ **AN ANGEL**: He resembled angels in coming from God; even so, he was much more than a powerful messenger (see Hebrews 1, p.236), and "even the angels long to catch a glimpse of these things" (I Peter 1.12).

✝ **A GNOSTIC MEDIATOR** (p.233): Gnostics claimed him as a teacher who revealed God; even so, his life in Palestine made God real on earth in a way that Gnostics would have thought impossible.

✝ **A GIFTED TEACHER AND HEALER**: He could have been promoted by God and adopted as Son – hence the words "You are my beloved Son; with you I am well pleased" (Mark 1.11). Jesus clearly was in a special relationship with God; even so, there is no evidence that he moved into a relationship that had not previously existed.

Jesus and God

One Being With the Father

The Prodigal Son
Luke 15.11–32 records one
of Jesus' many brilliant
stories which lie at the heart
of the Christian
understanding of God; the
unfailing love of God for
those who have lived wrongly
but who turn back in sorrow,
a love made real in Christ.
This sculpture by Rodin
(1840–1917) shows the
moment when the
prodigal son comes to his
senses, and knows that
his father will welcome
him back (see box,
opposite).

DURING THE REIGN of the Roman Emperor Trajan (98–117CE), Pliny, one of his provincial governors, wrote to him to ask how he should deal with some apparently disloyal people called Christians. Those who, under threat, worshipped the statue of the emperor and cursed Christ were fine, but was he right to execute those who would not? According to Pliny, "the whole of their guilt, or their error, was that they were in the habit of meeting on a certain fixed day before it was light, when they sang in alternate verses a hymn to Christ as though to a God" (*Letter* 96). In fact they were singing to Christ, not as *though* to a God, but to God. Any account, like that of Arius (p.242), saying of Christ that he was less than God, did not seem to them to do justice to the evidence – and evidence not just from the past but also of the present in the continuing Christian experience of God. To them, the only account that seemed to be true was to say of Jesus (as a creed later did say) that he was "God from God, light from light, true God from true God" (the so-called Nicene creed, though its final form came from a later Church Council).

Neither Arius nor all those who earlier attempted (p.243) to associate Jesus with God by adoption or promotion seemed to do justice to the person and the events that had brought the Church into being. It was not enough to say that Jesus was *like* God in some of the things that he did and said, or that he became *like* God in his own nature – or, in the Greek of the time, that he was *homoiousios* (of a like nature or substance). Jesus had done what only God can do: he had brought people from wrong to right (from sin to salvation) and from death to a new life beyond death. So, people felt, he could not have done that unless he was of the same nature or substance (*homoousios*) as God; the Nicene Creed therefore continues, "…begotten, not made, of one being (*homoousios*) with the Father: through him all things were made".

Those two Greek words (*homoiousios* and *homoousios*), differing by only a single letter, the Greek *iota* (i), point to the storm that raged around Arius. It seems absurd that people should fall out over a single letter – so that, as the historian Gibbon (1737–94) was later to put it mockingly, "the profane of every age have been able to deride the furious contests which the difference of a single diphthong excited".

Yet in fact the whole Christian understanding of God turns on the issue. Jesus did not live and act more or less like God in dealing with human need: to *deal* with that need, it had to be *God* who was at work in conjunction with the humanity of Jesus. Jesus did not *become* God, because the One united uniquely to the human nature of Jesus had always been God, pre-existing his manifestation, or incarnation, in the person of Christ. What God always is is always what God, united now with the human person of Jesus, must have been.

Only if that were so could Jesus have rescued people in the way that he did. As Athanasius (c.296–373, the main opponent of Arius) put it, God became human in order that humans might become God: drowning people cannot be rescued by exhortations from the shore, but only by one who knows and understands their crisis, and who enters into it in order to do for them what they cannot do for themselves. For that reason, the Creed goes on: "For us and for our salvation he came down from heaven; by the power of the Holy Spirit he became incarnate of the Virgin Mary, and was made man". In gratitude for this, those who see the point and realize what has been done for them, kneel before Christ (cf. the early hymn, p.234), as the Wise Men had knelt in the stable, in worship, adoration, and love. If Christ is not truly God, that worship is a kind of idolatry.

For reasons of rescue and salvation, the early Christians knew that Jesus was both God and man, and uniquely so. In all the many speculations about the ways in which people might be inspired or possessed by God, nothing like this had ever been claimed, let alone described. The Christians were left with the impossibility of trying to explain how this unique conjunction of the human and the divine in one person could have happened.

To some extent, it is easier now than then. We now know how information, in the technical sense, acts as a constraint over all human behaviour, including speech and action, without destroying that humanity. From the record, it is clear that God was, at least in the belief of Jesus, an invariant source of information acting as a constant constraint over his humanity without in any way destroying it. The source of information, therefore, remained independent while being wholly and effectively present in the transformation of that life. Hebrews 4.15 put the point more colloquially by saying that Jesus was tempted in every way like us and yet was without sin. That creates the paradox: God is both wholly present and wholly absent, both within the person of Jesus and yet apart from Jesus, being addressed as Father and supporting him as the Spirit. How could God live, suffer, and die in a small corner of Palestine while at the same time running the universe? It was in answer to that question that the understanding of God as Trinity began to emerge.

"When he came to himself he said, 'How many of my father's hired hands have bread enough and to spare, but here am I dying of hunger! I will get up and go to my father, and I will say to him, 'Father, I have sinned against heaven and before you; I am no longer worthy to be called your son; treat me like one of your hired hands.' So he set off and went to his father. But while he was still far off, his father saw him and was filled with compassion; he ran and put his arms around him and kissed him. Then the son said to him, 'Father, I have sinned against heaven and before you; I am no longer worthy to be called your son.' But the father said to his slaves, 'Quickly, bring out a robe – the best one – and put it on him,… and get the fatted calf and kill it, and let us eat and celebrate; for this son of mine was dead and is alive again; he was lost and is found!' And they began to celebrate"

(Luke 15.11–32)

Three in One

The Holy Trinity

The Holy Trinity
God lies far beyond human words or descriptions. Nevertheless, the ways in which God became known, as creator, redeemer, and sustainer, led to many conventional pictures in which God is represented in Biblical terms as the Father, the Saviour, and the Holy Spirit (the Dove). The threefold inner nature of God is known as the immanent Trinity, and the way in which it becomes known in the process of self-revelation is known (from the Greek oikonomia) *as the economic Trinity.*

T HE EARLY CHRISTIAN UNDERSTANDING of God was formed under the pressure of two apparently contradictory truths. On one side was the obvious and absolute truth that God, to be God, must be One. God cannot be a committee of superhuman beings living on Mount Olympus (p.206). The fundamental truth of the Shema (p.178), inherited from Judaism, was rapidly reinforced by increasing contacts with Greek philosophy. Looked at in that perspective, God must be the one source and origin of all things, the only sovereign Lord of all creation. God is, in another word, Monarch (Greek *monos* = "sole", "only", "alone"; *arche* = "source", "origin", "ruler").

On the other side, there was the equally certain view that God was uniquely present in Christ, whose life on earth had been initiated and then sustained by the Holy Spirit. How can God be and remain Monarch, while at the same time being present in Christ, and being also the One who sustains people, including Christ, in the world? The question was then inevitable: How are these ways of being God related to each other? Immediately after the New Testament period, the truths were simply stated (see box, right) but very soon a word in that question became the earliest answer to it – Christ and the Holy Spirit are *ways* in which God acts in the world. The Monarch remains sole and sovereign but acts in different ways or modes – and for that reason, this way of describing God is known as "modalistic monarchianism". Sabellius (of whom little else is known) argued this, saying that the way God acts in a threefold manner is like the sun which is a single object radiating both heat and light. That answer was inadequate because what had been experienced and recorded in

history was not the effect of God who remains "off stage" but of God present as the leading actor on stage. How could those two truths be held together? Not by splitting God into three separate individuals. When it was said (following the New Testament) that Jesus is the only-begotten Son of the Father, it did not mean a physical act of procreation:

"Let no one laugh at the idea of God having a Son! This is not a case of the myths of the poets who make the gods out to be no better than men. We have no such ideas about God the Father and the Son. The Son of God is the Logos [p.232] of God in thought and power"

(Athenagoras, 10.1)

B ut if it did not mean physical procreation, what did it mean? As with all language about God, it was a metaphorical way of saying that within the nature of God there is an eternal dynamic of relationship (i.e., one that has not had a beginning in time, but is what God is outside the domain of time): the universe is constituted in networks of relationships because it reflects the nature of the creator in whom relationship is of the essence.

Relationships are of many different kinds: they may, for example, be of tyranny or of cruelty. That the nature of the relationship constituting God is one of love is known from the way God has dealt with the world in creating, redeeming, and sustaining, as the New Testament makes clear. God as love is a relationship at least of two, the lover and the one loved, and in fact of three since, in what is known as "a metaphysic of relationship", love exists equally as the consequence (named in Scripture as the Holy Spirit) of the lover and the loved. Yet in the case of self-love (which must be the case in God's own nature since before creation there is nothing external to God), these three are also and at the same time one: the three are God and constitute what God is (see caption, left).

After three centuries, battles over how to express the Trinitarian nature of God, and how to understand the two natures in Christ led to agreement in the definition of the Council of Chalcedon (451CE). Or near agreement. To some Christians (mainly in the West) it seemed clear that the Father is the source from whom proceed (in an eternal, not temporal, relationship) the Son and then the Holy Spirit: hence the Nicene Creed says of the Holy Spirit, "...the Lord, the giver of life, who proceeds from the Father *and the Son*" (Latin, *filioque*). Others (mainly in the East) said that both the Son and the Spirit proceed from the Father, and they rejected, and still do, the addition *filioque*.

It seems a small point. But it split the Church – and still does.

During the 2nd century, Irenaeus, Bishop of Lyons, summarized the Christian understanding of God at that time:

"This is the rule of our faith: God the Father, not made, not material, invisible, one God, the creator of all things: this is the first point of our faith. The second point is this: the Word of God, Son of God, Christ Jesus our Lord,...through whom all things were made; who also, at the end of the age, to complete and gather up all things, was made man among human beings, visible and tangible, in order to abolish death and show forth life and produce perfect reconciliation between God and human beings. And the third point is this: the Holy Spirit, through whom the prophets prophesied, and those of old learned the things of God, and the righteous were led into the way of righteousness, who at the end of the age was poured out in a new way upon people in all the earth, renewing humanity to God"

(*The Demonstration of the Apostolic Preaching 6*)

The East-West Debate

The Same Truth in Different Words

IN TRYING TO SPEAK OF GOD in Christ and of God as Trinity, Christians in the Eastern (Greek-speaking) and Western (Latin-speaking) parts of the Roman Empire fell into serious disputes. Eventually those and other arguments, reinforced by political rivalries, led to the major schism or divide between the Eastern Churches (the Greek Orthodox and subsequently other Orthodox Churches) and Western Churches (mainly, but not entirely, under the Pope in Rome, hence eventually Roman Catholic): the schism was confirmed in 1054, when Rome excommunicated the Patriarch of Constantinople.

The earlier disputes about the person of Christ and the Trinity arose in part because translating each language into the other gave rise to critical misunderstandings. Thus the East spoke of three underlying hypostases (Greek *hupostasis*, "that which stands under") in one Being (*ousia*). The Latin equivalent of *hupostasis* is *substantia*, as in the English words "substance", "substantial". That sounded to the Latin West as though the East was placing in the Trinity three separate and substantial realities, or, in other words, three Gods.

Eventually it was recognized that the same truth was being expressed in different words, but in the meantime the debate was deeply felt – although to the outsider it seems esoteric and arcane. Gibbon had mocked the battles over a single letter (pp.244f), and his contemporary, Laurence Sterne (1713–68), was equally scathing about these other battles as well (see box, left).

But words matter, even when trying to speak about that concerning which, as both East and West agreed, nothing can be said, since God is beyond words and description – as Clement of Alexandria (c.150–215), at the heart of the debate, made plain:

> "What a pudder and racket in Councils about ousia and hupostasis; and in the Schools [the scholasticism associated with Aquinas, pp.266–9] … about essences and quintessences; about substances and space. What confusion… from words of little meaning, and as indeterminate a sense!"
>
> (Sterne, p.77)

"John the apostle wrote: 'No one has seen God at any time; it is the only-begotten God, who is close to the Father's heart, who has made him known' (I John 1.18). He used the word "heart" of God to refer to his invisibility and ineffability; for this reason some people have used the word "depth" to indicate that he is inaccessible and incomprehensible but embraces and enfolds all things. This is the hardest part of the discussion about God. The first cause of anything is hard to discover. It is therefore particularly hard to describe the first and original cause, which is the source of the existence of everything else that is or has been. For how is one to speak

about that which is neither a genus nor a differentia nor a species nor an individuality nor a number – in other words, which is neither any kind of accidental property nor the subject of any accidental property? Nor can one properly speak of him as a "whole", for a whole is a matter of size and he is "Father of the whole universe". Nor can one speak of him as having parts, for that which is "One" is indivisible and therefore also infinite – infinite not in the sense of measureless extension but in the sense of being without dimensions or boundaries, and therefore without shape or name. If we do give it a name, we cannot do so in the strict sense of the word: whether we call it "One", "the good", "mind", "absolute being", "Father", "God", "Creator", or "Lord", it is not a case of producing its actual name; in our impasse we avail ourselves of certain good names so that the mind may have the support of those names and not be led astray in other directions. For taken individually none of these names is expressive of God but taken together they collectively point to the power of the Almighty"

(Wiles & Santer, *pp.6f*)

"The vision of God consists in this: that God cannot be seen, since what we seek is beyond all knowledge, being wholly concealed in a cloud of incomprehensibility. Therefore St John, who also entered into this bright mist, says that no one has seen God at any time, meaning by this negation that the knowledge of the divine nature is impossible not only for humans but for every created intellect"

(Gregory of Nyssa, p.376d)

E ven so, it is still vital not to say of God things that are clearly misleading or wrong. It is much easier to say what God is not than to say what God is – a perception that leads in all religions to different versions of "the negative way" (see box, right and, e.g., pp.220f, 268). But having fenced off error (and that is what was achieved in creeds and Council declarations, as of Nicaea and Chalcedon), it is then far better to stop speaking and to seek God – God who invites us into a union of complete and perfect love.

God and Prayer
The human imagination, not least in art, cannot avoid thinking of God as though God is like a human being but more so (cf. analogy on p.268). Prayer leads in the opposite direction, into a deeper and deeper silence in the presence of God.

This approach to God is known as the apophatic way, from the Greek *apophatikos*, "negative". It is to approach God beyond the words about God: it is to move from reading the menu to starting the actual meal. God is known only through negation of concepts and ideas about God, and of one's own attachments to the world: it is a way, not of knowing about God, but of unknowing everything until one is left with nothing but God. It was a way much emphasized in Eastern Christianity.

Darkness and Light

God Beyond Words

EASTERN CHRISTIANS WERE CLEAR that the essence of God is totally beyond human understanding. And yet the awareness of God fills people with such a longing for God that "the true sight of God consists in this, that the one who looks up to God never ceases in that desire" (Gregory of Nyssa, *Life of Moses*, 233).

These two themes – the unknowability of God, combined with the desire for God that begins already in this life, in prayer, to be satisfied – were brought together in immensely influential works by a writer (c.5th century CE) known as Pseudo-Dionysus or (in Latin form) Ps.-Denys. He was thought to have been Dionysus the Areopagite converted by Paul, Acts 17.34. For Ps.-Dionysus, the apophatic (p.249) way was reinforced by Neoplatonism (p.233), which also held God to be far beyond human knowledge. There was a vital difference, however: Neoplatonism kept God free from entanglement in the world by proposing a series of emanations. Ps.-Dionysus knew that the One involved in creation and incarnation was not the end-term of a series of emanations, but the true reality of God. God may thus be known *directly*, but only mediated through the things we sense and apprehend (i.e., notice in appropriate ways: it is God who is known through the effects of God, but God is still not seen "face to face"; cf. p.20).

Ps.-Dionysus wrote of the ways in which a life can be lifted up to God in worship and contemplation until that life is "divinised" (made God-like) and then united with God. The two are known as *theosis* (Greek, *theos*, "god") and *henosis* (Greek, *hen*, "one").

Ps.-Dionysus realized that the utterly unknowable God is nevertheless so sufficiently manifest in creation and revelation that all beings, starting from that point, are able to attain union with the unmanifest source. *The Divine Names* explores what can be said positively about God (i.e., kataphatic theology in contrast to apophatic) as

According to Ps.-Dionysus, to seek God is:

"to leave behind everything perceived and understood, everything open to perception and understanding, all that is not and all that is, and then, with your understanding set aside, to strive upward as much as you can toward union with him who is beyond all being and knowledge. By an undivided and absolute abandonment of yourself and everything, shedding everything and freed from everything, you will be uplifted to the light of the divine darkness which transcends everything that is"

(*The Mystical Theology* 997b)

THE HESYCHASTIC PRAYER

The words of this simple prayer were originally "Lord Jesus Christ, Son of God, have mercy on me".
The words "a humble sinner" were added to the end to increase the feeling of joy-filled sorrow and love.

Elements of this prayer are very early, but they were first offered in a formal way by Diadochos of Photiki in the 5th century. By the 13th century, Nicephorus the Hesychast was writing of the

physical preparation needed for the prayer, with head bowed and breathing increasingly slowed down until it accompanies the rhythm of the words, creating a sense of joy-filled sorrow.

a foundation for the ascent (Greek *anagoge*) into God (see box, top left). These ideas were taken even further, in the East, by Gregory Palamas (died 1359), who believed that while the essence of God cannot be known, what can be known of God is real and important. He distinguished between the essence and the "energies" (*energeia*, the effects) of God. The *energeia* are themselves uncreated and are therefore not other than God, and since they permeate all things (as God's creative act sustains all things in being), God can be known through them directly, though not immediately. To experience God in this way, it is essential to empty oneself of all else and to find God within, and as a way to this, Gregory advocated the Jesus prayer (the constant repetition of "Lord Jesus Christ, Son of God, have mercy on me, a humble sinner"). This creates quiet (Greek, *hesuchia*) concentration on God, and is known as Hesychastic prayer (see box, bottom left). In this state, a feeling of warmth is often experienced, leading to contemplation of the light that is God.

On this point the Hesychasts were fiercely attacked, not least by Barlaam of Calabria (c.1290–1348). He maintained that neither God nor the light that is God can possibly be seen immediately by anyone in this life; claims to such seeing were a mistaken interpretation of experiences brought about by the techniques of Hesychastic prayer. Gregory's defence (distinguishing essence from energies, above) he dismissed as a confusion: it introduced division into the simplicity of God. In contrast, Hesychasts insisted that the experience of God is real because it is bestowed by God in anticipation of the final vision: it is, in other words, an embodiment of grace.

The debate continued, but Hesychasm remained a part of the Orthodox way of attending to God at all times. It is deeply embedded in *The Philokalia*, an 18th-century collection of major texts on the spiritual life that were written from the 5th century onwards. The purpose of this, as of all prayer, is union with God, as Diadochos summarized the point: "Only God is good by nature, but with God's help, people can become good through careful attention to their way of life. They transform themselves into what they are not when their soul, by devoting its attention to true delight, unites itself to God, in so far as its energised power desires this. For it is written: 'Be good and merciful as is your Father in heaven' [Luke 6.36; Matthew 5.48]".

Ladder to God
The Neoplatonic idea of "climbing" up to God was a strong image in later developments of Christian spirituality, which describe the "ascent" or "the ladder" that leads to God. John (7th century) became known as Climacus (Greek, klimax, "ladder") after he described the 30-step ladder, from what were thought to be the 30 years of Christ's life, that leads up to God; The Ladder of Perfection (Scala Perfectionis) of Walter Hilton (died 1396, p.274) describes the stages through which the lost image (p.252) of God in humans can be restored.

The Negative Way

The Greek Fathers

URING THE 4TH CENTURY, Gregory, the Bishop of Nyssa, returned from a visit to Constantinople, the capital of the Eastern Empire, and said that it was a city buzzing with theology (the ferment of debate described on the previous pages, see box, left). Why did it all matter so much? Because, as Gregory of Nyssa wrote (p.249), the vision of God is the finest destiny that anyone can hope for, but it is no simple matter. Gregory had no doubt that human beings belong naturally to God. He used the story of Adam and Eve to show what it is to live at ease with God and with each other:

> *"By its likeness to God human nature is made as it were a living image [Genesis 1.26] partaking with the Godhead both in rank and name, clothed in virtue, resting in the blessedness of immortality, wearing the crown of righteousness, and thus a perfect likeness to the beauty of the Godhead in all that belongs to the splendour of majesty"*

(De Hominis Opificio 4.136)

"It is a city full of profound theological disputes!…If you ask a man to change a piece of silver, he tells in what way the Son differs from the Father; and if you ask for a loaf of bread, you get in reply that the Son is inferior to the Father; and if you ask whether your bath is ready, you are solemnly told that the Son was made out of nothing"

(Concerning the Godhead of the Son, 4)

And he knew equally that that is meant to be our final end, when "Paradise lost is found again, and the tree of life springs up once more, and the grace of the image and the splendour of sovereignty are restored" (13.8).

In the meantime, in the time between what we have been in origin and what we may yet be, the wisest way is to move towards God in deeper commitment and love, even though it is by the apophatic (p.249) way: the nearer we approach, the more we realize that God lies far beyond our knowledge and understanding (see box, top right). How can

ANTONY AND GOD

Antony, one of the Desert Fathers, emphasized the importance of inner tranquillity, obedience, and love:

✝ **ON INNER PEACE:** "Just as fish die if they stay too long out of water, so the monks who loiter outside their cells or pass their time with people of the world lose the intensity of inner peace. So, like a fish going toward the sea, we must hurry to reach our cell, for fear that if we delay outside we will lose our interior watchfulness."

✝ **ON LOVE:** "I no longer fear God, but I love him. For 'love casts out fear' [1 John 4.18]".

✝ **ON OBEDIENCE:** "Obedience with abstinence gives people power over wild beasts."

humans do this? They can't. Or at least they cannot do so out of their own effort. It can only be, as Gregory says, "by the work of the Spirit". Even so, it is important to be open to that work of the Spirit and at the very least to be looking in the right direction when that gift is offered. For that reason, Basil, the elder brother of Gregory, believed that the way to God becomes more obvious if people make the kind of radical choice for God that Jesus had demanded – forsaking everything for God's sake, giving up father, mother, sisters, and brothers, leaving the dead to bury the dead. Already there had been Christians who had taken this literally, and had gone out to the edges of the desert, to abandon the world and to live only for God. Stories were beginning to be told of the heroic battles of the Desert Fathers, as they are called, against temptations and the devil; and Athanasius, the great opponent of Arius (p.242) wrote an influential life of one of them, Antony, who led the way in the founding of Christian monasticism (see box, below left). It was said that an old man asked God to let him see the Fathers, and he saw them all except Abba Antony. He asked his guide, "Where is Abba Antony?" The guide told the old man that in the place where God is, there would Antony be (Ward, pp.3,7,8).

Basil took up the theme of radical choice for God and wrote two Rules for monastic orders, believing that it is, for most, better to live in a community than as hermits. Like his brother, he was clear that no one can know the essence of God, but that does not prevent us offering ourselves to God in an ordered way:

"That *God exists, I do know. But what his essence is, I regard as beyond my understanding. How then am I to be saved? By faith. Faith is sufficient for the knowledge* that God *is, not of* what *he is – and of the fact that he rewards those who seek him [Hebrews 11.6]. So knowledge of the divine essence consists in the perception of his incomprehensibility. What we worship is not that of which we comprehend the essence, but that of which we comprehend that the essence exists…Thus we believe in him of whom we have knowledge, and we worship him of whom we have faith*"

(Wiles & Santer, p.11f)

"*As the soul makes progress, and by greater and more perfect concentration comes to appreciate what the knowledge of the truth is, the more it approaches this vision, the more it realizes that God's nature cannot be seen. It therefore leaves all appearances that lie on the surface, not just those that can be taken in by the senses, but those also that the mind can imagine, and it keeps on going deeper and deeper until by the work of the Spirit it penetrates the invisible and the incomprehensible, and there it sees God.*"

(On the Life of Moses)

The Cappadocians
This 18th-century Russian icon depicts the Eastern Fathers, also known as the Cappadocian Fathers.

Celtic Christianity

God In and Through Nature

Praise

"Almighty Creator, it is you who have made
The land and the sea…
The world cannot comprehend in song bright and melodious,
Even though the grass and trees should sing,
All your wonders, O true Lord!…
He who made the wonder of the world
Will save us, has saved us.
It is not too great a toil to praise the Trinity"
(Old Welsh poem, c.9th century).

THE WAYS IN WHICH CHRISTIANS in the East developed their prayer and their understanding of God lay outside the influence of Rome. So too until 664 (when the Synod of Whitby affirmed the authority of Rome in establishing the date of Easter against local custom) did the Christianity of at least some Celts.

The word "Celtic" refers, not to a Church, but to tribes and people who spoke a related group of languages although it could not be said that they shared a common culture. They lived in areas ranging from central Europe to Ireland and Scotland. Many were absorbed into the Roman Empire and subsequently became part of Western Christianity. But beyond the boundaries of the empire, and especially in Britain when the Romans withdrew by the 5th century, the Celts continued with their own beliefs and customs (as well as their own way of dating Easter).

Since the 19th century, the term "Celtic Christianity" has referred also to a style of prayer and spirituality associated with those Celts, emphasizing the discernment of God in and through nature. This was partly a result of Alexander Carmichael making a record in the 19th century of what people in Scotland told him about their lives and their beliefs. In 1900 he published the first of what became after his death six volumes under the title *Carmina Gaedelica* (Gaelic Songs). In those collections, he caught a strong sense of spiritual presence in all things and at all times that can be found also in the earliest surviving Celtic literature:

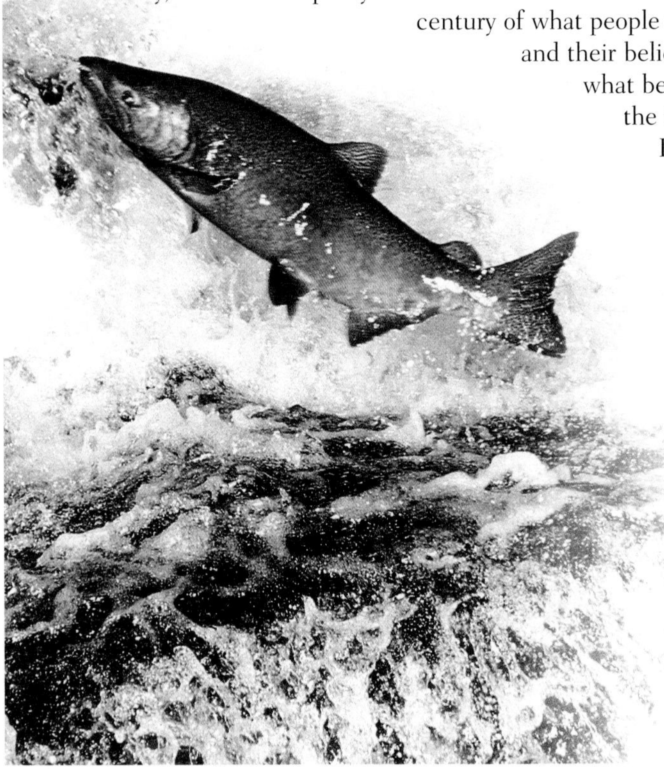

"I am the wind which breathes upon the sea,
I am the wave of the ocean,
I am the murmur of the billows,…
I am the beam of the sun,
I am a salmon in the water,
I am a lake in the plain,
I am word of knowledge,…
I am the God who created the fire in the head"

(Mackey, p.78)

Ultimately the presence is that of God, though it may often be the presence of the agents of God. In the morning, for example, this prayer of presence was said while lighting the fire:

"I will kindle my fire this morning
In presence of the holy angels of heaven,
In presence of Ariel of the loveliest form,
In presence of Uriel of the myriad charms,
Without malice, without jealousy, without envy,
Without fear, without terror of anyone under the sun,
But the Holy Son of God to protect me…

God, kindle Thou in my heart within
A flame of love to my neighbour,
To my foe, to my friend, to my kindred all,
To the brave, to the knave, to the thrall,
O Son of the loveliest Mary,
From the lowliest thing that lives,
To the Name that is highest of all"

(Carmina Gaedelica I, 82)

God is seen through the whole of the natural order as a shining and certain presence. All things come from God as their creator, and they become the window through which the beauty and majesty of God can be seen. In this spirit, Thomas Jones (1756–1820) wrote of a thrush:

"Lowly bird, beautifully taught,
You enrich and astound us,
We wonder long at your song,
Your artistry and your voice.
In you I see, I believe,
The clear and excellent work of God.
Blessed and glorious is he,
Who shows his virtue in the lowest kind.
How many bright wonders (clear note of loveliness)
Does this world contain?
How many parts, how many mirrors of his finest work
Offer themselves a hundred times to our gaze?
For the book of his art is a speaking light
Of lines abundantly full,
And every day one chapter after another
Comes among us to teach us of him"

(Parry, pp.332f)

Song Thrush
Welsh poet Thomas Jones wrote a poem celebrating the beauty of the lowly thrush's song, believing it to be part of the "excellent work of God".

The created order, however, is not a place of safety and innocence. It contains destructive dangers, some natural, some created by its inhabitants. God is looked to as a shield and defence, as in prayers known as Loricae, "breastplates". A famous example of these "breastplate" prayers is the one attributed to St Patrick, though it came from a later tradition (see box, left).

The battle against evil and danger was literal and fierce. In early Celtic Christianity, for example, monks stood in icy streams to pray and built their huts in places remote from the inhabited world. In this battle with the elements, God's presence is one of powerful help (of grace), protecting people in every detail of their lives. On rising in the morning they would pray:

"O great God, aid Thou my soul
With the aiding of Thine own mercy;
Even as I clothe my body with wool,
Cover Thou my soul with the shadow of Thy wing.

Help me to avoid every sin,
And the source of every sin to forsake;
And as the mist scatters on the crest of the hills,
May each ill haze clear from my soul, O God"

(CG, III, 231)

And at night they would pray:

"In thy name, O Jesu who wast crucified,
I lie down to rest;
Watch Thou me in sleep remote,
Hold Thou me in Thy one hand;
Watch Thou me in sleep remote,
Hold Thou me in Thy one hand"

(CG, III, 327)

In response, the Celtic Christians offered praise and prayer spoken from God-centred lives:

"I am bending my knee
In the eye of the Father who created me,
In the eye of the Son who redeemed me,
In the eye of the Spirit who sanctified me
In love and desire"

(CG, I, 34)

It was a love and desire expressed eloquently by Augustine.

For my shield this day I call:
The mighty power:
The Holy Trinity!
Affirming threeness,
Confessing oneness,
In the making of all
Through love…

For my shield this day I call:

Heaven's might,
Sun's brightness,
Moon's whiteness,
Fire's glory,
Lightning's swiftness,
Wind's wildness,
Ocean's depth,
Earth's solidity,
Rock's immobility…"

(Mackey, pp.46f)

OPPOSITE:

◈

Iona
Iona, a small island off the west coast of Scotland, was given to Columba (c.521–97) when he arrived in Scotland from Ireland as "a pilgrim of Christ". Here he founded a monastery from which missionaries went out. The recent Iona Community was founded in 1938 to bring the incarnation into the modern world.

Augustine

A Searching Soul

Augustine in the Cell
Botticelli (1445–1510)
painted his idea of Augustine
at work. Augustine wrote
hundreds of letters and
sermons (some were
rediscovered only in the 20th
century: see Brown
pp.442–5) and many major
works such as Confessions,
On the Trinity, *and* The
City of God.

AUGUSTINE LAID FOUNDATIONS in the Christian understanding of God on which many subsequent generations built. He was born at Tagaste, in North Africa, in 354CE. He received a thorough Roman education, becoming familiar with Neoplatonism (p.233) and being for some years attracted by Manichaeism: Mani (216–76CE) had taught a strong dualism (p.196), with good trying to free itself from the material bondage of the world; in this struggle the Elect (frontline troops) assisted by Auditors (helpers, the highest that Augustine advanced in their ranks) tried to disentangle the sparks of light from within themselves to return to the Source.

In 383 Augustine went to Rome as a teacher, and from there (in 384) to Milan as an orator. But for all his education, he was still restless to find the enduring truth that lies beyond the passing fashions and philosophies of the day. Fundamental to human nature is *cor inquietum*, a restlessness at the heart of our being that drives us in the search for what is true, whether in life or in love, in science or in art: "Our yearning sees far off the land we seek, it throws out hope as an anchor that pulls us toward that shore" (*Understanding the Psalms* 64.3).

One afternoon, sitting with a friend beneath a fig tree (cf. John 1.48), he heard from next door a child's voice chanting repeatedly, *"Tolle lege, tolle lege'"* – "take up and read" or, in another meaning of the verb *lego*, "take up and choose" (the child was perhaps demanding a story or a game). Doing what it seemed he had been bidden, Augustine opened at random the copy of Paul's letters lying beside him and read: "Let us live honourably as in the day, not in revelling and drunkenness, not in debauchery and licentiousness, not in quarrelling and jealousy. Instead, put on the Lord Jesus Christ, and make no provision for the flesh to gratify its desires" (Romans 13.13f). He wrote: "In that instant,… it was as though a light of utter confidence shone in all my heart, and all the darkness of uncertainty vanished away" (*Confessions* 8.12).

Augustine became a Christian. He "put on Christ" by being baptized, and later he was ordained. He returned to North Africa where he became Bishop of Hippo. There he had to deal with a rival branch of Christianity, the Donatists, who refused to re-admit to the Church those who had abandoned Christianity under persecution and the threat of death. Augustine realized from this that on earth the good and the wicked continue to live side by side entangled with each other (cf. the parable of the wheat and the weeds in Matthew 13.24–30): the *final* judgements are made not by humans but by God.

L ater in life, Augustine wrote an account (*Confessions*) of how it had felt as God drew him, and draws all people, to the truth. It was done, not as a result of his own effort or merit, but entirely by God. From the unmerited way God had dealt with him, Augustine emphasized the absolute sovereignty of God in dealing with creation. On a strict account, all humans deserve to be condemned: it is only by God's decisive act (i.e., grace) that any are rescued. Augustine also realized that his search for God outside himself in the works of creation had been a good start (they are, after all, made and kept in being by God). But he had to move from seeking God outside to finding God within and to finding his true self within the nature of God (see box, right).

Augustine knew that "what God is" is far beyond human understanding: "Since it is God of whom we are speaking, you do not understand it – if you did understand it, it would not be God" (*Sermons* 117.5). But humans, created to reflect God, understand themselves almost as little: "Our mind cannot be understood, even by itself, because we are made in the image of God [Genesis 1.26]" (*Sermons* 398.2). It would seem, then, that the human search for God is a puzzle in pursuit of a conundrum. But God has taken the initiative to search for us and to find us:

> "Late have I loved you, Beauty so ancient and so new, so late have I loved you! But look! You were within me and I was outside, and there I searched for you, and into those things of beauty that you made I threw my defective self. You were with me, but I was not with you. Those things were holding me far from you, yet if they were not from you, they could not even exist... [Through them] you touched me, and I burned for your peace"
>
> (*Confessions* 10.27)

> "Our life came down to this earth of ours and took away our death, killed death with the abundance of his own life: and he thundered, calling to us to return to him to that secret place from which he came forth to us – coming first into the Virgin's womb, where humanity was wedded to him, our mortal flesh, though not always to be mortal... He did not delay, but rushed on, calling to us by his death and life, by his descent and ascension, to return to him. And he withdrew from our sight that we might return to our own heart and find him. For he went away and behold he is still here. He was not with us long, and yet he never left us"
>
> (*Confessions* 4.12)

"Think of it this way. Only what is good holds your love. The earth with its high mountains, gentle hills, level plains is good. The lovely and fertile land is good; the sturdy house with its proportions, its spaciousness and light is good. The bodies of living things are good; the mild and healthy air is good; pleasurable and health-giving food is good; health itself, a freedom from pain and exhaustion, is good. The human face with its symmetrical features, its glad countenance, its high colouring is good; the heart of a friend whose companionship is sweet and whose love is loyal is good; a righteous man is good; wealth for what it enables us to do is good; the sky with its sun, moon, and stars is good; the angels by their holy obedience are good; speech which teaches persuasively and counsels suitably is good; the poem of musical rhythm and profound meaning is good.
But enough! This is good and that is good; take away 'this' and 'that' and gaze if you can upon good itself: then you will behold God,... he is the goodness of every good... So our love must rise to God as the Good itself, not in the way we love this or that good thing. The soul has to seek that Good over which it does not act as judge in some superior way but to which it will cleave in love. And what is that Good but God? -- not the good soul, the good angel, the good heavens, but the good Good!"

(On The Trinity 8.3)

It is that *cor inquietum* (that restless centre of our being) which drives us on to find truth and to find within truth God: "You made us for yourself, and our heart is restless until it finds its rest in you" (*Confessions* 1.1). All else is transient – "time takes no holiday" (*Confessions* 4.8). In the midst of profound grief when his closest friend died suddenly, Augustine realized that only God endures: "This is the root of our grief when a friend dies, and the blackness of our sorrow,... and a feeling as though we were dead because he is dead.... Wherever the soul turns, unless towards God, it cleaves to sorrow, even though the things outside God and outside itself to which it cleaves may be things of beauty... Things pass that other things may come in their place and this material universe be established in all its parts. 'But do I depart anywhere?' says the Word of God. Fix your dwelling in him, commit to God whatsoever you have: for it is from God. O my soul, wearied at last with emptiness, commit to truth's keeping whatever truth has given you, and you shall not lose any; and what is decayed in you shall be made clean, and what is ill shall be made well, and what is transient shall be reshaped and made new and established in you in firmness; and they shall not set you down where they themselves go, but shall stand and abide and you with them, before God who stands and abides for ever" (*Confessions* 4.9ff).

This certainty of God means that the good things of creation remain good, but they are not the *final* good: that can only be God, in whom the reality of goodness is defined (see box, left). Augustine knew well that there is much disorder in creation, an absence of the good that might be, the defect, as he called it in his own being. Much of that disorder arises from our diverting into selfish preoccupation (self-love) the kind of generous love that led God to the work of creation. The pattern of that love and friendship is manifest in the world:

"Friendship is a precious thing because it brings into harmony different souls. Sin arises from this, and from things like this, only if a disordered fastening onto good things at a lower level pulls us down from good things that are higher, or from the highest good of all, you, my God, my Lord, your truth and your law"

(*Confessions* 2.5)

The rediscovery of an unselfish and generous love, made so obvious in Christ, is the beginning – and the end – of our rescue. It is indeed to see into the nature of God. The revelation of God as love made God inevitably, for Augustine, the Trinity, since love cannot be other than that: "Love is the act of a lover by being the love given to the loved person. It is a Trinity, the lover, the loved person and love itself" (*On the Trinity* 8.14). Humans (made in the image of God) reflect that Trinitarian nature in their own experience of themselves in memory, understanding, and love. They become that Trinitarian nature when they use their memory, understanding, and love to unite themselves with God (14.12).

It is love, therefore, that finds us at our finest because in love we are caught up into the being of God who is love:

> *"The striving after God is the desire of beatitude, the attainment of God is beatitude itself. We seek to attain God by loving him, we attain to him, not by becoming entirely what he is, but in nearness to him, and in wonderful and sensible contact with him, and in being inwardly illuminated and occupied by his truth and holiness. He is light itself; it is given to us to be illuminated by that light... This is our only and complete perfection, by which alone we can succeed in attaining to the purity of truth"*
>
> (*On the Customs of the Church*, 1.11, 25)

Gateway of the Senses
Augustine interrogated the whole of creation: "'What is this God?' he asks the earth, the sea, the animals, the air, the heavens and 'all the things that throng about the gateway of the senses', and each in turn answers, 'I am not God'. 'Then tell me something of him'. And with a mighty voice they answered, 'He made us'" (*Confessions* 10.6).

Benedict and Dominic

Ordered Lives of Prayer and Preaching

Augustine's Rule has inspired many religious orders down to the present day. Its aim is to draw people into union with each other in a common love of God, and at the end of the Rule Augustine prays:

"May the Lord grant that you observe all these things in love, like lovers of spiritual beauty; may you burn with the sweet savour of Christ in your good way of life, not as slaves under the law, but as free people established under grace"

The Lord's Service
Benedict *"established a school for the Lord's service"* in Monte Cassino. His Rule is *"the single most important document in the history of western monasticism, and arguably the most significant text from the whole late antique period"* (McGinn, II, p.27).

WHILE AUGUSTINE WAS STILL ALIVE, the Visigoths under Alaric captured Rome (in 410CE). Although Alaric was a Christian (an Arian, p.242), the fall of Rome felt to many like the end of the world. Why had it happened? Was it, as some said, because Christians had rejected the pagan gods who had protected Rome, or because the Christian God was too weak (cf. p.180)?

Augustine tackled those questions in *The City of God*. He showed how disasters had happened to Rome even when the pagan gods were worshipped, but far more he used his lesson from the Donatists (p.259) to show that God allows two cities to grow up together, "the earthly city marked out by the love of self, even to the contempt of God, and the heavenly city marked out by the love of God, even to the contempt of self". Only the final judgement makes clear who truly belongs to the city of God, where, in the final words,

"we shall rest and we shall see; we shall see and we shall love; we shall love and we shall praise. Behold what will be in the end and will not end! For what is our end but to arrive in that Kingdom which has no end?"

Augustine did much to prepare Christians in the West for the centuries that followed the fall of Rome. He did this by his emphasis on the absolute sovereignty of God who cannot be dislodged by "the changes and chances of this fleeting world", and also by the Rule he wrote (in c.397) to encourage the growth of religious communities (see box, top left) in common life.

Between 400 and 700 at least thirty Rules appeared, including translations of the Rules of Pachomius and Basil (p.253). By far the most far-reaching and influential was the Rule written by Benedict (c.480–.550) which has been followed by many orders (e.g., Benedictines, Carthusians, Cistercians). Benedict, often regarded as the founder of Western Christian monasticism (though Augustine has an equal claim), abandoned his studies as a young man, and in devotion to God lived as a hermit in a cave at Subiaco, south of Rome. He attracted many followers, but after some locals tried to poison him, he moved with a small number of loyal monks to Monte Cassino, where he wrote his Rule ("a little rule for beginners") toward the end of his life.

It was written to help those seeking God in community to live their lives in the presence of God and for the praise of God. Every action and every activity is to be directed toward God through prayer, reading, and work – not randomly, but in an ordered way under an abbot who "holds the place of Christ" (Rule 63) and to whom therefore, as the Prologue makes clear (see box, right), obedience is owed.

The Rule of Augustine was also important in the life of Dominic (1170–1221), a Spaniard whose experience of a wealthy Church in the midst of a religious war led him to believe that the gospel of Christ must be preached by those who share the poverty of Christ. His contemporary, Jordan of Saxony, wrote of him: "God gave him a special grace to weep for sinners, for the distressed, for the afflicted; he carried their troubles in the sanctuary of his compassion" (*Account of the Beginning of the Order of Preachers* 12).

He and his followers, basing themselves on the Rule of Augustine, determined to become "the humble servants of preaching" and they became known as the Order of Preachers. The Word (*Logos*, p.236) who has spoken in creating and in scripture continues to speak through those who preach following the example of the early apostles; and the Word still speaks also to those who seek God in scripture and in prayer. Prayer thus becomes a direct encounter with God, as the description of Dominic in prayer makes clear: "It was as if he were arguing with a friend; at one moment he would appear to be feeling impatient, nodding his head energetically, then he would seem to be listening quietly, then you would see him disputing and struggling, and laughing and weeping all at once, fixing then lowering his gaze, then again speaking quietly and beating his breast… The man of God had a prophetic way of passing over quickly from reading to prayer and from meditation to contemplation… Often [in prayer with others] he seemed suddenly to be caught up above himself to speak with God and the angels" (Koudelka, pp.89ff).

Rules and Orders were designed to help people make a radical and complete offering of themselves to God, with vows of obedience, poverty, and chastity. That offering was made by another man in the 13th century in a very dramatic way.

Subiaco
This monastery at Subiaco (south of Rome) is built into the cliff that contains the cave in which Benedict lived as a hermit. The cave is kept as a shrine.

"*Our minds and bodies must be made ready to fight under a holy obedience to what the Lord commands; and let us ask God that he be pleased, where our nature is powerless, to give us the help of his grace. And if we are to escape the pains of hell and reach eternal life, then, while there is still time, while we are in this body and this life, we must make haste to do now what may profit us for eternity*"

Francis

Living in Imitation of Christ

I N THE YEAR 1206, a young man was brought before his local bishop charged (by his father) with having misused his father's money and property. True, he had taken goods to market and had sold not only them but also his horse and had given the money away. In any case, he did not defend himself. He simply stripped naked and returned his clothes to his father.

The young man's name was Francesco Bernadone (1181/2–1226), better known now as St Francis – of whom the French writer Renan said that he was "after Jesus, the only perfect Christian". He acted as he did to make a complete commitment to the poverty of Christ who had himself hung naked on the cross.

Francis was born into the family of a wealthy cloth-merchant in Assisi, but his life of exuberant enjoyment was changed when he met a leper in the plain below Assisi. In his *Testament*, written shortly before he died, Francis recalled how the ruined bodies of lepers had revolted him, and how he was moved to embrace the man he met:

"The Lord granted to me, Brother Francis, to begin to do penance in this way: while I was in sin, it seemed very bitter to me to see lepers. And the Lord himself led me among them and I had mercy upon them. And when I left them that which seemed bitter to me was changed into sweetness of soul and body; and after that I lingered a little and left the world"

(Armstrong & Brady, p.154)

Stigmata

Giotto (c.1267–1337; see also p.24) painted this picture of Francis receiving the stigmata, the appearance on his own body of the wounds inflicted on Christ. Others have experienced the pain of the wounds without marks appearing.

What happened to Francis is told in a series of Lives, each of which develops the story in order to relate it to the needs of the Order that he founded, so details are not always certain. But all the early Lives agree on the central importance of the encounter with the leper, in whom Francis recognized Christ – whose words concerning acts of compassion Francis knew well: "Inasmuch as you have done it to the least of one of these, you have done it to me" (Matthew 25.40).

Francis sought to live in the imitation of Christ, not as a vague aspiration, but as a constant turning to God in complete dependence and trust. At first he was not sure what form that life should take. He repaired dilapidated churches until in one of them, Santa Maria degli Angeli, he heard in 1208 a sermon on the instructions Jesus gave to his disciples when he sent them into the world ("Take no gold, or silver, or copper in your belts, no bag for your journey, or two tunics, or sandals, or a staff", Matthew 10.9f.): he resolved immediately to follow that way of life himself. Gradually others joined him, leading to the Franciscans – first men, but later, after the decision of Clare to follow his way of poverty, an order for women (Poor Clares) followed.

> "…Glory, my Lord, to you for all your creatures
> Especially our brother, the sun,
> Who is the day, and by whom you give us light:
> He is beautiful and radiant with great splendour
> And bears witness to you, most high One"

God, for Francis, is the constantly generous creator, from whom every detail of creation comes as gift – Francis would move worms off the road in case they were run over by a cart. In 1225, the year before he died, he wrote *The Canticle of the Sun*. It is a celebration of the goodness of God experienced at every moment in a world that is received as gift. Anyone committed to poverty must necessarily experience all things as gift, as the birds and animals do. *The Canticle* calls on creation to praise God, starting with the sun (see box, top right). It goes on to praise God for sister moon and the stars, for brother wind "and all the different weathers", for sister water and brother fire (who is "beautiful and joyful and robust and full of power"), for our sister mother earth, and for our sister death of the body. Francis had the *The Canticle* set to music, because song and music were for him the most joyful form of praise: "For what are God's servants but his minstrels, whose task is to strengthen people and move them to the joys of the spirit?"

Since God is the origin of all creatures, Francis lived with them in gratitude and peace, and many stories are told of Francis celebrating with animals, birds, and fish the gift of having been created. Because he trusted God completely, he was entirely without fear – for as he read in his simple dependence on scripture, "perfect love casts out fear" (1 John 4.18). When his habit caught fire and a brother rushed to put it out, Francis told him not to harm brother fire. Even the fearsome wolf of Grecchio was rebuked by Francis and told to rely on the people to feed him and not to plunder them – and the people did exactly that.

In 1223, when Francis created a replica of the Nativity (see caption, right), he stood before the manger immersed in the humility and poverty of the One from whom all the riches of creation have come. He had drawn so close to God in the imitation of Christ that the following year the wounds and the marks of Christ's passion (the Stigmata) appeared in his own hands and body. He had taken nothing for his journey (Matthew 10.9) and had received the whole world.

The Nativity
It was at Grecchio, at Christmas in 1223, that Francis brought together the people and their animals to recreate the manger in which Jesus had been born – a custom that has extended throughout the world. It is said that the woods rang out with prayers of joy and thanksgiving, and that the rocks responded with praise.

Thomas Aquinas

The Angelic Doctor

Saint and Scholar
Thomas Aquinas taught in Paris before returning to Italy in 1260. After a further period in Paris (1269–1272), he lived again in Italy, and died near Naples in 1274. Shortly before he died, he experienced a vision of such power and beauty that it made him say that all his writings were, in comparison, like straw.

AT ABOUT THE TIME FRANCIS DIED, Thomas Aquinas was born (c.1225). In newly emerging universities, people explored the ideas of Aristotle (pp.231f), especially as they were brought to the West by Muslim philosophers (pp.340f, 352–59). Aquinas took advantage of both developments. He became a Dominican in 1242, and was sent to Paris, arriving there in 1246, where he became a pupil of Albert, later to be known as the Great (Albertus Magnus).

God was to him more important than his writings (see caption, left) but they were a great achievement, especially his *Summae* or *Summas* (*Contra Gentes* and *Theologiae*). Writers before him like Augustine (pp.258–61) had started with scripture and revelation, and from the stories of God creating, redeeming and sustaining the world, moved on to the nature of God. Aquinas began by reflecting on what the nature of God must be in order to create, redeem, and sustain as God has done.

Aquinas was well aware that God lies far beyond our comprehension, and certainly beyond description. Something, however, is known of God through our observation of the way the world is, and through worship and love. Furthermore, if God is the creator, the works of creation will reveal something of the nature and purpose of their creator, just as an artist's work reveals something of the nature and purpose of that artist.

How, then, do we begin to know God? We have to start with the things we see and know around us. When we look at the way things are, we must, if we are intelligent and rational, infer a sufficient cause of their being like that, even if we take that cause to be a set of scientific laws. This kind of argument is extremely common in the natural sciences of our time; it is known now as "abductive inference".

Thus neutrinos (fundamental particles, p.17) cannot be seen: their reality is inferred from the observation of their effects and from the necessity of their being in existence in order to account for the conducive properties (or evidence) in what can be observed. Even so, it is impossible to describe what neutrinos would look like if you could see them.

Aquinas thus believed that reason can reach the conclusion that God exists, and he put forward five ways (known from the Latin as *Quinque Viae*) leading to that conclusion (see box, right). Briefly summarized, the arguments put forward in the Quinque Viae may not seem convincing, but they continue to be argued down to the present day, and certainly they exemplify the way in which Aquinas believed that faith is rational. But why do we bother? Many people live successfully (or so it seems) without a belief in God. Aquinas believed that humans have a natural longing for God because they have a natural longing for truth. If you seek truth diligently, you will arrive at the conclusion *that* God is. Even so, you will not know fully *what* God is. In fact, you will never know, in this life, what God is: that only becomes evident in the final vision of God, the so-called Beatific Vision. In the meantime, however, we do know something of God as a consequence of the way in which God has acted toward us and has revealed something that we can apprehend. In scripture, we read of the way in which the love of God creates and rescues us. But, in the same way as the work of the artist reflects the nature and the purpose of the artist, Aquinas argued that the love revealed by God in his dealings with the world reflects the nature of God as perfect and absolute love.

This means that God is not a barren cipher, the conclusion of an academic argument. The nature of God is in itself the perfect reality of love. That is why God is three Persons in one Being, because without plurality, love could not exist, and without perfect union, love would not be complete. There must be three Persons in One Being.

Put in technical language, this means that there is the unoriginated origin, from whom proceeds the expression of that divine nature, in which the consequence is ever present to them. In more ordinary, human language, these are called the Father, the Son, and the Holy Spirit: from the unproduced Producer of all that is, the Word is ever spoken as the means of self-expression, and in that self-expression the consequence of love exists. They are not three "bits" of God, still less three Gods: the One who is God is constituted in this dynamic relatedness of love.

The nature of God as Trinity (three Persons in One Being) is, according to Aquinas, something like the way in which the mind of any person knows itself uniquely as being itself and not another; but the mind (without losing any part of itself) puts forward thoughts, and the two are

Quinque Viae

Five ways that reason reaches the conclusion that God exists:

✝ **ONE**: From the fact that everything is in movement and transition to that which sets everything in motion but is itself unmoved.

✝ **TWO**: From the observation that everything is caused to the conclusion that if you move back through the chain of cause and effect, you reach the origin of all cause which is itself uncaused.

✝ **THREE**: From the fact that we live in a world of contingent possibilities (whatever is, might not have been) to the conclusion that for anything to be at all, there must be a necessary guarantee of contingent being, which means that God is the reason why there is something rather than nothing.

✝ **FOUR**: From the fact that we make comparisons (taller, wiser, smaller, etc.) to the conclusion that there must be some absolute standard against which comparisons are made, and that the "standard" must exist since to be perfect is to exist in the fullest possible way.

✝ **FIVE**: From the observation that all things exist in such a way that they are directed towards their own end, in the way that seeds turn into plants, and arrows, properly aimed, hit their target (since they are designed to reach their goal, in Greek, *telos*, hence this is called the teleological argument), to the conclusion that where there is organized design it is rational to infer a designer.

distinct and yet constitute one reality; this reality, the mind with its thoughts, utters words (and in doing this, neither mind nor thoughts are diminished); and again, when that happens, the word is both distinct from mind and thought, and yet together they constitute and are one reality.

Looked at the other way round, the uttered word is not something other than the mind and the thought, nor is the thought detached from the word that is uttered: all are one, and at the same time three, while thought and word proceed from the mind as their origin and source. Yet even this analogy, which Aquinas took from our own experience of ourselves, only points to the truth that God is Love, and that as God's loving is identical with God's existence, so what proceeds (is set forth) in God as loving is God also.

The Angelic Doctor
Thomas Aquinas was known in his lifetime as Doctor Angelicus, and was called by Dante il maestro che color che sanno, "the master of those who know". Dante describes him in Paradiso as singing the glories of truth as it brings light and illumination from heaven to the deepest abyss.

I t was this perception of the inner nature of God as Trinity, and as being necessarily one in will and love, that enabled Aquinas to answer the question of the Muslim philosophers about why perfect and self-sufficient Being would ever create a universe external to itself. There cannot be any *reason* to do so, since that reason would then be the cause of the *First* Cause acting, and the first Cause would then be second. ibn Sina had said that creation, being strictly speaking unnecessary, must arise from *jud* (p.355); in Latin, for Aquinas, that was *liberalitas* (unconstrained generosity), but because God's nature is known to be a Trinity of love, it is pure love that leads to creation. God does not create to "get anything out of it" but simply in order to share the generosity of that nature of love.

Of course, we cannot speak descriptively of the inner nature of God, because we only know the cause through its effects. By abductive inference we can infer that there must be in reality that to which we give the name "God", but we cannot describe what God would be like if we could see God (because we can't). We can only say what God is not. This is usually known as the *via negativa*, the negative way (or the *via remotionis*, the removing from God of what God cannot be): God is not square or round or taller than a tree.

On the other hand, because we know something of God in revelation, worship, and love, as also through the absolutes of truth, beauty, and goodness, and because something is known of the artist through what the artist has brought into being, we can speak about God through analogy: God is something like an artist, but much more than an artist; God is something like a human lover, but much more than human love. God is like many things in human experience, but more eminently so – and that is why this way of thinking about God is known as *via eminentiae*. It is analogy and the analogy of being that point to the radical difference between God and all that has been created. In the universe, there is a distinction between essence (what a thing is) and existence: what it is to be a lion (its essence) is determined by whatever constitutes a lion in distinction from a lamb or from anything else; but nothing in the form or essence of a lion requires that it exists. Whether a particular lion happens to exist or not is a contingent matter, entirely separate from its essence (from what makes it what it is in distinction from anything else). In the case of God, however, the essence of God (what it is to be God) requires that God exists: God could not be what God is understood to be if God did not exist: God's essence *is* to be.

It follows that creatures combine essence (being what they are) with existence (being here at all) in a contingent way – we know what they are, but, like dodos, they might happen not to exist. By analogy from what we know in the universe about essence and existence, we can see that in God essence and existence must be combined *non*-contingently. It could not be the case that God might not exist, since then the essence of God (what it is to be God) would fall apart in contradiction.

The argument is clear. But God is not simply the conclusion of an argument. God can be known through worship, prayer, and love, and this, in the view of Aquinas, is the true and best meaning of our existence. The supreme *telos* (goal, point, purpose) of human life is to be caught up in the dynamic and undying nature of God, who is Love, and to abide in it forever. Another story is told of Aquinas toward the end of his life in Naples. He was kneeling one day in prayer before the crucifix, and suddenly he seemed to hear the voice of Christ speaking to him from the cross, and offering to him anything he wanted as a reward for his work. It was the creator offering creation to his child. Not surprisingly, Aquinas was silent for a long time. Then he slowly raised his head, and he said, "I will have – only yourself." The story may not be true, but even so, it tells the whole truth about Aquinas.

The Triumph
Aquinas' ideas were contested by those who rejected the use of Aristotle in theology, and he came close to being formally condemned in Paris in 1277. In contrast, Pope Leo XIII made his work the foundation of Christian philosophy for Roman Catholic theological students in 1879.

Dante

God and the Poetry of God

IN THE YEAR THAT AQUINAS DIED (1274), a boy nearly nine years old met a girl a year younger than himself at a children's party and fell instantly in love. The boy was Dante Alighieri, the girl was Beatrice. Of that first sight of Beatrice, Dante wrote 20 years later, in *Vita Nuova*: "She came before me dressed in a most noble colour, a rich and subdued red, girded and adorned in a manner becoming to her very tender age." His inner being cried out, "Now is your bliss [*beatitudo*] made manifest", and he said, "Now has a God stronger than I come to rule over me."

That encounter was not a transient infatuation or friendship. It was an overwhelming awareness that there exists beauty of such a perfect kind that it is unforgettable. Many, perhaps nearly all, know and remember exactly what that experience is like. Wordsworth as a child saw a girl struggling in a strong wind, and never forgot her (see box, below left). Some know the experience but attach no meaning to it – "the sudden illumination – we had the experience but missed the meaning" (Eliot, p.28). Those who are willing (and Dante knew very well that it is an act of will) to consider the meaning frequently find themselves led directly to God as the source of all beauty and goodness. So it was with Dante. Beatrice did not even speak to him for another nine years, and had by then married another. But that moment of impact, that crash of absolute beauty surging through human senses into the mind and intellect that convert the accident into amazement and wonder, stayed with Dante for life. It evoked first *Vita Nuova* and then eventually the supreme poem of the Christian vision of God, and of how that vision can be seen for oneself, *The Divine Comedy* (see caption, left). He insisted (in a letter to his patron) that he was describing a real journey – unlike, for example, John Bunyan: Bunyan stated of his *Pilgrim's Progress From This World To That Which is to Come*, even in the title, that it was a dream (*Delivered Under the Similitude of a Dream*), and he gave examples of the hindrances and encouragements that humans receive on their pilgrimage in the names of both people (Mr Worldly Wiseman, Giant Despair) and places (Doubting Castle, Vanity Fair).

Dante, in contrast, states that he was describing a real journey, one that all have to undertake, and certainly there are real people in Hell and Purgatory, although he allows that his text can be read in the four different ways in which the text of the Bible was also read at that time – the literal, the allegorical (where the text stands for another truth), the moral (engaging

Dante Explains His Work
In this painting by Michelino, Dante explains how, in his work The Divine Comedy, *he made a journey from "the dark wood" of human ignorance and error in which he was lost, down into the 24 circles of Hell, onto the terraces and ledges of the mountain of Purgatory, up into the spheres of Heaven until he glimpsed the vision of God.*

*"There are in our existence
spots of time,
That with distinct pre-eminence
retain
A renovating virtue..."*

(*The Prelude* 12.208–10)

readers in some correction in their own lives), and the anagogical (from the Greek *anagoge*, "leading up", lifting readers to the contemplation of God in Heaven).

How does Dante (or anyone else) find his way out of the dark wood? His first guide is the Roman poet, Virgil (70–19BCE), who represents the best (and it is much) that humans can achieve on their own in wisdom, art, and poetry. Even so, the capital sins hold people in hell (see caption, right), because they live only for themselves. In *The Sea and the Mirror*, by W.H. Auden (1907–73), Antonio chooses to remain outside the circle of the reconciled, (see box, above right). Dante likewise emphasized the freedom people have to will their own destiny. In the end, Antonio "dances for death alone", as do those in Dante's Hell. In Purgatory, people are still in the field of fault, but fault that is being dealt with (purged). Through Purgatory, Dante is brought by Virgil to the edge of Paradise, but Virgil can guide him no further. He is replaced by Beatrice, for she had been to Dante the first "God-bearer", the first manifestation of the grace of God made visible in beauty. So Beatrice is the figure of other "God-bearers" – those who carry God into our midst – the Church, the Virgin Mary, even Christ himself. Paradise is the unqualified light of God: it can be seen on earth, except that humans often close the shutters of their lives against it:

> *"The glory of him who moves everything*
> *Penetrates the universe and shines*
> *In one part more and, in another, less"*

> (*Paradiso* 1.1–3)

In this light, made manifest in love, humans find their complete and unending joy: all the anticipations that come to them in moments of love, beauty, goodness, and truth become the final and unending condition of their being, for in Paradise they are in union with God. Dante knew (and wrote) that that vision could not be put into words. But he ended with a brilliant glimpse of all those hints of love gathered into the Being of God

> *"My will is all my own:*
> *Your need to love shall never know*
> *Me: I am I, Antonio,*
> *By choice myself alone"*

> (Auden, p.412)

Circles of Hell
In a scene from The Divine Comedy, *Virgil guides Dante through the different circles of Hell, in which people are trapped by what are called, inaccurately, "the deadly sins"; in fact, as Dante knew well, they are "the capital sins", from the Latin* caput, *"head": actions and attitudes that at root are good (e.g., hunger, desire), but become destructive when they take control of a human life (as greed, lust, etc.). The capital sins then isolate people from the love of God and of their neighbour by becoming a destructive obsession.*

Beatific Vision

Through Beatrice, Dante finally experiences the unqualified light of God, the so-called Beatific Vision, of which Aquinas wrote: "Final and complete bliss cannot be anything other than the vision of what God essentially is" (Summa Theologiae, 2.3.8).

*"O how my speech falls short,
how faint it is
For my conception!
And for what I saw
It is not enough to say that
I say little.*

*O eternal light, existing in
yourself alone,
Alone knowing yourself; and
who, known to yourself
And knowing, love and smile
upon yourself!"*

(33.121–126)

("I saw gathered there in the depths of it, Bound up by love into a single volume, All the leaves scattered through the universe", *Paradiso* 33.85–7). That essential nature of God is one of constant and consequential love (necessarily, therefore, a Trinity: three circles of deep light, in Dante's image), far beyond description though it is (see box, below left).

Dante knew, finally and forever, that he too is caught up in that love: "At this point high imagination failed; But already my desire and my will Were being turned like a wheel, all at one speed, By the love which moves the sun and the other stars" (33.142–5).

Dante is a reminder that the story of God is told at least as much in poetry as it is in prose. The paradoxes and sharp ear for language of the so-called Metaphysical Poets (17th-century poets including Traherne and Herbert, in whom "thought is *fused* into poetry at a very high temperature" (Eliot, p.50), the thought often being Christian) turned the story of God into a vivid drama of human redemption and of the soul's longing for God. Traherne wrote of "The Bible":

*"That! That! There I was told
That I the son of God was made, His image. O divine!
And that fine gold,
With all the joys that here do fade,
Are but a toy, compared to the bliss
Which heavenly, God-like, and eternal is;*

*That we on earth are kings;
And, tho we're cloth'd with mortal skin,*

Are inward cherubins, have angels' wings;
Affections, thoughts, and minds within,
Can soar through all the coasts of Heaven and earth;
And shall be sated with celestial mirth"

The poetry of God became particularly powerful and honest during the 20th century. With Auden and Eliot, the nature of poetry itself was changed, as they wrestled (as Dante had before them) to find words with which to carry the continuing truth of God – a truth challenged (as it had been for Dante) by the horrors of human evil translated into strife, murder, and treachery – in the 20th century on a scale that even Dante's imagination of Hell could scarcely have believed possible. Auden recalled the opening words of *The Divine Comedy* when he wrote: "Alone, alone, about a dreadful wood Of conscious evil runs a lost mankind, Dreading to find its Father lest it find The Goodness it has dreaded is not good: Alone, alone, about our dreadful wood" (p.352). Dante's hell and Hitler's Germany show how robustly evil grows in the soil of a papal court or of a cultured civilization. Auden realized in 1939 that in Christian understanding, the meaning of God's redemption is that we are moved beyond understanding why evil happens, to accepting the responsibility of resistance (see box, top right).

Eliot, too, looked back to Dante throughout his life, from a short work on Dante in 1923, to *Four Quartets*, where he not only made allusions to *The Divine Comedy* and adapted Dante's *terza rima* in a section of *Little Gidding*, but also made the same journey as that of Dante, transposing its imagery into the equally real world of the 20th century: from the hints of love, all go into the dark; but a further exploration remains possible for those who are willing to "fare forward" into the trial of the sea; and for these, the prayers of the Lady whose shrine stands on the promontory, the Queen of Heaven, avail:

"Who then devised the torment? Love.
Love is the unfamiliar Name
Behind the hands that wove
The intolerable shirt of flame
Which human power cannot remove,
We only live, only suspire,
Consumed by either fire or fire"

(*Little Gidding* IV)

The final vision is as far beyond words as it was for Dante – so much so that the word "God" scarcely appears in *Four Quartets*, and then only in precise and restricted contexts. Nevertheless, *Four Quartets* glimpse the same truth about God (see box, right).

"I sit in one of the dives
On Fifty-Second Street
Uncertain and afraid
As the clever hopes expire
Of a low dishonest decade:
Waves of anger and fear
Circulate over the bright
And darkened lands of the earth,
Obsessing our private lives;
The unmentionable odour of death
Offends the September night.
Accurate scholarship can
Unearth the whole offence
From Luther until now
That has driven a culture mad,
Find what occurred at Linz,
What huge imago made
A psychopathic god:
I and the public know
What all schoolchildren learn,
Those to whom evil is done
Do evil in return…

Defenceless under the night
Our world in stupor lies;
Yet, dotted everywhere,
Ironic points of light
Flash out wherever the Just
Exchange their messages:
May I, composed like them
Of Eros and of dust,
Beleaguered by the same
Negation and despair,
Show an affirming flame"

(Auden, pp.245–7)

"Quick now, here, now, always –
A condition of complete simplicity
(Costing not less than everything)
And all shall be well and
All manner of thing shall be well
When the tongues of flame
are in-folded
Into the crowned knot of fire
And the fire and the rose are one"

(*Little Gidding* end)

The Way of Unknowing

Eckhart and the English Mystics

WHEN PS.-DIONYSUS (p.250) was translated into Latin by Erigena in the 9th century, the apophatic way (p.249) became as important in the West as in the East. For the German Meister Eckhart (died 1327), God lies so far beyond thought and language that even the names of the Trinity (Father, Son, and Holy Spirit) are simply human words for God's self-revelation: they are a point of access, yet God's essence, although it is known to be love, lies beyond even those names (cf. immanent and economic Trinity, p.246). Eckhart wrote:

"The eternal wisdom is born by the Father's power, for the Son is wisdom and the Holy Spirit is goodness, and both are love – one in nature and distinct in person...
The soul enters the unity of the Holy Trinity but it may become even more blessed by going further, to the barren Godhead, of which the Trinity is a revelation. In this barren Godhead, activity has ceased and therefore the soul is most perfect when it is thrown into the desert of the Godhead, where activity and forms are no more, so that it is sunk and lost in this desert where its identity is destroyed and it has no more to do with things than it had before it existed. Then it is dead to self and alive to God"

(Blakney, pp.200f)

"There never was another such union [as between the soul and God], for the soul is nearer to God than it is to the body which makes us human. It is more intimate with him than a drop of water put into a vat of wine, for that would still be water and wine; but here, one is changed into the other [theosis, p.250] so that no creature could ever again detect a difference between them"

(Blakney, p.29)

For Eckhart, union with God is the proper end and purpose of our existence (see box, left). The quest for union with God was equally important for the English mystics of the 14th century, above all Walter Hilton (c.1343–96), Richard Rolle (c.1300–49), Julian of Norwich (c.1342–post 1416), and the author of *The Cloud of Unknowing*. They had a wide influence through the many people who came to seek advice from them, and eventually through their writings. Each of them was clear in slightly different ways that through the adventure of prayer, the individual soul begins to know God and "to see some what of the nature of Jesus, and eventually to perceive the properties of the Blessed Trinity". They were all connected with the north-east of England, the East Midlands, and East Anglia. They were influenced possibly by the Franciscans and by the Rhineland Mystics, but they were far more obviously based on scripture, making use especially of the Psalms and of the New Testament. The immensely rich way in which the Bible led them to God made them ask urgently what God meant to them in their lives. The answer they found was one of "paring down", a reducing of the requirements of God in prayer to an apostolic minimum ("apostolic" because they believed that this was the fundamental practice of prayer established by the apostles). They all lived lives of total poverty, and Hilton required of himself and of those whom he counselled deeper and deeper conversion of lifestyle: "A man must be truly turned to Christ, and in his innermost mind turned away from all visible things before he can experience the sweetness of divine love." This might mean experiencing considerable suffering, as it did for Julian of Norwich: in her *Showings* (her visions of Christ) the suffering became her sharing in the passion of Christ. For Rolle and Hilton, suffering was a purging process that made possible an apophatic kind of prayer. Feelings did not matter. The "sharp dart of longing love" from the human to the divine, described in *The Cloud of Unknowing* (6), they recognized as an act of divine grace, an act initiated by God out of love: "The stirring of love, that is the work of the only God." The grace of God is always "the chief stirrer or worker… and thou only the consenter and sufferer". Even if sin is the cause of pain, nevertheless in the end "all shall be well, and all shall be well, and all manner of thing shall be well" (Julian of Norwich, *Showings* 13/27).

God is love and the source of love. Julian, therefore, came to think of God as Mother – God who is beyond all words and description nevertheless becomes known to us with the effects not just of Father but also of Mother: "As truly as God is our Father, so truly God is our Mother. Our Father wills, our Mother works, our good Lord the Holy Spirit confirms. And therefore it is our part to love our Lord God in whom we have our being, reverently thanking and praising him for our creation, mightily praying to our Mother for mercy and pity, and to our Lord the Holy Spirit for help and grace" (Colledge, p.296).

Eckhart and the English Mystics combined in their understanding of God two truths: God lies beyond intellectual knowledge, and yet God is known, both as and in a relationship of love (see box, above right). This means, as Augustine (p.259) also knew well, that those who love God no longer live in the created world looking for God outside it, but, prompted by the signs of God in creation, they start to live within God, and it is creation that is now outside.

This meant that the love of God was increasingly expressed through created things, not least through art, music, and architecture.

"God cannot be comprehended by the intellect of humans or for that matter of angels, for both are created beings. But God is incomprehensible only to our intellect, never to our love"

(*The Cloud of Unknowing* 4)

Eckhart
As a Dominican, Eckhart preached sermons (above) and may have studied under Albertus Magnus (as did Aquinas) in Paris. He was condemned in 1328 for 28 unorthodox propositions, but he was declared to have recanted (or never intended them in a heretical sense) before he died. His purpose was to break through the words and pictures in order to find the simple ground and source of all that is.

Architecture

The Houses of God

Cathedral St-Denis
Suger's work on this cathedral pioneered what became known as Gothic style. The massive thrust from the building was taken from pillars inside and distributed outside onto flying buttresses. Delicate ribbed vaulting replaced the barrel-and-groin vaulting of earlier churches. As a result, the "walls" became spaces to hold brilliant and beautiful stained glass.

"Out of my delight in the beauty of the house of God,… it seems to me that I see myself dwelling, as it were, in some strange region of the universe which neither exists entirely in the clay of this earth nor entirely in the purity of Heaven; and that, by the grace of God, I can be transported by spiritual ascent (anagoge) from this lower to that higher world"

(Administration 32)

I N 1091, A TEN-YEAR OLD BOY entered the Benedictine Abbey of St-Denis near Paris. By 1122, he had become Abbot, and from then until his death in 1151, he began to rebuild the abbey church in such a way that it would express his beliefs about God and enable others to share them. His name was Suger, and his rebuilt church led the way into what became known as Gothic architecture.

The original abbey had been founded by Clovis in 507. The St Denis to whom it was dedicated was a 3rd-century martyr who, according to legend, had been decapitated and then walked two miles to the spot where the church was later built. However, this St Denis was soon identified with the Denis (Dionysus) converted by Paul (Acts 17.34), to whom were attributed immensely influential works on the way in which humans can be united with God (p.250). It is *that* Denis (Ps.-Dionysus) whom Suger took as his guide and inspiration, writing *Concerning Consecration* and *Concerning his Administration* to describe his work.

Suger accepted from Ps.-Dionysus that the essence of God is unknowable, but that there are innumerable manifestations of God in revelation and in the created order, on which people can base their ascent to God. According to Ps.-Dionysus, "any thinking person realizes that the appearances of beauty are the signs pointing to invisible Beauty as real" (*Celestial Hierarchy* 1). Suger expressed those beliefs in building and decoration (see box, below left).

The recognition of beauty requires light. "God is light" (I John 1.5), and Jesus, in the words of the Nicene Creed, is "God from God, Light from Light". Suger therefore insisted that his masons and architects should open the interior to light (see caption, left). Suger even removed the screen bearing a rood (cross) that separated the chancel (the space for choir and sanctuary) from the nave, so that all could draw near to the adoration of God and the sacrifice of Christ in the Eucharist: "The sacred vessels should be enhanced by outward adornment, and nowhere more than in serving the Holy Sacrifice, where inwardly all should be pure, and outwardly all should be noble" (*Administration* 32).

Suger's view that a church and its ornaments may, by their splendour and beauty, lead through Christ to God (see box, above right) was profoundly influential, but it was not uncontested. Bernard of Clairvaux (1090–1153) had joined the newly founded Cistercians because they wished to emulate the poverty of Christ. He therefore denounced the new architecture:

"I say nothing of the astonishing height of your chapels,…the costly decorations and curious carvings and paintings, which distract those who would worship and keep them from contemplation… I do say to my brother monks, poor as you are – if in fact you are poor – what is all this gold doing in your churches?… Oh vanity of vanities!… The church has splendid walls, while her poor are beggars; her stones are gilded, while her children are naked; the eyes of the rich find plenty to satisfy them, while those in need find nothing to help them"

(Letter to William of St–Thierry)

The conflict continues throughout Christian history: how shall honour best be given to God in and through the houses of God? Cistercian churches achieved their own kind of beauty through their austere simplicity. Luther and Calvin (p.290) led the Reformed Churches into protest against what they took to be the attempted incarnation of God and the saints in statues and images, much as the Iconoclasts in the East (p.287) had been suspicious of idolatry.

Church architecture thus expresses the ways in which particular communities respond to what they believe God has done for them and for the world. The *form* of churches remains remarkably constant, often being built in the shape of a cross, but the interior use may change. Where, for example, it is thought that the priest offers again the sacrifice of Christ, a church will lead up to a high altar, far removed from the congregation; where it is thought that people are gathered to remember the Last Supper, the altar is moved into the middle of the congregation.

What remains true is that architecture surrounding the symbols of faith can be for many as life-giving as it was for the German poet Rilke (1875–1926) when he first entered a Russian Orthodox Church:

"For him the simple folk kneeling and praying before their Madonnas were not ensnared in superstition: their worship in such wondrous surroundings was the manifestation of a creative process which he saw in art, in which God himself was still in the forming: 'From the people's every gesture there streams out the warmth of his growth like an infinite blessing'"

(Prater, p.53)

To step into a church should, in Suger's view, be to take a step towards God. He therefore wrote an inscription for the porch:

"…Being nobly bright, the work Should enlighten souls that they may pass through light To the True Light, through Christ, the true door [John 10.7,9]… The earth-bound soul rises to truth through that which is material, And from being bowed down, a dead thing, it is raised to new life"

Pontigny Abbey
This abbey was built in the 12th century in austere Cistercian style. It portrayed Bernard's belief that monastic buildings should reflect the simple poverty of monastic lives. The abbey churches usually lack belfries because the monks live not to attract others, but to draw closer to God in separation from the world.

Liturgy and Drama

In the Presence of God

Do this in Remembrance of Me

"Was ever another command so obeyed? For century after century, spreading slowly to every continent and country and among every race on earth, this action has been done, in every conceivable human circumstance, for every conceivable human need from infancy and before it to extreme old age and after it, from the pinnacles of earthly greatness to the refuge of fugitives in the caves and dens of the earth. Men have found no better thing than this to do for kings at their crowning and for criminals going to the scaffold; for armies in triumph or for a bride and bridegroom in a little country church; for the proclamation of a dogma or for a good crop of wheat; for the wisdom of the Parliament of a mighty nation or for a sick old woman afraid to die; for a schoolboy sitting an examination or for Columbus setting out to discover America;... one could fill many pages with the reasons why men have done this, and not tell a hundredth part of them. And best of all, week by week and month by month, on a hundred thousand successive Sundays, faithfully, unfailingly, across all the parishes of Christendom, the pastors have done this just to make the plebs sancta Dei – *the holy common people of God"*

(Dix, p.744)

CATHEDRALS AND CHURCHES were not built only for the glory of God. They were built also for use, and above all for liturgy. Liturgy means, in general, the worship of God (p.214), but in Christianity it refers especially to the ways in which Christians obey the command of Jesus at the Last Supper to "Do this" in remembrance of him – his way of saying that through the bread taken as his body, and through the wine taken as the blood that marks the start of the new covenant, he will be present with his followers "until the end of the world".

The liturgical way in which this command has been obeyed has been called by many names – the Last Supper, the Eucharist, the Mass; and these names reflect different understandings of what Jesus meant by it. Obedience to the command "Do this" remains the central way in which Christians are united with God and with each other (see box, left).

The drama of liturgy surrounding obedience brings the past event (and person) into the present and makes it an eventuality now, as R.L. Grimes puts it: "Liturgies do two things. They 're-present' events and 'event-ualize' structures. An event is literally unrepeatable... So every event, not just the exodus of the Hebrews, the incarnation of Christ, or the enlightenment of Buddha, is unique... We, by our ritual action, save such events from becoming mere artefacts from the past. Without rituals such events have no presence" (Grimes, pp.44f).

Churches and cathedrals were not restricted to the performance of liturgy alone. They became stages for drama, bringing God directly to human experience. Early examples of this are the medieval miracle plays (dramatizations setting forth the life, miracles, and/or martyrdom of a saint); the mysteries (cycles of plays telling the story of humanity from the Creation to the Last Judgement – in England the cycles of Chester, Coventry, Wakefield, and York have survived); and the moralities (dramatized allegories – early examples are *The Castle of Perseverance* and *The Summoning of Everyman*, more usually known simply as *Everyman*). Although these dramas were based on Scripture, they went far beyond the text, introducing characters with whom the audience could identify themselves. For that reason, they were opposed in the Reformation (although biblically based plays were written as a substitute). One consequence was to accelerate the development of a theatre detached from the Church. Even so, religious themes continued to be important (e.g., Faust), and a specifically Christian theatre was developed by the Jesuits (p.294–5), partly in reaction to Protestant productions, but even more as a natural development of the Ignatian (p.294) emphasis in prayer on the imagination of place and circumstance. When music was added (for example, di Lasso's choruses for *Samson*), this contributed to the development of opera and oratorio.

In Spain, the *auto sacramental* was an even more direct development from the medieval morality plays, which led to the powerful transformations of the form effected by Calderon (1600–81). He wrote more than 70 *autos*, which expound the meaning of faith, but which are devotional as well. A.A. Parker, in *The Allegorical Drama of Calderon*, called Calderon "the dramatist of Scholasticism [medieval philosophical theology] in general, as Dante (p.270) was the poet of Thomism [Aquinas, p.266] in particular".

As theatre has become increasingly detached from its place in liturgy and ritual, so its connection with religion has depended on the outlook of the dramatist. Corneille and Racine could not have written as they did without a Christian background. As the French writer and poet, Charles Péguy (1873–1914) observed, "In Racine we discover our wounds, in Corneille we discover ourselves"; and R. Speaight, in *The Christian Theatre*, regarded Corneille's *Polyeucte* as "among the rare masterpieces of the Christian theatre... standing on a lonely eminence".

In the 20th century there were notable attempts in the theatre to explore Christian faith by dramatists who held Christian beliefs themselves, notably T.S. Eliot and Charles Williams. In TV and film, the connection between human experience and God beyond the realms of sentiment has become increasingly rare and accidental. The "option for options" (p.316) still means that those who control the media do not regard God as a serious human option; but those controlled by money cannot deny the human spirit forever.

Medieval Mystery
In medieval times sound effects were used to make mystery plays as realistic as possible. The thunder barrel, a quarter full of pebbles, was vigorously turned, drums were beaten, and horns were blown.

Big Screen Crucifixion
Surrounded by Roman soldiers, Jesus carries his cross in a crowd scene from the film Golgotha.

Music

Praise or Performance?

The harmony of creation became known as "the music of the spheres", of which Thomas Browne (1605–82) wrote:

"There is a music wherever there is a harmony, order or proportion; and thus far we may maintain the music of the spheres;… for even that vulgar and tavern music, which makes one man merry, and another mad, strikes in me a deep fit of devotion, and a profound contemplation of the First Composer, there is something in it of divinity more than the ear discovers

(*Religio Medici*, p.111)

Handel's Messiah

Luther saw that music could tell God's story, culminating in works that became vast oratorios like Handel's Messiah. *Below is the score for the* Messiah *written in the composer's own hand.*

IN THE LETTER TO THE EPHESIANS (5.18), Christians are commanded to "sing psalms and hymns and spiritual songs", and they have been singing in praise of God ever since. In early days, much was inherited from synagogue and Temple (pp.214f), with special emphasis on chanting Psalms on a single note – the kind of chanting known as Gregorian because it was associated inaccurately with the reforms of Pope Gregory.

New hymns were also written, many of which, from both Greek (on Orthodox music, see p.288) and Latin, are still sung – e.g., *Phos hilaron*, "O gladsome light, O grace/ Of God the Father's face/ The eternal splendour wearing"; or, probably written by Ambrose, 340–97, *Rerum Deus tenax vigor*, "O God, creation's secret force,/ Thyself unmoved, all motion's source".

Ambrose helped Augustine (p.258) to become a Christian, and Augustine recognized music as a gift from God: "This is the way of singing God gives you; do not search for words. You cannot express in words the sentiments which please God: so, praise him with your jubilant singing… What is this jubilation, this exultant song? It is the melody that means our hearts are bursting with feelings words cannot express. And to whom does this jubilation most belong? Surely to God who is unutterable. And does not unutterable mean what cannot be uttered? If words will not come and you may not remain silent, what else can you do but let the melody soar? What else, when the rejoicing heart has no words and the immensity of your joys will not be imprisoned in speech? What else but 'sing out with jubilation?'" (*Sermon on Psalm 32, 1.7–8*)

Music was thus believed to take people into harmony with the whole of creation and with God. Thomas Browne wrote of music in harmony with creation (see box, left), but long before then polyphony (many voices singing the same text to different but harmonious notes) had been invented, reinforcing the sense of symphony (Greek *sun*, "with" + *phone*, "voice") in God's creation. Luther's encouragement of music in the service of God gave rise to composers like J.S. Bach (1685–1750), who wrote in the margin of his rules for accompaniment, "The end

and goal of thorough bass is nothing but the honour of God". Luther (see box, right) believed that people should approach God, not in Latin but in their own language. He encouraged hymn singing, writing both the words and the music of *Ein' feste Burg ist unser Gott* ("A safe stronghold is our God"). On the other side of the Reformation, Roman Catholics also saw what music offered in telling God's story and helping people to sing God's praise. Above all, it allowed increasingly splendid and dramatic settings of the liturgy surrounding the Eucharist, the Mass. The Council of Trent declared: "In the case of those Masses which are celebrated with singing and with organ, let nothing profane be intermingled, but only hymns and divine praises. The whole plan of singing should be constituted, not to give empty pleasure to the ear, but in such a way that the words may be clearly understood by all, and thus the hearts of the listeners may be drawn to the desire of heavenly harmonies, in the contemplation of the joy of the blessed" (Hayburn, pp.25–31).

All this outpouring of music was certainly splendid, but was it praise or performance? Long before music took off in so many new directions, the reformer, John Wycliffe (c.1330–84), observed: "When there are forty or fifty in a choir, three or four proud and lecherous rascals perform the most devout service with such flourishes that no one can hear the words, and all the others are dumb and watch them like fools".

To allow music to be of service to all people, a search was made for congregational music. Metrical versions of the Psalms were produced, and many new hymns were written. In the case of John and Charles Wesley (p.296; Charles alone wrote more than 5,000 hymns), these were not just to be rousing or pleasing to the ear: they carried Biblical and Christian teaching. When John Wesley put together *A Collection of Hymns for the Use of the People Called Methodists* (1780), he wrote: "The hymns are not carelessly jumbled together, but carefully ranged under proper heads, according to the experience of real Christians" (Manning, p.11).

In 1940, a community called Taizé was founded to bridge the divide between Protestants and Catholics: its music draws people together in the recognition of God. It also points to the way in which music is genuinely ecumenical (Greek *oikumene*, "inhabited world"). It is music not for an audience outside, but within the symphony that can be regarded as the nature of God:

> "What is this big thing? God, if you like. What's it, or shehit, like? I would say,' Enderby said thoughtfully, 'like a big symphony, the page of the score of infinite length, the number of instruments infinite but all bound into one big unity. This big symphony plays itself for ever and ever. And who listens to it? It listens to itself. Enjoys itself for ever and ever and ever. It doesn't give a bugger whether you hear it or not"
>
> (Burgess, p.31)

Abide With Me
The Christian hymn Abide With Me *is sung on secular occasions, notably at football matches. In music and hymns, human emotions continue to be reached and connected with God, whether in the revival of Gregorian chant, in charismatic choruses, or in other chants.*

In the Reformation, Luther (pp.290f) understood the power of music:

"Next to the word of God, music deserves the highest praise. She is a mistress and governess of those human emotions... which control people or more often overwhelm them... Whether you wish to comfort the sad, to subdue frivolity, to encourage the despairing, to humble the proud, to calm the passionate, or to appease those full of hate, what more effective means than music could you find?"

(Blume, p.10)

OPPOSITE:

Blake's Jerusalem
William Blake said of
himself: "Inspiration and
vision was then, and now is,
and I hope will always
remain, my element, my
eternal dwelling place".

Art and Feeling
By expressing the feelings
associated with
events, art is able
to create the same
feelings in others,
as here in the
descent of Jesus
from the cross by
Michaelangelo
(1475–1564).

Art

Instruction and Vision

THE POET AND ARTIST WILLIAM BLAKE (1757–1827), who saw the purpose of art as the transcendence of the ordinary, wrote "'What,' it will be question'd, 'when the Sun rises, do you not see a round disk of fire somewhat like a guinea?' 'Oh no, no, I see an Innumerable Company of the heavenly Host crying "Holy, Holy, Holy, is the Lord God Almighty!"' I question not my Corporeal or Vegetative Eye any more than I would question a Window concerning a Sight. I look thro' it and not with it." In the same way, the art critic Clive Bell concluded in the days preceding World War I: "Art and religion are two roads by which men escape from circumstance into ecstasy". Immediately after World War II, Pablo Picasso (1881–1973) came to a very different conclusion: "Painting is not done to decorate apartments; it is an instrument of war for attack and defence against the enemy". Christian art comes into being between these two extremes: art lifts people from the world to see something of the glory of God, but art also serves many purposes in the affirmation of God's kingdom on earth. Examples of these are:

❖ instruction: wall paintings and stained glass windows served as "texts" for instructing the faithful in the days before books and widespread literacy

❖ persuasion: the life of Christ and above all his crucifixion are displayed in ways that might appeal to people to convert their lives into greater conformity with his

❖ propaganda: beyond persuasion, art might be used to entice people with the prospects of paradise or terrify them with the torments of hell

- protest: art can become an expression of prophetic anger against evil, not least corruption in the Church
- participation: art can take people through the scene or person portrayed into the reality that lies beyond it: an obvious example is the series in many churches of the Stations of the Cross: these portray 14 episodes (some legendary) in the events of Christ's Passion, leading up to his death; the purpose is to draw those who follow the 14 Stations into the suffering of Christ, and into reflection on the high cost of their redemption
- prayer: art builds a bridge between people and God, so that they are taken through the work of human hands to the One to whom it points – and from whom it has come (for the example of icons, see pp.286f): art becomes a window through which people look, as the priest and poet, George Herbert (1593–1633), wrote:

"A man that looks on glass,
On it may stay his eye;
Or if he pleaseth, through it pass,
And then the heaven espy"

- interpretation: art often takes the verbally expressed ideas of Scripture and translates them into sight
- decoration: art endeavours to dignify buildings or objects associated with God; with this was connected the immense economic consequence of patronage and of the employment of so many skills and crafts
- analogy: philosophical analogy recognizes the limits of language but tries nevertheless to say that God is "something like this" though not exactly (p.268); art may do the same; Mark Cazalet's *Christ Nailed* hangs Jesus on a fence with a scrap metal smelter in the background, suggesting that out of the wreck comes new life. Analogy has become particularly important in Christian art since cinema has moved to an increasingly realistic portrayal of both Jesus and God. Film has moved from God being heard but not seen, through Pasolini's *Matthew* and *Jesus Christ Superstar*, to *Jesus of Montreal* – a repeat of the move in painting from symbol to realism

Christian art may therefore be a direct expression of praise, adoration, and glory, or it may serve some other purpose that points less directly to God. What all art has in common is the way in which, like music, it goes directly to human emotions and feelings. This leaves all art (not just Christian art) open to manipulation, open to the attempt of artists to control people through their emotions – the grotesque and often grim side of art as propaganda for ideology.

Where Christian art is not propaganda, it is "the invisible made visible" – the title of a chapter in Richard Harries' book, *Art and the Beauty of God*, a title that reflects Francis Thompson's poem (see box, right).

"O world invisible, we view thee,
O world intangible, we
touch thee,
O world unknowable, we
know thee,
Inapprehensible, we
clutch thee…

Not where the wheeling
systems darken,
And our benumbed
conceiving soars!
The drift of pinions, would we
hearken,
Beats at our own
clay-shuttered doors.

The angels keep their
ancient places;
Turn but a stone and start a
wing!
'Tis ye, 'tis your estrangéd faces
That miss the many
splendoured thing"

(Thompson, pp.132f)

OPPOSITE:

Christ Nailed
This is one of Mark Cazalet's
14 Stations of the Cross (see
text), painted in 1999, all of
which are set in areas of
London, making the same
point about incarnation as
the Chinese and African
crucifixions on pp.242–3.

Icons

Veneration and Adoration

Madonna and Child
This Byzantine-Serbian icon was made in 1350. Icons of Mary were hung on city walls to ward off attackers. Some were believed not to be the work of human hands: a human artist might be involved, but only as the agent of the Holy Spirit.

"In the image the features of the emperor have been preserved unchanged, so that anyone who looks at it recognizes him in the image... Thus the image could say, 'I and the emperor are one'... He who honours the imperial icon, therefore, honours in it the emperor himself"

(Belting, p.153)

ART HAS FREQUENTLY IN CHRISTIAN history raised the issue of idolatry, of whether worship is being offered to an image. This was one issue in the break between Eastern and Western Christianity. That schism (p.248) seemed mainly to be about issues of authority and doctrine, but another was the use of images. When the legate of the Pope proclaimed the schism at Constantinople in 1054, he criticized the Greeks for showing Jesus on the cross, thereby implying that Jesus was dead and not risen.

By that date, Greek paintings, known as icons, were well-established. They depicted God, angels, saints, and many other sacred subjects and were displayed in churches. Icons were used in liturgy and personal devotion, but they became popular only after great argument. The fundamental objections were, first, that God cannot be represented in a picture, and second, that even if that were possible, any respect shown to the picture would be idolatry – exactly that grievous offence condemned so fiercely in the Bible (p.183).

In the earliest Christian art, no attempt was made to portray Jesus or the events of his life. Instead, signs and symbols were used (e.g., a fish, because the Greek letters of *ichthus* ("fish") are the initials of Jesus Christ Son of God Saviour). But as Christianity became the religion of the Roman Empire, Christians took over two uses of images:

❖ to commemorate the dead: from the Roman veneration of the dead through portraits on their tombs, the veneration of saints through icons developed in about the 3rd century

❖ to make present among people the power and authority of the emperor: from the time of Diocletian (245–313), images of the emperor were sent to distant provinces to receive ritual homage as a sign of loyalty

On that basis, Athanasius (p.253) put forward an argument (see box, left) that Basil (p.253) showed could be applied to God without supposing that God was being divided into parts:

"Just as no one who looks at the imperial image in the marketplace and acknowledges the emperor would deduce the existence of two emperors, first the image and then the real emperor, that is the situation here, too. If the image and the emperor can be one (for the

*image does not cause a multiplication of the emperor),
the same holds true of the divine Logos and God"*

(Belting, pp.152f)

According to this argument, whatever is portrayed on an icon can be approached as present through the icon. The more theologians argued that God's essence cannot be known, the more helpful icons were in making worship possible, as, not surprisingly, Ps.-Dionysus (p.250) realized: "It is quite impossible that we humans should, in any material way, rise up to imitate or to contemplate the heavenly hierarchies without the aid of those material means capable of guiding us as our nature requires" (Belting, p.494). Some objected that God cannot be depicted in the way an emperor can. That is true, but as the incarnation of Christ shows God united with human nature, so an icon shows God united with this created object – without, in either case, the essence of God being divided or diminished.

Because icons belong to God or to the spiritual realm, and are thus holy (cf. p.188f), it was believed that they possess great power. Many icons were believed to be miraculously created and were known as *acheiropoieteis* "not made with hands" (see caption, left). Icons were therefore revered: as Gospel books are honoured because the Word of God saves people through them, so icons can be honoured because God saves people through them (the argument of the Synod of 869). But honoured in what way? That remained the divisive question. The suspicion of idolatry would not go away, and there were two periods in the Eastern empire (the Iconoclastic Controversies, 726–87 and 813–43) when icons were banished and destroyed, at times when Islam, with its ferocious rejection of idolatry (p.321), threatened the borders.

In the end, a distinction was drawn between veneration and adoration: to respect and venerate divine and spiritual realities through icons is different from worshipping an icon as though it is the reality to be worshipped – a distinction of great importance in Indian religions. The distinction was clearly stated in a resolution of the 2nd Council of Nicaea in 787 (see box, right). On this basis, icons became "windows into eternity", access on earth to God and the things of God.

Speaking of "images of our Lord, God and saviour, Jesus Christ, and of our Lady without blemish, the holy God-bearer, and of the revered angels and of any of the saintly holy people", the 2nd Council of Nicaea declared:

"The more frequently they are seen in representational art, the more are those who see them drawn to remember and long for those who serve as models, and to pay these images the tribute of salutation and respectful veneration. Certainly this is not the full adoration in accordance with our faith, which is properly paid only to the divine nature, but it resembles that given to the figure of the honoured and life-giving cross, and also to the holy books of the gospels and to other sacred cult objects"

Icon of Christ
Christ is depicted as a wise man and teacher in this richly coloured icon crafted in Macedonia in 1393/4.

From Greece to Russia

Incarnation, Freedom, and Beauty

IN ORTHODOX CHRISTIANITY, icons encourage worship and are therefore important in liturgy (p.278). So too is music. In the 6th century, Greek musicians such as Anastasios, Kyriakos, and above all Romanos (known, for his skill, as Melodos) developed the chanting of *Kontakia* (Greek *kontos*, the pole around which scrolls of text were wound), poems in which each verse leads to the same refrain. The poems retell scripture in dramatic ways to encourage deeper understanding of God (see box, left). The beauty of Greek liturgy soon spread throughout the world of Orthodox Christianity. Envoys sent by Vladimir of Kiev in the 10th century to assess other religions gave poor marks, not only to Judaism and Islam, but also to Western Christianity. When they arrived in Constantinople, the capital of the Eastern (Byzantine) Empire, they were overwhelmed by the liturgy in the cathedral of Hagia Sophia (Holy Wisdom): "We could not tell whether we were in heaven or on earth, because on earth such beauty does not exist, and we cannot describe it. We know only that God abides there among the people."

Vladimir proclaimed Greek Christianity the religion of his realm in 988, and its influence continued even after Moscow replaced Kiev as capital in the 14th century. The painting and veneration of icons remained a path to God, as did Hesychasm (p.250) in prayer. But distinctive Russian understandings of God emerged, not least in the way in which *startsi* (pl. of *staretz*, "old man") became living symbols of God in the way they lived their lives of holiness. Seraphim of Sarov (1759–1833) spent ten years of unceasing prayer in his monastery, mostly in total isolation, until he emerged to share God with the thousands who came to him: he lived the meaning of life possessed entirely by the Holy Spirit. In conversation with Motovilov in 1831, he said, "Prayer, vigil, fasting, and all other Christian practices may be good in themselves, but they are nothing if they are not the means through which we gain the Holy Spirit."

All this came home to a man who, in 1849, was taken to Semyonovsky Square in Moscow to be shot. He and 16 other so-called revolutionaries were allowed to kiss a cross, and three were then blindfolded and tied to posts. They heard the command "Take aim!" – and a long minute went by. Then they were told that they were to be spared and sent to the grim depravity of Siberia. The man was the Russian novelist Dostoevsky (1821–81). The experience seared into his deepest being the unconditional authority of Christ's command to forgive

---

Romanos on the Nativity stresses the paradox of incarnation:

"Today the Virgin gives birth to him who is above all being, and the earth offers a cave to him whom no one can approach. Angels with shepherds give glory, And magi journey with a star, For to us there has been born a little child, God before the ages.

Bethlehem has opened Eden, come, let us see; we have found delight in secret, come, let us receive the joys of Paradise within the cave… For this, let us hasten to this place where there has been born a little child, God before the ages…

The kings of the East seek your face, and the rich among your people beg to see you, for truly your people are those to whom you have been made known as a little child, God before the ages.

(Lash, pp.3, 5)

and to love – and also recognition of the dark complexity of the human soul. Where does God enter in? *Notes from the Underground* (1864) portrays human life as, so often, self-contradiction in pursuit of self-interest: one part parades rationality, offering reasons for using others for its own ends; the other, despising reasons, simply treats others as enemies. Dostoevsky claimed that the censors prevented him including a third option, the force of Christian love (see box, right). But Dostoevsky did not restore the suppressed passages when later he might have done so. His turmoil remained: where is God in the midst of darkness? The question continues in *Crime and Punishment* (1866), *The Idiot* (1868), *The Devils* (1871), and supremely *The Brothers Karamazov* (1880). Here, Dostoevsky set the dissolute father Karamazov against the admirable *staretz* Zosima, for whom the true goodness that he embodies issues in happiness and joy:

"Those swines of censors! Where I mocked and sometimes blasphemed for form's sake – that is allowed; where I deduced from this the need for faith and Christ, that is suppressed"

"People are made for happiness... All the righteous, all the saints, all the martyrs, were happy people"

Hell is then the inability to love which turns people from bearing each other's burdens into isolated individuals no longer related to others in love but alone with their own selfish interest. God, in contrast, is the possibility of real goodness; and one of the brothers, Alyosha, approaches it. But will humans in general ever take the risk of God? Dostoevsky saw human freedom as something so awesome that most people prefer to relinquish it. This is epitomized in the "Legend of the Grand Inquisitor", which follows the elder brother Ivan's probing question to Alyosha whether, if he foresaw the extreme suffering of even only one child, he would create a universe. Alyosha concedes that he would not, but suggests that Ivan has left out Christ. Ivan tells his story of the Grand Inquisitor to show how the Catholic Church has subjected Christ to its own ends: the miracle, mystery, and authority rejected by Christ in the wilderness temptations (p.238) are made instruments by the Church in order to take away from people the burden of free will and choice. Christ refused to rob people of their freedom, leaving them open to seek that victory of beauty which some lives do achieve: "The awful thing is that beauty is mysterious as well as terrible. God and the devil are fighting there, and the battlefield is the human heart."

The Firing Squad
The kind of execution faced by Dostoevsky was painted by Goya (1746–1828) in 1814. When the rebellion of the people of Madrid against the French was put down in 1808, their leaders were executed. Goya shared with Dostoevsky a realistic passion against human cruelty and evil, against which reason is impotent: "The Dream of Reason produces monsters".

Luther and Calvin

The Reformation

IN 1517, MARTIN LUTHER (1483–1546), an Augustinian (p.262) Professor of Theology, was said to have nailed to a church door in Wittenberg 95 theses criticizing indulgences (see text below). In fact, he may not have nailed them to the door but perhaps had simply circulated them for discussion. He had already distributed 97 theses for debate, arguing that people are saved not because they do meritorious works, nor because they have obtained from the Church remission of just penalties for their faults, but solely because God wills to save them.

In arguing this, Luther was striking at the heart of the way the medieval Church had taken control of salvation, much to its own profit. In that Church system, people are born in the condition of original sin – "original" because it comes from the fault of Adam transmitted to all his descendants. Its effect is removed by baptism. But what about sins committed after baptism? Confession of sins removed the guilt, and penance paid the penalty. If any outstanding penalty remained after death, it could be paid off through suffering in Purgatory (cf. Dante, on p.271), or it could be cancelled by indulgences.

Indulgences rested on a belief that Christ, Mary, and the saints had built up a vast treasury of merit on which the Church could draw in order to "pay off" the penalties that were owing, not just of the living but also of the dead in Purgatory. Sin might be forgiven but the penalty still had to be paid. The Church, with its devotion to Mary and the saints (hoping for their help), had become very much "a cult of the living in the service of the dead". The immediate trigger of Luther's protest was the widespread sale of indulgences, with its promise:

"So soon as coin in coffer rings The soul from Purgatory springs"

His protest, however, went much deeper, because indulgences raised the whole question

Cranach Triptych
This three-panel work by Cranach (1515–86) shows the great Reformers at work basing all they do on the crucifixion of Christ, preaching the unearned and unmerited goodness of God. In the words of Augustine (pp.258–61): "Grace is given, not to reward good works, but to enable us to do them – not because we have kept the law, but to enable us to do so" (Augustine, On the Spirit and the Letter 17).

of the nature and character of God and of how humans are saved. The Church, under Neoplatonic influence (p.250), had come to see God as the goal of a spiritual quest that humans, although disordered by sin, are competent to undertake. The help of God (*gratia,* grace) comes to people through Christ and through the sacraments, above all through baptism, penance, and the re-enactment of Christ's sacrifice in the Mass. Grace enables people to live and act in ways that acquire merit. On this view faith is thus fundamental, but on its own it is not enough. It has to be perfected by love – hence the formula of Aquinas (p.266), *fides caritate formata,* ("faith formed by love"): faith is the basic material on which love works to bring it to a perfect form of expression, much as clay is the matter that a potter brings to the form of a pot (see caption, right).

How can we be sure that we have done enough good works in this life to merit salvation? That was exactly the question that had troubled Luther as a young monk (see box, right). He found the answer – and God found him – by going back to Scripture. Luther accepted that we know nothing "of God's incomprehensible and unsearchable will" and that "to aim at a perfect comprehension [of God] is dangerous work in which we stumble, fall and break our necks… We look with the blind eyes of moles on the majesty of God" (*Table Talk* 118).

In that case, we have nothing to rely on except what God has revealed: Scripture alone (*sola scriptura*). Luther, therefore, translated the New Testament into German so that all people could have access to God through the word of God. Scripture reveals that God has acted to save us not in response to works of merit but solely because it is the will of God to do so. This is done by grace alone (*sola gratia*), to which humans respond by faith alone (*sola fide*). But faith is not a matter of assent on which love builds. Faith is total and absolute trust from which love flows as from a surging spring (*quellende Liebe*).

L uther wrote as occasions demanded, and printing spread his words widely. A Frenchman, Jean/John Calvin (1509–64) gave order to these beliefs, especially in successive editions of *The Institutes of the Christian Religion.* Calvin recognized both the sovereignty of God over all life, and the supremacy of Scripture as the sole rule of faith and practice, an authority confirmed by the inward witness of the Holy Spirit. The effects of God can be seen in creation, but it is impossible to understand what has been revealed of God without the "spectacles" that Scripture provides. Inherently sinful people, lost in the labyrinth of iniquity, can only be delivered by the Bible's message which, like Ariadne's thread, leads them out to a totally undeserved salvation. All this is in the control of God, which led Calvin's followers to develop strong doctrines of predestination, of the elect to salvation and of others to damnation. But for Calvin, as for Luther, salvation leads to union with Christ through the Spirit, by which people find peace with God and begin a transformed life.

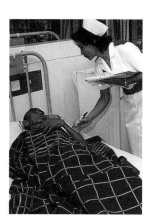

Good Works
According to Aquinas, baptism removes the fault inherited from Adam, but people still have to work on the material of their own lives to bring them to a form that merits salvation. This means that no one can be sure they have done enough until the final judgement: there can be no absolute assurance of salvation.

In one of his sermons, Luther looked back on his early life:

"For more than 20 years in my cloister… I sought God with great toil and with severe mortification of the body, fasting, watching, singing, and praying. In this way I shamefully wasted my time and found not the Lord.
The more I sought and the nearer I thought I was to him, the farther away I got. No, God does not permit us to find him so. He must first come and seek us where we are. We may not pursue and overtake him. That is not his will"

(Twentieth Sunday After Trinity)

Teresa and John

The Wounds of Love

L
UTHER AND CALVIN were not alone in seeking a reformation of the Church even though, in their case, it led to a break from the Church under the Pope. Others recognized the need for reform but hoped that this could be done under Papal rule. Notable was Erasmus (c.1466–1536), known as "the wisest man in Christendom". He was brilliant at pointing out the Church's many faults, but he hoped that it would reform itself. The Council of Trent (in three sessions between 1545 and 1563) made moves in that direction, though it reaffirmed indulgences, Purgatory, and the veneration of saints – the system to which Luther objected since it seemed to turn God into the manager of a supermarket of salvation (p.290).

For others, the reaffirming of Papal authority opened the way to a new confidence in living God-centred and God-directed lives. New religious orders came into being (see pp.294f) and others were reformed, among them the Carmelites in Spain.

In 1535, Teresa (later Saint Teresa, 1515–82) entered the Carmelite Convent of the Incarnation at Avila. After years of lax discipline, she became drawn to a stricter life, encouraged by her visionary experiences of God (p.41). In 1562 she founded the convent of St Joseph at Avila, the first of the houses of the Carmelite Reform (called "discalced", i.e. without shoes). Alongside her reform, she wrote several books for her nuns, notably her *Autobiography*, *The Way of Perfection*, and *The Interior Castle*. In these she traced the spiritual life from its beginnings to union with God in the "spiritual marriage", illustrating its stages (recollection, quiet, and union) from her own experience.

Teresa's reforms were much opposed, but she found support from a monk known as John of the Cross. He had joined the Carmelites in 1563, but because of laxity in the Order, he was close to leaving when Teresa persuaded him to support her reform. He did so, suffering imprisonment and banishment from opponents. Out of passion (in both senses, of his suffering and of his love of God), his life was changed and his great books on God's work in the soul were written.

John of the Cross's writings show how he came to the living God whose life is love, a love that searches for the beloved. They are extended commentaries on three of his own poems. *The Spiritual Canticle* unfolds the love of the Biblical Song of Songs in his poem of that name:

"You looked with love on me,
and, deep within, your eyes imprinted grace;

Teresa's desire for God was described by Carmelite nun Ruth Burrows in this way:

"All that made Teresa a great mystic, a passionate lover of God, is available to each of us if we would take the same path of faithful prayer, humble perseverance, and generosity in doing God's will and not our own, and a tireless effort to love others as Jesus has loved us. The Teresa of visions and ecstasies (p.41) remains on the pedestal, out of reach; an object of delight and admiration but unchallenging. The real Teresa speaks directly to us: true union can be attained, 'with our Lord's help, if we really try for it by surrendering our own will to whatever is the will of God... Oh how much to be desired is this union! Happy the soul that has attained it!'; and again, 'Beg our Lord to give you perfect love for your neighbour and leave the rest to him'"

(Burrows, p.9)

this mercy set me free,
held in your love's embrace,
to lift my eyes, adoring to your face…
Your look that can endow
All things, sought me – see how
Your eyes on me left grace and beauty there!"

(Flower, p.16)

"So dark the night! At rest
and hushed my house, I went
with no one knowing
upon a lover's quest
– Ah, the sheer grace! – so blest,
my eager heart with love aflame
and glowing"

(Flower, p.9)

The Ascent of Mount Carmel and *The Dark Night of the Soul* explore the poem that "rejoices at having reached the high state of perfection, which is union with God, by the path of spiritual negation" (see box, right). *The Living Flame* explains the poem that begins

"Flame, living flame, compelling,
yet tender past all telling,
reaching the secret centre of my soul!
Since now evasion's over,
Finish your work, my Lover,
Break the last thread, wound me and make me whole!"

(Flower, p.18)

The wound is real. To love God like this demands the loss of everything that is less than God – including one's ideas about God – and this is the Dark Night of the soul. That is not a kind of depression. It is a realization that even God seems to have gone – but only to draw us deeper, through darkness into light: "If the living God, and not our image of God, is to fill the emptiness of the human spirit, even that image – the closest we have got to God himself – may need dismantling… When John later had time to relate this experience in prison, he perceived it as 'the loving mother of the grace of God, undoing him to recreate him'" (Matthew, p.83).

"O lamps of fire bright-burning
with splendid brilliance, turning
deep caverns of my soul to pools of light!

Once shadowed, dim, unknowing,
now their strange new-found glowing
gives warmth and radiance for my Love's delight"

(Flower, p.18)

For both Teresa and John, God was not a truth to be considered, but Truth to be lived with daily and forever.

John and Teresa
John and Teresa receive their commission from Christ and respond, "I will sing the mercies of the Lord forever".

Ignatius

The Jesuit Vision

I N MARCH, 1522, a young courtier and soldier knelt before the Black Madonna of Monserrat, a wooden figure dating from the 11th century to which many pilgrims came, and there he offered up his dagger and his sword. He had already given away his mule and his elegant clothes. He was setting out on an entirely different campaign.

The young man was Ignatius. Teresa and John sought the conversion of religious Orders: he sought a new kind of Order altogether. Born in 1491 with the name Inigo Lopez de Onaz of Loyola (Ignatius is the Latin form), he began life as a soldier, devoted to women and involved in duels and fights. But a serious wound led to a long convalescence. Having no exciting stories to read, he read a Life of Christ and some lives of the saints – and found them exciting in an entirely different way. Bravery in battle and romance were as nothing compared to the way in which he was moved by the stories of Francis (p.264) and Dominic (p.262). In discerning the utterly different feeling within himself, he had already begun on what became a vital part of Ignatian prayer, the discernment of what God is doing within the soul.

When he was sufficiently recovered, he made the journey to Montserrat to offer himself to God, and from there he went to Manresa where he lived in poverty as a beggar. Although he found much of that life repellent, and even thought of suicide, he also began to experience the deepest meaning of the Trinity, of creation and of the humanity of Christ. In a cave near the river Cardoner, all this was confirmed in a vision that gave direction to his life. He began, through prayer, to seek and find God in all things, and to see Christ as the gentle Lord and King who calls humans to work with him in extending the kingdom of God.

Ignatius began to write down what he had learned in the Manresa vision in the book that eventually became *The Spiritual Exercises*. This contains exercises in various forms of prayer, thematically arranged and designed to be used several times a day over 30 days. They help those undertaking them to probe the depth of faith or of doubt, to journey alongside Christ, and to begin to understand what that journey might mean, in practice, for life, values, and vocation. *The Exercises* may be undertaken as a part of daily life, or removed from it – either in a monastic house or in a retreat centre. In either case, people are guided by someone called a director, who suggests to them what exercises to do, and helps them to discern what God is asking of them.

Ignatius of Loyola
Ignatius had been born in 1491 with the name Inigo Lopez de Onaz of Loyola – much later he changed his name to the Latin form, Ignatius.

The Exercises rest on the certainty that all people can know God and are known by God: God is always with them and committed to them. The aim is "the praise, reverence, and service of God" through a conversion of life *away* from self-centred attachments and *to* a freedom which makes for a "graced collaboration" with the Spirit. Whatever decisions follow, those who undertake *The Exercises* realize that in *all* lives "two sets of values, two wisdoms" (cf. Augustine, p.262) are at work, and that following the Christ of the Gospels is a risky business. That the risk is worth taking is a grace that may dawn and deepen in the second and third weeks of *The Exercises*. It takes different forms in different people, because God does not jump to attention according to the timetable: "God acts according to his sovereign freedom and his action cannot be scheduled" (Ivens, p.69). But it is *God* who is acting in them and whose way within them can be discerned. Ignatius followed that insight throughout the rest of his life. He made pilgrimages to the Holy Land, studied in Paris and ended up living in Rome. A small group gathered around him, and together they formed Compania de Jesus, the Society of Jesus, recognized by the Pope in 1540.

Jesuits are strongly bound by their obedience to the Pope, and by their understanding that they must go to promote the faith wherever they are sent. They were often the first missionaries in the Americas and in India, Japan, and China. At the heart of the Jesuit vision is God's love for the world. That is why the Jesuit vocation is to be always *in via*, "on the way" to any place where God's glory can be proclaimed. A Jesuit of the 20th century, Karl Rahner, described the Ignatian experience in this way:

"God 'becomes flesh' in his creature and yet his creature does not falter the nearer she comes to God but, for the first time, feels her true worth: this is the experience, yet not all the experience. Incomprehensible as it may seem, God's descent into finiteness takes place through his creature who has attained his very presence. The nameless, incomprehensible, inflexible, incalculable God does not disappear from the sight of the person who prays and acts, God does not become like the sun which makes everything visible and itself is not seen… The creature who is singled out from every other creature by the bestowal of God's love appears in this unremitting light as the one beloved and preferred, as the one chosen for existence among many empty possibilities:… [She] is loveable, beautiful, of ultimate, eternal validity, because God himself can and does bring to fulfilment the inconceivable miracle of his love by giving himself to his creature"

(Rahner & Imhof, p.18)

Karl Rahner
Rahner (1904–84) was a Jesuit who explored the philosophical foundations of Christian theology. This must begin with humans as they know and experience the world, each other, and themselves. Humans come to know God not by trying to solve puzzles of Christian teaching (doctrine), but by constantly extending their knowledge of the world and themselves until they find that they are led beyond themselves and their immediate knowledge, first to the meaning, then to the source of it. Then they can forget themselves and begin to know God in faith, hope, and love; and that is the meaning of spiritual life.

John Wesley

An Urgency of Salvation

The name Methodist had been used of Wesley and some others when they were students at Oxford, "either in allusion to the ancient sect of physicians (so called from their teaching that almost all diseases might be cured by a specific method of diet and exercise), or from their observing a more regular method of study and behaviour than was usual with those of their age and station"

(The Character of a Methodist, 1747)

John Wesley
Wesley undertook "field-preaching" because he believed that existing Churches failed to bring true religion to the world – "the love of God and of all mankind": "This love we believe to be the medicine of life, the never-failing remedy, for all the disorders of a disordered world"
(Wesley, p.3).

IGNATIUS WAS NOT ALONE IN INSPIRING MISSIONARIES. So too did the brothers John and Charles Wesley (1703–91, 1707–88). The conversion they brought to others they had experienced themselves in 1738. On 21 May 1738, Charles Wesley was lying ill in a house in London, and not only ill but also in utter despair about the cruel treatment of slaves in Georgia in America. Suddenly, he said, "I found myself at peace with God". Three days later, "towards ten, my Brother [John Wesley] was brought, in triumph, by a troop of our friends and declared, 'I believe'".

John Wesley had begun that momentous day by reading the words in 2 Peter 1.4: "Exceeding great and precious promises, that by them... you might be partakers of the divine nature". A little later he read, "You are not far from the kingdom of God" (Mark 12.34). That afternoon he went to St Paul's Cathedral, where he heard sung, "Out of the deep have I called unto Thee, O Lord: Lord, hear my voice" (Ps.130). Not long after came the famous moment when he felt God in a new way:

"In the evening I went very unwillingly to a society in Aldersgate Street, where one was reading Luther's [p.290f] preface to the Epistle to the Romans. About a quarter before nine, while he was describing the change which God works in the heart through faith in Christ, I felt my heart strangely warmed. I felt I did trust in Christ, Christ alone, for salvation; and an assurance was given me, that he had taken away my sins, even mine, and saved me from the law of sin and death"

John Wesley founded the movement, eventually Church, known as Methodism (see box, left). He was ordained in the Church of England and did not intend to set up a separate movement. But he was accused of enthusiasm when he followed the Moravians in saying that all Christians should feel in their hearts the faith they professed in their heads. He answered: "Now cannot you join in all this? Is it not the language of your heart? O when will you take knowledge, that our whole concern, our constant labour is, to bring all the world to the religion which you feel, to solid, inward, vital religion" (Earnest Appeal to Men of Reason and Religion). For Wesley, the knowledge of God was a matter, not just of intellectual conviction, but of deeply felt realization that God has dealt with sin, and that the Holy Spirit works powerfully in the lives of those who turn to God in trust. He took this message to the furthest parts of the land, travelling on horseback about 8,000 miles a year, and preaching wherever he went until he reached the age of 87 (see box, right). This burning desire to share the truth and consequence of God, as it has been made known uniquely in Christ, took missionaries to the furthest parts, not just of England, but of the world. The American novelist, Pearl Buck, was brought up in China by her missionary father. Looking back, she could see in him a blindness to much that was good in China, but she also recognized his passion to help others to feel the truth of God. She called it "an urgency of salvation, a very madness of necessity". This understanding of God involves necessarily the whole of life. God is not a proposition waiting for consent or rejection: God is an immense power bringing change in people who then bring change to others in the world, especially to those in need – a reason why Christian missions did so much to establish schools and hospitals worldwide.

In that spirit, John Wesley, on 24 February 1791, took up his pen and wrote his last letter, less than a week before he died. He wrote it to William Wilberforce, who had already begun his campaign for the abolition of slavery. It was a campaign that Wesley had himself supported with passion in one of his most powerful tracts, *Thoughts upon Slavery*, in 1774. In his letter to Wilberforce he wrote:

My Dear Sir,
Unless the Divine Power has raised you up to be as Athanasius [p.245], contra mundum, I see not how you can go through your glorious enterprise in opposing that execrable villainy which is the scandal of religion, of England, and of human nature. Unless God has raised you up for this very thing, you will be worn out by the opposition of men and devils; but if God be for you, who can be against you? Are all of them together stronger than God? Oh, be not weary in well doing. Go on, in the name of God and in the power of His might, till even American slavery, the vilest that ever saw the sun, shall vanish away before it... That He who has guided you from your youth up may continue to strengthen you in this and all things is the prayer of,...
Your affectionate Servant,   John Wesley

Wilberforce saw the abolition of the slave trade and slavery in 1807 and 1833. Slaves were freed in America by the Proclamation of 1863. There are now more people in slavery than at the height of the slave trade; and opposition to that continues as part of the Christian story of God.

A lady once asked John Wesley, "Suppose, Mr Wesley, that you knew that you were to die at 12 o'clock tomorrow night, how would you spend the intervening time?" He replied, "How, Madam? Why, just as I intend to spend it now. I should preach this evening at Gloucester, and again at five tomorrow morning. After that, I should ride to Tewkesbury, preach in the afternoon, and meet the society in the evening. I should then repair to my friend Martin, who expects to entertain me, converse and pray with the family as usual, retire to my room at 10 o'clock, commend myself to my heavenly Father, lie down to rest, and wake up in glory"

Methodist Meeting
A preacher delivers a sermon to a group of Methodists during a church camp meeting in Eastham, Massachusetts, in 1852. At such meetings, hymns played a powerful part (p.281).

America

Old and New England

Quaker Settlement
This Friends Meeting House was built by Quakers in 1808. It stands in Mullica Hill, New Jersey.

CHRISTIAN MISSIONS SPREAD RAPIDLY as part of the exploration of what were, to the Europeans, "new worlds". But the sense of mission was not the only reason why European Christians settled in those new worlds. One was trade; another was to escape persecution and religious conflict in their home countries. As a result, the settlements in North America reflected the different ways in which God had been understood and characterized in the places of origin (see box, below).

Christians brought with them from their home countries radical differences in the understanding of God and of God's dealings with the world. To give one example, the Puritans – of whom Perry Miller and Thomas Johnson wrote (p.1), "Without some understanding of Puritanism… there is no understanding of America" – emerged in England in the 1560s as "the hotter sort of Protestants". As Protestants, Puritans accepted the fundamental principle of God's grace, through which people are justified by faith alone (p.291), as Luther had expressed it: "There is no other beginning than that your King comes to you and begins to work in you… You do not seek him but he seeks you, and

---

NORTH-AMERICAN SETTLEMENTS

Moving from south to north on the East coast, these North-American settlements tended to reflect the way God had been worshipped "back home".

✝ **ENGLISH COLONY, VIRGINIA**: This attempted to translate across the Atlantic Anglican episcopalianism (Greek, *episkopoi*, "bishops") "according to the constitution of the Church of England", with "all atheism, prophaneness, popery or schism to be exemplary punished to the honour of God" (Bemiss, p.57).

✝ **QUAKER SETTLEMENTS, NEW JERSEY AND PENNSYLVANIA**: William Penn (1644–1718) sought to establish colonies in which the Quaker principles of non-violence and the inner light of conscience would be guarded constitutionally: he received the grant of Pennsylvania in 1681, confirmed in 1682.

✝ **PURITAN SETTLEMENTS, MASSACHUSETTS**: In 1620, William Bradford established Plymouth, so named after the town they had left; later they were called

"pilgrims", and the Pilgrim Fathers led the way for much larger settlements from 1630 onwards; they had a vision of establishing a new Israel, a holy commonwealth under God. John Winthrop (1588–1649), their first governor, wrote: "We must consider that we shall be as a city upon a hill, the eyes of all people are upon us" (Miller & Johnson, p.199).

✝ **ROMAN CATHOLIC SETTLEMENT, NEW FRANCE (CANADA)**: Initially (following the Edict of Nantes, 1583, which had allowed in France extensive rights to the Huguenots), this was to coexist with Protestants. Cardinal Richelieu, however, reorganized the Company of Quebec in order to remove the toleration extended to Protestants, and to ensure that Roman Catholicism would dominate.

where he does not come, you remain outside". That raised the question for both Luther and Calvin (pp.290f) of why God does not seem to come to some people: as the Geneva Catechism asked, "Are not all ordained unto eternal life?" To that question, the robust answer came back, echoing both Paul (p.235) and Augustine (p.259), "Some are vessels of wrath ordained unto destruction, as others are vessels of mercy prepared to glory." A further question and answer follows in a catechism, *Certaine questions and answeres touching the doctrine of Predestination*, bound up with the Breeches Bible (the Geneva Bible of 1560, so-called because the word "breeches" is used in Genesis 3.7):

> *"Question: How standeth it with God's justice, that some are appointed to condemnation?*
> *Answer: Very well: because all men have in themselves sin, which deserveth no less: and therefore the mercy of God is wonderful in that he vouchsafeth to save some of that sinful race, and to bring them to the knowledge of the truth"*

On the Continent, battles raged over whether God saves some or all, or whether God has predestined only some for salvation, and over the question also of whether anyone could be sure that they were saved and not damned.

English Protestants from Tyndale in the 1520s, through Cranmer, Latimer, and Ridley, to Queen Elizabeth and well beyond, tried to find a middle way between extreme answers to these questions. They rejected the authority of the Bishop of Rome over the English Church (allied as it was to threats of invasion from the Continent), and they resisted the certainty that some are predestined to damnation; they rejected also the belief that after conversion and baptism, no fall from grace would be forgiven by God. They thought God's judgements were "very deep", so that that people could be sure of salvation but not secure in it: they were "saved but not safe".

Pilgrim Fathers
The Pilgrim Fathers (see box, left) build their first communal dwelling in New Plymouth. Of their landing in America, William Bradford (1590–1657), first governor of the Plymouth colony wrote: "Being thus arrived in a good harbor and brought safe to land, they fell upon their knees and blessed the God of heaven, who had brought them over the vast and furious ocean, and delivered them from all the periles and miseries therof, againe to set their feet on the firme and stable earth, their proper elemente" (History of Plimouth Plantation, in Miller & Johnson, p.100).

This middle way, between despairing of salvation and neglecting the grace of God, was well expressed in the catechism of the Book of Common Prayer in 1662 (see box, top left). In this view, it follows that all people are called to the life of grace and can indeed live it. There developed, therefore, in England a spirituality that was for all people and not just for a privileged few. Benjamin Whichcote put this strongly during the 17th century (see box, bottom left).

"Know this, that thou art not able to do [good] things of thyself, nor to walk in the commandments of God and serve him, without his special grace: which thou must learn at all times to call for by diligent prayer"

(BCP, 1662)

"We are now under God's call and invitation. There is no man in the world, that hath the Bible in his hand, or that hath heard anything out of it, who hath any reason to doubt but that he is called of God. What we read in the Bible, we may build upon, and apply to ourselves, with as good assurance as if God did despatch an angel from heaven to us. We are in this day of grace God's invited guests; and we are all of us under the operation of the divine spirit and may depend upon the assistance of the divine grace"

(Porter, p.428)

The Puritans shared many beliefs with other English Protestants, not least justification by faith. But they took issue with the religious settlement in England which put into effect that middle way between extremes, a way that had endorsed episcopacy, the liturgy of the Book of Common Prayer, and the discipline and instruction of the people, not by gatherings of the congregation (which might result in a gentleman being placed on the penitent's stool), but by courts and sermons.

The Puritan ambition to promote a more thorough-going Protestantism ranged from those who attempted to introduce legislation for change in Parliament, to those who actively pamphleteered, notably in the Marprelate Tracts, for the abolition of episcopacy and of the Book of Common Prayer – which, in their view, contained in its prayers too much "vain repetition". Even more radical were those who thought that the Queen's governorship of the Church should be abolished.

Common to them all was an understanding of how life should be lived according to God's word, in a way that distinguished them from others. They abhorred excess in drink and clothing; their families were to be centres of prayer and instruction; they liked to hear sermons; they would not allow sport on Sundays; they made a point of instructing their servants in the duties of the godly. It was the more theologically and morally extreme of this group who recognized that Jacobean England was unlikely to put into effect their wishes, and that they needed to distance themselves from a range of laws which might lead to their condemnation and imprisonment. They set sail for the New World.

Many other examples could be given of conflicts in Europe from which the early settlers sought to escape. This background of dispute about God (or at least about the ways in which God and the expected consequences of God in behaviour should be understood) had a profound effect on the search for a Constitution in America after the successful war of independence from Britain which took place in 1776–83.

Those seeking a form of government that would hold a balance between the States and a central Federal authority knew well the background of wars in the name of religion, and they were aware also of the political mood heading towards the French Revolution. In 1814, John Adams (1735–1826), US President from 1797 to 1801, wrote on religious passion (see box, right). He had written 40 years earlier why he was not inclined to preach: "The frightful engines of ecclesiastical councils, of diabolical malice and Calvinistical good-nature never failed to terrify me exceedingly whenever I thought of preaching" (Lasley, p.38).

Faced with so many religious rivalries, it was necessary to set up what Thomas Jefferson called (in a letter to the Danbury Baptist Association, 1802) "a wall of separation between Church and State": "Believing with you that religion is a matter which lies only between a man and his God, that he owes account to none other for his faith or his worship, that the legislative powers of government reach actions only, and not opinions, I contemplate with sovereign reverence that act of the whole American people which declared that their legislature should 'make no law respecting an establishment of religion, or prohibiting the free exercise thereof' [1st Amendment], thus building a wall of separation between Church and State".

This does not imply an antagonism against God. The majority clearly prayed, as most presidential (and other) speeches still end, "God Bless America". It is simply that, as Senator George Mitchell said at the Iran-Contra hearings in July 1987, "Although he's regularly asked to do so, God does not take sides in American politics".

This has left a situation in which the human imagination of God has received the maximum freedom, and new religions, even newly found revelations (as in the case of the Mormons), have flourished. In God we trust; but at a distance from public statement.

"Touch a solemn truth in collision with a dogma of a sect, though capable of the clearest proof, and you will soon find you have disturbed a nest, and the hornets will swarm about your legs and hands, and fly into your face and eyes"

(Lasley, p.40)

Shakers
Members of The United Society for Believers in Christ's Second Appearing became known as Shakers because of their ritualistic shaking in prayer.

America

Out of Africa

THROUGH ABOUT FOUR CENTURIES at least ten million (perhaps as many as 18 million) Africans were sold into slavery in North and South America. Everything was taken from them. Except God. Indeed, from one point of view, God (in Christian understanding) was imposed on them, because some slave traders justified their work by saying that they were bringing Africans out of darkness to the light of Christianity. One of these Africans, Phyllis Wheatley, was taught to read and write, and she published a book of poems in 1773 (only the second to be published by a woman in colonial America) in which she expressed those feelings:

> "'Twas mercy brought me from my Pagan land,
> Taught my benighted soul to understand
> That there's a God, and there's a Saviour too:
> Once I redemption neither sought nor knew.
> Some view our sable race with scornful eye,
> 'Their colour is a diabolic die.'
> Remember, Christians, Negroes, black as Cain,
> May be refined and join th' angelic train"

(Fishel & Quarles, p.37)

But people in Africa already knew well that "there's a God", and travellers had been reporting this frequently. One of them, William Bosman, wrote of the beliefs of Africans on "the Slave Coast" (i.e., West Africa) that they had a clear idea of "the True God and ascribe to him the Attributes of Almighty and Omnipresent": "It is certain that ... they believe he created the Universe, and therefore vastly prefer him before their Idol-Gods. But yet they do not pray to him, or offer any Sacrifices to him; for which they give the following Reasons. God, they say, is too high exalted above us, and too great to condescend so much as to trouble himself or think of Mankind; Wherefore he commits the Government of the World to their Idols; to whom, as the second, third and fourth Persons distant in degree from God, and our appointed lawful Governours, we are obliged to apply ourselves. And in firm Belief of this Opinion they quietly continue" (*A New and Accurate Description of the Coast of Guinea*, p.368a). This meant that Africans brought to America a strong sense of God high above humans and the world, who delegates gods and goddesses to act as intermediaries on earth (cf. the Canaanites, p.178). The High God is known by different names in different tribes, as are the very numerous gods and goddesses, though they may be given a

Phyllis Wheatley
A portrait of the author of Poems on Various Subjects, Religious and Moral, *printed in London in 1773. Wheatley was kidnapped from Senegal at the age of nine and taken as a slave to Boston, where she began to write poetry in English five years later. She was quickly recognized as a prodigy, and her writings became particularly popular in England.*

collective name. The Yoruba, for example, call them *orishsa*, the Ibo *alose*, the Ashanti *abosom*, and the Fon *vodun*. The merging of African and South American beliefs that resulted from the slave trade (see caption, right) led to the creation of new yet old ways of worshipping God. Thus the Fon *vodu* was believed to be the spirit of God present everywhere but able to be summoned to a local place or person, and much of their religion focused on rituals to summon *vodu* and bring their powers into effect. In Haiti, the word was used first to speak of God, but then of their religion in general, appearing in English as Voodoo.

The Africans also took with them their way of worshipping God in drumming and dancing. In South America, especially in Brazil, Uruguay, and Argentina, African dancing was known by the European settlers as *macumba* and *candomblé*, but those words soon became the names of distinct religions in which the African understanding of God and gods remained alive, combined with Christian and indigenous beliefs.

Increasingly, the God and gods of Africa became associated with Christian beliefs and symbols. In Mexico and the West Indies in particular, the gods as the agents of God were associated with the Virgin Mary and with the saints, to whom non-Protestant Christians addressed so many devotions and prayers. For African Christians this was natural, since God remains high (beyond words and description) yet acts through agents bringing power and mercy into the world.

Furthermore, the distinction between adoration and veneration (p.287) seemed completely unreal when Africans observed Christians addressing their prayers to images and pictures of the Virgin Mary and of the saints. The gods as agents were clearly the same as saints, and did much the same things. Thus Shango was identified with St Barbara (despite the gender difference) because both were protectors against thunder. Eshu-Elegba is a trickster who carries messages to heaven, so he was identified in Trinidad with the devil (the trickster) and in Cuba with St Peter (who carries the keys to the kingdom).

In North America, this process happened much less, but even so, African Americans continued their own ways of understanding God, even when many of them became Christian, especially in dancing and drumming, and eventually in the songs of tribulation and hope known as Spirituals. Of these the great African American writer, W.E.B. DuBois (1868–1963) wrote: "Through all the sorrow songs there breathes a hope, a faith in the ultimate justice of things". They and the Bible enabled Martin Luther King "to have a dream" that spoke directly from God. All these are examples of ways in which Africans pioneered in America the naturalization of the imagination of God. But for some Christians, that was extremely threatening.

Slave Trade
When Africans were captured and taken (with hideous brutality) to South and Central America to be sold into slavery, their fundamental understanding of God went with them. This allowed them not only to continue their own religion in a strange land but also to link God and the agents of God to the beliefs they encountered, not least those of Christianity.

W.E.B. DuBois wrote about God from an African perspective in *The Smoke King*

"I am the smoke king,
I am black…

I am carving God in night,
I am painting hell in white.
I am the smoke king,
I am black…

Sweet Christ, pity toiling lands!
Hail to the smoke king,
Hail to the black!"

(Chapman, pp.359f)

New Clothes for Old Beliefs

God in Religions Outside Christianity

I N 1968, THE JOURNALIST, RENE CUTFORTH, wrote of an uncle of his who was "an Anglican clergyman about 80 years old who closely resembled a tortoise: he'd been in India for 60 years, completely immersed in Sanskrit roots and the translation of bits of the New Testament into Marathi. He was also wildly eccentric to the point, some people said, of insanity... In the end, he left India under a cloud":

"He'd been in charge of a little church at Miri on the Bombay side, and...he'd begun to fashion the Anglican Service more to his own way of thinking, and when some ecclesiastic called in there at the time Charles was nearly 80, he found a very odd state of affairs. There was a cross on the altar, but there were also Shiva [p.104] and the Elephant God [p.108], and others of the Hindu Pantheon. Most of the service consisted of dancing and singing with elaborate chants in Sanskrit all written to the tune of 'Champagne Charlie is me name'. Nowadays he'd be regarded as an ecumenical pioneer, but in those days they simply shunted him back to England with the suggestion that he was off his rocker."

(The Listener, 4/4/68)

Missionaries
Missionaries (shown here in a painted wood carving) were divided by the beliefs about God that they encountered in the lands to which they went. Were they the worship of idols (and therefore to be condemned) or did they represent a consequence of God and a real knowledge of God expressed in local ways?

Cutforth's uncle was not alone in seeing that words and imaginations about God do not have to be European only. Wherever Christian missions from Europe went, they encountered people who believed in God and not some rival to God. Christians could not doubt that Christ had, in the phrase of the poet Gerard Manley Hopkins, "let all God's glory through" in a unique way:

"...God's glory which would go Through her [Mary] and from her flow Off, and no way but so"

But they had no doubt, either, that it was *God*, and not some other kind of "God", who had entered into covenant with the Jews: there can only be the One who is God, no matter how much Christians might claim that Christ had brought into being a new reconciliation with the One God. From the start, therefore, Christians put God at the centre of the entire religious universe, just as the Jews had done before them. The Jewish *Letter of Aristeas* (c.100BCE) therefore argued that Jews should not be imprisoned by the Egyptian Pharaoh, because they worship "the God who maintains your kingdom, the same God, the Lord and Creator of the universe, as other people, although they call him by different names, such as Zeus or Dis" (15).

As Christianity spread, in its earliest years, into the Roman Empire, it attacked whatever brought God down to a human level – for example, the immorality of the myths (p.206) taken as literal descriptions of how gods and goddesses behave. But equally the Christians recognized much that was true in life and thought. They therefore argued that the Word and Wisdom of God, the Logos of God (pp.232, 236), is planted as a seed in all people: it is what the Stoics called *spermatikos logos*, the "seed

Ricci
The Jesuit missionary Matteo Ricci, shown here with an early convert, immersed himself in Chinese ways and learning until eventually he was recognized by the Chinese as "a wise man" (like one of their own), and therefore deserving the utmost respect.

Logos" that "in each generation enters into holy souls and makes them friends of God" (Wisdom 7.27; p.205). From this God-given reason arises a natural knowledge of God and of moral law that is not in conflict with the Christian understanding of God – so much so that Plato could be regarded as Moses speaking Greek.

This attitude allowed an alliance between the Christian understanding of God and Greek philosophy, so that correctly expressed ideas about God (orthodoxy, Greek, "right opinion", in contrast to orthopraxy, "right behaviour") led to the emergence of creeds as signs or marks of those who belonged to the true Church: a creed was originally called *sumbolon*, or symbol, a word that meant a password in the Roman army showing whether you were friend or foe.

As Christianity spread, this search for points of connection was repeated, as in the conversion of Norse ideas of God (p.39). In the 16th century, the only possible entry into China was achieved when a Jesuit (pp.294f), Matteo Ricci (1552–1610), adopted the same principle, just as another Jesuit, Alessandro Valignano (1539–1606), had put it into practice in Japan: Christian missionaries must adopt the ways of the country in which they had come to live provided those ways did not conflict with the fundamental Christian understanding of God.

Ricci therefore learned Chinese and became a master of the Chinese classics, and he dressed as the expert in their learning that the Chinese recognized him to be. He encouraged Chinese Christians to continue to bow before Confucius and to make food offerings to their ancestors, because he realized that the Chinese were not worshipping either as God, but simply showing gratitude and respect for them. But he did forbid anything that showed lack of trust in God, as, for example, in funeral rites summoning additional help for the deceased against the perils of death. He recognized what Shang Di and Tian (pp.144–7) meant to the Chinese, but extended the meaning of God by calling God Tianzhu, Master of Heaven.

The foundations of Christianity in China were relaid. But as other Christians arrived, particularly Franciscans and Dominicans, they rejected the sinification (making Chinese) of Christianity: as happened in South America, they insisted on a European statement of the meaning of God. The Rites controversy was resolved by the Pope in Rome against the Jesuits in 1742 (in the bull *Ex quo singulari*), and the Chinese emperor expelled Christians unless they followed the Ricci way.

Can the Christian imagination of God be clothed in Chinese (or Indian or African or other) garments, or does this compromise the unique revelation of God in Christ on which salvation depends? This battle over so-called syncretism continues, but "the Ricci way" has in fact extended widely as Christians in different cultures offer their own approximate and corrigible words in speaking of God – in, for example, *minjing* theology in Korea or "water buffalo" theology in Thailand.

All this has led to a liberation of the human imagination of God, in which René Cutforth's uncle was indeed a pioneer.

OPPOSITE:

———◇———

The Wise Men
In this Indian miniature
from the Mughal school of
the 17th century, the Magi
(Zoroastrian ritual experts)
are seen bringing their gifts
and adoration to the infant
Jesus. This is expressed in
Indian terms, although
influenced by the earlier
traditions (for example, the
halo; cf. p.38).

God and Myth

The Challenge of Science

I N 1835, THE FIRST RAILWAY IN GERMANY was opened, running 20 km (12.5 miles) between Fürth and Nürnberg. In the same year, David Strauss (1808–74), published *Das Leben Jesu Kritisch Bearbeitet* (*The Life of Jesus Critically Examined*, Eng. trsl. 1846). Strauss saw a connection between the two events when writing about his first journey on the line (see box, left). In his *Life of Jesus*, Strauss was responding to the view that the science which has produced steam engines (and much else) has the right to decide other matters of truth, as well as claims about what God can and cannot do. Those claims were made widely in the 19th century. John Tyndall said in 1874:

"The impregnable position of science may be described in a few words. We claim, and we shall wrest from theology, the entire domain of cosmological theory. All schemes and systems which thus infringe upon the domain of science must, insofar as they do this, submit to its control, and relinquish all thought of controlling it."

(Tyndall, p.197)

Science and Success
This contemporary picture shows the opening of the railway in 1835, taken by Strauss to be an example of "a modern miracle" achieved by science (see box, above).

The immense success of post-Newtonian science led to what is known as "the nomothetic ambition" (Greek *nomos*, "law"), the determination to find the laws that govern all that happens in the universe, including human behaviour. Laplace, when Napoleon observed that he had left God out of his system, replied, "Sir, I have no need of that hypothesis"; Lemaitre wrote a book with the title *L'homme machine* (humans understood in terms of mechanisms that "make them go"). Darwin's account of the origin of species by means of evolution reinforced the nomothetic ambition, so that Freud initially hoped that he would become "the Newton of the inside of the human head".

How could God intervene in such a universe? Deists (a term used loosely of varying writers defending God against scepticism in the 17th and

18th centuries) hoped to rescue God as the one who initiates creation and then allows it to run according to God-created laws. But that produces a remote and ineffective God, "all brain, like a watch", as Herman Melville (author of *Moby Dick*) put it in 1851 (p.35), very different from the traditional pictures.

Perhaps, however, it is the traditional pictures that are wrong – or at least misunderstood. That was Strauss' conclusion. In his view, the traditional characterizations of God in the Bible were being taken far too literally, as he wrote in the Preface to *The Life of Jesus* (see box, right), in words that seem to be a straightforward surrender to science. But Strauss was far more subtle. Science may have the right to adjudicate on the truth or otherwise of many factual propositions, and facts may have to be the foundation of truth, but there is more to life, and the meaning of life, than science. There is also the world of myth.

The word "myth" has become in modern times a word of abuse, meaning a story that is put about but is false. In the 19th century (and earlier), it meant a way of telling the truth about ourselves and the world when other words and equations have failed us (see further pp.46f). It is that positive understanding of myth which Strauss brought to bear on the Gospels and their portrayal of God.

The philosopher Hegel (1770–1831) had drawn attention to the distinction between idea and fact: ideas may be based on facts, but they go beyond the bare facts in order to show what they mean. Religions are the great communities of "meaning-making", or, to use Strauss's own term, "myth-making" – as indeed are the sciences when they produce theories, such as evolution, based on facts: they are myths in the older, not the more recent, sense.

Myth may have no connection with any event, and may simply be a way in which people have tried to explore and share with each other the meaning of the world and of themselves and of their relationships. But equally, myth may arise from events in order to draw out their meaning. Events are not left "back there" in the past as bare happenings. They are given meaning. So when Strauss called attention to the primary role of myth in relation to Jesus, he was not denying that there were facts and events which had happened. He was rejecting the approach that tries to sort out scientifically which claimed facts are factual, and then discards everything else as useless fiction, or as worthless invention. Clearly *something* happened in the case of Jesus. But which is more important? The archaeology which attempts to establish the certain details of his biography (which are in fact, from a historian's point of view, extremely few)? Or the meaning of his life? In truth, both are important, but what mattered to Strauss is to understand the way in which the followers of Jesus used the mythological opportunities of their Bible to convey why he was important and significant in making God real for them and for others. It follows that God cannot be destroyed (or for that matter rescued) by science. How then can God be known?

"The exegesis of the church of old was based on two presuppositions: first, that the gospels contain a history; and second, that this history was a super-natural one. Rationalism rejected the second of these presuppositions, but only in order to hang on more tenaciously to the first, insisting that these books present plain, though only natural, history. Science cannot remain satisfied with this half-measure. The other presupposition must also be given up, and the investigation must first be made whether in fact, and to what extent, the ground on which we stand in the Gospels is historical"

David Strauss
Strauss was a German theologian who tried to build a bridge between the claim that Newtonian science will explain everything and human emotions, the quality of which cannot be "explained away".

Beyond Reason

Barth, Pascal, and Kierkegaard

Isenheim Altarpiece
This panel forms part of the centre of the Altarpiece by Grünewald (d.1528). It again insists on the reality of the incarnation, as the critic J.K. Huysmans points out: "As for the Child, who is very lifelike and skilfully portrayed, he is a sturdy little Swabian peasant, with a snub nose, sharp eyes, and a pink, smiling face" (in Ruhmer, p.16).

STRAUSS RESCUED GOD from remoteness, but at a price that seemed to others to be too high: humans become judges of what God can and cannot do. To a young pastor of the Swiss Reformed Church, Karl Barth (1886–1968), the consequence was a disaster made all too evident during World War I, when he observed Christians on both sides using "God" to support and justify the war. God had been nurtured, like a pack animal, to carry whatever ideas people wanted to load on.

During the War Barth read carefully Paul's Letter to the Romans, and then wrote a Commentary in which he totally rejected any idea that God is subordinate to human reason. Exactly the reverse, God to be God must be utterly distinct from human ideas, not to be found as the conclusion of an argument, still less as the goal of a human experience or mystical quest: "There is no way from man to God". There is an infinite, qualitative difference between the creator and creatures, and God can only be known through revelation, in "the strange new world of the Bible". We can never see God as God is, but only through the revelation that culminates in the supreme paradox of Jesus. Looking at Grünewald's Isenheim altarpiece (left), Barth wrote: "Over there, but quite lonely, the child Jesus lies in His mother's arms, surrounded with unmistakable signs reminding us that He is a child of earth like all the rest. Only the little child, not the mother, sees what is to be seen there, the Father. He alone, the Father, sees right into the eyes of this child. On the same side as Mary appears the Church, facing at a distance. It has open access on this side, it adores, it magnifies, it praises, therefore it sees what is indeed the glory of the only-begotten of His Father, full of grace and truth. But it sees it indirectly. What it sees directly is only the little child in His humanity; it sees the Father only in the light that falls upon the Son, and the Son only in this light from the Father. This is the way, in fact, that the Church believes in and recognizes God in Christ... Because of this light streaming down from above, it worships before this human being as before God Himself, although to all visual appearance He is literally nothing but a human being.... It faces the mystery. It does not stand within the mystery. It can and must adore with Mary and point with the Baptist. It cannot and must not do more than this. But it can and must do this" (*Church Dogmatics*, I.2, p.125).

None of this diminishes the achievements of human intelligence, science among them, but it emphasizes that God is greater than, and different from, them all. Three centuries earlier, the scientist and philosopher Blaise Pascal had emphasized the glory of reason (see box, right) so that thought can show *that* God is (or at least that it is prudent to bet one's life on God, since if God exists one has gained everything, and if God does not exist, one has lost nothing – Pascal's wager). But only God can show *what* God is, as he did memorably to Pascal in 1654:

"Fire
God of Abraham, God of Isaac, God of Jacob, not of
philosophers and scholars.
Certainty, certainty, heartfelt, joy, peace.
God of Jesus Christ.
God of Jesus Christ.
My God and your God …
Everlasting joy in return for one day's effort on earth.
I will not forget thy word"

(ed. Krailsheimer, pp.309f)

Blaise Pascal
Pascal (1623–62) invented the calculator and syringe, and discovered "Pascal's Law" on pressure. Human intelligence was for him supreme (see box, below) but there is further still to go.

God can be known directly (even though not seen immediately) only in the inward recognition of faith. "Truth consists precisely in inwardness", a remark made by Søren Kierkegaard (1813–55) in *Training in Christianity*, who went even further in emphasizing the unbridgeable abyss between humans and God – an abyss that nevertheless *is* bridged by what he called the absurd, miraculous, and absolute paradox that in Christ the eternal has entered time and God has become human. To this Absolute Paradox of grace (of God's initiative) there can be only two serious responses: offence that anything so absurd could be proposed, or faith that it is so – *Either/Or* as he entitled one of his works:

"Faith is precisely the contradiction between the infinite passion of the individual's inwardness and the objective uncertainty. If I am capable of grasping God objectively, I do not believe, but precisely because I cannot do this, I must believe"

(Kierkegaard, p.182)

Life then becomes a radical choice of a Christ-like life (cf. Francis, pp.264f) – a seeming impossibility, so that despair is at the heart of ethics. But the true foundation of life before God is not to "get it right" but to live with passion in God's world: "The ethical demand is that one become infinitely interested in existing" (*op. cit.*, p.280). Living in that way became the demand of God in Liberation Theology.

"*Man is only a reed, the weakest to be found in nature; but he is a thinking reed. It is not necessary for the whole of nature to take up arms to crush him: a puff of smoke, a drop of water, is enough to kill him. But, even if the universe should crush him, man would still be more noble than that which destroys him, because he knows that he dies and he realizes the advantage which the universe possesses over him. The universe knows nothing of this. All our dignity, then, consists in thought. It is upon this that we must depend, not on space and time, which we would not in any case be able to fill. Let us labour, then, to think well: this is the foundation of morality*"

(Pensées 33)

Liberation Theology

The Option for the Poor

I N THE FINAL MONTHS before he died in 1961, the social philosopher Frantz Fanon published a book called *The Wretched of the Earth*. It was a passionate appeal on behalf particularly of the poor and exploited in Africa: change cannot be engineered by yet more "shifting around of the chairs on the deck of the Titanic": liberation is to be achieved, not by a return to African culture, not by an enlightened middle class, not by benevolent African dictators, not by "a new negritude", but by a collective – and violent – catharsis (see box, below).

Fanon's heartfelt cry met a response in South America, where the divisions between rich and poor, and the widespread exploitation of the poor, led to "an ethical indignation at the poverty and marginalization of the great masses of our continent". Those words were written by Leonardo Boff, one of the leaders of what became known as Liberation Theology. In that understanding of God, the priority is not to think and write, in an unbelieving world, as correctly as possible about God (orthodoxy), but "how to tell the non-person, the non-human, that God is love, and that this love makes us all brothers and sisters" (Gutierréz). This immediately demands a priority, not so much for orthodoxy as for orthopraxy (acting rightly: for the distinction, see p.306). This led H. Assman to define Liberation Theology as *teologia desde la praxis de la liberación* ("theology starting from the praxis of liberation").

"Liberation Theology" is more accurately theologies in the plural, because it contains several different understandings of God in relation to the poor. Its origins stem from the 16th century when at least some missionaries (e.g., Antonio de Montesines [died 1545] and Bartolomé de Las Casas), helping to establish the extremely strong presence of Roman Catholicism in South

Catharsis
Cockfighting is a popular sport in Bali. The ways in which people "enjoy" violence may be linked to a cathartic effect (see box, below).

CATHARSIS AND ENFORCEMENT

The ways in which people express themselves and their feelings about God are not always straightforward:

Why do Utku Eskimo men (normally peace-loving) beat chained-up dogs and enjoy it? Why do Balinese people enjoy cock fights in which birds tear each other apart? For the Utku, the experience is cathartic (Greek *katharsis*, "cleansing", "pruning") giving expression to feelings of violence in a way that does not harm other humans.

For the Balinese, the experience expresses and reinforces rivalries between groups in society in a way that again does not harm other humans. Catharsis and enforcement both occur in the many different ways in which people express their feelings about God and their membership of particular religions or religious groups.

America, began to protest on behalf of indigenous populations against colonialist exploiters. The modern movement began with the book by Gustavo Gutiérrez, *Hacia una teologia de la liberación*, in 1969. In a later book, Gutiérrez took as his title a phrase from St Bernard, *We Drink from Our Own Wells: The Spiritual Journey of a People*, and he applied to South America Bernard's argument that, in matters of the spirit and in relation to God, people must draw first on their own experience (see caption, right). In contrast, the emphasis in the Church had been, for centuries, the spiritual formation and deepening experience of individuals according to norms established in European Christianity. Liberation theologians seek a Church that arises from among the people by the power of the Holy Spirit: the agenda is set by the poor.

I n the *Power of the Poor in History*, Gutiérrez argued that the Biblical picture of God repeatedly demanding the liberation of the oppressed means that God has "a preferential option for the poor". By this he meant that "the poor deserve preference, not because they are morally or religiously better than others, but because God is God, in whose eyes "the last are first" (Matthew 19.30)". In other words, a mother with a sick child does not love her other children less because she spends more time with the sick child.

All this raised the possibility that violence may be a necessary means of bringing about justice: "We cannot say that violence is alright when the oppressor uses it to maintain or preserve order, but wrong when the oppressed use it to overthrow this same order." This evoked a hostile reaction from the Vatican (involved because these were Catholic writers in mainly Catholic countries), since it seemed to imply the validity of a Marxist criticism of traditional teaching about God, and also that, in the case of violence, the end justifies the means.

Even so, the final Vatican response, *Instruction on Christian Freedom and Liberation* (issued in 1986), emphasized the importance of liberation in the Biblical understanding of God (see box, above). The issue remains of what, in the eyes of God, the "true solidarity" of that instruction means, and of whether, in secular societies, obedience to the demand of Christ (that to help those in need is to help God in them) can seriously be obeyed without changing the structures within those societies. As Walter Rauschenbusch (1861–1919) put it: "Christian asceticism called the world evil and abandoned it: humanity is waiting for a Christian revolution which will call the world evil and change it."

The Vatican's Instruction takes the example of liberation achieved by God in the Exodus (p.181), and goes on to state:

"The Church is firmly determined to respond to the anxiety of contemporary man as he endures oppression and yearns for freedom. The political and economic running of society is not a direct part of her mission. Divine love, which is her life, impels her to a true solidarity with everyone who suffers. If her members remain faithful to this mission, the Holy Spirit, the source of freedom, will dwell in them, and they will bring forth fruits of justice and peace in their families and in the places where they work and live"

Communal Poverty
In South America poverty is communal, often a matter of solidarity for survival: "Spirituality is a community enterprise: it is the passage of a people through the solitude and dangers of the desert, as it carves out its own way in the following of Jesus Christ: this spiritual experience is the well from which we must draw."

Thealogy

God as Mother and Father

Christa
The portrayal of Christ or of God as feminine is, for some, disturbing. But for others it is a statement, following that of Paul, that in Christ "there is neither Jew nor Greek, slave nor free, male and female" (Galatians 3.28).

AMONG MANY LIBERATION GROUPS is one called *mujerista,* which is concerned with the oppression of women in general, and of Hispanic women in particular. The subordination of women to men exists in all religions and certainly in Christianity, where some Christians still derive it from Genesis as a creation principle (i.e., as belonging to the intention of God in creation, an argument that used to be used to justify slavery), reinforced by passages in Paul's letters.

Women have increasingly reclaimed God from male-dominated language and imagination. Many prefer to speak of thealogy (reflection on Goddess) rather than theology (reflection on God) because the Greek words for God and Goddess are gender specific, *theos,* masculine, *thea,* feminine. On 19 April 1984, a bronze statue of a woman as the crucified Christ was set up in the Cathedral Church of St John the Divine in New York. It was called Christa (again, gender-specific in Latin, *-us* masculine, *-a* feminine). After 11 days, protests led to its removal.

Do words matter? Certainly, because it is in words and language that we express our fundamental beliefs and our thoughts. Those who refuse to change their language continue the history of oppression: consider the shift from "nigger" to "Negro" to "black" to "Afro-American" to "African American": every step is a move towards the goal of human worth, equality, and dignity. That is why change in the masculine language of God is so urgent for many, both women and men. All words about Deity are inadequate, but some are a great deal more inadequate than others. Christa and Thealogy are early steps in reminding Christians that God is far beyond gender, but that a predominantly male vocabulary in relation to God damages Christian understanding and action. Maybe the next step would be to abandon both theo- and thea- and speak instead of Deology: Latin is also gender-specific (*deus, dea*), but both can be abandoned in speaking of Deo-.

Associating Mary with God has seemed to many Christians a way in which the feminine can be brought closer to God, but that too has become increasingly problematic, because of the way in which Mary has been held up as a model of submissive obedience, and because the claim that she was immaculately conceived and remained a virgin reinforced the denial of women's sexuality (through the claim that virginity is a higher vocation). But here, conversely, the claim has been made that Mary is a model of liberation because she brought into the world the redeemer without the help of a man.

The liberation of women is very recent and far from completed. The test of how far it has been achieved will be shown by the extent to which it enters into worship and liturgy. The Community of St Hilda was formed in 1987 to develop liturgy in which images precious to women rest easily among those of the older tradition. This liturgy can be compared with any in Prayer Books and Missals, as equally with the Wicca ritual for creating a circle on p.35:

"God is with us.
Her Spirit is here.
Lift up your hearts.
We lift them up to God.
Let us give thanks to the One who inspires us.
It is right to offer her thanks and praise.
Spirit of God, who breathes fire into our very existence, filling us with heavenly joy and holy indignation at the plight of our world; we worship you, we praise you, we recognize the symbol of your presence, your promise of solidarity with us on our journey.

We claim the sign of renewal given to a broken and discouraged community, now as then in Jerusalem. For you came to your own, filling them with confidence, gusting through their lives, bringing ecstasy and wholeness, clarity and vision, hope and peace. You enlightened their existence, enabled their mission, empowered them to be disciples of your word.

So, with all the women who followed you through your ministry, who watched you die and rise again, and with all those who inspired and supported the early Church, with Tabitha who showed solidarity with the poor, Lydia who welcomed the tired and travel weary, and Priscilla who knew the meaning of persecution, we praise you, singing:
Holy, Holy, Holy, God of all power! Heaven and earth are full of your glory. Come and deliver us, come and deliver us, come and deliver us, God most high. Blessed is One who comes in the name of our God! Come and deliver us, come and deliver us, come and deliver us, God most high.
Blessed is Christ our brother, who fills us with a sense of being one people, one community. On the night he was betrayed, he took bread, gave thanks, and broke it, saying: 'This is my body, which is given for you. Do this to remember me.' In the same way, after supper he took the cup, blessed it and said: 'This cup is the new covenant made in my blood. Do this whenever you drink it to remember me.'
Christ has died. Christ is risen. Christ will come again.
As one community we rejoice in your gifts, we accept responsibility for our world; we trust in your Spirit of challenge; we welcome your presence in this bread and wine.

Drunk with longing for your deep and disturbing presence to be revealed to us, we praise you with all who have derived inspiration from this story of renewal and refreshment. Come now, pour your Spirit on us so we are better able to proclaim your message, see new visions, dream new dreams. In the name of Christ.
Through him, with him, in him, in the unity of the Holy Spirit, all honour and glory be given to you, O God our Source and Inspiration, now and forever. Amen."

Mary
This 15th-century limewood carving from Upper Swabia (possibly by Friedrich Schramm or Michel Erhart) shows Mary gathering into her care those who pray for protection. It expresses the meaning of prayer for others.

Secularization

The Consequence of Options

FLYING OVER INDONESIA, the sociologist Peter Berger came close to being God. He was in a plane covered with symbols of the Indian bird of heaven, Garuda, the name also of the Indonesian national airline. Garuda is half-man, half hawk-like bird who is the *vahana* ("mount") of Vishnu (pp.92ff). Flying, like Vishnu, on the wings of Garuda, Peter Berger realized that to villagers gazing up from earth, he was "a god perhaps, or at least a demigod, soaring through the sky with unimaginable speed and served by machines of unimaginable power". For Berger, therefore, "the jet traveller in the Third World is a pretty good metaphor of modernity. He moves on the same planet as those villagers, and yet he moves in an altogether different world. His space is measured in thousands of miles, theirs by the distance a bullock cart can go. His time is expressed in the controlled precision of airline schedules, theirs by the seasons of nature and of the human body" (Berger, pp.1f).

The greatest difference is that travellers with their credit cards have many more choices or options than the villager. The post-Enlightenment world has endorsed, not a preferential option for the poor (p.313), but a preferential option for options, for securing the maximum freedom for individuals within the boundary of law. This means that religion and belief in God have also become optional, in an unprecedented way. That is the true meaning of secularization – a diminishing number of people who believe in God, and a diminishing influence of religion in society.

Secularization is not an ideology set up in competition with God: it is the consequence of options, of people choosing to do or believe a multitude of different things, although within the other options there are certainly critiques of God. Of these, the most searching has been the question of "theology after Auschwitz": where was God when people in a civilized society, many of them

Bird of Heaven
The sun shines on an airborne Garuda Indonesia Boeing 737–400 – the plane in which sociologist Peter Berger felt that he became close to being God.

Christians, enacted or allowed the Holocaust (pp.224–27)? Some resisted: Dietrich Bonhoeffer (1906–44), a Lutheran pastor, was arrested in 1943 and executed in 1944. But even before his final *Letters and Papers from Prison*, he had argued that the traditional understanding of God as one who intervenes from the outside (a *deus ex machina*, as in the classical Greek Theatre) was dead, and that the time had come for "religionless Christianity": "Our coming of age forces us to a true recognition of our situation vis-à-vis God. God is teaching us that we must live as people who can get along very well without him. The God who is with us is the God who forsakes us (Mark 15.34)" (*Prisoner of God* p.163).

The Death of God became a common phrase after World War II, implying not the disappearance, but the re-characterization of God. One who had already proposed this was the mathematician and philosopher, A.N. Whitehead (1861–1947). He realized that science presupposes a metaphysic of some sort (*meta + physic* = beliefs based on and transcending the elementary observations of nature; cf. Hegel on fact and idea, p.309).

In Whitehead's view, the most fundamental metaphysic is the belief that the universe is a matter of process through which possibilities are realized as actual occasions. God is the aim and sum of all occasions, so that everything is comprehended in God (panentheism), but God is also involved in the process, working like an artist to win order and beauty out of opportunity – but suffering also within the process when it is obdurate or resistant. God is "the great companion, the fellow-sufferer who understands".

This Process Theology was developed by Charles Hartstone (1897–2001), arguing that God as the sum of true perfection must include change, since perfection includes perfect relatedness. Thus God is "dipolar", embracing both the absolute and the relative, both eternity and time, and is therefore both world-transcending and world-including. God does not determine all things but is the means through which even the chance interactions of decision-making creatures are worked into a good conclusion. In contrast, others continued to live with God in prayer and worship (and thought) as the One who is and continues to be, even though this or any other universe may cease to exist, the One who is the source of all things, the absolute guarantee that our glimpses of goodness, beauty, truth, and love are not a matter of chance or illusion: they are the reality that endures because they reflect the reality that is God. But after Auschwitz (and other savagery during the 20th century) this could only be expressed quietly – a reason why that century produced astonishing poetry of God (e.g., Eliot and Auden p.273) much of which was a "wrestling with God". Of this, the Welsh poet R.S. Thomas was a major voice. If God is at all, it is "patiently with invisible structures he builds" (see box, right).

"Never known as anything
but an absence, I dare not name
    him
as God. Yet the adjustments
are made. There is an unseen power,
whose sphere is the cell
and the electron. We never catch
him at work, but can only say,
coming suddenly upon an
    amendment,
that here he has been. To demolish
a mountain you move it stone by
    stone
like the Japanese. To make a new
    coat
of an old, you add to it gradually
thread by thread, so such change
as occurs is more difficult to detect.
Patiently with invisible structures
he builds, and as patiently
we must pray, surrendering the
    ordering
of the ingredients to a wisdom that
is beyond our own. We must
    change the mood
to the passive. Let the deaf men
be helped; in the silence that has
    come
upon them, let some influence
work so those closed porches
be opened once more. Let the bomb
swerve. Let the raised knife of the
    murderer
be somehow deflected. There are no
laws there other than the limits of
our understanding. Remembering
    rock
penetrated by the grass-blade,
    corrected
by water, we must ask rather
for the transformation of the will
to evil, for more loving
mutations, for the better ventilating
of the atmosphere of the closed
    mind"

(Thomas, p.345)

ISLAM

ISLAM, THE RELIGION OF "allegiance to God", began historically with the prophet Muhammad in Arabia in the 7th century CE. However, according to its own account, it began as the way of life, or *din* (often translated as "religion") that God intended for all people from the start. God constantly sent prophets, including Moses (Arabic Musa) and Jesus ('Isa) to summon people to that *din*, but all were rejected, often killed. Some, however, accepted Muhammad and the revelation (Quran) proclaimed through him, so that Muhammad is the final prophet. Muslims bear witness to the fact that "there is no god but God [Allah, *the* God], and Muhammad is Allah's messenger." This witness is the Shahada, the first of the Five Pillars of Islam (p.349) which give structure and unity to Muslims all over the world.

The Quran is the non-negotiable authority in Muslim life and belief. The words and actions (and silences) of Muhammad and his companions are accepted as a living commentary on what the Quran means and how it should be applied. They were gathered in six revered collections of traditions (*ahadith*), known collectively as Hadith. Quran and Hadith make up Sharia, the way that Muslims should live.

After the death of Muhammad in 632CE (10AH in the Muslim dating), the Muslim community split. Some thought Abu Bakr was best qualified to be leader, and they became the Sunni Muslims (following the Sunna or custom of Muhammad). Others thought that his nearest relative, Ali, should succeed, and they became the Shia Muslims (*shi'at 'Ali*, "the party of Ali"). Shia Muslims exalt Ali and their Imams, a succession of leaders whom they regard as inspired teachers. There have consequently been bitter political divisions.

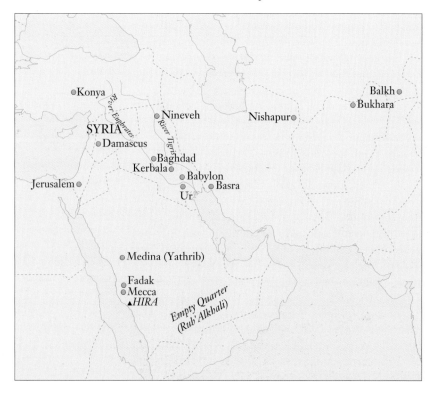

Within 100 years of Muhammad's death Islam had reached the Atlantic and the borders of China. It continues to expand, with about a quarter of the world's population being Muslims, living in most parts of the world. The worldly Muslim empires led some to react and draw closer to God in love and devotion. These were the Sufis (perhaps from *suf*, the rough wool cloak that they wore). Sufis spread widely in the 12th century and have remained influential ever since.

ISLAM TIMELINE

Prayer
Muslims are a single people (umma) *united in allegiance, or Islam, to Allah. They are united by the Five Pillars (p.349) including prayer, undertaken together facing Mecca.*

Muslim dates are given AH, After the Hijra, and follow a lunar calendar, but to make reference and comparison easier, dates are given here according to the Western calendar

Dynasties are shown in **bold**

Birth of Muhammad . Revelation of Quran begins . Hijra (move to Medina, 622) . Night Journey . Death of Muhammad (632) . 1st four caliphs, arRashidun . Abu Bakr . Umar . Uthman: forming of Quran . Ali	570–661
Umayyad dynasty . Disputes over succession . Formation of Shia (party of Ali) . Battle of Kerbala . Death/martyrdom of Husain . Dome of the Rock built in Jerusalem . Great Mosque of Damascus	661–750
Abbasid dynasty (750–1517) . Mutazilites . Hasan alBasri . Baghdad founded . abu Hanifa (Hanafites) . Ibrahim ibn Adham . Malik (Malikites) . Rabia . ashShafii (Shafiites) . ibn Hanbal (Hanbalites) . alHallaj . alFarabi . alAshari	750–1000
Ghaznavids in India (976–1186) . ibn Sina (Avicenna) . alGhazali . ibn Rushd . **Almohads in Spain** (1130–1269) . Jilani (Qadiriyya) . Kubra (Kubrawiyya) . Hasan (Chishtiyya) . ibn alArabi . Attar	1000–1200
ashShadhili (Shadhiliyya) . Rumi & Mawlawis . Naqshband (Naqshbandi) . Nimat Allah (Nimatullahi) . **Ottoman dynasty** (1299–1923) . Timur (Tamerlane) sacks Delhi . Capture of Constantinople . **Mughals in India** (1526–1858) . Siege of Vienna . Akbar in India . Wahhabis capture Mecca . Babis & Bahais in Persia	1200– PRESENT

319

Muhammad

A Young Man's Quest

I N THE YEAR 610CE, a man weary with prayer fell asleep in a cave on a mountainside near Mecca in Arabia. In the moments that followed, the religion of Islam and the Muslim story of God began.

From a Muslim point of view, that religion and that story began long before, with the creation of the world. But historically, the story began with the quest of a young man, Muhammad, to find the absolute truth of God in the midst of the many conflicting claims about the nature of God that he encountered as he grew up. In Mecca (where he was born in the year c.570CE) and in the surrounding territories (which he came to know when he travelled with the trading caravans as far away as Syria) there were many such claims: there were Jews, polytheists, animists, and Christians of different kinds, often in conflict (sometimes ferocious) with each other. All of these groups, and many more, were claiming to have not just *a* but *the* true knowledge of God. How, then, could they be arguing against each other? If there is a God, then logically there can only be what God is – so, at least, Muhammad began to reason: if these different groups or different religions were claiming to worship *God*, it must be God (however inadequately described or understood) that they were worshipping. Why, then, were they in dispute with each other?

Those were the questions that began to worry Muhammad as a young man. How could those who claim to worship God, the only theistic reality that there is, be in

Makkah alMukarramah (Mecca the Blessed) was a trading and pilgrimage centre long before the birth of Muhammad. The Quran (3.96) says, "The first house appointed for humans was that at Bakkah [sic] full of blessing and guidance for all who dwell in the world." The Ka'ba, a large cubic structure covered with a black cloth, stands at the centre of Mecca and contains the Black Stone (alHajar alAswad), possibly in origin a meteorite. Neither of these is any longer an object of worship, as at least the Black Stone may have been in pre-Islamic days, but together they represent a sanctuary consecrated to Allah at the heart of the world. They are the focus of Muslim prayer and pilgrimage (see p.349).

constant disagreement? In fact, Muhammad was not the first or the only one of those in Mecca or in that part of Arabia who had come to recognize the costly folly of religious and political divisions. Others were also attempting to recover the unity implicit in devotion to one God alone.

The most important of these were the people known as Hanifs. They were deeply religious people who had encountered highly moral and monotheistic Jews in Arabia and who were therefore trying to follow what they called "the religion of Ibrahim" (they are commended in the Quran in 2.129; 3.60, 89; 4.124; 6.79; 161; 10.104–5; 16.121, 124; 22.31–2; 30.29–30; 98.4–5). Ibrahim is simply the Arabic form of Abraham, whom they regarded as the ancestor of the Arabs – not surprisingly, since Arab Jews knew that the Arabs are identified as descendants of Abraham in Genesis 25.

What was particularly important about Abraham in the context of Mecca, with its worship of many gods and goddesses, was that Abraham himself had turned away from the worship of many gods to the worship of one God alone. The Jews told many stories (some of which appear in the Targums, p.200, and in the Quran) of the way in which Abraham destroyed the idols of the polytheists, and those of the Chaldaeans (the original home of Abraham had been Ur of the Chaldees, Genesis 11.31), and of how he had exposed the futile impotence of idolatry and polytheism – exactly the kind of worship that was going on in Mecca. The stories were widely told and known, and Abraham had thus become the role model of those who reject polytheism and adhere to God alone. But Abraham was the father of Ishmael, and Ishmael, as Genesis itself affirms, was the father of the Arabs. So any Arab who gave his allegiance to the one God could legitimately regard himself as following the religion of Abraham, without necessarily becoming a Jew or a Christian. Muhammad began to follow the example of the Hanifs without actually joining them: to join them would be to join one more party among many. Muhammad, in contrast, was seeking the One who is God behind all the conflicting and divisive claims about God.

He took himself to a cave on the mountain of Hira, close to Mecca, trying to find *alHaqq*. That means in Arabic "the True": what Muhammad was seeking, as he went out to the cave in silent prayer, was the underlying and fundamental truth of God.

It was on one of those visits to Hira that the blinding, overwhelming moment of vision occurred: he suddenly saw the direct and obvious truth of God, breaking through the conflicting beliefs and rituals of the world he knew, and establishing with Muhammad the direct sense of God's reality beyond any kind of speculation.

Muhammad later told Aisha, his wife, that he had already, before this single moment, received visions of great brightness and splendour in his sleep, and that these had driven him into his increasingly solitary struggle with God. According to Aisha's later account, he had seen "true visions, resembling the brightness of daybreak, which were shown to him in his sleep; and Allah made him love solitude so that he liked nothing better than to be alone". But this great moment of truth was something far beyond those previous visions.

Mecca

The Meccans originally rejected Muhammad's message about the nature of God as Allah, the only one who is God. To avoid persecution he moved to Yathrib (p.350), soon to be known as Madinat anNabi, the City of the Prophet, shortened to Medina. He returned to Mecca after its conquest in 8/629 to hear Bilal (p.351) issue the summons to prayer from the roof of the Ka'ba, shown here in 17th-century diagrams.

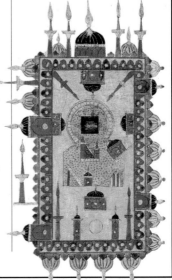

The Vision in the Cave

The Muslim Story Begins

MUHAMMAD'S EXPERIENCE in the cave on Mount Hira was the beginning of the specifically Muslim story of God. The episode is recorded in many sources. Here is the version given by alBukhari (alBukhari made a collection of Hadith, or traditions, about Muhammad that became one of the most authoritative in Islam), a tradition that went back to one of his wives, Aisha:

"Aisha said: The first part of revelation was granted to the apostle of God in a true dream during sleep, so that he never dreamed a dream without there coming the likeness of the light of dawn. Then solitude became dear to him, and he used to isolate himself in the cave of Hira, where he devoted himself to God [literally, practised *tahannuth*, perhaps 'as a Hanif']; and he remained there several nights before coming back to his family and taking refreshment for that purpose. Thus he used to return to Khadija [the first of his wives] and take refreshment for a similar period until *alHaqq* [the Truth] came while he was in the cave of Hira. And the angel came and said, 'Recite [or 'read']'. He answered, 'I am not one of those who recite [or 'read']'. He said: 'Then he took me and pressed upon me until it was unbearable; then he let me go and said: "Recite". I said, "I am not one of those who recite". So he took me and pressed upon me a second time until it

The Cave
In this cave Muhammad experienced the direct presence of Allah and the command of the angel Jabra'il or Jibril (Gabriel) to utter the words that now stand as the Quran: "This is nothing but a gift given [a revelation revealed]: one mighty in power taught him"
(53.4f).

was unbearable; then he let me go and said: "Recite". I said, "I am not one of those who recite". So he took me and pressed upon me a third time; then he let me go and said: "Recite in the name of your Lord who created – created man from a drop. Recite! and your Lord is most generous" [*Quran* xcvi 1–3]. Then the apostle of God returned with it, with his heart trembling, and went into Khadija and said, 'Hide [or 'wrap'] me, hide me!' So she hid him until the awe left him. Then he said to Khadija (telling her what had happened): 'I am terrified for my life'. Khadija answered: 'No, by God! God will not bring you to disgrace, for you bind together the ties of relationship, you carry the burdens of the weak, you earn what you earn to give to the destitute, you welcome the guest and you help where there is genuine distress'". The sense of fear did not diminish when the vision receded. At first, Muhammad thought that he had gone mad (*majnun* "possessed by the jinn of the desert") or that he had become one of the *kahin*, a *sahir*, or a *sha'ir* – wild people who went into ecstatic states and received what they claimed to be messages from God. Muhammad decided that suicide would be better than that. He actually set out to throw himself off a cliff. Yet on his way there he had an overwhelming impression of Jabra'il (the angel Gabriel) restraining him. When he came back to Khadija, he told her that he was sure he had seen something on the mountain, but that he feared that he was now possessed. Khadija advised him to wait and see what transpired – "After all", she added, "perhaps you did see something", "Yes", he answered, "I really did".

From this point on he knew, with unshakeable simplicity, that for God to be God, he must be *God*, Allah, the One who is God: there cannot be bits of God or less than God if there is God at all: there cannot be other gods, or divisions of one god from another. There can only be what there is, Allah, one true theistic reality, the one source of all creation, the unproduced Producer of all that is, a belief summarized in the famous Sura (chapter) of Unity in the Quran (see box, left). Muslims who say that Sura, with absolute sincerity, will find that their sins fall off them like leaves from a tree in autumn. In a sense, Muhammad's life and message became a working out of the consequences of that basic vision: all life, every aspect of life, is derived from the fundamental unity of Allah: consequently, every aspect of life – the creation of every thought and action – must be recognized as being derived from Allah and as returning to Allah for judgement after death: every word and every action must "bear witness that there is no god but Allah". So what happened after that amazing vision? To begin with, nothing. Then, after a while, Muhammad began to utter the words that now stand in the Quran, the foundation of Muslim life and of the Muslim story of God.

HADITH

Sources for the life of Muhammad are the maghazi *books, giving accounts of his campaigns and of those who took part in them – that of alWaqidi survives. Early lives were written within a hundred years of his death, culminating in that of ibn Ishaq (died 151CE), which survives in a recension by ibn Hisham. The other major source is the collection of Hadith, or traditions (Arabic pl.* ahadith*). The things that the Prophet and his companions said and did (and the matters on which they were silent) were remembered and passed on orally until in the 9th century CE they were gathered in great collections. Six of these (those of alBukhari, Muslim, ibn Maja, abu Dawud, atTirmidhi, and anNasai) have authority in guiding Muslim life. The Quran is fundamental, but Hadith have a reinforcing authority because they are a living commentary on what the revelation from Allah meant in the practice of life.*

Not all Hadith have equal authority: they are evaluated as strong, good, possible, weak, etc., according to the strength of the chain of people who transmitted the tradition, and according to content.

The Quran

The Word from Allah to the World

AFTER THE DRAMATIC vision in the cave, Muhammad felt further pressure to speak words directly from Allah/God, but then there was an interval of about three years (known as the *fatra*) during which nothing further happened. Muhammad lapsed into a state of bewildered despair, but at the end of that period, he again felt words being spoken through him (see box, top left).

For the rest of his life, Muhammad continued on various occasions to speak words that came, he believed, directly from Allah. He was described as a prophet (*nabi*) and an apostle (Arab *rasul*, = Greek *apostolos*, "one who is sent", i.e., "apostle"). The difference between the words he spoke as a prophet (that is, as a mediator or communicator of words coming from Allah) and the words spoken by him as an ordinary person, was unmistakable – both to himself and to others. In the first place, Muhammad looked and sounded entirely different. There are many traditions that record this (see box, below). Quite apart from the change in Muhammad's appearance, the rhythmic and rhyming sound of the words he used was totally different from ordinary human speech. Muhammad was described as *ummi*, a word that might mean "ordinary", "belonging to the people", but also means "illiterate", and that is how Muslims understand it: Muhammad did not create or write the Quran. He received it directly from Allah, from the Mother of the Book in heaven: "With Allah is the mother of the

MUHAMMAD AS PROPHET

When speaking the words of Allah, Muhammad changed in a number of ways that were subsequently recorded. These are from the Collections made by alBukhari and Muslim:

☾ **RED IN THE FACE**: "Over the apostle of Allah was a garment with which he was covered; then Safwan ibn Yala put his hand under, and saw that the apostle of Allah was red in the face, and that he was snoring."

☾ **DRIPPING WITH SWEAT**: Aisha said: "I saw him when revelation came down on him, when the day was extremely cold, then it left him, and his forehead was dripping with sweat."

☾ **A GREAT WEIGHT**: Zaid ibn Thabit said: "Allah sent down [the word] on his apostle,

when his leg was resting on mine, and the weight was so great on me, I feared my leg would be crushed."

☾ **A CLANGING BELL**: Harith b.Hisham asked the apostle of Allah: "How does revelation come to you?" He answered: "Sometimes it comes to me like the clanging of a bell, and that is heaviest upon me; then it leaves me and I remember what he said; and sometimes the angel comes to meet me resembling a man and speaks to me, and I remember what he says."

book" (13.39). The Quran contains the eternal word of Allah applied to the circumstances in which Muhammad found himself. Thus the Quran mentions events and people of the time, but it remains the same eternal message in essence.

It follows that the same Quran has been revealed to all true prophets, including Musa/Moses and Isa/Jesus (see box, centre left). Moses, Jesus, and other prophets before Muhammad received the same eternal word, though obviously it was applied to the circumstances of their own time. Why, then, are the revelations or scriptures of the Jews and Christians different from each other and from the Quran? Because, according to Muslim belief, those scriptures have been changed through the course of time in order to suit the needs or the corrupt inclinations of people who were beginning to drift away from God – so that the Quran remains the only version of the one revelation from Allah that has not been corrupted, and Muhammad is therefore the last prophet through whom Allah will reveal the content of the Mother of the Book. He is the Seal of the Prophets.

For Muslims, therefore, the Quran is the absolute and uncorrupted word of Allah. The writing and the reciting of it are human works, but the Quran itself is, like Allah, uncreated. This issue, of whether the Quran is created or uncreated, was fiercely debated in the early centuries of Islam, but the orthodox and prevailing opinion is as one of the early and great Muslim theologians, alMaturidi, put it:

The Ascent to Heaven
Traditions (Hadith) record how Muhammad went on a night journey (alIsra) to Jerusalem on the mount Buraq, and from the site now marked by the Dome of the Rock on the Temple Mount in Jerusalem, made the ascent (alMiraj) to heaven. There Allah commanded him that people should pray 50 times a day, but Moses encouraged him to get the number reduced to five
(see p.349).

> *"The Quran is the speech of Allah, written in the copies, preserved in the memories, recited by the tongues, revealed to the prophet. Our pronouncing, writing, and reciting the Quran are created, but the Quran itself is uncreated"*

The Quran, therefore, brings the Word from Allah to the world. Its words are open to interpretation, especially as new circumstances arise, but they cannot be changed. They cannot even be translated, because Arabic is the language in which revelation was transmitted to Muhammad. Versions in other languages are simply pointers to the supreme revelation sent down through the Prophet to the earth.

Once the Quran was collected and made uniform, it was as near to the presence of Allah on earth as anyone can come. Of course, Allah is far above all heavens and earth, and is not contained in anything at all. Even so, the word that comes from "the Mother of the Book" is rightly revered and honoured. It was this feeling that led to the copying of the Quran in ways that would be a worthy act of reverence and thanksgiving.

Calligraphy

Script Worthy of Revelation

THE VERSES OF THE QURAN that were first revealed to Muhammad (p.316) continue by telling of "your Lord", "…who taught by means of the pen, taught people what they never knew" (xcvi.4f). One of the earliest suras (chapters) to be revealed (according to some, the second) is called *AlQalam*, The Pen (lxviii), pointing to the guidance Allah gives in a sure and certain way.

That guidance is now contained, in uncorrupted and uncompromised form, in the Quran. Initially, the Quran was not written down: it was memorized and transmitted by people known as Huffaz, but as some of these were killed in battle after the death of Muhammad, it was realized that a more permanent record was needed. Under the 3rd Caliph, Uthman (died 655CE), an authorized text was completed and sent out to people in the rapidly extending parts of the Muslim Empire.

Here, then, was put into their hands the words, not of Muhammad, but of Allah. Important though the Prophet is, the word of Allah is even more so, since it contains all that anyone can possibly need to know in order to pass what Mohammad Jamali, writing to his son from political imprisonment in Iraq in 1961, called "the examination of life":

Kufic Script
Kufic script (khatt alKufi) came into prominence in the 8th century. This example from the Great Mosque in Kairouan in Tunisia shows the end of Sura 53 and the heading of Sura 54: "[Will you laugh] and not weep, wasting your time in vanities? Prostrate yourselves before Allah and worship Him."

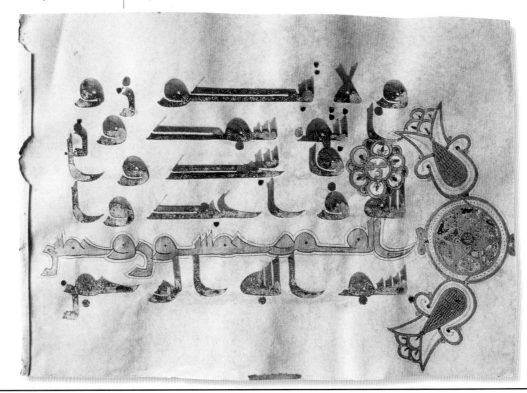

"My view is that all life is an examination and that Allah created man in order to examine him in this world. Every one of us has to pass an examination every hour and every day of his life in every act which he performs. We must therefore do our best and work well to succeed in life. Success is required not only in mathematics and chemistry but in everything, and we must seek the help of the Holy Koran every day for success in the examinations of life"

(Jamali, p.3)

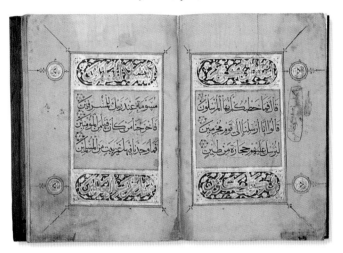

The Six Styles

Six styles of cursive writing (known in Arabic as alAqlam asSittah) were developed under the rules of ibn Muqlah (see text). One of these was the Naskhi script shown here. It was developed further by ibn alBawwab so that ordinary people could read the word of Allah more easily, and it has become the most popular of the cursive scripts.

With this understanding of the way in which the Quran brings the guidance of Allah directly to the life of every person, it is not surprising that the writing and the copying of the Quran became a way in which Allah could be revered and praised. Even the writing of Arabic was carefully reformed so that it would be more worthy of the revelation that was being written down.

Eventually, the writing of the Quran developed into the highest form of art in Islam, with many different scripts produced. When Islam was established in Basra (p.335) and Kufah, one of the most important of these became *khatt alKufi*, the Kufic script (see opposite), characterized by short vertical strokes to the letters, and long, extended horizontal strokes. It was not governed by unbreakable rules, so that scribes were free to develop ornamental forms of great beauty.

Not that rules necessarily conflict with beauty: abu Ali Muhammad ibn Muqlah (died 940CE) laid down a systematic set of rules based on geometric proportion and the size of letters, intended to reflect the proportions and beauty of the created world. Right down to the present, calligraphy has been a way of offering thanks to Allah for the gift of revelation, in accord with the saying of Muhammad, "Good writing makes the truth vivid".

The truth made vivid in such brilliant ways is the truth of Allah displayed in creation and the Quran.

Allah in the Quran

The One Who is God

THE QURAN WAS REVEALED at various stages in Muhammad's life. The text is divided into chapters (known as suras) and verses (known as *ayat*, a word that means, basically, "signs"). Each sura has its own name (for example, 112 is *alIkhlas*, Purity, 113 is *alFalaq*, Dawn, 114 is *anNas*, Humanity), but in modern works references are often given with the sura number first and the verse number second, although the numbering of the verses differs in different editions of the text. The suras are arranged with the longest first, except for *alFatiha*, The Opening, which stands at the head of the whole Quran.

*"In the name of God the merciful,
the compassionate.
Praise be to God, the Lord of all being,
the merciful, the compassionate,
Sovereign of the Day of Judgement.
You we serve [or 'worship'],
and to you we pray for help.
Guide us by the straight path,
The path of those on whom you have
bestowed your favour,
Not of those against whom is the wrath,
nor of those who are straying in error"*

*"Do not they who doubt the truth
see the skies above,
How we made them,
and arrayed them,
without fault or flaw?
And the earth,
how wide we spread it,
setting mountains rooted firm,
And within it fruitful growing,
beautiful in form?
And we send down from the
heavens
rain charged with blessing;
From it we produce the gardens
and the harvest grain…
These to nourish the servants
of Allah
with life from a lifeless land:
Like that
will be the going forth
from the grave [the
Resurrection]"*

(Sura 50.6–11)

The shortest suras at the end of the Quran are, generally speaking, those that were revealed first, while Muhammad was still in Mecca. In 622, he made the *Hijra*, or move, to Medina, and from that year the Muslim calendar begins, with years dated AH, after the Hijra.

In the Quran, Allah is the sovereign Lord of all creation. Allah is the creator, and the works of creation are themselves signs (*ayat*), pointing to the obvious truth of Allah (see box, left).

Allah is therefore the sovereign Lord from whom all creation comes and to whom all creatures return after death. Allah is utterly distinct from the created universe, and cannot be described in words. The most one can say is that Allah is like unceasing light illuminating those who seek in faith: "Light upon light! Allah guides to his light those whom he wills" (24.35). The Sura of Light and this verse in particular are of great importance in Muslim prayer, consummately in *Mishkat alAnwar* (The Niche of Lights) of alGhazali (p.356ff).

As sovereign Lord, Allah is the final Judge. On the last day, good and evil deeds will be weighed on an exact balance, and Allah will reward people according to their works. The consequences in heaven or hell are graphically described, and must, from a Muslim point of view, be literally true. Allah is therefore one to be feared as well as worshipped. But Allah is also *Rahman waRahim*, "merciful and compassionate". Going back to a tradition from Abu Huraira, a Companion of the Prophet, there are 99 Beautiful Names of God, divided between names to evoke fear and names to evoke reverence and worship. Most of them are derived from the Quran. Allah is also described with many Attributes, some of which resemble those of humans, such as having a hand or a face, or being seated on a throne.

"He is the first and the last, the manifest and the hidden, and he knows all things. He it is who created the heavens and the earth in six days, then he established himself on the throne. He knows what enters into the earth and what comes forth from it, what comes down from heaven and what goes up to it. He is with you wherever you are, and he sees whatever you do"

(Sura 57.3f; cf.7.52/4)

In the dramatic poetry of the Quran, to say that Allah sees all things and sits on a throne might be simply a way of talking of sovereignty and power. But was that so? Was it the case that these Attributes are metaphors derived from human language and experience, or might it not have to be said (since the Quran comes from Allah who is not bound by the limits of human language) that they are more literally descriptive? Does Allah literally sit on a throne and see all that is going on? The issue became a fierce battle in the early centuries of Islam.

So too did the question of the extent to which Allah knows and determines the outcome of all events. The Quran stresses the omnipotence of Allah. As sovereign Lord, nothing can happen unless Allah wills it. 81.29 says, "You shall not will except as Allah wills, the Lord of all being"; and 13.27 reports the challenge of the unbelievers, "Why is there not sent down upon him [Muhammad] a sign from his Lord? Say: Allah leads astray those whom he wills, and guides to himself those who repent." According to 3.123/8, "Allah forgives whom he wills and punishes whom he wills."

If Allah wills and determines all things, including the "choices" that humans make, how can humans possibly be judged at the Last Day according to their works? If Allah has brought their works into being, they can hardly be blamed or praised for what they do. These two issues, of the Attributes and the power of Allah to determine all things, compelled Muslims to ask how literally the language of the Quran must be taken in telling the story of God.

OPPOSITE:

Allah the Creator
For Muslims, the "works of creation" are themselves signs pointing to the truth of Allah.

God's Power

Human Freedom

I N ABOUT THE YEAR 912CE, a bright student of theology, alAshari (873–935CE), asked his teacher, alJubbai, a series of searching questions:

❖ What account do you give of a believer, an unbeliever, and a child [after their deaths]? alJubbai answered, "The believer is in heaven, the unbeliever is in hell, and the child is in a place of safety"
❖ What if the child asks why he was not allowed to grow up, so that he could earn a larger reward? alJubbai replied that Allah knew that he would be a sinner if he grew up
❖ What if the unbeliever should ask why Allah did not kill him when he was young so that he might not sin?

alJubbai had no answer to this, so alAshari began to wonder what use theology is in telling the story of God.

The problem comes from the strong statements in the Quran of Allah's power to determine all things, summarized in the Arabic words *qadar* and *qada'*. In the Quran those words mean something like "to command", "to plan", "to decide", but in the early Muslim attempts to understand the Quran, the words were taken to mean something much stronger, the absolute impossibility of anything happening outside the control and knowledge of Allah. Taken to an extreme, as it was by a group known as the Jabariya (from the Arabic *jabr*, "compulsion"), this amounted to Allah predestining everything.

Others rejected this, because it took away human responsibility and accountability: if Allah predestines everything we think or say or do, what point is there in our making a moral or religious effort? To everything we would have to say, *InshAllah*, if Allah wills it. A group began to form called the Mutazilites (from an Arabic word *'itazala*, "to separate from") to address this and other questions.

They came into being in the period of war and conflict about the true successor (Caliph) of Muhammad, the conflict that led to the division between Sunni and Shia Muslims. An issue in that conflict was whether the third Caliph, Uthman, had so deviated from Islam that it was a justified act to assassinate him, as happened in 656CE. This time the key question was asked by Hasan alBasri (642–728CE): is a Muslim who commits a serious sin still a Muslim (in which case he cannot be killed), or has he ceased to be a Muslim (in which case he can be)? Some (the

Shia Muslims
Some Muslims believe that Ali, the nearest direct descendant of Muhammad, should have succeeded him as Caliph, and they believe that his descendants are the true leaders (Imams). They are "the party of Ali", shiat Ali, hence Shia Muslims. At Kerbala, Ali's son Husain was killed by the Sunni Caliph's army in 61/680, becoming a martyr. Pilgrims participate in his bloody suffering in annual festivals.

Kharijites) said that he was no longer a Muslim. Hasan alBasri, however, said that he remained a Muslim but was also a hypocrite (strongly condemned in the Quran). The Mutazilites "separated themselves" from both and took an intermediate position between the two, asking what light reason (itself created by Allah) can throw on questions thrown up by the Quran. In effect, they introduced philosophical theology into Islam.

The first principle identified by the Mutazilites, Tawhid (see box, below) led them to address the problem of Attributes (p.330), because these seemed, if taken literally, to compromise the unity of Allah. Put crudely, if Allah speaks, hears, sees, and sits on a throne, does Allah have a body with parts that can be enumerated? If so, it cannot be said that Allah is One. Between the extremes of literalism and metaphor, the Mutazilites divided the Attributes into those that are what Allah essentially is (it is in the essence of God to be knowledgeable) and those that are inferred from the consequence of Allah's acts. To be established on a throne is to say that Allah is established always according to the essence of what it is to be Allah.

However, this rational approach to understanding Allah as described in the Quran proved unsatisfactory, not least because it did not in fact answer questions like those of alAshari. He argued that reason is not superior to revelation: it can only be used to defend traditional, Quran-based belief. On the Attributes, he affirmed their truth "without knowing how" (*bila kaif*) they relate to Allah's essence or essential being. On determinism, he argued that all possibilities, including those that lead to the punishment of hellfire, are created by Allah, but that humans have the responsibility to acquire those that are good. Acquisition (see caption, right) means that the power and the foresight of Allah are uncompromised but that humans have the freedom to act and to be held responsible for their actions. It was a neat doctrine, but it was not the end of debates.

Acquisition
alAshari argued that the teaching of acquisition (kasb, iktisab) is like shopping in a supermarket: the manager puts all the possibilities on the shelves and knows what the stock is, but the shoppers have to acquire what they think is good and suitable. If they buy nothing but toothpaste, the consequences for their health will be bad but the fault is all their own.

THE FIVE PRINCIPLES

The Mutazilites came to be identified by five principles, the first two of which gave them the name by which they called themselves, ahl al'Adl wa'lTawhid, the People of Justice and Unity:

☾ **ONE**: *Tawhid*, the absolute and uncompromised unity of Allah.

☾ **TWO**: *'Adl*, the justice of God defended by insistence on human free will, through which evil enters the world and is punished by Allah.

☾ **THREE**: *alWa'd wa'lWa'id*, threat and promise, which are real and necessary in the Quran because of human free will.

☾ **FOUR**: *alManzilah bain alManzilatayn*, a position between two positions, their attempt to find a rational middle ground between extremes in the early controversies.

☾ **FIVE**: *alAmr bi'lMa'ruf wa'nNahy 'an alMunkar*, commanding the good and prohibiting the evil, a succinct statement of social responsibility and obligation.

Sufis

The Beginning

HASAN ALBASRI (HASAN OF BASRA) was a man of searching intellect. He asked not only that question about the state of a Muslim who had sinned (p.332) but many other questions as well. The Mutazilites had taken a different view on that particular issue, but they still regarded him as one of the founders of their own way of rational reflection on all that Allah means and implies.

Hasan was also revered as the key person in establishing another exploration of faith in Islam, that of union with Allah in adoration, ecstasy, and prayer. After Muhammad and Ali (the fourth Caliph and inspiring figurehead of Shia Muslims), Hasan was regarded as "the Third Master", who founded "the science of the inner life" (*'ilm alqulub*, literally, "knowledge of the hearts").

In this exploration of Allah through obedience, devotion, and prayer, it is clear that Hasan regarded this world as an arena in which humans are tested and trained in their devotion to Allah: "Allah created fasting as a training ground that his servants may learn to run to him." He once described the world as a bridge on which it is sensible to put one's feet in order to walk from one side to another, but on which it is foolish to build.

All this was taking Islam in the direction of asceticism, of giving up the attractions of this world in order to give everything to Allah. That seemed at first sight to contradict a strong emphasis in the Quran on the goodness of the world and on the generosity of Allah in bestowing so many gifts. If asceticism means turning away from the world as something evil, then it is a kind of blasphemy, because it is rejecting the gifts and the providence of Allah. The Quran warns against spurning the gifts of Allah, and in 57.27 it seems to be condemning monasticism (*rahbaniya*) as an invention by Christians that Allah did not command. Even though the Arabic may mean something different, it has always been taken by Muslims as a statement that Allah did not want an ascetic celibacy of that kind.

So was Hasan taking Islam down forbidden paths? Actually, he understood

Dancing Sufis
Many Sufi orders (pp.346f) use dance as a means to bring worshippers out of the world and into the presence of Allah. The form and meaning of dance were taken furthest by the Mevlevis (Mawlawis), followers of Rumi (pp.344–6), where it is called muqabalah, *"encounter". But dance has also been regarded with suspicion by those who see it as a human attempt to become one with Allah.*

asceticism in a different way. It was not that he despised the good things all around him (and within him), but that he wanted to give all his time and energy to an even greater love than he had for any of those other things: he wanted to put Allah first in this world as Allah will clearly be first in the world to come. So he wrote:

"Sell this present world of yours for the next world, and you will gain both of them completely, but do not sell the next world for this or you will lose both of them completely… Those who know Allah treat him as a friend, while those who know this world treat him as an enemy"

(Attar, I, p.40)

A danger in the attractions of the world is that those attractions become, not a means through which people give glory to God, but an end in themselves: the possessions that people seek take possession of them, as Hasan wrote in a letter to Umar II, the Caliph at the time (see box, right). Jesus was not the only one who was content that his "clothing is wool" (see box, right). Out of this complete devotion to Allah, searching for Allah at all times and in all ways, came the Sufis.

Sufis are Muslims who seek direct and personal experience of Allah. The original meaning of their name is not clear, but it is often understood as coming from an Arabic word meaning "wool", because of the humble garment they usually wore. They first appeared at a time when Islam was spreading rapidly: within a hundred years after the death of Muhammad, Muslims had reached the Atlantic in the West and China in the East. Great wealth and power came to the Caliphs, and from a simple life in the desert, many Muslims began to live in splendid style. Sufis were determined to remain close to the simple desert life, making real in themselves the absolute sovereignty of Allah.

Sufism opened up a way of love that took many of the Sufis into poverty, as was certainly the case with Ibrahim b.Adham. He was happy only three times, of which one was when he looked at his coat and could not distinguish fur from lice because the lice were so numerous: "Poverty," he wrote, "is a great treasure that Allah keeps in heaven and gives only to those he loves."

That love of poverty did not contradict the emphasis in the Quran on the love of all good things in creation, nor did it conflict with the equal delight of Muslims in knowledge and understanding, since the aim of both knowledge and poverty is the same, to enter into an ever deeper union with Allah. But Sufism offered a way of giving complete priority to Allah, and before long, the Sufis became a major part of Muslim life.

"Beware of this world with all its deceit: it is like a snake, smooth to the touch, but deadly in its poison. This world has in itself no particular weight or worth with Allah. It is so slight that it weighs with him less than a pebble or a speck of dust. As the Word ['Isa/Jesus] used to say, 'My daily bread is hunger, my emblem is fear, my clothing is wool, my mount is my foot, my lantern is the moon, my fire is the sun, my food is whatever the earth brings forth for the animals and cattle; by nightfall I have acquired nothing, but there is no one richer than I'"

(Hasan of Basra)

Basra
As Islam extended into Iraq, Basra became a major centre of learning. The wife of the famous azZuhri (d.742) said, "By Allah, these books of yours are worse to me than three rival wives."

Rabia

A Sufi Devoted to Allah

ASRA BECAME A FAMOUS centre for Sufis, and it was here that the remarkable Rabia alAdawiya was born (c.713–801CE). Her name means "fourth", because she was the last of four daughters, yet she became one of the first women to be regarded in Islam as the equal of men. "If anyone asks me", wrote Attar (p.342) in his *Memorial of the Friends of God*, "why I included Rabia alongside men, I answer in the words of the Prophet, 'Allah does not regard outward forms. The heart of the matter is not in the form but in the intention…When a woman becomes a man in the path of Allah, she is a man and one cannot any longer call her a woman.'"

Hasan (p.334) met Rabia and wondered whether they were meant by Allah to marry. Rabia responded, "Marriage is for those who have their being. For me, 'being' has disappeared, because I have become nothing in my self, and live only through Allah, under whose shadow I dwell. If you want to marry me, ask Allah." Where, he wondered, had she discovered how to live with Allah? "You know how", she answered. "I only know 'not-how'."

She did, however, reveal the key to the "how" of knowing Allah when she was seen one day running through the market with a bucket of water in one hand and a tray of burning wood in the other. When asked what she was doing she replied, "I am going to light a fire in Paradise and to quench the fires of hell, so that the veils [i.e., impediments to the true love of Allah] will be removed, and people will look for Allah without hope of reward or fear of punishment." In that spirit she prayed, "O Allah, if I worship you for fear of hell, burn me in hell; if I worship you in hope of Paradise, exclude me from Paradise; but if I worship you for your own sake, do not deny me your everlasting beauty."

She so loved creation as a gift from Allah that Hasan found her one day surrounded by deer and other wild animals. When Hasan approached, the animals ran off. He asked her why. "Because", she replied abruptly, "you eat them". She lived in complete poverty. Malik i-Dinar visited her and listed all her possessions: they were a broken jug, an old reed mat, and a mud brick that she used as a pillow. Malik said that his rich friends would care for her. "Malik", she said, "how could you make such a disastrous mistake? Do I not have the same Provider as they?" "Of course", said Malik. "And does Allah, who provides, care less for the poor because of their poverty, and more for the rich because of their wealth?" "Certainly not". "Then", she said, "since Allah knows my condition, why should I keep worrying him about it? All this is the will of

Rabia had the last word on the subject of male superiority. Some men rebuked her for exceeding her place as a woman, saying:

"All the great virtues belong to men: the crown of being prophets has been placed on their heads, the belt of authority has been fastened round their waists: no woman has ever been a prophet."

"All that is true," she answered.

"But total selfishness and pride in their own achievements, and words like 'I am your lord and master', never came from women… All these things are the special concern of men."

Allah, so it is my will also". Rabia, like other Sufis, accepted alms, but only if they were offered and used for the sake of Allah. Once she was given four dirhams, and because her last clothes had fallen to bits, she gave them to a man to go and buy a blanket to cover her nakedness. The man started out, but turned back and asked her what colour she wanted. "How does colour come into it?" said an exasperated Rabia. She demanded the money back and threw it into the Tigris.

For Rabia, poverty simplified human allegiance to Allah. It meant nothing in itself, everything if it was what Allah truly willed. Even miracles were not to be trusted if they distracted from Allah. One day Rabia was eating her usual crust of bread when a neighbour said, "Have a change! Let me make you an onion stew." Rabia raised no objection, so the neighbour boiled up a pan of water and then looked for some onions – in vain. The neighbour said, "Let me go and ask next door". "What!" said Rabia: "For 40 years I have had an agreement with Allah never to ask for anything except from him. Never mind the onions!" At that moment a bird flew down with peeled onions in its beak and dropped them in the pan. "It's just a trick", said Rabia, and left her neighbour to eat the stew.

Anecdotes abound about the lovers of God in every religion. It is irrelevant whether the events happened "exactly like that". They illuminate what those who are still pilgrims on the way believe and hope may be the transformation of human life. In one of her prayers, Rabia cried out: "My peace is in solitude, because my Beloved is always with me… O Healer of souls, it is the striving toward union with you that has healed my soul. You are my joy and my life to the end of time… My hope is for union with you, and that is the goal of my quest."

Prayer of Rabia:

"O God, whatever you have set aside for me from the things of this world, give to your enemies; and whatever you have set aside for me from the things of the world to come, give to your friends; for you alone are more than enough for me"

Old Baghdad
Baghdad, called Dar asSalam, the House of Peace, was made the capital of a new succession of Caliphs, the Abbasids, after they defeated the Umayyads in 750. Bagdad was founded in 762 by the Caliph Mansur. Its prosperity (reflected in The Thousand and One Nights) *reached its height while Rabia lived there, under Harun arRashid (died 809).*

alHallaj

The Lightning Strike of Allah's Love

SUFIS ARE THOSE WHO "set out from the first to reach Allah, *alHaqq* [the True], the One who brings all things into being. Until they find what they seek, they take no rest, nor do they pay any attention to any people. For your sake I race over land or water, I skim over the open ground, I split mountains in half, and I turn my eyes away from anything I meet, until the moment when I reach the place where I am alone with you" (quoted in alGhazali, *Maqsad alAsna*). That was the definition of a Sufi offered by one of the most famous of them, Abu 'lMughith alHusain ibn Mansur (died 922CE). He was known as alHallaj because the Arabic *halaja* means "he carded cotton," and his father worked at that trade; but the name was soon taken to mean "the one who cards [or searches] consciences" (alHallaj alAsrar), because alHallaj became a passionate advocate of the love of Allah which finds the presence of Allah within the self. He once said of Allah – and he was weeping at the time:

"With the One make me one
You who uniquely are that One,
As I bear witness,
There is only God,
The Way to whom no way can
ever come!
I am the True [ana alHaqq],
made so by Truth,
Truth to become:
So let our separation cease
And Truth be One,
With You in me, and I
Found in your form,
As lightning strikes all clear
In blazing storm"

(Massignon, p.93)

"Your distance from us is not brought about by your withdrawing from us, but in your removing from us awareness of your presence: becoming aware of your presence does not mean that you have changed your place, but that we have changed our knowledge: your absence means that you have set a veil between us, not that you have moved any distance from us"

(Akhbar alHallaj, Massignon & Kraus, no.5)

alHallaj began to write poems of the presence of Allah that seemed to obliterate distinction (see box, left). His love of Allah was so immediate and real that, as with Rabia (p.336), heaven and hell were irrelevant to him:

"If you were to offer to sell me Paradise for a moment of my time with you here, or for one moment of the least of my states of spirit with you now, I would not buy it. If you were to place the fires of hell before me, with all the torment it contains, I would think nothing of it compared with my desolation when you are hidden from me. Forgive everyone, but do not forgive me; have mercy on them but not on me. I do not plead with you for myself, nor ask you for reward: do with me what you will"

(Massignon, p.78)

The Quran tells people that Allah is nearer to them than the vein in their neck (50.51). Sufis experience that closeness of Allah and dissolve the gap between creator and creature (see box, right). That ecstatic union with Allah was pressing much too far for other Muslims, however. What did alHallaj mean when he claimed, *ana alHaqq*, "I am the True"? It seemed as though he was claiming to have become Allah, because *alHaqq* is one of the most profound names of God (p.328) in the Quran: the absolute foundation of all being, the True, that which alone truly is. In the end, alHallaj was brutally executed in Baghdad, saying, "All who have known ecstasy long for this, alone with the Alone."

But did he actually say "*Ana alHaqq*"? According to some texts, he said only, *ana haqq*, "I am true", and "I am true in what I say about our union with Allah in love". And was he executed for that, or was it more because he had brought with him from the years he spent in India some beliefs and practices which seemed to orthodox Muslims subversive of Islam? Ibrahim ibn Fatik visited him in prison and found him, as he later said, "resting on the crown of his head" – in other words, in one of the postures of Indian yoga. And alHallaj once spoke these enigmatic words: "Go and warn my friends that I am launched on the ocean and my boat is shattered: my death will be in the religion of the scaffold; I do not wish for Mecca or Medina" (*Akhbar* 52). Did he mean that once people have seen and felt the presence of Allah as being truly closer than the vein in their neck, then that experience dissolves the partitions of human religion as it did for Kabir (p.120)? Even so, bringing Allah down to earth was a risky procedure: could any account be given of the Sufi experience that would not seem threatening to others?

I am he whom I love, and he whom I love is I.
We are two spirits dwelling in one body.
When you see me, you see him.
When you see him, you see us"

(Massignon, no.93)

Lightning Strike
Through his long years of Sufi practice and training, alHallaj felt that the veil had been ripped through, as by a lightning strike: "You have unveiled yourself to me so openly that you are in my soul itself" (Massignon & Kraus, no.38).

ibn Arabi

Light Refracted Through a Prism

Refraction and Dispersion
Muslims inherited Greek science and extended it greatly, because the study of nature was the study of Allah's creation. They were aware that an apparently colourless ray of sunlight is in fact made up of constituent colours that can be dispersed or separated as, for example, when it passes through a prism. They observed refraction (the effect on the electromagnetic waves that constitute light when they cross the boundary from one transparent medium to another) although they did not understand it and did not use that language. These observations provided a powerful metaphor and analogy of the effect of Allah in human lives.

THE SUFIS' CLAIM that their union with Allah seemed to obliterate all separation and distinction raised disturbing questions for many Muslims. The Quran is emphatic and insistent that the Creator is utterly and always different from creation. Could the experience of union be explained without compromising the transcendence of Allah?

One of the greatest Muslim philosophers, who was himself a Sufi and knew at first hand what the Sufis were struggling to express in words, set out to do so. He was ibn Arabi (Abu Bakr Muhammad Muhyiddin ibn al-Arabi, 1165–1240CE). He was born in Murcia, Spain, and was called *ashShaykh alAkbar* "the greatest of teachers". He travelled widely in search of truth, and his tomb in Damascus remains to this day a shrine.

The early Sufis had shown that the way to find Allah is to lose one's self, and that the way to lose one's self is to concentrate on Allah so completely that one becomes oblivious of all other things – a state, called by Sufis *fana*, "annihilation", in which one "dies before one dies". That concentration is summed up in the practice of *dhikr*, "remembrance": the practice of keeping God always in mind. Of *dhikr*, a practice common to all Muslims, ibn Arabi wrote: "When beginners forget their *dhikr* for one breath, Satan is with them at once. When forgetfulness of Allah creeps in, so does Satan, but when there is *dhikr*, he has to depart."

Dhikr leads to the experience of union with Allah that ibn Arabi explored further. He was clear that nothing can be said about the nature of Allah who is far beyond words and understanding: "All these words about Allah are pointers to profound mysteries and illuminations given to me by Allah. Far better, you who read this, to turn your thoughts from words to seek the hidden truth behind the words, that you may enter into understanding" (*Tarjuman alAshwaq*).

What, then, is to be said about the Attributes (p.330)? If they are real, then Allah has a number of eternal "partners". But one of the greatest sins in the Quran is *shirk*, associating anything with Allah as though it is equal to Allah. Against that, Islam declares that Allah is absolute and undivided, uniquely One: "Allah," wrote ibn Arabi, "is far apart from all likeness as well as from every rival, contrast, or opposition" (*Risalat alAhadiya*).

What *are* the Attributes? ibn Arabi argued that when Adam (humanity) was created, human nature began to refract through itself (like a prism) the nature of Allah in such a way that the Essence of Allah (*dhat alHaqq*, the self of the Real, the essential nature) was made discernible in partial ways and with different qualities, as Attributes. Just as light refracted through a prism still remains light, so the essence of Allah is refracted through creation without diminishing Allah. In a comparable way, aspects of Nature can be seen without diminishing what Nature is: "Nature remains distinct from the particulars that make her manifest, nor is Nature diminished by that which makes her manifest" (*Fusus alHikam*: the name means "the polished edges/bezels of wisdom"). Equally important, creation, and especially the creation of Adam, is capable of reflecting back to Allah exactly what Allah is in Essence: "For Allah to know his own Essence required an object outside that Essence to make it apparent, and in that way to manifest his mystery to himself" (*Fusus alHikam*). The purpose of Sufis is to polish the mirror of human nature within themselves until it reflects ever more perfectly the nature of Allah: "Allah is the mirror in which you see yourself, just as you are the mirror in which he contemplates his attributes: these are nothing other than himself, so that the analogy from one to the other is turned inside out."

ibn Arabi wrote:

"My heart has become capable of every form: it is pasture for gazelles and a monastery for monks; it is a temple for idols and the Ka'ba [p.321] for pilgrims; it is the tables of Torah and the copies of Quran. I follow the religion of love, wherever his camels lead on. My religion and my faith are the true religion"

(*Tarjuman alAshwaq*, 13–15)

In the end, the exchange between Allah and the servant of Allah can become so perfect that they are indistinguishable from each other, and that is the complete union with Allah in which Allah is truly present but remains transcendent. Allah becomes for the Sufi "the hearing with which he hears, the seeing with which he sees, the hands with which he touches, the feet with which he walks, the tongue with which he speaks".

Allah can thus be seen in refracted form anywhere in creation. Even so, the most certain place to find Allah is not outside oneself in the refracted glimpses of

glory, but within, where that glory strikes home in mirrored reflection: "People must know their own souls before they can know their Lord, for their knowledge of the Lord is, as it were, the first fruit of their knowledge of themselves" (*Fusus alHikam*).

Put in words, this way of approaching Allah may seem academic; put in life, Allah became vivid and real. Out of the vivid reality of that experience, the great Sufi poetry of devotion began to be written.

Journey to Allah
For Sufis, the pilgrimage to Mecca became another powerful metaphor of the soul's journey to Allah (see box above and p.345).

The Conference of Birds

Pilgrims Seeking Allah

The Desert
*The deserts of Arabia alone
cover more than a million
square miles and are so
desolate and barren that
Arabs call them* Rub
alKhali, *the Empty Quarter:
"It is a bitter, dessicated land
which knows nothing of
gentleness or ease" (Thesiger,
p.xii). But that is where
Allah can be found.*

MANY OF THE STORIES of the early Sufis come from Farid adDin Attar's *Memorial of the Friends of God (Tadhkirat alAwliya)*. Attar (died c.1221CE) was himself a Sufi who expressed his love of Allah in some of the greatest poems written in Persian. More than a hundred are attributed to him, of which the finest is the long *Mantiq atTair, The Conference of Birds.* Attar took his basic idea from Quran 38.18/19, which speaks of creation joining with David in the praise of Allah: "The birds gathered; all with him turned [to Allah]." In the poem, the birds are all pilgrims seeking Allah: so they assemble to seek the true king, and they choose the Hudhud (the hoopoe) to be their guide. The Hudhud tells them that such a king, the Simorgh (the Rare Bird), can indeed be found, but that the way is difficult and the distractions from it many:

*"We have a king; beyond Kaf's mountain peak
The Simorgh lives, the sovereign whom you seek,
And He is always near to us, though we
Live far from His transcendent majesty.
A hundred thousand veils of dark and light
Withdraw His presence from our mortal sight...
His creatures strive to find a path to Him,
Deluded by each new, deceitful whim,
But fancy cannot work as she would wish;
You cannot weigh the moon like so much fish!
How many search for Him whose heads are sent
Like polo-balls in some great tournament
From side to giddy side – how many cries,
How many countless groans assail the skies!
Do not imagine that the way is short;
Vast seas and deserts lie before His court.
Consider carefully before you start;
The journey asks of you a lion's heart.
The road is long, the sea is deep – one flies
First buffeted by joy and then by sighs;
If you desire this quest, give up your soul
And make our sovereign's court your only goal.
First wash your hands of life if you would say:*

'I am a pilgrim of our sovereign's Way';
Renounce your soul for love; He you pursue
Will sacrifice His inmost soul for you." (p.34)

The birds at once begin to doubt whether they can make the effort, and the Hudhud starts to encourage them with stories, which make up the main part of the poem. Ultimately, only two things are required of those who seek the true king. The first is exactly what virtually all the Sufis had found (cf. Rabia, pp.336–37): those who wish to find God must love and pray to God neither for reward, nor even to avoid punishment, but simply because God is beyond all else to be desired (see box, below right). The second major lesson from Attar and the Hudhud is this. Those who wish to love Allah without reserve must first forget, or even annihilate, self (see box, left).

It is not that the things of this world are evil or bad. It is simply that those who love Allah have a greater love than anything this world can offer. In the end, not all of the birds persist. But 30 (*si morgh*) attain Simorgh, and that play on words makes the point that the self is not other than the Self, in a final union of love:

Migrating Swallows
"Like deep-sea sailors
from afar
Drawn home by their
mysterious star,
They sport, they sing
in unison,
Their noble perils make
them one"
(Pitter, p.162).

"Their souls rose free of all they'd been before;
The past and all its actions were no more.
Their life came from that close, insistent sun
And in its vivid rays they shone as one.
There in the Simorgh's radiant face they saw
Themselves, the Simorgh of the world – with awe
They gazed, and dared at last to comprehend
They were the Simorgh and the journey's end.
They see the Simorgh – at themselves they stare,
And see a second Simorgh standing there;
They look at both and see the two are one,
That this is that, that this, the goal is won…
Then, as they listened to the Simorgh's words,
A trembling dissolution filled the birds –
The substance of their being was undone,
And they were lost like shade before the sun;
Neither the pilgrims nor their guide remained.
The Simorgh ceased to speak, and silence reigned"

(Darbindi & Davis, pp.219f)

Even in his own lifetime, Attar was revered not just as a poet, but as a guide to Allah. A man slightly younger than Attar said of him, "Only once in a hundred years does an Attar appear." Only once in a thousand years (or even longer) does there appear one like the man who said that. His name was Jalal adDin Rumi.

"God said to David: 'Tell my
servants: prayer
Should be creation's
all-consuming care;
Though hell were not his fear
nor heaven his goal
The Lord should wholly occupy
man's soul…
True prayer seeks God alone;
its motives start
Deep in the centre of a
contrite heart…
If it is paradise for which you pray
You can be sure that you have
lost your way"

(The Conference of Birds, p.158)

Rumi

Living Through Love

*"O incomparable giver of life,
cut Reason loose at last!
Let it wander grey-eyed from
vanity to vanity.
Shatter open my skull, pour in it
the wine of madness!
Let me be mad, as mad as You,
mad with You, with us.
Beyond the sanity of fools is a
burning desert
Where Your Sun is whirling in
every atom; drag me there,
Beloved, drag me there, let me
roast in Perfection!"*

(Harvey, p.209)

Rumi

Rumi said, "A Sufi is a man or a woman with a broken heart. Someone who is always sensitive to the heartbreak of the world and who is always sensitive to the Divine Beauty of the world. Once you see it, your heart breaks open forever and goes on breaking at the beauty and majesty and agony of the experience" (Harvey, p.70)

IN THE YEAR 1219CE, Attar happened to be in Nishapur, and there he came across a family on their way to Mecca on pilgrimage (p.348). Seeing their ten year-old son, Attar said: "This boy will open a gate in the heart of love."

The boy was Jalal udDin Muhammad Balkhi. As the name states, he was born at Balkh in Afghanistan in 1207CE, at a time when Mongol invasions were threatening the Muslim world. Under the threat to Balkh, Jalal udDin's father, a prominent Sufi and teacher, fled with his family in 1219CE. After ten years of wandering, a school was built for him at Konya in South Turkey, an area known, from an earlier occupation, as Rum (Rome). Jalal udDin spent his life there, and so became known as Rumi.

In 1231CE, Rumi's father died and Rumi succeeded him. By 1244CE, his fame had spread and people flocked to him for instruction. In that year, he met Shams-i-Tabrizi (Sun of Tabriz), and his life was blown apart. Shams was a famous Sufi who, in a wild passion for Allah, had struck out on a totally independent path, urging people to cut loose from books and teachers in order to cling, in utter devotion, to Allah alone:

*"All theologies are straws that His Sun burns to dust:
Knowledge takes you to the threshold,
but not through the door.
You cannot learn anything
if you do not unlearn everything.
How learned I was, before God's revelation
struck me dumb!"*

Shams had asked Allah to send him to someone who would understand and practise this total love, and Allah sent him to Rumi. Shams arrived in Konya in 1244, and Rumi immediately recognized Allah in him – Allah as refracted (p.340) through the messenger. Through the person of Shams, he fell in love with Allah totally and without reserve:

*"Love is here like the blood in my veins and skin
He has annihilated me and filled me
only with Him
His fire has penetrated all the atoms of my body
Of 'me' only my name remains; the rest is Him"*

(Harvey, p.181)

The philosophy of ibn Arabi (p.340) enabled Rumi to see Allah in all aspects of the world, and especially in Shams, through whom Allah was manifest, and in a sense he put that philosophy into the supreme poetry of mystical love (see box, left). Rumi was so immersed in Allah through Shams that his pupils became jealous and drove Shams away. The sense of loss made Rumi almost lose his mind. But Shams returned, and once more they lived in a communion of love, praying, dancing, chanting together in a union with God:

"I was snow, I melted in your rays
The earth drank me: mist now, and pure spirit,
I climb back to the Sun"

(Harvey, p.182)

In 1247, there was a knock at the door. Shams stood up and said, "It is time. I am going. I am called to my death." Rumi was grief-stricken, but the parting, he realized, was necessary. He spent the rest of his life trying to share in words with others the ecstasy of that enduring and unending love of Allah. He wrote poetry (including *Mathnawi* and *Divan-i-Shams-i-Tabrizi*), and a prose work of advice on spiritual life, much of it sharp and concise: "If you look in the mirror and see an ugly face, you are not going to improve matters by smashing the mirror with your fist." For Rumi, each day of his life was a new stage of his journey to Allah, much as a caravan prepares each day to move on:

"O lovers, the time has come to move on from this
world. The drum is sounding in the ear of my
soul, calling us to the journey. The camel-driver
is rubbing his eyes and setting his camels in
order and asking us to let him depart. Why
are you still sleeping, you who travel?
Each moment that passes, a soul is
passing out of this life and setting out
for the world of Allah. O heart, depart
to the Beloved, O friend, go to your
Friend. Watchman, keep awake, for
sleep is foolish for those who should
be keeping watch"

(*Divan-i-Shams-i-Tabrizi*)

Rumi summarized his life by saying, "My religion is to live through love." He died at sunset in December 1273CE, saying, "My death is my wedding with eternity" (see box, above).

"If you are seeking, seek us with
joy
For we live in the kingdom of joy.
Do not give your heart to
anything else
But to the love of those who are
clear joy.
Do not stray into the
neighbourhood of despair
For there are hopes: they are
real, they exist –
Do not go in the direction of
darkness:
I tell you: suns exist"

(Harvey p.3)

Life as Pilgrimage
"Be off! Be off!
O soul, leave behind this
world of separation
And come with us to the
world of union...
Cast away the burdens of
the earth
And fly upward toward
heaven!"
(Star, p.13).

Sufi Orders

Dancing in Ecstasy

AROUND RUMI GATHERED followers who became known as Mevlevis, or Mawlawis. They emphasized rhythmic dance that leads out of the body into union with Allah. For that reason, they became known colloquially as the Whirling Dervishes. *Sama*, dance around the centre who is Allah, is common among Sufis, but it is of great importance to the Mevlevis (see box, right). The Mevlevis are only one among many Sufi Orders in Islam. By the end of the 19th century, more than half of all Muslim men were attached to one. The Orders usually had different great teachers as their distinctive guides, and are named after them, but all of them trace their line of succession back to Muhammad, often through Hasan alBasri (p.334).

Ecstatic Dance

Rumi said: "Dancing is not rising to your feet painlessly like a whirl of dust blown about by the wind. Dancing is when you rise above both worlds, tearing your heart to pieces and giving up your soul"
(Harvey, p.224).

❖ Abd alQadir Jilani (born 1077CE) of the Qadiriyya emphasized how indispensable it is for all Muslims, not just for an elite, to follow the law laid down in Sharia (p.348) as a precondition of entering into the true knowledge of Allah. Because he put that before entering into states of ecstatic union with Allah, he is known as the founder of "sober Sufism". He was regarded as the Pole (*Qutb*) around whom revolved the manifestation of Allah in the world, and he demonstrated through his own life that Allah is not an idea or a philosophical abstraction but the presence in whom people can learn to live and from whom each moment of life is then transformed

❖ Abu 'l Jannab Najm adDin Kubra (1145–1221CE) of the Kubrawiyya, known as "the Maker of the Friends of God" (*wali tarash*), based his teaching on visionary experiences of Allah, and insisted on absolute dependence on the *shaykh*, or teacher, as the director and interpreter of the disciple's way: that way is a journey inwards, discovering and dealing with realities that are talked about as external (e.g., devils, angels, and eventually even Allah) within the reality of one's own being

❖ Khwajah Muin adDin Hasan (1141–1236CE) of the Chishtiyya (from Chisht in Afghanistan) stressed the importance of austerity and ascetic poverty (cf Rabia, p.336): we should neither earn nor borrow money, and if we come by possessions (for example, as gifts from others), we should not keep them beyond the dawn of the next day; we are responsible for our own acts, and therefore should fear the judgement of Allah and refrain from anything that might lead to his adverse judgement, even from speaking too often, and then only to say words that will be pleasing to Allah; at the same time, we should recognize that our good actions come not from ourselves, but from the teaching of the *pir* (guide) and the prompting of Allah

❖ Abu 'lHasan ashShadhili (1197–1258CE) of the Shadhiliyya wrote special litanies of prayer (*Hizb alBahr*, the Litany of the Ocean, *Hizb alAnwar*, the Litany of Lights) to bring people into a full realization of the Oneness (*tawhid*) of Allah: through *dhikr* (p.340) especially, the truth takes hold that Allah is all there is: people should learn now to dissolve their attachment to the world, so that when this world disappears, they will remain attached to "all that remains", i.e., Allah; the effect of this is that life must be lived in total self-effacement

❖ Shah Nimat Allah (1331–1431CE) of the Nimatullahi believed that people should work in the world (he was himself a farmer) in order to manifest Allah's possession of their lives through generosity to others and the service of society

❖ Khwaja Baha adDin Muhammad Naqshband (1317–1389CE) of the Naqshbandi insisted upon strict obedience to the laws of Sharia (cf. the Qadiriyya, left) so that knowledge of Allah might permeate the whole of society: the path to follow towards a spiritual knowledge of Allah is mapped with great precision

The differences are matters of emphasis. The purpose of all the Orders is the same, to teach the ways in which believers can bring themselves constantly into the presence of Allah (especially through *dhikr*, remembering the qualities of Allah through the Beautiful Names, p.328) and in which Allah can therefore become present in their lives.

Important for most is music (*Sama*) and dance (*Hadrah*, "presence", and *Imarah*, "fullness", names that show how sacred dance empties people of themselves in order to be filled by Allah), despite the fact that music is suspect in Islam. Any singing or dancing in the context of other forbidden activities (for example, while drinking alcohol) is always forbidden; if it amuses people and distracts them from remembering Allah, it is "detested" (*alMakruh*). But for the Sufis, *Sama* simply extends the way in which both the call to prayer (*adhan*, p.350) and the Quran are recited as a kind of music. As one of them (alJunaid, died 910, himself one of the "sober Sufis") wrote:

"My ecstasy is that I remove myself from existence here By the grace of the One who shows me the Presence"

Rumi's son, Sultan Walad, described what dance meant to Rumi:

"Day and night, he danced in ecstasy. On the earth, he turned and turned like the heavens. His ecstatic cries scoured the skies, and everyone around heard them… He was constantly lost in music and ecstasy, never resting for a moment… Everyone was amazed that so great a leader should be behaving like a man possessed. But the people abandoned everyday religion, and went mad with love"

Whirling Dervishes
For the Mevlevis music annihilates one's self: it takes one "out of oneself" into the presence of Allah. Through their music, therefore, Sufis do not have to wait for death to enter into the presence of Allah: they do so now.

Sharia

The Path That Leads to Allah

ALL SUFI ORDERS ASSUME – and some explicitly demand – that their members live as Sharia requires. But what is Sharia? The word *sharia'* means basically the well-worn path made by camels leading to the watering-place. In Islam, it came to mean the rules and laws that must be obeyed by all who call themselves Muslim – the well-tried path that leads to Allah. It is thus fundamental to Muslims that Allah gives clear guidance, commands, and prohibition, in the essential aspects of life. These rules and laws are gathered from the Quran (p.324) and from the way in which Muhammad and his companions lived. There have been many prophets to whom Quran (revelation) has been entrusted (p.325) but, in Muslim belief, only the Arabic Quran has been preserved in uncorrupted form. It follows that Muhammad and his companions form the first "living commentary" on the Quran, expressing in their "words, deeds, and silent approvals" its meaning in everyday life.

The record of these words, acts, and silences is gathered in *Hadith*, an Arabic word meaning "narrative", "speech", or "report". The plural is *ahadith*, but the word Hadith is now used as a collective, meaning not only a single tradition, but also the whole collection of *ahadith* recognized in Islam.

The laws of the Quran, interpreted in Hadith, were drawn together into schools of Sharia, of which four, known from their leading

THE FIVE PILLARS OF ISLAM

These represent the foundations of Islam laid down in recognition of Allah:

◦ **WITNESS**: The Witness (ashShahada) makes the connection between Allah and Muhammad as the exemplary Messenger: "I bear witness that there is no God but Allah, and that Muhammad is his messenger."

◦ **PRAYER**: Formal prayer, five times a day, has 18 required acts and 51 that are customary. Details differ in the different schools of Sharia.

◦ **TITHE**: Money must be set aside for the poor.

◦ **PILGRIMAGE**: It is necessary for the faithful to travel to Mecca.

◦ **FASTING**: This must be carried out during the month of Ramadan.

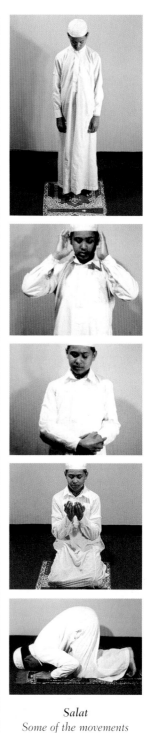

Salat
Some of the movements in Salat (prayer) that bind Muslims together before Allah.

proponents or founders as Hanafite, Hanbalite, Malikite, and Shafi'ite, prevail in the Muslim world. They differ from each other in some matters and in the extent to which they allow rules of exegesis and interpretation, but they agree that a life of Islam should be lived within these boundaries laid down by Allah.

Islam is often translated as "submission", but it comes from the same root as the Hebrew word *shalom*, meaning "peace" or "safety"; and therefore the word Islam means something more like "entering into a condition of safety in allegiance to Allah". Achieving that goal is not a matter of vague aspiration. It is a matter of following the commands of Allah and of applying their implications: "Then we set you on the right path [*sharia'*], so follow it, and do not wander after the fancies of those without knowledge" (Quran 45.17/18). All people will be judged on the Last Day exactly according to their works. But they need have no fear, because Allah has told them what is expected of them (cf. Micah, p.224); and in any case, Quran and Hadith make it clear that the judgement of Allah is always controlled by mercy. The very first of anNawawi's famous collection of the Forty (most important) Hadith is: "When Allah decreed [*qada*, p.332] the creation, he pledged solemnly in his book, and it is preserved carefully with him: my mercy conquers my wrath" (*Matn al-Arba'in anNawawiya*)

The fundamental rules are summarized (see box, above) in the Five Pillars of the way of life pleasing to Allah (*Arkan udDin*). *Salat* is by no means the whole of Muslim prayer, as the Sufis, for example, have already made clear. The prayer known as *dua'*, supplication, is a way in which it is possible for all Muslims to bring themselves and their needs before Allah at any time. It is possible for them always to take refuge with Allah; indeed, as they enter a mosque, many Muslims say exactly that, "I take refuge with Allah". So personal and private prayer saturate Islam. But the prayer made following the rules of Salat brings the whole community together in a common and corporate acknowledgement of Allah. In the Quran, Allah states the intention to make the whole of humanity into a single community (*umma*): if Allah is one, all people belong to Allah and to each other. That is given visible expression in the mosque.

The Mosque

◇

Place of Prostration

*"Oh you who believe, when the
call is made for prayer on the
day of assembly make haste to
the remembrance [dhikr, p.340]
of Allah, and leave your
business. That is best for you, did
you but know!
And when the prayer is finished,
then you may disperse through
the land and seek the good
things of Allah; and remember
Allah often, that you may prosper"*

(62.9f)

AT THE TIME WHEN MUHAMMAD was alive, the people of the town of Yathrib, north of Mecca, were divided in a conflict that seemed unending because the rules of blood vengeance require that a victim's family should secure a victim from the offender's family. They invited Muhammad to come as a new leader, in the hope that, by offering a new start, the divided parties might be reconciled. He made the move, the Hijra, in the year 622CE, the first year of the Muslim calendar.

For the first time, Muhammad found himself in a community in which Islam, the meaning of life lived in obedience to Allah, could be worked out in practice. When he arrived, almost his first act was to build a mosque – a fundamental statement in visible form of the Muslim understanding of Allah.

A mosque is basically the place where Muslims assemble for prayer on Fridays. The word "mosque" comes, via French, from the Arabic *masjid*, the place of prostration in worship and prayer: *sajadu* means "they prostrated themselves". A mosque is known also as *jami'*, from the Arabic *jama'u*, "they assembled".

The mosque, therefore, symbolizes the intention of Allah to create a single community of worshippers in the world. The prayer on Friday

---

COMMON FEATURES OF THE MOSQUE

For all their variety in materials and architecture, all mosques have certain features in common that reflect the Muslim understanding of Allah:

◇

☾ **THE MINARET**: Tower from which the call to prayer is made incorporating the fundamental witness of faith: 1. Allahu akbar (God is greater than everything); 2. I bear witness that there is no God but Allah; 3. I bear witness that Muhammad is the Messenger of Allah; 4. Come to prayer; 5. Come to wellbeing/salvation; 6. [Morning call] Prayer is better than sleep; 7. Allahu akbar (God is greater than everything).

☾ **THE MIHRAB**: A niche in the wall indicating the direction of prayer, originally Jerusalem but changed during Muhammad's lifetime to Mecca.

☾ **THE MINBAR**: A pulpit from which the preacher (*khatib*) delivers his address.

☾ **THE KURSI** ("footstool", used as a synonym of "throne"): The stand on which the Quran is placed; reflecting the "Verse of the Throne" in the Quran (2.256) that summarizes the majesty of Allah, in whose honour the mosque is built and before whom the worshippers bow: "Allah, there is no God but he, the living, the eternal: no slumber can seize him, nor sleep. His are all things in the heavens and the earth. Who is there that can intercede with him except by his leave? He knows what is before them and what is after them, nor shall they comprehend anything of his knowledge except what he wills. His throne [*kursi*] extends over the heavens and the earth, and preserving them does not weary him: he is the exalted, the mighty."

(whose Arabic name, *yaum alJumu'a or Jum'a*, means "the day of assembly") draws together all able-bodied Muslim men (women may attend but are separated from men, it being an act of mercy on Allah's part that they are not under this obligation); and it draws them together in the same actions of obedience to the command of Allah, in adoration, worship, and prayer (p.349).

Although the mosque gathers together the whole Muslim community in the recognition and remembrance of Allah, mosques are not uniform in style or construction. They take on local features, making use of the materials and architecture of the places where they are built. They may be simple, amounting to little more than a single room, or they may be vast and brilliantly ornate in ways that themselves give praise to Allah.

The "Verse of the Throne" (see box, below left) lies at the heart of the Muslim understanding of Allah – as One, utterly distinct from all else that is or can ever be, and as One who is sovereign Lord over all that is. Among the earliest to grasp the message of Muhammad and to follow him in the worship of Allah was a slave, Bilal – later freed by Abu Bakr, Muhammad's successor: Bilal became the first "summoner to prayer" (*mu'adhin*). Before that, he was persecuted by two Meccans, who:

> *"during the hottest part of the day used to take him to an unshaded valley and hold him down with a large rock on his chest. Then they said to him, 'You will stay here until you die or until you reject Muhammad and worship alLat and alUzza' [Meccan deities]. He used to murmur while he was enduring this, 'Ahad, Ahad' ['One, One'; cf Akiba, p.211]"*

(ibn Ishaq, I, p.317f)

Mosques
The entrance to a mosque may be similar to a house entrance (as above).
In contrast, the Mosque of the Prophet in Medina (below) illustrates the way in which mosques remind a whole town or city that they live under Allah. Masjid anNabi is the second most holy (after the Great Mosque of Mecca) in the Muslim world, containing the Tomb of the Prophet.

Allah as One is complete and perfect and needs nothing to add to that perfection. But given that this must be so, the questions that had been raised almost from the start continued to be asked, of how so complete and perfect a Being could ever create something outside, or in addition to, that perfection (the problem of the One and the many), and of how it is possible to say anything of One who lies beyond the possibility of description (the problem of the Attributes of Allah). In response to questions like these, the great philosophers of Islam came into being.

alFarabi

The Essence of Being

Existence

It is possible to imagine what must essentially (in essence) belong to unicorns (e.g., they must have a single horn; Latin unus + cornus = *one horn) while accepting that there has never been an instance of one (a unicorn has never been instantiated). To claim that God exists is to claim simply that there is an instance of God (God is instantiated). It is then possible to imagine what must essentially (in essence) belong to God, including existence, since to imagine God without existence is as impossible as to imagine a unicorn without a horn – like the son of a barren woman, p.119. Existence is not "added on" as it is (or is not) with tigers and unicorns. Whether God is instantiated remains the issue of belief.*

WHAT DO YOU THINK? And does it matter? In Islam, it certainly does. It is possible to praise Allah or to offend against Allah as much in the head as in the body. Islam puts great emphasis on the way in which Allah has provided for humans all the guidance they need to pass "the examination of life" (p.327); and it puts equal emphasis on the way in which a final judgement will be made by an exact balance between good and evil deeds.

But deeds are not enough. When alBukhari made his great Collection of Hadith (p.322), he began the whole Collection with a saying of the Prophet that actions will be judged only by their intention (*biniyya*) – so that if, for example, people made the Hijra (p.328) for the sake of Allah and the Prophet, it would be rewarded, but not if it was made for the sake of gaining a wife.

What people think about Allah and how they think about Allah are both immensely important, and that is why the Mutazilites (p.332) placed such emphasis on reason in religion. As Islam spread over the Mediterranean world, that commitment to reason met the developed forms of Greek philosophy (pp.230ff), and above all the Neoplatonic (p.233) interpretation of Plato and Aristotle (see box, right). From this composite philosophy, Muslim philosophers saw an exhilarating opportunity to answer sceptical questions and to elucidate the brief statements in the Quran about the nature of Allah and about Allah's relation to creation. One of them achieved such fame that he became known as "the second teacher", the first being Aristotle. He was Abu Nasr Muhammad alFarabi (870–950CE).

Like all Muslims, alFarabi knew that Allah is the creator of all things who remains absolutely distinct from creation. He argued that all existing beings are divided into the necessary and the possible. Necessary beings exist in their own right, without any external cause. Possible beings might or might not exist, and their existing needs a cause external to themselves to bring them into being. In any existing being, most of its features are therefore unnecessary or accidental – they might or might not happen to be. But if you take away those accidental attributes, you will be left with the essence of what that being is. Particular people may have long hair, short hair, or no hair at all, two arms, one arm, or no arms at all. Those are accidental attributes. The essential feature remains – whatever the accidents – that they are human. This means that it is possible to conceptualize the essence of something quite apart from the accident of whether it happens to exist or not. It is possible to understand what essentially a Siberian mammoth is even though none happens any longer to exist. To bring one into existence would require a cause external to itself – for example, by cloning cells from a frozen carcass. It is even possible to conceptualize the essence of imaginary things (unicorns) or logically impossible things (the present-day king of Connecticut), even though they cannot possibly be brought into existence, for the different reasons that obtain in each case. From this, alFarabi argued that all existing beings are made up of an essence to which existence with its accidental attributes is added. However, there are no accidental features in Allah because there is nothing in Allah that might or might not happen to exist. Even if Allah were imaginary, that logical point would still be true because that is what would have to be the case for Allah to be Allah, even if only as a matter of definition. In Allah, essence and existence cannot be separated. In fact, alFarabi was entirely clear that there are abundant signs (p.328) in creation, prophecy, and revelation that point to Allah. But in any case, logic insists that it is the essence of Allah (the essential nature of Allah) to exist: it is only in the case of Allah that essence and existence must necessarily be the same, since otherwise the definition of Allah would collapse in self-contradiction (see caption, left).

How, then, can it be possible for an absolute, perfect, and self-contained being to bring anything into existence outside itself? There cannot be any *need* for such a being to do so because that would imply some contingent deficiency (something that was lacking that needed to be brought into being). It must be a consequence of what the essence of Allah is. It was here that that the Neoplatonists were most influential. From them, alFarabi saw that the interior life of Allah would bring into being the Intellect that could contemplate itself, otherwise there would be nothing but a lifeless abstraction. The Intellect thus produced would be what Allah is, but would also start a further series of emanations until there emerges the Tenth Intellect, which produces the created order as its own means of self-reflection (cf. ibn Arabi, pp.340f). But why would the process begin? It was left to another to answer that question.

Aristotle

Aristotle was revered among Muslim philosophers, who did much to rescue and preserve his works, The Caliph Mamun (d.833) dreamt that he saw Aristotle seated on a throne, and as a result he sent to the West for his works to be found and translated into Arabic (Fihrist, p.243). Other Muslims were suspicious of this enthusiasm because it seemed to be subordinating revelation to reason.

ARISTOTELIANISM

"Aristotelianism" was a fusion of genuine works of Aristotle and Plato with works and commentaries of Neoplatonists.

When work began in Europe (especially in Spain where the three monotheisms – Judaism, Christianity, and Islam – met) of translating Arabic texts into Latin, works were attributed to Aristotle that came from Neoplatonists: the widely influential *Theologia Aristotelis* (*The Theology of Aristotle*) was in fact a text compiled from *The Enneads* of Plotinus, and another, *Liber Aristotelis*, usually known as *De Causis* (*Concerning Causes*), was drawn from a work by Proclus. This fusion of ideas brought in beliefs about God (such as emanation and a chain of being) that are not in Aristotle.

ibn Sina (Avicenna)

A Necessary Existent

ibn Sina

Arberry, the great interpreter of Muslim thought, wrote of ibn Sina: "To read Avicenna on theology…is to be aware of standing in the presence of one of the profoundest and most courageous thinkers in history" (p.7).

"So I bought the book and found that it was written by Abu Nasr alFarabi, On the Objects of the Metaphysica [i.e., Aristotle's Metaphysics]. I rushed home and started to read it, and at once I saw clearly what it was about – for I had it all in my memory. I rejoiced greatly, and on the next day I gave much to the poor in the way of alms because I was so grateful to Allah"

(Autobiography of ibn Sina)

NOT LONG AFTER ALFARABI DIED, a young man, 18-years old, was browsing in a secondhand bookshop in Bukhara. He was widely read and passionate in his search for knowledge: he had already read the *Metaphysics* of Aristotle at least 40 times and had indeed learned it by heart, but, as he recalled in his autobiography, "even then I did not understand it or what the author meant". On this momentous afternoon, the bookseller offered him a book at half-price because the owner needed to sell it (see box, below left).

The young man was ibn Sina (980–1037CE), known outside Islam in a Latinized form as Avicenna. Through translation, he had an immense influence on Christian thought, especially on Aquinas (p.264), who quoted him many times. His summary of medical knowledge at the time, *AlQanun fi'l Tibb* (*The Canon of Medicine*), became the foundation of medical training for many centuries to come, and one of his works on philosophy and metaphysics, *AshShifa* (*The Healing*), became a standard work of reference. He was known as "the leader of the wise" and "the proof of God". Like alFarabi, ibn Sina believed that reason points to the conclusion that there must be what he called in Arabic *wajib alwujud* – roughly, "that which must as a matter of absolute necessity be existent", or more briefly "a Necessary Existent":

"Whatever exists must either have a cause or reason for its existing, or not have a cause or reason for it. If there is a cause or reason, then it is contingent. But if it has no cause or reason of any kind whatsoever for its existing, then it is necessary [existing for its own reason and in its own right]. This rule having been established, I will now move on to prove that there is in being a being that has no cause or reason for its being"

(arRisalat al'Arshiya)

His proof is that a Necessary Existent is either necessary or contingent. If it is necessary, the point has been proved. If it were to be contingent, it would then be preceded by an infinite regress of reasons and causes which, because they are contingently related to that which they bring into being, cannot bring into being that which has no reason or cause for its being because it is not contingent. The point about a Necessary Existent is that its essence must, by definition, be none other (and nothing more) than its existence, since if there were more to be said about it (e.g., that it is a substance), it would be possible to determine whether that substance is of such a kind and reality that we can know whether it happens to exist or not. But a Necessary Existent does not "happen" to exist or not exist: it exists necessarily. It then becomes possible to look at the chain of causes and reasons the other way around, and to realize that the Necessary Existent is the ultimate cause of all causes and reasons (of all contingent beings) in the sense that it is logically the first cause. The question then immediately arises how or why the Necessary Existent moves to bring into being anything outside itself. ibn Sina, like alFarabi, gave the same answer as the Neoplatonists: by a succession of emanations. There is no external necessity for this, since otherwise the Necessary Existent would be under contingent constraint: emanation arises from the nature of the Necessary Existent to contemplate its own nature and produce the first self-awareness or Intellect, from which further emanation occurs. This is an effect of pure grace or generosity (*jud*): it exists within the nature of the Necessary Existent without looking for any reciprocity or return.

All this is advanced as a rational argument and does not in itself seek to identify the Necessary Existent with any characterization of God, not even with Allah as revealed in the Quran and as apprehended by Sufis (p.334) in experience. The Necessary Existent is simply an ontological principle required if the puzzles of essence and existence, or of causes and contingency, are to be solved. But ibn Sina was himself a religious man and a Muslim – as he wrote in his *Autobiography* (see box, top right). ibn Sina therefore realized that the Necessary Existent is the One whom the Sufis encounter as they ascend (cf. pp.250f) through the stages and stations (*ahwal and maqamat*) that lead to the loss of themselves in Allah – just as the Necessary Existent is the One who is revealed in the Quran in pictorial images and language that ordinary people can understand. It was, incidentally, a misunderstanding of this that led Christians to accuse Avicenna of proposing a notion of double-truth. Truth for ibn Sina is truth however it happens to be expressed, whatever forms it is expressed in. In his view, the truth about God can be expressed in the most rigorous philosophical terms without even mentioning the word Allah, since reason is itself the most precious gift that humans receive. His was a massive achievement, as influential in Christianity as in Islam. And yet, little more than 40 years after his death, sharp and destructive questions began to be raised by another philosopher about what he had done.

> "When I found myself perplexed by a problem, or when I could not find the middle term of a syllogism, I would take myself to the mosque and pray in adoration of the Creator, until the problem was resolved and my difficulty was made easy"
>
> (Autobiography of ibn Sina)

The Arts as Praise
This title page of a work by ibn Sina illustrates the importance and beauty of book production and illustration in Islam. The revelation of the Quran in Arabic led to the development of calligraphy and other arts.

alGhazali

The Search for Reliable Truths

IN THE SUMMER OF 1095CE, one of the most eminent Muslim teachers of the time – indeed, of all time – stood in front of a class of students. His lectures were always well attended, because he was, as near as could be, an absolute master of his subject – not simply Islamic law (*fiqh*), but also philosophy, theology, and those subjects that would now come within the scope of natural sciences. So he should have had no worries about giving this particular lecture. And yet when he stood up to speak he found that his voice was paralyzed: he was completely unable to speak, and he stood before his class in silence.

What was the crisis? It was his realization that he did not know what he was talking about – or rather, *whom* he was talking about. He was talking with profound skill about Allah, and yet he did not know the One about whom he was talking.

It was not the first crisis he had experienced of that kind. Earlier in his life, he had, like many philosophers before and since, set out to establish the certain and unshakeable foundations of knowledge: what can we know for certain and beyond doubt? alGhazali was clear that we cannot know anything for certain simply because someone with authority tells us, although accepting things on the basis of authority (*taqlid*) was widely respected in Islam. He was clear also that nothing can be established by miracles (see box, left).

Absolutely certain knowledge cannot even be established by sense-perception without further thought, because our senses frequently deceive us: it is impossible to observe a shadow moving, and yet its progress from one end of a day to the other makes it clear that it has been moving all the time. So where can we find the certain and unshakeable foundations of knowledge on which we can rely without doubt or argument? Without that secure foundation being established (and the quest for it in philosophy is known as "foundationalism"), how can anyone be sure of anything? alGhazali could not find it, and, in despair, he became a complete sceptic.

He emerged from that earlier crisis by recognizing that some certain and some reliable truths obtain. Some truths are what we would now call analytic – for example, that 3+7=10; some truths are reliable if we can specify the circumstances in which we could verify them for ourselves without being deceived. For instance, someone may tell us that Fadak is a village near Mecca (see caption, right); that claim is a candidate for reliable knowledge because we could verify it for ourselves by making a journey to that place and either finding it there or not. So alGhazali concluded that genuine knowledge (what he called in Arabic *'ilm*

> *"Supposing someone says to me, '3 is greater than 10, and in order to prove it I will change this stick into a snake', and let us suppose that he actually does it: the only consequence to me is to wonder how he did the trick. So far as establishing knowledge is concerned,* fala – *nothing at all"*

alyaqini) "is that in which whatever is to be known presents itself in such a way that no doubt accompanies it, that no possibility of falsification or illusion accompanies it, that the person involved cannot envisage even the possibility of such an illusion or falsification."

That approach, in the way in which it combines verification and falsification, resembles modern empiricism, and it helped alGhazali to establish genuine (*yaqin*) knowledge. But it did not help to establish genuine knowledge of Allah, because Allah cannot be produced as an object among objects, like a village among the villages near Mecca; and supposing that one did propose some kind of verification of that kind, what would be the result? The Quran, for example, affirms that Allah sits on a throne: does this mean that a throne with Allah sitting on it will one day present itself to observation? If it does, the fatal Muslim offence against Allah of *tashbih* (of anthropomorphism, of reducing Allah to human stature) has been committed. If it does not do so, then how can we be sure that any propositions about Allah are true – if nothing is ever offered to verify them?

This is the long-running problem of the Attributes of Allah (the status of the things that the Quran attributes to God, like sitting on a throne and having hands and a voice: see p.330). Traditional theology had accepted the Attributes as true statements about Allah, but without knowing how they could be so (*bila kaif*). But for alGhazali, that came too close simply to accepting things on authority (*taqlid* above).

It soon became clear to alGhazali that the philosophers, turning to Aristotle and the Neoplatonists, had not in fact solved these problems, and he wrote, not long before the crisis in 1095CE, *Tahafut alFalsafah* (*The Incoherence of the Philosophers*) to show why and where they had failed, both in general and in particular.

In general, he took 20 points on which they could be shown to be wrong or inconclusive: the latter showed, much like Kant in the famous "antinomies of reason", that from the arguments of the philosophers two contradictory sides of an argument can be proved with equal validity.

In particular, he argued that their reliance on Neoplatonism did not in fact achieve what they had hoped. The theory of emanation did not protect Allah from involvement in creation, since Allah is the source of the first movement into separate and contingent being. Therefore emanation does nothing to solve the problem of why Allah, being perfect and self-sufficient, would want to create anything external to that complete perfection – the classic problem of the One and the many. Their solution had

Seeking a Village
How do we know that a claim (e.g., about the existence of unicorns, p.352) is true or false? Some have answered, By going and finding (or not finding) one, and by thus verifying or falsifying the claim by direct observation. The claim that there is a village called Fadak can be verified by going and taking a look. The claim by some 20th-century philosophers (positivists) that meaningful propositions can be established only in this way was shown to be false, in arguments anticipated by alGhazali, not least the recognition that genuine human knowledge and insight build on sense experience but go far beyond it.

been to claim that the world must itself be eternal, and that all substances, whatever form they may happen to take, must also be eternal. But that too was incoherent to alGhazali because it would make substances equal to Allah, and yet the philosophers wanted to keep a distinction between the Necessary Existent and creation.

For that reason also they had claimed that Allah cannot know particular things, but has only a general knowledge, since otherwise Allah would be less than perfect: at one time Allah would be ignorant of something, and only later aware of it. alGhazali argued that to know the unknowable is a *logical*, not a practical, impossibility, and therefore is not a necessary condition of omniscience.

It is, however, one thing to expose the incoherence of arguments about Allah, quite another to put something in their place. How can Allah be known, given that the philosophers had failed to give a rational answer to this question? It was that crisis that reduced alGhazali to silence in front of his class. He could talk about Allah fluently, but he did not know Allah personally and in his life.

He glimpsed a solution by remembering that there were other Muslims who did claim a genuine (*yaqin*) knowledge of God, and who claimed also to show how in practice that knowledge could be attained. These were the Sufis, and alGhazali's immediate response to his crisis was to take himself away into solitude – in the first instance to Damascus and to the minaret of the mosque – in order to learn and to put into practice what the Sufis were teaching (see box, top right).

Damascus

Claims have been made that Damascus is the oldest continuously inhabited city in the world – it is mentioned in an Ebla tablet c.3000BCE. It was captured by Khalid ibn Walid in 14/635 and became the capital city of the first dynasty, the Umayyads, in 41/661. Its greatest building is the Umayyad mosque, to which alGhazali went during the first part of his Sufi quest.

In his ten years of withdrawal from the world, or at least from public life, alGhazali found the truth which he had sought: he found it in the Sufi way of direct and immediate devotion to Allah that passes into love (see box, below right). On that basis he wrote his greatest work to show people how to come to that knowledge of God, and above all how they can live in that condition of devotion and love. He called the work "a bringing to new life of the knowledge that religion makes possible" (*Ihya 'Ulum udDin, The Revival of the Sciences of Religion*). He maintained his critique of the philosophers, but went on to offer a practical guide to the way in which this world can become the gateway to the world to come.

The achievement of alGhazali was that he rebuilt the bridge between the quest for knowledge and the service of Allah. He showed how the often ecstatic love of Allah among the Sufis was not an end in itself but was a part of the entire life of Islam embedded in Sharia (p.348). In that way, the spiritual energy of the Sufis was integrated into the wider life of Muslims as they sought their way, in obedience to Allah, from death to life.

P hilosophy continued in Islam after the time of alGhazali (for an example, see ibn Arabi, p.340): ibn Rushd, known outside Islam as Averroes, even wrote *The Incoherence of the Incoherence.* But philosophy could never again be an end in itself. It became, particularly in Persia, the exploration of the way in which love leads, as alGhazali had both argued and experienced, to a direct mode of cognition, not just between one person and another, but between all those who learn to live this way and Allah.

But how could that be verified? In the end (the final End and last judgement of all things) it must be verified to us, or else the claim would turn out to have been false so far as we are concerned. There must be sufficiently what there is about a person that continues from this life into the next for the verification to occur to that person (much later, this argument came to be known as eschatological verification). That is why alGhazali insisted that the philosophers must be wrong in claiming that the descriptions of the physical resurrection were pictorial ways of speaking about a purely intellectual satisfaction. Here, along with his refutation of the arguments that the world is eternal and that Allah does not know particulars, alGhazali established for subsequent Islam that the Quran controls philosophy and sets an impassable limit on speculation.

In 1106CE, alGhazali took up teaching again in Nishapur, though in a more communal style with students sharing his life. He retired finally in 1109CE and died in 1111CE. On the day of his death, he performed the dawn prayers and then asked for his shroud. He kissed it, laid it on his eyes and said: "In obedience I enter into the presence of the King." He then lay down facing the *qibla* (the direction of Mecca) and died before the day was fully come.

In his own account of how he was delivered from error (his *Munqidh min adDalal, The Deliverance from Error*), alGhazali wrote:

"At last I turned to the way of the Sufis, a way that combines both knowledge and action. Its purpose is to remove from oneself the faults and defects of character until the heart is stripped of everything that separates from Allah and is constant in the remembrance (dhikr) of Allah's name"

(3.4)

alGhazali heeded at last a voice within that had called out to him long before:

"The love of lesser things had kept me chained in my place, until the herald of faith had cried out to me: 'On the way! On the way! The day is short and the journey before you is long. Your knowledge and action are deceit and self-deception. If you do not prepare for the world to come now, when will you prepare? If you do not cut through your attachments now, when will you do so?'"

Jihad and Martyrdom

The Supreme Effort

"To those against whom war is made, permission is given [to fight], because they have suffered wrong; and truly Allah is their most powerful help – those who have been driven out of their homes contrary to justice [haqq] simply because they say, "Our Lord is Allah"; and if Allah did not hold back one set of people by means of another, there would have been devastation of monasteries, churches, synagogues, and mosques where the name of Allah is so much remembered [dhikr]"

(22.40f)

Martyrs
To become a martyr may mean dying "in the cause of Allah" but it may mean any costly witness, such as accepting patiently the death of three sons (Bowker, p.122).

IN APPROACHING THE GREAT "examination of life" (p.327), it is not necessary to answer all the questions correctly, because in Muslim understanding it is fundamental that Allah is *rahman wa rahim*, merciful and compassionate (p.328). But it is necessary always to be making an effort to put into practice the guidance that Allah has given, and to observe the commands and prohibitions. The Arabic word *jahada* means "he made an effort", from which comes the word *jihad*. Jihad is often translated as "holy war", but that is only one small part of what effort "in the cause of Allah" (*fi sabili'lAllah*) means, as Muhammad made clear when he and his troops were returning to Medina from a battle. He told them that they were returning from the lesser Jihad to the greater Jihad, by which he meant the constant effort to overcome all temptations to stray from "the straight path" (Quran 1.6). Nevertheless, Jihad "in the cause of Allah" may include *Qital* ("killing") in the cause of Allah, and this is certainly envisaged in the Quran, although there it is also made clear that such killing can only be defensive (see box, left). A defensive war could also be fought on behalf of the oppressed in general (4.77/75):

"What reason have you for not fighting in the cause of Allah and of those who are weak among men, women, and children, who say, 'Our Lord, take us out of this town whose people are oppressors, and give us from yourself a protector, and give us from yourself a friend'"

In both Quran and Hadith, clear limits are set on the ways in which war can be fought (e.g., 2.186/190ff). Abu Dawud (one of the six "sound" or recognized collectors of Hadith, p.323) recorded how Muhammad instructed those setting out on campaigns: "Undertake Jihad in the name of Allah and in the cause of Allah. Do not touch the old, close to death, women, children, or babies. Do not steal anything from the spoils of war, and play your part in collecting whatever falls to you on the battlefield; and do good, for Allah loves those who are good and devoted" (*Kitab alJihad*). The 2nd Caliph, Umar, gave instructions for the army invading Syria (see box, right). Those who flew planes as bombs into buildings on 11 September 2001 so flagrantly broke those rules that they cannot be regarded as martyrs, perhaps not even as Muslims (cf. pp.332–3). So killing (but within limits) in the cause of Allah is one way in which Muslims recognize the authority of Allah. It is not an obligation on all Muslims (it is, in other words, *fard kifayah*, not *fard 'ain*): apart from the fact that those involved must be Muslim, male, sane, past puberty, and able to maintain their families while away, it is also the case that other obligations may have priority. Both alBukhari and Muslim (collectors of Hadith) record, for example, how obligation to one's parents comes first: "Abu Huraira told how a man came to the Messenger of Allah (peace be upon him) and asked, 'Who deserves the best treatment from me?' He replied, 'Your mother.' He then asked, 'Who next?' He replied, 'Your mother.' Again he asked, 'Who next?' and he answered, 'Your mother.' He said, 'Who after that?' and he said, 'Your father.'… Abdullah b. Amr reported that a man came to the Messenger of Allah and asked to take part in Jihad. He answered, 'Are your parents living?' The man told him, 'Yes', so he replied, 'You should make all your effort in caring for them" (Muslim, *alJami asSahih*, 30.553. 6180, 6184).

"Wait, my people, while I give you ten rules for your guidance in battle. Do not act treacherously; do not stray from the straight path; do not mutilate the dead; do not kill children; or women; or old men; do not harm trees; do not burn trees, especially those bearing fruit; do not kill the flocks of the enemy except for your own food; do not search out those who have dedicated their lives as monks – leave them alone"

(atTabari, *Tarikh arRasul* 1.3.1580)

Even so, the lesser Jihad is precious in the sight of Allah, who favours those who die during the course of it and thus become martyrs. Just as the Greek word *marturos* means literally "one who bears witness", so the Arabic *shahid* is "a witness", as in the fundamental witness (*ashShahada*, p.349). A Shahid who dies in the course of the lesser Jihad is exempted from the interrogation in the grave by the two angels and has a privileged place in Paradise. Because martyrs are pure and clean, their bodies do not have to be washed before burial – indeed, they should be buried in the clothes they were wearing when they died, since they will appear in Paradise displaying the wounds that killed them (Muslim, 18.781.4629); they have no need of the help or intercession of others, and instead they become those who intercede on behalf of others. For Shia Muslims (p.332), martyrdom is even more important because their first Imams, Ali, alHasan, and alHusain were believed to be martyrs at the hands of other Muslims, and their deaths have a redemptive power for Shiites. For all Muslims, Jihad in its two senses (greater and lesser) shows the way in which they must be devoted to Allah. It has reference not just to this life, but even more to the world to come.

War and Peace
Muslims divide the world into three domains: Dar alIslam (the domain of Islam), where Allah is acknowledged; Dar alHarb (the domain of War), where hostility to Islam must be resisted; and Dar asSulh (the domain of Truce), where treaties allow coexistence.

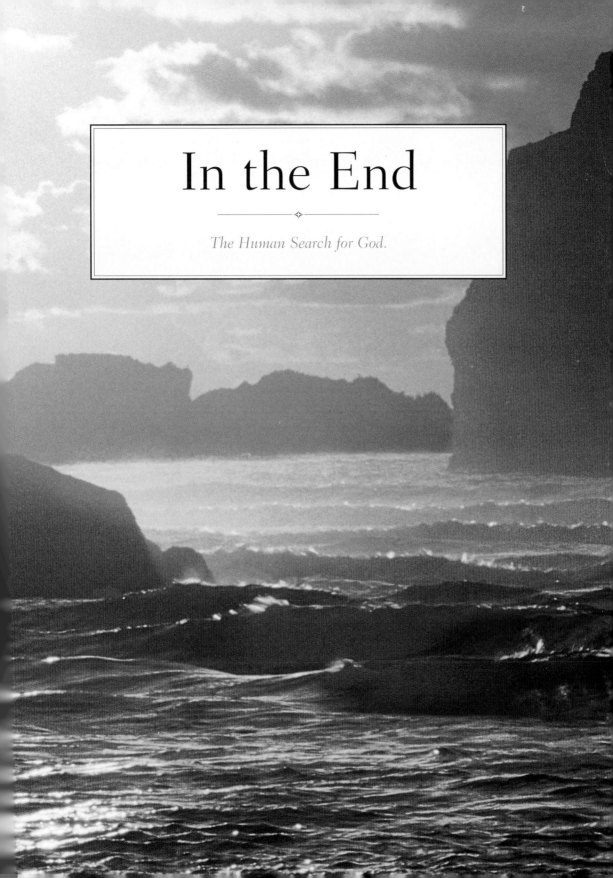

In the End

◆

The Human Search for God.

Conclusion

The Human Search for God

THERE IS NO CONCLUSION to the human search for God. That is so in two senses. The first is obvious. There is no end to all that might be written about the many ways in which humans have explored and discovered something of the meaning and nature of God – and still do. There are new religions, and new ways in old religions, in which the language of God is translated into life, and no book could mention them all.

What I have tried to do in this book is show why and how those who lived before us came to the *second* sense in which there is no conclusion to the human search for God. This too is obvious on almost every page of this book: the more you come to know God, the more you realize that God is more than you can know, at least in this life.

This means that the knowledge people enter into of God is real, but the ways they speak of it are incomplete. Their words and poems and pictures, as well as their lives, try to share something of the character of God as One of whom they know much more than a distant rumour of a far-off place; but their characterizations of God are always inadequate and are constantly being changed from one generation to another.

Some characterizations do, of course, persist – for example, God in the character of Mother and God in the character of Father. Even so, we know that God is not exactly like any human parent: and what, in any case, of those whose experience of their human mother or father has been disastrous?

So, as we saw from the outset (pp.16f), all characterizations of God are necessarily approximate, provisional, corrigible, and mainly wrong. But they point, nevertheless, to the One who evokes these words and pictures, but remains beyond the verbal net in which we try to catch our fish. *Deus semper maior*: God is always greater.

Something like that, however, is also true for scientists as they try to describe and characterize the universe. Of course their methods are entirely different, and the universe presents itself in ways very unlike those through which God becomes a living presence. Even so, when scientists, playing their part in the human search for truth, describe and characterize the universe, their words are approximate, provisional, corrigible, and often wrong from the point of view of later generations. But they achieve, all the same, great

Unconditional Love
Human beings begin to learn the meaning of love long before they learn the meaning of words. They learn it first with their mothers. If that does not or cannot happen, they can still learn the meaning of love in later relationships – though no one is compelled to do so.

That we love others is miracle enough. That others love us is, for many, the first glimpse of what God is like.

reliability (see caption, p.369). What this book illustrates is that the same is true in the human search for God: it too has achieved great reliability in the ways, well-tested and well-winnowed, through which people can know for themselves, in body, mind, and spirit, the reality of God. These ways then take people beyond knowledge (though surely on the foundation of knowledge) to worship, penitence, adoration, and love. Beyond knowledge lies invitation into relationship.

The nature of that relationship with God has often been one of fear, even of terror – in the past excessively so. But if we are to be responsible and accountable for what we are, what we think, and what we do, then the contrast between ourselves and God is bound on occasion to produce fear. "I tremble sometimes for my country", wrote Thomas Jefferson (third President of the United States), "when I reflect that God is just." Beneath the carved scene of the Last Judgement on the Church at Autun in France, the sculptor Ghiselbertus inscribed: *Terreat hic terror quos terreus alligat error*; "May this terror terrify those bound in terrestrial error."

But what is clear from the many people described in this book is that those who live with God find that it is a relationship of love, and that perfect love casts out fear (I John 4.18). Augustine (pp.258–61) wrote the sane advice, "Fear God that you may not fall back, love God that you may move forward" (*Letter* 144.2); and certainly for Augustine, love was the final word: *dilige et quod vis fac*; love, and what you will [in the character of love], do.

I t is true that the word "love" means many different things in different times and places. Take the sentence "He cannot really, then, have loved her." The poet Walter de la Mare (1873–1956) pointed out how different the people are of whom that might be said, and how different their circumstances (see box, right). The particular examples he gives may not all be familiar, but it is easy to think of others of whom the same statement might be made. Love means so many different things that comparisons with God are not simple. It means that all analogies, including the analogy of love, are imperfect. But human love is the nearest parallel in experience to what it feels like to be intensely immersed in God.

Certainly, God does not feel like that all the time: for example, in the Indian poetry of Bhakti (of devotion to God, p.95) there is much more of absence (p.96) than of presence: "One day Caitanya [p.137] was sitting in a state of desolation, writing with his fingers in the sand and lamenting: 'Where are the banks of the Yamuna [p.134]! Where is the Lord who infatuates even the god of Love himself!'" (Hardy, p.5).

But when God *is* known in love, even if only once for a moment, it is never forgotten. This is true (as this book illustrates), not just in India, but in universal human experience. It is, for those who have known it, the most memorable of all possible human experiences. The experience of God as love does not diminish or "explain away" the counteravailing

> "He cannot really, then, have loved her"
>
> *"With how much of this will any other 'he' or 'she' be likely to concur in regard to those to whom the sentence might be actually applied? To Shelley and Harriet, or Swift and Vanessa, let us say; to Bothwell and Mary Stuart; George IV and Perdita; to Paolo and Francesca; Abélard and Héloise; Thomas and Jane Carlyle; to Christian and his wife; Othello and Desdemona; to Gibbon and the young lady of whom (when on parental advice he had resigned her hand) he said, 'I sighed as lover, I obeyed as a son'"*
>
> (de la Mare, xxxivf)

experience of suffering and pain, still less the fall of a sparrow or the affliction of those whom we would help but cannot. But suffering has to be seen in the entire context of love, because love is at least as real as suffering. And since love only rarely seeks to cause suffering (and even then, in cases of remedy, it is an act of love), and since suffering cannot destroy love, it is an act of faith that love is as strong as death (*Song of Songs* 8.6), stronger by far than suffering, and that it will in the end prevail. It is faith based on reason and experience. Even so, it is an act of faith.

It is this faith that enables God to create the miracles of human hope and love by which people begin to live in entirely new ways. Even the world itself becomes a new place, when it is lived as the creation and the miracle of God. The word "miracle" comes from the Latin *miror*, to marvel at something, to be amazed. To call something "a miracle" is to say that it is something worth looking at, something that should open our eyes, and in that sense every consequence of God in creation is a miracle. The English poet Thomas Traherne (c.1638–74) caught the feeling of very many in this book when he wrote the words in the box, left.

> "You never enjoy the world aright, till you see how a sand exhibits the wisdom and power of God…. Your enjoyment of the world is never right, till every morning you awake in heaven, and see yourself in your Father's palace, and look upon the skies and the earth and the air as celestial joys…. You never enjoy the world aright, till the sea itself floweth in your veins, till you are clothed with the heavens and crowned with the stars…. The world is a mirror of infinite beauty, yet no man sees it. It is a Temple of majesty, yet no man regards it. It is a region of light and peace, did not men disquiet it. It is the paradise of God, it is the place of angels and the gate of heaven"
>
> (*Centuries, Poems and Thanksgivings*, 1st Century, 27ff)

Seeing and living in the world in this way, as a gift received from one who gives it with generous grace but is not a part of it, means that there cannot be any final or ultimate conflict between science and God, because God is not an object, like a universe, waiting to be investigated – although there is at least *something* about God that is open to exploration and even experiment, as this book repeatedly shows. Even so, to engage with God is not to seek additional information about the universe. For that, we go to science. But when we do go to science we are brought inevitably to the question "Why is there a universe at all?" As the philosopher Wittgenstein (1889–1951) put it, "Not *how* the world is, but *that* it is, is the mystery."

It was this that led another philosopher, Martin Heidegger (1889–1976), to claim that the question "Why is there something rather than nothing?" is the most fundamental question that humans can ask. Heidegger began his lectures *Introduction to Metaphysics* in exactly that way:

"Why are there beings at all instead of nothing? That is the question. Presumably it is no arbitrary question. 'Why are there beings at all instead of nothing?' – this is obviously the first of all questions. Of course, it is not the first question in the chronological sense. Individuals as well as peoples ask many questions in the course of their historical passage through time. They explore, investigate, and test many sorts of things before they run into the question 'Why are there beings at all instead of nothing?' Many never run into this question at all, if running into the question means not only hearing and reading the interrogative sentence as uttered, but asking the question, that is, taking a stand on it, posing it, compelling oneself into the state of this questioning.

And yet, we are each touched once, maybe even now and then, by the concealed power of this question, without properly grasping what is happening to us. In great despair, for example, when all weight tends to dwindle away from things and the sense of things grows dark, the question looms… The question is there in heartfelt joy, for then all things are transformed and surround us as if for the first time… The question is there in a spell of boredom, when we are equally distant from despair and joy, but when the stubborn ordinariness of beings lays open a wasteland in which it makes no difference to us whether beings are or are not – and then, in a distinctive form, the question resonates once again: Why are there beings at all instead of nothing?" (Heidegger, pp.1f).

Of course, Heidegger recognized that there are those who cannot see the point of the question at all, and who say that the universe (and ourselves in the universe) happen to be here, and that's an end to it.

Absolute Beauty
We see examples of beauty, goodness, truth, and love in particular people, places, or acts. But we experience them and recognize them as being absolutely what they are (beautiful, good, true) no matter what the particular circumstances (which change) may be. To recognize this is to recognize that in the midst of time and change, the Absolute exists; to realize that we can relate in personal terms (e.g., of thankfulness, praise, sorrow, and love) to that which is Absolute, the source of beauty, goodness, truth, and love, is to realize that that which is Absolute is more like a person than an abstract, philosophical conclusion. Instead of the Absolute, we speak in human language of God.

Science, however, like other human knowledge, depends on our determination to go on asking the questions "why" and "how": it is abject and irrational to say that the final questions are not to be asked – not least because whatever answer we give to the question, why is there something rather than nothing, is the foundation of what we understand by "God": God is what we mean when we say that there is a reason why there is something rather than nothing: "A potter is necessary to produce a jar; mere clay is not sufficient" (Shankara, p.365).

The point is that "why" and "how" questions are basic to human wisdom and truth. Why and how are you a person alive and reading these words? Because your parents procreated you that way. Yes, but why and how did they do that? Because they wanted a child and the genes and proteins enabled them to achieve their wish. Yes, but why and how do genes and proteins do this? Because the biochemistry of reproduction enables this. Yes, but... The questions, *if they are pursued*, take us eventually into the fundamental consistencies of physics whose regularities allow us to call them 'laws'. The remaining question will always be, Yes, but why are there laws at all? To refuse to ask the question on the grounds that we just happen to have laws is as abjectly irrational as to say that we just happen to be here and that there is no point asking how or why. With *that* attitude there would be no biology, chemistry, or physics.

Of course, we could stop asking questions at any point, and most of us don't have time to pursue the answers to all questions down to the level of the laws of physics. Nor should we: there are true and worthwhile answers to human questions *at every level*, and in no way can they all be reduced to biology, chemistry, or physics: biology, chemistry, and physics are the necessary but never sufficient condition of answers to human questions.

Even so, the questions of "how" and "why" remain, even if we prefer not to ask them. Heidegger simply asked the most fundamental of all questions, Why is there a universe rather than nothing? What is more, he asked it knowing that it cannot be answered by science. Nor can it be answered demonstratively by anyone, since whatever it is that is the answer to that question is what is meant by God. But at least by extending the metaphor of the recipe (see box, left), it is obvious that where there is a recipe, it is a reasonable abductive inference (pp.17 & 266) to conclude that there is One who devises the recipe and produces the product in the way that it appears. It makes far more sense of the universe as we know it to conclude that there is One from whom it comes and by whom it is sustained – and that is true even if the universe has neither a beginning nor an end: it can still be in that relationship of dependence. In that case, the One (whom we call God) cannot be a part of what the universe is, although God can clearly become known through the way the universe is. *Deus semper maior*. In this context, the consistent reliability of the universe is unsurprising. God is the guarantee that there is enduring coherence in the universe of such

In a recent book, the mathematical physicist John Taylor has shown how through the ages (the winnowing process) scientists have explained more and more very different phenomena with fewer and fewer underlying principles, and how these in turn reveal *"the hidden unities in nature's laws"*. This enables him to produce *"a simple recipe for a universe"* (pp.395–99), which allows the speculation, *"how must the universe have 'started off' to be consistent with what is known?"* (p.396) His answers are a good example of abductive inference: see in this book pp.17 & 266.

a kind that it can be investigated and understood. It was this trustworthiness of the universe as we explore it that led Albert Einstein to make his famous remark, "The Lord God is subtle, but malicious he is not." For that reason, both God and the universe are, in their different but connected ways, invitations to this brilliant human architecture of atoms and molecules to move with integrity into truth. And that *is* a miracle.

So there cannot be any ultimate conflict between science and God. However, between the sentences that try to speak of science with the discoveries of science, and the sentences that try to speak of God with the consequences of God, there may be, and often are, conflicts. The most serious of these arise from sentences that are (to use the technical phrase) propositions about putative matters of fact – sentences that make claims about what purports to be, as a matter of fact, either true or false.

Thus when, for example, a scientist recently (in 1992) claimed that God is a virus, that was a claim (expressed metaphorically) about a putative matter of fact, and it was in conflict with other claims about God. It is easy to show, as I have done in my book, *Is God a Virus? Genes, Culture and Religion*, that the claim is completely and unequivocally wrong, not only because the metaphor cannot work, but also because the scientist in question was not familiar with the latest work on the ways in which genes and culture interact in human evolution.

Conversely, when believers in God make claims that God made the universe in six literal days, that God gets hungry and needs sacrifices to keep going until tomorrow, or that God is rightly represented as an old man with a beard, then scientists (and not only scientists) rightly protest that those claims about God are completely and unequivocally wrong if they are advanced as claims about putative matters of fact.

These conflicts about putative matters of fact are undoubtedly one major reason why characterizations of God change. A far more important reason in the case of God is the fact that those who live with God in worship and prayer come to realize very deeply indeed that their words and pictures about God cannot in any way represent adequately the wonder of what God is. This means that characterizations of God are bound to change, just as characterizations of the universe change, but only because there is sufficiently what there is in each case (entirely different though the two cases are) making an independent demand on us, so that the winnowing process of change is both required in terms of truth and is sustained.

In the case of God, I have tried to show in this book something of this process of change as it has happened, and scientists (many of whom have been and are believers in God) have played a major and creative part in demanding, and often in leading, the necessary changes and corrections.

An obvious problem arises when God-fearing people are reluctant to change – when, for example, they believe that a particular narrative or characterization of God has God's authority for it, and that change is not

Discovering DNA
Looking back on the moment when he thought he had discovered how the structure of DNA is formed, James Watson wrote: "My pulse began to race. If this was DNA, I should create a bombshell by announcing its discovery... For over two hours I happily lay awake with pairs of adenine residues whirling in front of my closed eyes. Only for brief moments did the fear shoot through me that an idea this good could be wrong" (Watson, pp.103ff). But it was: "My scheme was torn to shreds by the following noon"(p.105). Yet he was only a step away from the correct solution.
This illustrates the winnowing way in which science proceeds by its own corrigibility. But it does proceed because there is sufficient consistency and reliability in what is being investigated.

permissible. When it is claimed that a narrative or characterization has been revealed, it may also be felt that it cannot be changed without implying the fallibility of God.

But that is a problem within religion, not within science, and certainly not within the essential nature of God. This book has shown repeatedly that claims to revelation and authority do not have to lead to that feeling (above), since all revelation (supposing there is any) is made into contingent, historical circumstances and languages. It means that the understanding of revelation and inspiration changes in step with changes in the understanding of God, without in any way affecting the authority of scripture (see the discussion of the relation between 'author' and 'authority' in Bowker, *The Complete Bible Handbook*, DK, 1998, pp.9f).

Scriptures are thus an invitation and opportunity to learn more of God on the basis of what is already known, received, and believed. God does not change but the characterizations of God must. Even then, the praise of God will frequently be expressed in the language of poetry, which is often the language of the past (see caption, opposite). That is why in worship and prayer many old images endure, although, as a putative matter of fact, they happen to be wrong. Even scientists talk about the sun rising.

What becomes clear, therefore, is how important it is to distinguish the poetry of praise from the prose of description. Only then can we understand why the characterizations of God will be both stable (where they have proved reliable in leading to God) and yet open always to change. If you come across a person who knows more about God than God, or a religion that captures in words "what God is like", you will know at once that this is a person in error and a false religion.

In the immediate future, the far more serious conflict between human experience of the world and human experience of God lies in the area of ethics. People continue to do evil and wicked things, myself surely among them. There is a particular malevolence when people do evil and wicked things in the name of God, and give God a character that is worse than the worst person we know. There are at least some people who seem cheerfully to describe God behaving in ways that in human terms would lead to instant arrest.

For God's sake, that too has to be challenged. It is very difficult to do, or at least to do so with any discernible effect. There are those who hang on to their defective characterizations of God as though their lives depend upon it – as psychologically they may well do. But the earth does not remain flat simply because there are those who think that their lives depend on not sailing over the edge. It is not that "the latest is always best" – far from it in the case of speculations about God or in the case of revisions of liturgy and prayer. It is simply that people who respond to the invitation of God to travel further into truth come to realize that some things that have been believed about God are incompatible with what God is now known (provisionally and incompletely) to be: love is incompatible with terror, hatred, and malice. To say this is not easy and is often fiercely resisted. Even so, we can take courage from this book.

Take, for example, the characterization of God as a Mafia gangster (p.186): that was challenged and changed within that tradition itself, and within the texts that were themselves believed to have been revealed by God. The gods no longer eat babies for breakfast, though it was once believed that they did.

Nevertheless, people still go to God to justify actions that the character of love condemns. From this, it is easy to see why God can be extremely bad news, and why the death of God has occurred so often. That happens, in part, because evil is real and because there are people who choose evil and who, like the first murderer in *Macbeth*, are "reckless what they do to spite the world". But it happens also because of the absurd things that have been claimed about God, even more because of the cruel and wicked things that have been done in the name of God. On 11 September 2001 four planes were made into flying bombs in the name of God (but see p.360; and Bowker, 1995, pp.121–91).

The consequent death of God has been for some people absolute and complete. Atheists are not agnostics. Nevertheless, the persistence of God is certain, not least because the recognition of God is so deeply embedded in the human brain and body, as I have tried to make clear in the Introduction. That may make God-belief extremely easy to manipulate and profitable to exploit, but it remains also the reason why so many people have found God, often in great simplicity, to be in fact true and real.

This means, to adapt my "paradox of religious urgency", that God is such bad news only because God is such good news: if God were not the highest good that humans can imagine and know, if God did not change lives to become that goodness in relations of love, God would indeed have "gone down the chute" for ever, as Mencken said (p.10). No one would bother about God if God were only bad news, or if God were only the invention of ruthless, unhappy, or neurotic people.

Of course to some extent God *is* a human invention, but then so is everything else, not least the world of science. The word "invention" is often used to mean "something made up", a fiction rather than a fact. But the underlying Latin words, *in + venio*, mean "I come into", "I find" or "I discover". Thus the universe is a human invention, but there is something there that we come into in order to understand it better. So too with God: I have tried to show in this book some of the many ways in which people have left a record of their invention of God, of the ways in which they came into a relationship with God, and of how others can do the same. But God is not an object like a universe

Poetry of Praise
Traditional words and images endure, even though they are transformed in each generation. Well-achieved, such images become timeless. When Henry Moore was asked to carve a Madonna and child, he asked himself how it would differ from an ordinary mother and child: "I have tried to give a sense of complete easiness and repose, as though the Madonna could stay in that position for ever (as being in stone she will have to do)"
(Read, p.154).

that can be "invented" or discovered in anything like the same way that discoveries are made in science. God is, whether this or any other universe happens to exist or not, and is far beyond human description. The gap – some would say abyss – between God and humans is necessary if any kind of voluntary relationship is to exist: we are created, not coerced, with sufficient freedom to recognize or to refuse God, and if that were not so, the relationship could not be one of exploration and love. God means that people are called into consequence, not coerced into compliance.

One result of this is that there will always be many different accounts of God, and that some of the claims made about God in different religions will be in conflict with each other. If God is not an object among objects, there is no simple appeal to "what God is like" in order to resolve these conflicts, not even if appeal is made to revelation, because revealed characteristics of God may also be in conflict.

There is, of course, one apparently simple way to resolve these conflicts. It is to say that because God is beyond words and description, all these conflicting ways are at least pointing to the same reality, and that all religions are thus different languages through which people talk about God, or that they are different roads leading to the same goal. There is undoubtedly a logical truth that if people are talking about God, it is God that they are talking about. But they may still be talking *falsely* about God. Despite the saying that 'all roads lead to Rome', roads do *not* all lead to Rome simply because they are roads.

Suppose you have never been to Siberia: you hear reports about Siberia, some from people who have lived there and know what they are talking about. If people are talking about Siberia, it is Siberia that they are talking about, and not some other country. If Siberia is real, it is Siberia that Siberia turns out to be. Nevertheless, when you visit Siberia, you may well find that some of the reports were false, even though they were (logically) reports about Siberia.

So also with God: if God is real, it is God that God turns out to be. Even so, reports about God may turn out to be false, even though they are (logically) reports about God. But how can we judge between true and false reports without visiting God as we might visit Siberia? The answer is, we can't. Certainly we can make many discriminating judgements: common-sense and philosophy pick out claims and propositions that are false, incoherent or just plain daft; and that is so even though some believers may refuse to be persuaded.

To visit God, however, is only possible in the preliminary ways of worship, prayer, and meditation, and in the practice of the presence of God in life. To that end, the initiatives of God, including not only the unique initiative claimed by Christians of Christ, but also the many others described in this book, are points of access. In the end, we will arrive and we will know as we are known, but in the meantime (in time and space) we are only on the way.

How, then, are we to deal with the conflicting claims about God? And do the conflicts matter? In a practical sense, they clearly matter, because religious people who believe in God are involved in some of the most intransigent and long-running conflicts in the world – as, for example, in Northern Ireland, the Middle East, the Balkans, Cyprus, the Sudan, Kashmir, Sri Lanka, the Philippines and Indonesia; and others, like Nigeria, are not far away. It is not that belief in God causes these conflicts, but belief in God may undoubtedly reinforce them, not least when there are specifically God-derived commands that endorse violence. As the Irish poet and Nobel prize-winner, Seamus Heaney, put it: "The problem with the IRA is that you're dealing with theology rather than politics. It's a metaphysical republic to which they are dedicated. And they are entrapped in vows" (*Sunday Telegraph Magazine*, 1 April, 2001, p.23).

Issues, therefore, between religions and between conflicting claims about God need urgently to be addressed, not just for pragmatic reasons of peace, but for reasons also of truth and salvation. Already religions have been drawn together to seek a global ethic that will encourage them to pursue common actions. But if issues of truth and truth claims are to be addressed without glossing over the serious conflicts that exist, then we have to begin at an even more fundamental level.

H ow can this be done? There is only one way, and that is the way of worship. If, as this book shows, all religions (including those of Jains, or of Buddhists, with an understanding of God restricted to this apparent universe) know that God is beyond human words and descriptions, and yet can be approached in worship, penitence, and praise, that is the one all-important way of being human that they all have in common. If God is truly greater (*Deus semper maior*), it is worship that says so.

Worship at present is as much entangled in conflict as everything else, but the forms of *common* worship need to be deliberately sought and found, even though it will be a dauntingly difficult task. In the context of worship, and only in that context, is there any chance of going on to address, in a completely different style, the divisions that could yet destroy us all. For in that context it turns out that the human search for God has always been God's search for humans, but in ways that respect and endorse their freedom.

The basic meaning of prayer, therefore, is extremely clear. All prayer is an act of love in response to love. Prayer is an act of pure love that looks for nothing beyond itself, but looks only to God in a simple way: here am I; You know me; help me to know You. Yes, more may well happen in addition to that – sorrow and penitence, for example, thanksgiving and praise, prayer for others, a loving caress of this beautiful though often painful world. But even if nothing more does happen, everything has happened, and nothing more is needed.

Rodin's "Cathedral"
"Prayer is,
my patient Lord,
my reach to you
and you at endless work
in making love from life:
shape this cold clay
into such work of art
that it may rest in peace
in You."

BIBLIOGRAPHY

❖

The following is a list of books and texts used in this book. The author's own translations are not listed. University Press is abbreviated to U.P. throughout.

Every effort has been made to secure permission for quotations from potentially copyrighted material and to ensure that all quoted material is properly credited. In the event that proper credit for any quoted material in *God – A Brief History* has been inadvertently omitted, please notify the publisher so that subsequent editions may be revised accordingly.

INTRODUCTION
Bible: the translations used are those of the New Revised Standard Version and The New Jerusalem Bible, London, Darton, Longman & Todd, 1985

Bowker, J., *Is God a Virus? Genes, Culture & Religion*, London, SPCK, 1995

Brooke, R., in ed. G.Keynes, *The Poetical Works of Rupert Brooke*, London, Faber & Faber, 1963

Bryson, B., *The Lost Continent*, London, Abacus, 1996

Cicero, *De Natura Deorum*, trsl. H.C.P. McGregor, London, Penguin, 1972

Damasio, A., *Descartes' Error: Emotion, Reason & the Human Brain*, New York, Putnam, 1994; *The Feeling of What Happens: Body, Emotion, & the Making of Consciousness*, New York, Vintage, 2000

Grou, J., *Spiritual Maxims*, 1786

Hume, D., *An Enquiry Concerning the Principles of Morals*, 1751; *Dialogues Concerning Natural Religion*, 1779

le Doux, J., *The Emotional Brain*, London, Weidenfeld, 1998

Mencken, H., *Prejudices*, New York, Vintage, 1958; *Minority Report: H.L. Mencken's Notebooks*, Baltimore, John Hopkins, 1997

Moscati, S., *The Face of the Ancient Orient*, London, Routledge, 1960

Nicholson, N., *The Lakers*, London, Robert Hale, 1955

Nietzsche, F., *Die fröhliche Wissenschaft*, in *Nietzsches Werke*, V, Leipzig, Naumann, 1899-1912

Rilke, R., *Sämtliche Werke*, Frankfurt, Insel-Verlag, 1955–97; *Rodin* in *ibid.*, 5, 1965

Rolls, E.T., *The Brain & Emotion*, Oxford, Oxford U.P., 1999

Sacchetti, F., *Il Trecentonovelle*, Rome, Salerno, 1996

Shaw, G.B., *The Adventures of the Black Girl in Her Search for God*, London, Constable, 1932

Stoppard, T., *Jumpers*, London, Faber & Faber, 1972

Taliaferro, C., *Consciousness & the Mind of God*, Cambridge, Cambridge U.P., 1996

Thompson, R.F., *Flash of the Spirit*, New York, Vintage Books, 1984

Williams, O., & Honig, E., *Major American Poets*, New York, New American Library, 1962

Xenophanes, *Die Fragmente*, Munich, Artemis, 1983

Yandell, K.E., *The Epistemology of Religious Experience*, Cambridge, Cambridge U.P., 1994

IN THE BEGINNING
Adler, M., *Drawing Down the Moon*, Boston, Beacon Press, 1986

Anand, M.R., 'Lines Written to an Indian Air', in B.N. Pandey, *A Book of India*, London, Collins, 1965

Asimov, I., *A Choice of Catastrophes*, London, Hutchinson, 1979

Aveni, A., *Nasca*, London, British Museum Press, 2000

Bowker, J., *Is God a Virus? Genes, Culture & Religion*, London, SPCK, 1995; *The Meanings of Death*, Cambridge, Cambridge U.P., 1993; 'Science and Religion', in ed. F. Watts, *Science Meets Faith*, London, SPCK, 1998

Brown, J.E., *The Sacred Pipe*, New York, Penguin, 1973

Clottes, J., & Lewis-Williams,D., *The Shamans of Prehistory: Trance & Magic in the Painted Caves*, New York, Abrams, 1998

Courlander, H., *A Treasury of African Folklore*, New York, Marlowe, 1996

Deacon, T.W., *The Symbolic Species: The Co-evolution of Language & the Brain*, London, Penguin, 1998

Dream of the Rood, ed. M. Swanton, Exeter, Exeter U.P., 1996

Edda of Snorri Sturluson, trsl. A. Faulkes, London, Dent, 1987

Gimbutas, M., *The Living Goddesses*, ed. M.R. Dexter, Berkeley, University of California Press, 1999

Grimes, R.L., *Beginnings in Ritual Studies*, Lanham, University of America Press, 1982

Gutierrez, R., *When Jesus Came, the Corn Mothers Went Away: Marriage, Sexuality, & Power in New Mexico, 1500–1846*, Stanford, Stanford U.P., 1991

Hogan, L., in (no author) *The Way of the Spirit*, Time-Life Books, 1997

Husain, S., *The Goddess: Power, Sexuality & the Feminine Divine*, London, Duncan Baird, 1997

Hutton, R., 'The Discovery of the Modern Goddess', in ed. J.Pearson, *Nature Religion Today*, Edinburgh, Edinburgh U.P., 1998

Johnson, H. & Pines, J., *Deep Roots Music*, London, Proteus, 1982

Jung, C.G, *Collected Works*, ed. H. Read *et al.*, London, Routledge, 1968

Lindfors, B., *Forms of Folklore in Africa*, Austin, University of Texas Press, 1977

Luther Standing Bear, *Land of the Spotted Eagle*, Lincoln, University of Nebraska Press, 1978

Mackay, A.L. (ed.), *The Harvest of a Quiet Eye*, Bristol, Institute of Physics, 1977

Mellaart, J., *Catal Hüyük: A Neolithic Town in Anatolia*, London, Thames & Hudson, 1967; *et al.*, *The*

Goddess from Anatolia, Milan, Eskenazi, 1989

Melville, H., in ed. H. Hayford & H. Parker, *Moby Dick*, New York, Norton, 1967

Mooney, J., 'The Doctrine of the Ghost Dance', in D. & B. Tedlock, *Teachings from the American Earth: Indian Religion & Philosophy*, New York, Liveright, 1975

Okpewho, I., *Myth in Africa*, Cambridge, Cambridge U.P., 1983

Pliny, *Natural History*, trsl. H. Rackham *et al.*, London, Loeb, 1938–63

Powers, W.K., 'When Black Elk Speaks, Everybody Listens', in ed. D.G.Hackett, *Religion & American Culture*, New York, Routledge, 1995

Rouget, G., *Music & Trance*, Chicago, University of Chicago Press, 1985

Schelling, F.W.J., *Philosophie der Mythologie*, in *Schellings Werke*, VI, Munich, 1959

Schopenhauer, A., *Die Welt als Wille und Vorstellung*, Wiesbaden, Brodhaus, 1972

Shakespeare, W., *A Midsummer Night's Dream*

Simpson, K., *The Literature of Ancient Egypt*, New Haven, Yale U.P., 1973

Sjöö, M. & Mor, B., *The Great Cosmic Mother: Rediscovering the Religion of the Earth*, San Francisco, HarperCollins, 1991

Starhawk, *The Spiral Dance*, San Francisco, HarperCollins, 1979

Sullivan, M., *Symbols of Eternity: The Art of Landscape Painting in China*, Oxford, Clarendon Press, 1979

Teresa, *Her Life*, trsl. K. Kavanaugh & O.Rodriguez in *Collected Works*, I, Washington, ICS Publications, 1987

Turner, H., in ed. V.C. Hayes, *Australian Essays in World Religions*, Bedford Park, Australian Association. for the Study of Religions, 1977

Wagner, R., *Parsifal*, ed. N.John, London, Calder, 1986

Whitehouse, H., *Arguments & Icons: Divergent Modes of Religiosity*, Oxford, Oxford U.P., 2000

INDIA

Allchin, F.R., *Tulsi Das: The Petition to Ram*, London, Allen & Unwin, 1966

Appar: see Peterson

Aurobindo, Sri, *The Life Divine*, III, Pondicherry, Sri Aurobindo Ashram, 1955

Babb, L., *The Divine Hierarchy*, New York, Columbia U.P., 1981

Bailey, G., *The Mythology of Brahma*, Delhi, Oxford U.P., 1983

Basavanna: see Ramanujan

Behari, B., *Minstrels of God*, Bombay, Bharatiya Vidya Bhavan, 1956

Belvalkar, S.K., *et al.*, Mahabharata, Poona, Bhandarakar Oriental Research Institute, 1927–66

Beyer, S., *The Cult of Tara: Magic & Ritual in Tibet*, Berkeley, University of California Press, 1978

Bhadwaj, S.M., *Hindu Places of Pilgrimage*, Berkeley, University of California Press, 1983

Bhagavadgita: see van Buitenen

Bhagavata Purana, ed. J.L. Shastri, Delhi, Motilal Banarsidass, 1983

Bhai Vir Singh, *Purantam Janamsakhi*, Amritsar, Khalsa Samachar, 1948

Bhardwaj, S.M., *Hindu Places of Pilgrimage in India*, Berkeley, University of California Press, 1983

Bhatt, G.R., *et al.*, *The Valmiki-Ramayana*, University of Baroda, 1970–75

Bhattacharji, S., *The Indian Theogony*, Cambridge, Cambridge U.P., 1970

Bhattacharya, V. (ed.), *The Agamasastra of Gaudapada*, Delhi, Motilal Banarsidass, 1943

Brahma Sutra: see Date

Brihad-aranyaka Upanishad: see Radhakrishnan

Brooks, D.R., *Auspicious Wisdom: The Texts & Traditions of Srividya Sakta Tantrism in South India*, Albany, State University of New York Press, 1992

Brown, C.M., *The Devi Gita*, Albany, State University of New York Press, 1998

Campantar: see Peterson

Chakravarty, U., *Indra & Other Vedic Deities: A Euhemeristic Study*, New Delhi, D.K. Printworld, 1997

Chari, S.M.S., *Philosophy & Theistic Mysticism of the Alvars*, Delhi, Motilal Banarsidass, 1997

Clothey, F.W., *The Many Faces of Murukan: The History & Meaning of a South Indian God*, The Hague, Mouton, 1978

Coburn, T.B., *Encountering the Goddess: A Translation of the Devi-Mahatmya & a Study of its Interpretation*, Albany, State University of New York Press, 1991

Crossley-Holland, P., 'The Religious Music of Tibet…', in *Proceedings of the Centennial Workshop on Ethnomusicology*, Victoria, Aural History Provincial Archives, 1975

Daniélou, A., *Hindu Polytheism*, London, Routledge, 1964

Dasam Granth Sahib, Patiala, Punjabi U.P., 1973

Date, V.H., *Vedanta Explained: Samkara's Commentary on the Brahma Sutras*, Bombay, Booksellers' Publishing, 1954, 1959

Dayal, T.H., *The Vishnu Purana*, Delhi, Sundeep Prakashan, 1983

de Bary, W.T. (ed.), *Sources of Indian Tradition*, New York, Columbia U.P., 1958

de Nicolas, A.T., *Meditations Through the Rig Veda*, Boulder, Shambhala, 1978

Delmonico, N., 'How to Partake in the Love of Krisna', in ed. D.S.Lopez, *Religions of India in Practice*, Princeton, Princeton U.P., 1995

Deshpande, P.Y., *The Authentic Yoga: Patanjali's Yoga Sutras*, London, Rider, 1978

Devibhagavata Purana, trsl. H.P. Chatterji, Allahbad, Panini, 1921–3

Devimahatmya: see Coburn

Dhavamony, M., *Love of God According to Saiva Siddhanta: A Study in the Mysticism & Theology of Saivism*, Oxford, Clarendon Press, 1971

Dobbins, J.C., 'Shinran's Faith…' in ed. G.J. Tanabe, *Religions of Japan in Practice*, Princeton, Princeton U.P., 1999

Eck, D., *Banaras: City of Light*, London, Routledge, 1983; *Darsan: Seeing the Divine Image in India*, Chambersberg, Anima Press, 1981

Eschmann, A. *et al.*, *The Cult of Jagannath & the Regional Tradition of Orissa*, Manohar, 1978

Flood, G., *An Introduction to Hinduism*, Cambridge, Cambridge U.P., 1996

Futehally, S., *In the Dark of the Heart:*

Songs of Meera, London, HarperCollins/Sacred Literature Trust, 1994

Gandhi, M.K., *The Story of My Experiments with Truth*, Ahmedabad, Navajivan, 1929

Gaudapada, *Mandukyakarika*: see Bhattacharya

Gitagovinda: see Jayadeva

Gonda, J., *Notes on the Names of God in Ancient India*, Amsterdam, North-Holland Publishing, 1970

Gopal Singh, *The Religion of the Sikhs*, London, Asia Publishing House, 1971

Govindalilamrta: see Delmonico

Growse, F.S., *The Ramayana of Tulsi Das*, Allahabad, 1937

Guru Granth Sahib: see Kaur Singh; *Sri Guru Granth Sahibji*; Trilochan Singh

Harbans Singh, *Guru Nanak & the Origins of the Sikh Faith*, Patiala, Panjabi U.P., 1969

Hardy, F., *Viraha-Bhakti: The Early History of Krisna Devotion in South India*, Delhi, Oxford U.P., 1983

Jataka Stories, ed. V. Fausboll, London, Trubner, 1880

Jayadeva, *Gitagovinda*, trsl. D. Mukhopadhyay, *In Praise of Krishna*, Delhi, B.R. Publishing, 1990

Jha, M., *Dimensions of Pilgrimage: An Anthropological Appraisal*, New Delhi, Inter-India Publications, 1985

Kabir: see Vaudeville

Kalikapurana, ed., B.N.Shastri, Delhi, Nag, 1991–2

Kaur Singh, N-G., *The Name of My Beloved*, London, HarperCollins/Sacred Literature Trust, 1995

Klostermaier, K.K., *A Survey of Hinduism*, New Delhi, Munshiram Manoharlal, 1990

Kramisch, S., *Exploring India's Sacred Art*, ed. B.S. Miller, Philadelphia, University of Pennsylvania Press, 1983

Krishnadasa Kaviraja, *Govindalilamrita*; see Delmonico

Kunst, A., & Shastri, J.L., *Puranas in Translation*, Delhi, Banarsidass, 1969

Lata, P., *Chaitanya Mahaprabhu*, New Delhi, Ess Ess, 1989

Lopez, D. (ed.), *Religions of India in Practice*, Princeton, Princeton U.P., 1995

Ludvik, C., *Hanuman in the Ramayana of Valmiki & the Ramacaritamanasa of Tulsi Dasa*, Delhi, Motilal Banarsidass, 1994

Lynch, O.M., *Divine Passions: The Social Construction of Emotion in India*, Berkeley, University of California Press, 1990

Macfie, J.M., *The Ramayan of Tulsidas*, Edinburgh, T. & T. Clark, 1930

Mahabharata: see Belvalkar

Mahadeviyakka: see Ramanujan

Majumdar, A.K., *Caitanya: His Life & Doctrine*, Bombay, Bharatiya Vidya Bhavan, 1969

Maraini, F., *Secret Tibet*, London, Hutchinson, 1952

Mattosho: see Dobbins

Milner, M., *Status & Sacredness: A General Theory of Status Relations & an Analysis of Indian Culture*, Oxford, Oxford U.P., 1994

Mirabai: see Futehally

Moorhouse, G., *Om: An Indian Pilgrimage*, London, Hodder, 1994

Mundaka Upanishad: see Radhakrishnan

Nagarjuna, *Mulamadhyamakakarika*, trsl. J.L.Garfield, Oxford, Oxford U.P., 1995

Nammalvar: see Chari; Raghavan

Nayar, N.A., *Poetry as Theology: The Srivaisnava Stotra in the Age of Ramanuja*, Wiesbaden, Harrassowitz, 1992

Nilsson, U., *Surdas*, New Delhi, Sahitya Akademi, 1982

Obeyesekere, G., *The Cult of the Goddess Pattini*, Chicago, University of Chicago, 1984

O'Flaherty, W., *Siva: The Erotic Ascetic*, Oxford, Oxford U.P., 1981

Pancatantra, ed. F. Edgerton, New Haven, American Oriental Society, 1924

Patanjali, *Yogadarshanam*: see Deshpande

Patwant Singh, *The Sikhs*, London, John Murray, 1999

Peterson, I.V., *Poems to Siva: The Hymns of the Tamil Saints*, Delhi, Motilal Banarsidass, 1991

Puranas: see Kunst

Radhakrishnan, S., *The Principal Upanishads*, London, Allen & Unwin, 1968

Raghavan, A.S., *Nammalvar*, New Delhi, Sahitya Akademi, 1975

Raghavan, V., *The Ramayana Tradition in Asia*, New Delhi, Sahitya Akademi, 1980

Ramayana: see Bhatt

Ramanujan, A.K., *Speaking of Siva*, London, Penguin, 1973

Redfield, R., *Peasant Society & Culture*, University of Chicago Press, 1956

Rig Veda, ed. M. Müller, London, 1877

Sachinanand, *Culture Change in Tribal Bihar*, Calcutta, Bookland, 1964

Schromer, K., & McLeod, W.H., *The Sants*, Delhi, Motilal Banarsidass, 1987

Shankara: see Date

Shantideva, *Bodhicharyavatara*, ed. Poussin, 1902

Shinran: see Dobbins

Shulman, D.D., *Tamil Temple Myths: Sacrifice & Divine Marriage in the South Indian Saiva Tradition*, Princeton, Princeton U.P., 1980

Shiva Purana, ed. P. Kumar, Delhi, Nag, 1981

Sri Guru Granth Sahibji, Amritsar, Shiromani Gurdwara Prabandhak Committee, 1969

Surdas: see Nilsson

Tagore, R., *Gitanjali*, 1912

Tanabe, G., *Religions of Japan in Practice*, Princeton, Princeton U.P., 1999

Thiel-Horstmann, M. (ed.), *Bhakti in Current Research, 1979–82*, Berlin, Dietrich Reimer, 1983

Trilochan Singh, *The Heritage of the Sikhs*, Bombay, Asia Publishing House, 1964

Tukaram: see Behari

Tulpule, S.G., *The Divine Name in the Indian Tradition: A Comparative Study*, Shimla, Indian Institute of Advanced Study, 1991

Upanishads, Advaita Ashrama Editions, Calcutta, 1957–65; see also Radhakrishnan

Uttaradhyayanasutram, ed. R.D. Vadekar, Poona, 1959

van Buitenen, J.A.B., *The Bhagavadgita in the Mahabharata: A Bilingual Edition*, Chicago,

University of Chicago Press, 1981

Varadpande, M.I., *Religion & Theatre*, Delhi, Abhinav Publications, 1985

Vaudeville, C., *A Weaver Named Kabir*, Delhi, Oxford U.P., 1997

Vidyarthi L.P. & Rai, B.K., *The Tribal Culture of India*, Delhi, Concept Publishing, 1977

Waghorne, J.P., & Cutler, N., *Gods of Flesh, Gods of Stone: The Embodiment of Divinity in India*, Chambersberg, Anima, 1985

Welbon, G.R., & Yocum, G.E. (eds.), *Religious Festivals in South India & Sri Lanka*, Manohar, 1982

Whitehead, H *The Village Gods of South India*, Calcutta, Association Press, 1921

Younger, P., *The Home of Dancing Sivan: The Traditions of the Hindu Temple in Citamparam*, Oxford, Oxford U.P., 1995

Zvelebil, K.V., *The Smile of Murugan: On Tamil Literature of South India*, Leiden, Brill, 1973; *The Lord of the Meeting Rivers*, Delhi, Motilal Banarsidass, 1984

THE RELIGIONS OF ASIA

Analects: see Leys

Bank, W., *Das chinesische Tempelorakel*, Wiesbaden, Harrassowitz, 1985

Barnstone, T. *et al*, *Laughing Lost in the Mountains: Poems of Wang Wei*, Hanover, U.P. of New England, 1991

Book of Odes (*Shijing*): see Chan Wing-tsit

Book of History (*Shujing*): see Waltham

Chan Wing-tsit, *A Source Book in Chinese Philosophy*, Princeton, Princeton U.P., 1963; *The Way of Lao Tzu*, Indianapolis, Bobbs-Merrill, 1963

Daode jing: see Chan Wing-tsit; Henricks

de Bary, W.T. (ed.), *Sources of Chinese Tradition*, New York, Columbia U.P., 1966

Eno, R., *The Confucian Creation of Heaven*, Albany, State University of New York Press, 1990

Forke, A., *Me Ti des Sozialethikers und seiner Schüler philosophische Werke*, Berlin, Mitteilungen des Seminars für Orientalische

Sprachen, 22–25, 1922

Graham, A.C., 'Confucianism', in ed. R.C. Zaehner, *The Concise Encyclopaedia of Living Faiths*, London, Hutchinson, 1959

Grayson, J.H., *Korea, A Religious History*, Oxford, Clarendon Press, 1989

Hardacre, H., *Shinto & the State, 1868–1988*, Princeton, Princeton U.P., 1989

Havens, N., trsl *Kojikiden*, in ed. Inoue Nobutaka, *Kami*, Tokyo, Institute for Japanese Culture, Kokugakuin University

Henricks, R.G., *Lao-tzu Tao-te Ching*, New York, Ballantine, 1989

Huhm, H.P., *Kut: Korean Shamanist Rituals*, Seoul, Hollym, 1983

I Ching: see *Yijing*

Journey to the West: (*Xiyou ji*): see Jenner

Jenner, W.J.F., *Journey to the West*, Beijing, Foreign Language Press, 1984

Kim, J. (ed.), *Korean Cultural Heritage: Thought & Religion*, Seoul, The Korea Foundation, 1996

Kitagawa, J., *Religion in Japanese History*, New York, Columbia U.P., 1966

Knoblock, J., *Xunzi: A Translation & Study of the Complete Works*, Stanford, Stanford U.P., 1988, 1990, 1994

Kojikiden: see Havens

Laozi (*Lao-tzu*) see Chan Wing-tsit; Henricks

Leys, S., *The Analects of Confucius*, New York, Norton, 1997

Liji (*Li-chi*), trsl. J.Legge, Oxford 1885

Loehr, M., *The Great Painters of China*, Oxford, Phaidon, 1980

Malraven, B., *Songs of the Shaman: The Ritual Chants of the Korean Mudang*, London, Routledge Kegan Paul, 1994

Meyer, J.F., *The Dragons of Tiananmen: Beijing as a Sacred City*, Columbia, University of South Carolina Press, 1991

Motoori Norinaga: see Havens

Shijing: see Chan Wing-tsit

Shiji: see de Bary

Shujing: see Waltham

Sullivan, M., *Symbols of Eternity: The Art of Landscape Painting in China*,

Oxford, Clarendon Press, 1979

Tao-te Ching: see Chan Wing-tsit; Henricks

Tsunoda, R. *et al.*, *Sources of Japanese Tradition*, New York, Columbia U.P., 1964

Waltham, C., *Shu ching, Book of History*, Chicago, Regnery, 1971

Wang Wei: see Barnstone

Watson, B., *Mo Tzu: Basic Writings*, New York, Colombia U.P., 1963; *Complete Writings of Chuang Tzu*, New York, Colombia U.P., 1968

White, C.W., *Bone Culture of Ancient China*, Toronto, University of Toronto Press, 1945

Whitehead, A.N., *Science & the Modern World*, Cambridge, Cambridge U.P., 1926

Whyte, D., *Where Many Rivers Meet*, Langley, Many Rivers Company, 1990

Xiyou Ji: see Jenner

Xunzi: see Knoblock

Yao Xinzhong, *An Introduction to Confucianism*, Cambridge, Cambridge U.P., 2000

Yijing, trsl. R.J. Lynn, *The Classic of Changes*, New York, Columbia U.P., 1994

Zhuangzi (*Chuang Tzu*): see Watson

JUDAISM
The separate books of the Bible have not been given individual entries: for these see the extensive bibliography in J. Bowker, *The Complete Bible Handbook*, London, DK, 1998

Albeck, Ch., *The Mishnah*, Tel Aviv, Mosad Bialik, 1952–8

Altmann, A., *Moses Mendelssohn: A Biographical Study*, London, Routledge, 1973

Babylonian Talmud, trsl. ed. I. Epstein, London, Soncino Press, 1948–61

Bergman, H., *The Autobiography of Solomon Maimon*, London, 1954

Berkowits, E., *Faith After the Holocaust*, New York, Ktav, 1973

Bold, A., *In This Corner: Selected Poems, 1963–1983*, Edinburgh, Macdonald, 1983

Bowker, J., *Jesus & the Pharisees*, Cambridge, Cambridge U.P., 1973

Boyce, M., *Zoroastrians: Their Religious Beliefs & Practices*, London, Routledge, 1979; *Textual Sources for the Study of Zoroastrianism*, Manchester, Manchester U.P., 1984

Buber, M., *Tales of the Hasidim*, New York, Schocken, 1991; *I & Thou*, trsl. R. Gregor Smith, Edinburgh, T. & T. Clark, 1959

Carmi, T., *The Penguin Book of Hebrew Verse*, London, Penguin, 1981

Clendinnen, I., *Reading the Holocaust*, Cambridge, Cambridge U.P., 1999

de Breffny, B., *The Synagogue*, London, Weidenfeld, 1978

Dead Sea Scrolls: see Vermes (translation); Tov (text)

Driver, G.R., & Miles, J.C., *The Babylonian Laws*, Oxford, Oxford U.P., 1952, 1955

Eliach, Y., *Hasidic Tales of the Holocaust*, New York, Avon Books, 1982

Fine, S., *This Holy Place: On the Sanctity of the Synagogue during the Greco-Roman Period*, Notre Dame, University of Notre Dame Press, 1997

Garrett, D., *The Cambridge Companion to Spinoza*, Cambridge, Cambridge U.P., 1996

Guttmann, A., *Rabbinic Judaism in the Making*, Michigan, Wayne State U.P., 1970

Haggadah shel Pesach, Tel Aviv, Sinai Publishing, 1966

Heschel, A.J.: see Rothschild

Hesiod, *Theogony*, trsl. M.L. West, Oxford, Oxford U.P., 1988

Hinnells, J., *Persian Mythology*, New York, P. Bedrick Books, 1985

Hoerth, A.J. et al., *Peoples of the Old Testament World*, Cambridge, Lutterworth, 1994

Lachower, F. & Tishby, I., *The Wisdom of the Zohar*, Oxford, Littman Library, 1989

Levy, I., *A Guide to Passover*, London, Jewish Chronicle Publications, 1958

Leon, H.J., *The Jews of Ancient Rome*, Philadelphia, Jewish Publication Society, 1960

Maimon, S.: see Bergman

Maimonides, *Mishneh Torah*, trsl. *The Code of Maimonides*, 15 vols., Yale Judaica Series; *The Guide for the Perplexed*, trsl. Ch. Rabin, London, East West Library, 1952; see also Minkin

Mendelssohn, M.: see Altmann

Midrash Rabbah, ed. H. Freedman & M. Simon, London, Soncino Press, 1939

Minkin, J.S., *The World of Moses Maimonides*, New York, Yoseloff, 1957

Mishnah: see Albeck

Moscati, S., *The Face of the Ancient Orient*, London, Routledge, 1960

Passover Haggadah: see *Haggadah shel Pesach*

Piyyutim: see Carmi

Prayer Book: see Singer

Reifenberg, A., *Israel's History in Coins*, London, Horovitz, 1953

Rothschild, F.A., *Between God & Man: From the Writings of Abraham J. Heschel*, New York, 1959

Rubenstein, R.L., *After Auschwitz*, Indianapolis, Bobbs-Merrill, 1968; *Approaches to Auschwitz*, London, SCM Press, 1987

Shanks, H., ed., *Ancient Israel: A Short History…*, Washington, Biblical Archaeology Society, 1989

Singer, S., *The Authorised Daily Prayer Book*, London, Eyre & Spottiswoode, 1957

Sperling, H., *The Zohar*, London, 1970

Spinoza: see Garret

Talmud: see Babylonian Talmud

Tanakh: A New Translation of the Holy Scriptures According to the Traditional Hebrew Text, Philadelphia, The Jewish Publication Society, 1985

Texidor, J., *The Pagan God: Popular Religion in the Greco-Roman Near East*, Princeton, Princeton U.P., 1977

Tov, E., text of Dead Sea Scrolls, microfiche, Leiden, Brill, 1993

Vermes, G. et al., *The History of the Jewish People in the Age of Jesus Christ*, Edinburgh, T. & T. Clark, 1973, 1979; *The Complete Dead Sea Scrolls in English*, London, Allen Lane, 1997

Weisberg, D.B., *Texts from the Time of Nebuchadnezzar*, New Haven, Yale U.P., 1980

Yose ben Yose: see Carmi

Zohar: see Sperling; Lachower

CHRISTIANITY
For individual books of the Bible, see the note at the start of the Judaism section.

Anderson, S., *The Virago Book of Spirituality: Of Women & Angels*, London, Virago, 1996

Aquinas, *Summa Theologiae*, trsl. various, London, Blackfriars, 1964; *Contra Gentiles*, trsl. various, Notre Dame, University of Notre Dame Press, 1995

Aristotle, *Metaphysica*, trsl. W.D. Ross, Oxford, Clarendon Press, 1908

Armstrong, A.H., *Classic Mediterranean Spirituality*, London, Routledge, 1986

Armstrong, R. & Brady, I., *Francis & Clare: The Complete Works*, New York, Paulist Press, 1982

Aristeas, Letter of: see Meecham

Athenogoras: see Schoedel

Auden, W.H., *Collected Poems*, ed. E. Mendelson, London, Faber, 1994; *The English Auden*, ed. E. Mendelson, London, Faber, 1988

Augustine, *Opera Omnia*, ed. J-P. Migne, Paris, 1861; *The Works of Saint Augustine: A Translation for the 21st Century*, trsl. various, New York, Augustine Heritage Institute, 1990; see also Dyson; Lawless; Sheed

Barth, K., *Church Dogmatics*, Edinburgh, T. & T. Clark, 1936–69

Basil: see Deferrari; Holmes; Wiles & Santer

Bell, C., *Art*, London, Chatto & Windus, 1920

Belting, H., *Likeness & Presence: A History of the Image Before the Era of Art*, Chicago, University of Chicago Press, 1994

Bemiss, S., *The Three Charters of the Virginia Company of London*, Williamsburg, 1957

Benedict: see McCann

Berger, P., *The Heretical Imperative*, London, Collins, 1980

Bernard: see Diemer

Bindley, T.H., *The Oecumenical Documents of the Faith*, London, Methuen, 1899

Blake, W., *Complete Writings*, ed. G. Keynes, Oxford, Oxford U.P., 1972

Blakney, R.B., *Meister Eckhart: A Modern Translation*, New York, Harper, 1941

Blume, F., *Protestant Church Music*, London, 1975

Bosman, W., *A New & Accurate Description of the Coast of Guinea*, London, 1705

Bowker, J. (ed.), *The Complete Bible Handbook*, London, DK, 1998; *The Religious Imagination & the Sense of God*, Oxford, Clarendon Press, 1978; 'The Nature of Women & the Authority of Men', in *Is God a Virus? Genes, Culture & Religion*, London, SPCK,1995; "Merkabah Visions and the Visions of Paul", *Journal of Semitic Studies*, XVI, 1971

Brown, P., *Augustine of Hippo*, rev. edn., London, Faber, 2000

Browne, T., *Religio Medici*, ed. W.A. Greenhill, London, Macmillan, 1904

Burgess, A., *The Clockwork Testament*, London, Penguin, 1978

Burrows, R., *The Wisdom of St Teresa of Avila*, Oxford, Lion, 1998

Calvin, J., *The Institutes of the Christian Religion*, ed. J.T. McNeill, London, SCM, 1961

Campagnac, E.T., *The Cambridge Platonists*, Oxford, Clarendon, 1901

Carmichael: see *Carmina Gaedelica*

Carmina Gaedelica, ed. A. Carmichael, Edinburgh, Scottish Academic Press, 1928

Chalcedonian Definition: see Bindley

Chapman, A., *Black Voices: An Anthology of Afro-American Literature*, New York, New American Library, 1968

Clark, M., *Augustine of Hippo*, New York, Paulist Press, 1984

Clement of Alexandria: see Wiles & Santer

Climacus: see Luibheid & Russell

Cloud of Unknowing, trsl. C.Wolters, London, Penguin, 1978

Colledge, E., & Walsh, J., *Julian of Norwich: Showings*, New York, Paulist Press, 1978

Comper, F.M.M., *The Life of Richard Rolle Together with an Edition of His English Lyrics*, London, Dent, 1933

Cronin, V., *The Wise Man from the West*, London, Hart-Davis, 1955

Dante: see Sissons

Deferrari, R.J., *Saint Basil: The Letters*, London, Loeb, 1926–34

Diemer, P., *Love Without Measure: Extracts from the Writings of Bernard of Clairvaux*, London, Darton, Longman & Todd, 1990

Dix, G,, *The Shape of the Liturgy*, London, Dacre, 1943

Dolan, J.P., *The Essential Erasmus*, New York, New American Library, 1964

Dominic: see Koudelka

Dostoevsky, F., *The Brothers Karamazov*, trsl. R. Pevear & L.Volokhonsky, London, Vintage, 1990

DuBois, W.E.B.: see Chapman

Dunn, J.D.G., *The Theology of Paul the Apostle*, Edinburgh, T. & T. Clark, 1998

Dyson, R.W., *The City of God Against the Pagans*, Cambridge, Cambridge U.P., 1998

Eckhart: see Blakney

Eliot, T.S., *Four Quartets*, London, Faber & Faber, 1955; ed. R. Suchard, *The Varieties of Metaphysical Poetry*, London, Faber, 1993

Erasmus: see Dolan

Fanon, F., *The Wretched of the Earth*, London, Penguin, 1967

Finan,T., 'Hiberno-Latin Christian Literature', in ed. J.P. Mackey, *q.v*

Fishel, L.H., & Quarles, B., *The Black American: A Documentary History*, Glenview, Scott, Foresman, 1970

Fleming, D.L., *Draw Me Into Your Friendship: The Spiritual Exercises*, St Louis, Institute of Jesuit Sources, 1996

Flower, M., *Centred on Love: The Poems of Saint John of the Cross*, Varrowville, The Carmelite Nuns

Francis: see Armstrong & Brady; Robson

Gardner W.H., & MacKenzie, H. (eds.), *The Poems of Gerard Manley Hopkins*, Oxford, Oxford U.P., 1970

Gibbon, E., *Decline & Fall of the Roman Empire*, ed. cit., London, Dent, 1956

Giotto: see Maginnis

Glasscoe, M. (ed.), *The Medieval Mystical Tradition in England*, V, Cambridge, Brewer, 1992

Goldscheider, L., *Rodin Sculptures*, London, Phaidon, 1964

Gregory of Nyssa, *Opera Omnia*, ed. J.-P. Migne, Paris, 1863: see also Meredith; Musurillo

Gregory Palamas, *Works*, ed. P.C. Chrestou, Thessalonica, 1962

Grimal, P., *Churches of Rome*, London, Tauris Parke, 1997

Grimes, R.L., *Beginnings in Ritual Studies*, Lanham, University of America Press, 1982

Gutierrez, G., *We Drink from Our Own Wells: The Spiritual Journey of a People*, London, SCM, 1984; *Power of the Poor in History*, London, SCM, 1983

Happé, P., *English Mystery Plays*, London, Penguin, 1987

Harries, R., *Art & the Beauty of God*, London, Mowbray, 1993

Hartshorne, C., *A Natural Theology for Our Time*, La Salle, Open Court, 1967

Hayburn, R.F., *Papal Legislation on Sacred Music*, Collegeville, Liturgical Press, 1979

Hazlitt, F. & H., *The Wisdom of the Stoics*, Lanham, University of America Press, 1984

Herbert, G., *The Poems of George Herbert*, Oxford, Oxford U.P., 1907

Hilton, W., *The Ladder of Perfection*, trsl. L. Sherley-Price, London, Penguin, 1957

Holmes, A., *A Life Pleasing to God: The Spirituality of the Rules of St. Basil*, London, DLT, 2000

Hopkins: see Gardner

Ignatius: see Fleming; Ivens; Munitiz; Rahner

Instruccions Orders & Constitucions…to Sir Thomas Gates: see Bemiss

Instruction on Christian Freedom & Liberation, London, Catholic Truth Society, 1986

Irenaeus, *The Writings of Irenaeus*, Edinburgh, T. & T. Clark, 1868–9

Ivens, M., *Understanding the Spiritual*

Exercises, Leominster, Gracewing, 1998

John Climacus: see Luibheid & Russell

John of the Cross: see Flower; Kavanaugh; Matthew

Jones: see Parry

Kavanaugh, K., & Rodriguez, O., *The Collected Works of St John of the Cross*, London, Nelson, 1966

Kelly, J.N.D., *Early Christian Creeds*, London, Longman, 1981

Kierkegaard, S., *Concluding Unscientific Postscript*, trsl. D.F. Swenson, Princeton, Princeton U.P., 1944; *Either/Or*, trsl. H.V. & E.H. Hong, Princeton, Princeton U.P., 1987; *Training in Christianity*, trsl. W. Lowrie, Oxford, Oxford U.P., 1941

King, M.L., *A Testament of Hope*, ed. J.M. Washington, San Francisco, HarperCollins, 1991

Koudelka, V., *Dominic*, London, DLT, 1997

Krailsheimer, A.J., ed., *Pascal Pensées*, London, Penguin, 1966

Lash, E., *On the Life of Christ: Kontakia*, London, HarperCollins

Lasley, J., *Priestcraft & the Slaughterhouse Religion*, Cocoa, NISGO Publications

Lawless, G., *Augustine of Hippo & His Monastic Rule*, Oxford, Clarendon, 1990

Layton, B., *The Gnostic Scriptures*, London, SCM, 1987

Luibheid, C. & Rorem, P., *Pseudo Dionysus: The Complete Works*, New York, Paulist Press

Luibheid, C. & Russell, N., *John Climacus: The Ladder of Divine Ascent*, New York, Paulist Press, 1982

Luther, M., *Luther's Works*, trsl. various, Philadelphia, 1931

Mackey, J.P., *An Introduction to Celtic Christianity*, Edinburgh, T. & T. Clark, 1995

Maginnis, H.B.J., *Painting in the Age of Giotto: A Historical Reevaluation*, Philadelphia, University of Pennsylvania Press, 1997

Manning, B.L., *The Hymns of Wesley & Watts*, London, Epworth, 1942

Matthew, I., *The Impact of God:*

Soundings from St John of the Cross, London, Hodder, 1995

Maxwell, J.C., *William Wordsworth: The Prelude, A Parallel Text*, London, Penguin, 1971

McCann, J., *The Rule of St Benedict*, London, Burns Oates, 1963

McGinn, B., *The Presence of God: A History of Western Christian Mysticism*, London, SCM Press, 1991, 1994, 1998

Meecham, H.G., *The Letter of Aristeas: A Linguistic Study with Special Reference to the Greek Bible*, Manchester, Manchester U.P., 1935

Meredith, A., *Gregory of Nyssa*, London, Routledge, 1999

Miller, P., & Johnson, T.H., *The Puritans*, New York, Harper, 1963

Moule, C.F.D., *The Origins of Christology*, Cambridge, Cambridge U.P., 1977

Munitiz, J.A. & Endean, P., *Saint Ignatius of Loyola: Personal Writings*, London, Penguin, 1996

Musurillo, H., *From Glory to Glory: Texts from Gregory of Nyssa's Mystical Writings*, New York, St Vladimir, 1979

Mystery Plays: see Happé

Nicene Creed: see Kelly

Palmer, G.E.H. *et al.*, *The Philokalia*, London, Faber, 1979

Panofsky, E., *Abbot Suger on the Abbey Church of St.-Denis & its Treasures*, Princeton, Princeton U.P., 1946

Parker, A.A., *The Allegorical Drama of Calderon*, London, Dolphin, 1943

Parry, T., *The Oxford Book of Welsh Verse*, Oxford, Oxford U.P., 1962

Pascal: see Krailsheimer

Patrick: see Mackey

Paul: see Dunn

Péguy, C., *Basic Verities: Prose & Poetry*, London, Kegan Paul, 1943

Philokalia: see Palmer

Plato: see Armstrong, A.H.

Pliny, *Letters*, trsl. W. Melmoth, London, Loeb, 1915

Plotinus, *Works*, trsl. A.H. Armstrong, London, Loeb, 1966–88

Porter, H., *Reform & Reaction in Tudor Cambridge*, Cambridge, Cambridge U.P., 1958

Prater, D., *A Ringing Glass: The Life*

of Rainer Maria Rilke, Oxford, Oxford U.P., 1994

Ps.Dionysus, *Works*, Migne; see also Luibheid & Rorem

Quarles, B., *The Black American: A Documentary History*, Glenview, Scott, Foresman, 1970

Rahner, K., & Imhof, P., *Ignatius of Loyola*, London, Collins, 1979

Rauschenbusch, W., *Selected Writings*, ed. W.S. Hudson, New York, Paulist Press, 1984

Ricci, M., *The True Meaning of the Lord of Heaven*, trsl. D. Lancashire & P.H. Kuo-chen, Taipei, Institut Ricci, 1985: see also Cronin

Rolle: see Comper

Robson, M., *St. Francis of Assisi: The Legend & the Life*, London, Chapman, 1997

Romanos: see Lash

Ruhmer, E., *Grünewald: The Paintings*, London, Phaidon, 1958

Schoedel, W.R., *Athenagoras: Legatio*, Oxford, Clarendon Press, 1972

Sheed, F.J., *The Confessions of Saint Augustine*, London, Sheed & Ward, 1944

Sisson, C.H., *Dante: The Divine Comedy*, Oxford, Oxford U.P., 1998

Socrates, *Church History*, Oxford, Parker, 1891

Speaight, R., *The Christian Theatre*, London, Burns & Oates, 1960

Sterne, L., *The Life & Times of Tristram Shandy*, ed.cit., London, 1948

Strauss, D., *Das Leben Jesu Kritisch Bearbeitet (The Life of Jesus Critically Examined)*, Eng. trsl. 1846; see also Zeller

Suger: see Panofsky

Teresa, *Collected Works*, trsl. K. Kavanaugh & O. Rodriguez, Washington, ICS Publications, 1987

Thomas, R.S, *Collected Poems*, London, Dent, 1993

Thompson, F., *Selected Poems*, London, Burns Oates, 1921

Traherne, T., *Centuries, Poems, & Thanksgivings*, ed. H.M. Margoliouth, Oxford, Clarendon Press, 1972

Tyndall, J., *Fragments of Science*, London, 1889

Virgil, *Eclogues*, rev. trsl., London,

Loeb, 1999–2000

Ward, B., *The Sayings of the Fathers: The Alphabetical Collection*, Oxford, Mowbray, 1983

Wesley, J., *An Earnest Appeal to Men of Reason & Religion*, Dublin, 1806; *The Letters*, ed. J.T. Standard, London, Epworth, 1931; *Journals & Diaries*, ed. W.R. Ward & R.P. Heitzenrater, Nashville, Abingdon, 1990

Wheatley, P., *Poems on Various Subjects, Religious & Moral*: see Fishel & Quarles

Whichcote, B.: see Campagnac

Whitehead, A.N., *Adventures of Ideas*, Cambridge, Cambridge U.P., 1933

Wiles, M. & Santer, M., *Documents in Early Christian Thought*, Cambridge, Cambridge U.P., 1977

Winthrop, J., *A Modell of Christian Charity*: see Miller & Johnson

Wordsworth: see Maxwell

Zeller, E., *Ausgewählte Briefe*, Bonn, 1895

ISLAM

Abu Dawud, *Sunan*, ed. M.M.A. Hamid, Cairo, 1950

alAshari, *Kitab alIbana 'an Usul adDiyana*, Hyderabad, 1903

alBukhari, *Kitab alJami asSahih*, ed. Abu Abd Allah Muhammad, 1938

alFarabi: *Kitab Tahsil asSaada*, Beirut, Dar alAndalus, 1981: see also Hammond

alGhazali, *alMunqid min adDalal*, Beirut, Commission Internationale…, 1959; *Ihya Ulum udDin, Kafr alZaghari*, 1933; *Mishkat alAnwar*, Cairo, 1933: see also Kamali

alHallaj, *Akhbar alHallaj*, ed. L. Massignon & P. Kraus, Paris, Vrin, 1957; *Diwan*, ed. L. Massignon, Paris, Guenther, 1955: see also Massignon

alKhayyat, *Kitab alIntisar*, Beirut, 1955

alQaradawi, Y., *The Lawful & the Prohibited in Islam*, Indianapolis, American Trust

anNawawi, *Matn al-Arba'in anNawawiya…*, ed. E. Ibrahim, Cambridge, Islamic Texts Society, 1997

Arberry, A.J., *Muslim Saints & Mystics*, London, Penguin, 1966;

Avicenna on Theology, London, John Murray, 1951

Attar, Farid adDin, *Tadhkirat alAwliya*, ed. R.A. Nicholson, London, 1905

Bowker, J., *The Meanings of Death*, Cambridge, Cambridge U.P., 1993

Chittick, W., *The Sufi Path of Love: The Spiritual Teachings of Rumi*, New York, State University of New York Press, 1983

Conference of Birds, trsl. A. Darbandi & D. Davis, London, Penguin, 1984: see also Attar

Doi, A.R., *Shariah: The Islamic Law*, London, Ta-ha, 1984

Fihrist: see Fluegel

Fluegel, G., *Corani Textus Arabicus*, Farnborough, Gregg Press, 1965; ed., Muhammad ibn Ishaq alBagdadi, *Fihrist*, Leipzig, 1871–2

Gray, B., 'Arts of the Book', in *The Arts of Islam*, London, Arts Council of Great Britain, 1976

Gruner, O.C., *A Treatise on the Canons of Medicine*, London, Luzac, 1930

Guillaume, A., *The Life of Muhammad*, Lahore, Oxford U.P., 1967

Hammond, R., *The Philosophy of alFarabi & its Influence on Medieval Thought*, New York, Hobson Book Press, 1947

Harvey, A., *Light Upon Light: Inspirations from Rumi*, Berkeley, North Atlantic Books, 1996; *The Way of Passion*, London, Souvenir Press, 1995

Hasan alBasri, *Risala*, in *Der Islam*, V, 1921

Ibn Arabi, *Bezels of Wisdom*, trsl. R. Austin, New York, Paulist Press, 1980; *Tarjuman alAshwaq; alFutuhat alMakkiya*, Beirut, Dar asSadr

Ibn Ishaq, *Sirat Rasul Allah*, ed. cit., Cairo, 1955; see also Guillaume

ibn Sina: see Arberry; Gruner; Morewedge

Ihya Ulum udDin: see alGhazali

Jamali, M.F., *Letters on Islam*, London, Oxford U.P., 1965

Kamali, S.A., trsl., *Tahafut alFalasifah*, Lahore, Pakistan Philosophical Congress, 1958, 1963

Leaman, O., *Averroes & His Philosophy*, Oxford, Clarendon

Press, 1988

Massignon, L., *Quatres Textes*, Paris, 1914

Matn al-Arba'in anNawawiya: see anNawawi

Morewedge, P., *The Metaphysica of Avicenna (ibn Sina)*, London, Routledge, 1973

Muslim, *Sahih Muslim*, trsl. A.H. Siddiqi, Kitab Bhavan, New Delhi, 1977

Pitter, R., *Collected Poems*, Petersfield, Enitharmon, 1990

Quran: see Fluegel

Rabia: see Smith

Rumi: *Mathnawi*, London, Luzac, 1926–34; *Diwan-i-Shams-i-Tabriz*, R.A. Nicholson, Cambridge, Cambridge U.P., 1898; see also Harvey; Star

Safadi, Y.H., *Islamic Calligraphy*, Thames & Hudson, London, 1987

Seale, M.S., *Muslim Theology*, London, Luzac, 1964

Sharia: see alQaradawi; Doi

Smith, M., *Rabia the Mystic & Her Fellow-Saints in Islam*, Cambridge, Cambridge U.P., 1928

Star, J., *Rumi: In the Arms of the Beloved*, New York, Tarcher Putnam, 1997

Thesiger, W., *Arabian Sands*, London, Longmans, 1960

IN THE END

Bowker, J., *Is God a Virus? Genes, Culture & Religion*, London, SPCK, 1995; *The Complete Bible Handbook*, London, DK, 1998

Date, V.H., *Vedanta Explained: Śamkara's Commentary on Brahma-Sutras*, Bombay, Booksellers Publishing, 1954

de la Mare, W., *Love*, London, Faber, 1943

Hardy, F., *Viraha-Bhakti: The Early History of Krisna Devotion in South India*, Delhi, Oxford U.P., 1983

Heidegger, M., *Introduction to Metaphysics*, trsl. G. Fried & R. Pott, New Haven, Yale U.P., 2000

Shankara: see Date

Taylor, J.C., *Hidden Unity in Nature's Laws*, Cambridge, Cambridge U.P., 2001

Watson, J.D., *The Double Helix*, London, Readers Union, 1969

INDEX

❖

ACKNOWLEDGMENTS

IN ADDITION TO SEAN MOORE and Margaret Bowker (pp.6–7), my thanks go to many other people who helped in different ways with this book. Gavin Flood, Yao Xinzhong, and Professor C.F.D. Moule read parts of it and made suggestions and corrections; Quinton and Mona Deeley did the same, and Quinton wrote parts of the section on Ritual (pp.42–45) in which his new and important work on "the religious brain" is brought to bear; David Bowker, from his own knowledge of religions, was as always a source of wise advice and correction. The late Richard Tucker and Guy Welbon helped with the Metaphysicals and Indian temples respectively, and Madeleine Shaw guided me round the Cambridge University Library — whose staff also gave invariable support. Felicity Bryan saved me from innumerable practical errors. A clutch of doctors – Bill Aylward, Malcolm Kerr-Muir, and Stephen Wroe – kept me going through prolonged eye and other troubles and enabled me to write. Bill Broderick, Sarah Brunning, Maureen Thomas, Hayley Glen, and Ted Hardingham offered unfailing support.

Studio Cactus produced this book on behalf of Dorling Kindersley. The team was led by Damien Moore, Amanda Lunn, and Kate Grant, who were superb. Donna Wood and Sharon Rudd bore the brunt of the work and did so with great skill and tolerant good cheer: without them, this book would not exist.

JOHN BOWKER

Studio Cactus would like to thank Oxford University Press for allowing the author unlimited use of the anglicized version of the New Revised Standard Bible and for permission to use some of his own material from *The Oxford Dictionary of World Religions* (1999). Thanks also go to Jo Walton for Picture Research; Polly Boyd for proofreading; Jane Baldock for editorial help; Sharon Moore for amendments to the maps; and Hilary Bird for indexing.

PICTURE CREDITS

Abbreviations: BAL = Bridgeman Art Library, RHPL = Robert Harding Picture Library

half title: Lester Lefkowitz/Corbis Stockmarket
title verso: Victoria & Albert Museum, London, UK/BAL
title page: DK/Glasgow Museums/Ellen Howden
Contents (LHP): AKG London
(RHP): above: Oriental Museum, Durham University, UK/BAL
below left: AKG London
below right: Staatliches

Kunstmuseum, Minsk/AKG London
p.7: William Manning/Corbis Stockmarket
p.8 & 11: Pergamon Museum, Berlin, Germany/Bildarchiv Steffens/BAL
p.10: National Museum, Damascus, Syria/Peter Willi/BAL
p.12: AKG London
p.13: Prisma/Rex Features
p.14: DK/Alistair Duncan
p.15: Institut et Musée Voltaire, Geneva/Erich Lessing/AKG London
p.16: DK
p.17: Sistine Chapel, Rome/AKG London
p.18 & 19: DK

p.20: Musée Rodin, Paris/AKG London
p.23: Private Collection/BAL
p.24: Scrovegni Chapel, Padua/Cameraphoto/AKG London
p.25: DK/Glasgow Museums/Ellen Howden
p.27: Corbis Stockmarket
p.28–9 & 36: Haffenreffer Museum of Anthropology/Werner Forman Archive
p.31: Bettmann/CORBIS
p.32: Naturhistorisches Museum, Vienna/Erich Lessing/AKG London
p.34: Kevin Carlyon/Fortean Picture Library
p.37: AKG London
p.38 above: DK/Max Alexander
p.38 below: DK/Francesca York
p.39: Musée Municipal, Limoges/Erich Lessing/AKG London
p.40: Jean-Louis Nou/AKG London
p.41: DK/David Sutherland
p.42 & 43: Rex Features
p.44 above: GJLP/CNRI/Science Photo Library
p.44 below: GCA/CNRI/Science Photo Library
p.45: David & Peter Tumley/CORBIS
p.47: Wittelsbacher Ausgleichfonds, Munich/AKG London
p.48: AKG London
p.49: Janet Wishnetsky/CORBIS
p.50: Werner Forman Archive
p.51: Erich Lessing/AKG London
p.52: Hubert Stadler/CORBIS
p.53: Kimbell Art Museum/CORBIS
p.54–5: British Library, London, UK/BAL
p.58: DK/British Museum
p.59: DK/Barnabas Kindersley
p.60: Angelo Hornak/CORBIS
p.61: Angelo Hornak/CORBIS
p.62: Historical Picture Archive/CORBIS
p.63: Jalaram Temple, Bilimora, Gujarat, India/Dinodia Picture Agency, Bombay, India/BAL
p.64: Victoria & Albert Museum, London, UK/BAL
p.65: DK/Frank Greenaway
p.67: Ancient Art and Architecture Collection
p.69: Science Photo Library: Colin Cuthbert
p.70: DK/Glasgow Museums
p.71: Goldhill/Rex Features
p.72 & 73: Philip Goldman

Collection/Werner Forman Archive
p.75: Oriental Museum, Durham University, UK/BAL
p.76: Robert Harding Picture Library
p.77: Jean-Louis Nou/AKG London
p.78: National Museum of India, New Delhi, India/BAL
p.79: Jean-Louis Nou/AKG London
p.80: DK/Peter Anderson
p.81: Victoria & Albert Museum, London, UK/BAL
p.82 above: Jean-Louis Nou/AKG London
p.82 below: DK/Ashmolean Museum, Oxford
p.83: Rex Features
p.85: Resource Foto/Art Directors/Trip
p.86: Art Directors/Trip
p.87: Rex Features
p.88: DK/Ashmolean Museum, Oxford
p.89: Art Directors/TRIP
p.90 above: DK/Ashmolean Museum, Oxford
p.90 below: DK/Gables
p.91: Victoria & Albert Museum, London, UK/BAL
p.92: Surya Temple, Somnath, Bombay, India/Dinodia Picture Agency, Bombay, India/BAL
p.93: Oriental Museum, Durham University, UK/BAL
p.94: DK/Glasgow Museums
p.95: Explorer/Jean-Louis Nou/Robert Harding Picture Library
p.96: DK/Barnabas Kindersley
p.97: National Museum of India, New Delhi, India/BAL
p.98: Jean-Louis Nou/AKG London
p.101: Private Collection, India/Dinodia Picture Agency, Bombay, India/BAL
p.103: Private Collection/Werner Forman Archive
p.104: DK/Glasgow Museums
p.105: DK/Barnabas Kindersley
p.106: British Library, London, UK/BAL
p.107: Robert Harding Picture Library
p.108: DK/Glasgow Museums
p.109: DK/Barnabas Kindersley
p.110: Jean-Louis Nou/AKG London
p.111: Rex Features
p.113: Helene Rogers/Art Directors/TRIP
p.114: DK/Amit Pashricha
p.115: JR Naylor@ The Ancient Art and Architecture Collection Ltd

p.117: Jean-Louis Nou/AKG London
p.118: DK/Glasgow Museums
p.119: National Museum of India, New Delhi, India/BAL
p.120: DK
p.121: Robert Harding Picture Library
p.122, 123, 124 & 125: Helene Rogers/Art Directors/TRIP
p.127: DK/Gables
p.128: Art Directors/TRIP
p.129: DK/Glasgow Museum
p.130: Ronald Sheridan@ The Ancient Art and Architecture Collection Ltd.
p.131: British Library, London UK/AKG London
p.132: DK
p.134: Paul McCullagh/Robert Harding Picture Library
p.135: F Good/Art Directors/TRIP
p.137: Rex Features
p.138: Archiv Peter Ruhe/AKG London
p.139: DK/Gables
p.140: Mary Evans Picture Library
p.143: Seattle Art Museum/CORBIS
p.144: Lowell Georgia/CORBIS
p.145: British Library, London/Werner Forman Archive
p.147: Erich Lessing/AKG London
p.148: Bibliotheque Nationale, Paris, France/BAL
p.149: Sipa Press/Rex Features
p.151: Burstein Collection/CORBIS
p.152: Oriental Museum, Durham University, UK/BAL
p.153: DK/Alex Wilson
p.155 & 156: Mary Evans Picture Library
p.157: Werner Forman Archive
p.158: Mary Evans Picture Library
p.159: DK/Glasgow Museums/Ellen Howden
p.161: Sipa Press/Rex Features
p.162: Oriental Museum, Durham University, UK/BAL
p.163: Sakamoto Photo Research Laboratory/CORBIS
p.165: Asian Art & Archaeology Inc./CORBIS
p.166: Paul A Berry/CORBIS
p.167: Hulton Deutsch Collection/CORBIS
p.168: Peter Scholey/Robert Harding Picture Library
p.171: Gina Corrigan/Robert Harding Picture Library
p.172–73: Musée National de la Renaissance, Ecouen, France/Peter

Willi/BAL
p.176: Israel Museum, Jerusalem/AKG London
p.177: Zev Radovan
p.178: Bettmann/CORBIS
p.179: DK/Alistair Duncan
p.180: Richard T Nowitz/CORBIS
p.181: DK/Andy Crawford
p.183: Austrian National Library, Vienna/AKG London
p.185: Judaica Collection Max Berger, Vienna/AKG London
p.186: Musée Rolin, Autun/AKG London
p.187: AKG London
p.188: Vatican Museums, Rome/AKG London
p.190: Richard T Nowitz/CORBIS
p.191: Musée National de la Renaissance, Ecouen, France/Peter Willi/BAL
p.192: Dave Bartruff/CORBIS
p.194: Pergamon Museum, Berlin/AKG London
p.195: Gianni Dagli/CORBIS
p.196: Charles & Josette Lenars/CORBIS
p.197: Chris Hellier/CORBIS
p.198: AKG London
p.200: DK/Jewish Museum/Andy Crawford
p.201: Ted Spiegel/CORBIS
p.202: DK/Paul Harris
p.203: DK/Max Alexander
p.204: Science Photo Library/Claude Nurisdany & Marie Perennou
p.205: Science Photo Library/Colin Cuthbert
p.206: DK/Manchester Museum
p.207: Archaeological Museum, Tunisia/Gilles Mermet/AKG London
p.208–09: Bibliotheque Nationale, Paris/AKG London
p.210: Israel Museum, Jerusalem/AKG London
p.211: National Gallery, London, UK/BAL
p.212: DK/Joods Historisch Museum
p.213 above: DK/Alan Williams
p.213 below: DK/Barnabas Kindersley
p.215: Annie Griffiths Belt/CORBIS
p.216 & 217: AKG London
p.219: Bibliotheque Nationale, Paris/AKG London
p.221: Royal Library, Copenhagen/AKG London
p.222: Markisches Museum,

Berlin/AKG London
p.223, 224, 225 & 227: AKG London
p.229: Courtesy of Mark Cazalet
p.230: Vatican Museums, Rome/AKG London
p.231: DK/Francesca York
p.232: DK/Mike Dunning
p.233: DK/British Museum/Christi Graham, Nick Nichols
p.234: DK/Peter Wilson
p.235: Kunstmuseum Basel/AKG London
p.237: The Ancient Art & Architecture Collection Ltd
p.238: National Library, Athens/Erich Lessing/AKG London
p.239: DK/Peter Dennis
p.240: Ronald Sheridan@The Ancient Art & Architecture Collection Ltd
p.241: Staatl. Russisches Museum, St Petersburg/AKG London
p.242: Missions Etrangers de Paris, Pairs/Jean-Francois Amelot/AKG London
p.243: Bareiss Family Collection/AKG London
p.244: Musée Rodin, Paris, France/Peter Willi/BAL
p.246: Museo del Prado, Madrid/AKG London
p.249: Galleria Nationale dell'Umbria/S Domingie/AKG London
p.251: Kathareinenkloster, Sinai/Erich Lessing/AKG London
p.253: Staatliches Kunstmuseum, Minsk/AKG London
p.254: Science Photo Library/Pat and Tom Leeson
p.255: DK/Cyral Laubscher
257: RHPL
p.258: Galleria degli Uffizi/S Domingie/AKG London
p.261: RHPL
p.262: Gian Berto Vanni/Corbis
p.264: Musée du Louvre, Paris/Erich Lessing/AKG London
p.265: S. Croce (Bardi Chapel), Florence/Erich Lessing/AKG London
p.266: Musée du Louvre, Paris/Erich Lessing/AKG London
p.268: Museo de Arte, Lima/Weintmilla/AKG London
p.269: S Maria Novella, Cappellone degli Spagnuoli/AKG London
p.270: DK/John Heseltine
p.271 & 272: British Library, London/AKG London

p.275: Bayerische Staatsbibliothek, Munich/AKG London
p.276: F Jalain/RHPL
p.277: Michael Short/RHPL
p.279 above: Bettmann/CORBIS
p.279 below: Reinhard Eisele/CORBIS
p.280: British Library, London/AKG London
p.281: Peter Robinson/Empics
p.282: Museo dell'Opera del Duomo, Florence, Italy/BAL
p.283: AKG London
p.284: Courtesy of Mark Cazalet
p.286: Monastery Decani, Yugoslavia/AKG London
p.287: Ronald Sheridan@The Ancient Art & Architecture Collection Ltd
p.290: AKG London
p.291: Operation Raleigh/RHPL
p.293: Bibliotheque Nationale, Paris, France/Lauros-Giraudon/BAL
p.294: AKG London
p.295: Bettmann/CORBIS
p.296: Brian Wilson@The Ancient Art & Architecture Collection Ltd
p.297: CORBIS
p.298: Lee Snider/CORBIS
p.299: The Ancient Art & Architecture Collection Ltd
p.301: AKG London
p.302: CORBIS
p.303: The Ancient Art & Architecture Collection Ltd
p.304: DK/Ray Moller
p.305: Archivo Iconografico/CORBIS
p.307: Jean-Louis Nou/AKG London
p.308 & 309: AKG London
p.310: Unterlindenmuseum, Colmar/AKG London
p.311: Port-Royal-des-Champs, Abbaye/Erich Lessing/AKG London
p.312: Nik Wheeler/CORBIS
p.313: Paul Almasy/CORBIS
p.314: Courtesy of Edwina Sandys
p.315: SMPK, Berlin/AKG London
p.316: George Hall/CORBIS
p.319: Robert Frerck/Robert Harding Picture Library
p.320: Art Directors/Trip
p.321: AKG London
p.322: Art Directors/Trip
p.325: British Library, London, UK/BAL
p.326: Jean-Louis Nou/AKG London
p.327: Private Collection/Bonhams, London, UK/BAL
p.328: DK/Glasgow Museum

p.329: Art Directors/Trip
p.331: DK/Alistair Duncan
p.332: AKG London
p.333: Steve Rayner/CORBIS
p.339: Science Photo Library/Gordon Garradd
p.340: Science Photo Library/Alfred Pastieka
p.341: British Library, London, UK/BAL
p.334: Ronald Sheridan@The Ancient Art & Architecture Collection Ltd
p.335: Nik Wheeler/CORBIS
p.337: Westfalisches Schulmuseum, Dortmund/AKG London
p.342: RHPL
p.343: Peter Johnson/CORBIS
p.344: Art Directors/Trip
p.345: Bibliotheque Nationale, Paris, France/AKG London
p.346: Helene Rogers/Art Directors/Trip
p.347: AKG London
p.348: A Gamiet/Art Directors/Trip
p.349: Art Directors/Trip
p.351 above: R Bell@The Ancient Art & Architecture Collection Ltd
p.351 below: Art Directos/Trip
p.352: Viesti Collection/Art Directors/Trip
p.353: Musée du Louvre, Paris/Erich Lessing/AKG London
p.354: Art Directors/Trip
p.355: Bibliotheque Nationale, Paris, France/BAL
p.357: RHPL
p.358: Museum im Azm-Palast., Damascus/Jean-Louis Nou/AKG London
p.360: Iman Zahdah Chah Zaid Mosque, Isfahan, Iran/Index/BAL
p.361: Christie's Images, London, UK/BAL
p.362: Lester Lefkowitz/Corbis Stockmarket
p.364: JM Trois/Explorer/RHPL
p.366: DK/Alistair Duncan
p.369: Corbis
p.371: Reproduced by permission of the Henry Moore Foundation/St Matthew's Church, Northampton, Northamptonshire, UK/BAL
p.373: Musée Rodin, Paris, France/Peter Willi/BAL